INTRODUCING
Microsoft
WINDOWS®
SERVER 2003

Jerry Honeycutt

PUBLISHED BY
Microsoft Press
A Division of Microsoft Corporation
One Microsoft Way
Redmond, Washington 98052-6399

Library of Congress Cataloging-in-Publication Data
Honeycutt, Jerry.
    Introducing Microsoft Windows Server 2003 / Jerry Honeycutt.
        p. cm.
    Includes index.
    ISBN 0-7356-1570-5
    1. Microsoft Windows Server.   2. Operating systems (Computers).   I.
Title.

    QA76.76.O63H6632   2003

                                                                2002043103

Printed and bound in the United States of America.

2 3 4 5 6 7 8 9   QWE   8 7 6 5 4 3

Distributed in Canada by H.B. Fenn and Company Ltd.

A CIP catalogue record for this book is available from the British Library.

Microsoft Press books are available through booksellers and distributors worldwide. For further information about international editions, contact your local Microsoft Corporation office or contact Microsoft Press International directly at fax (425) 936-7329. Visit our Web site at www.microsoft.com/mspress. Send comments to *mspinput@microsoft.com*.

Acquisitions Editor: Martin DelRe
Project Editor: Valerie Woolley
Technical Editor: Dail Magee Jr.

Body Part No. X08-68164

Table of Contents

5   Security Services   95

Part III   Getting Started

About the CD-ROM

The CD-ROM contains a pre-release (RC2) 360-day evaluation edition of Microsoft Windows Server 2003.

- Hardware requirements are listed in the back of the book.

- Additional software is not needed to use this book.

- The CD is for evaluation purposes only.

- Windows Server 2003 is still in the pre-release phase and not yet fully supported.

> **Caution**   The 360-day Evaluation Edition provided with this book is not the full retail product and is provided only for the purposes of evaluation. Microsoft Press does not offer any support for the CD.
>
> For additional support information regarding this book, visit the Microsoft Press Technical Support Web site at *http://www.microsoft.com/mspress/support*. You can also e-mail *tkinput@microsoft.com*, or send a letter to Microsoft Press, Attn: Microsoft Press Technical Support, One Microsoft Way, Redmond, WA 98052-6399.

Acknowledgments

I'd like to thank the folks who made this book possible. Martin DelRe was my acquisitions editor. Valerie Woolley was the book's project editor and was responsible for managing the overall process. She did a great job of pushing me to keep schedules. A number of other people deserve thanks. First is the technical editor, Dail Magee, Jr. His technical input to this book was dead-on accurate. The book's copy editor, Shawn Peck, made sure that the book flowed well and was readable.

Important also are the authors of the content on which this book is based. These are Microsoft folks who wrote the outstanding white papers about Microsoft Windows Server 2003, which you can find at *http://www.microsoft.com/windows.netserver*. They include Mark Aggar, Perry Anton, Mary Alice Colvin, Joseph Davies, Brian Dewey, Jason Goodman, Todd Headrick, John Kaiser, Jenna Miller Kapczynski, David Martin, Asif Moinuddin, Manoj Nayar, Nancy Narraway, Daniel Queva, Jackson Shaw, Bill Staples, Andi Stark, David Zank, and Ethan Zoller.

Part I
Overview

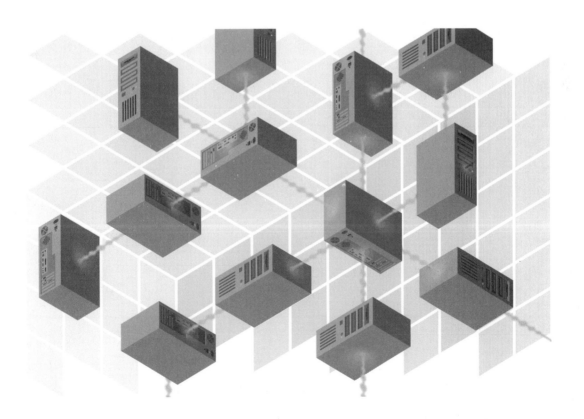

1

Product Family

This chapter introduces you to the Microsoft Windows Server 2003 family. It describes the different editions available and the features that are unique to each one. It also describes the hardware requirements for each edition. My goal with this chapter is to help you align your requirements with the appropriate edition of Windows Server 2003, of course, but the chapter is also a road map for what you'll find in the rest of this book.

This chapter and the next describe the compelling features of the Windows Server 2003 family and help you choose the edition that's right for your scenarios. After I've told you why Microsoft believes its newest server operating system is the best it has ever produced, I'll focus more on the technical details of new and enhanced features in Windows Server 2003 and a lot less on convincing you to upgrade. In the meantime, this chapter begins with an overview of the product family.

Meet the Family

The Windows Server 2003 family includes the following editions:

- **Windows Server 2003, Standard Edition,** is a reliable network operating system that delivers business solutions quickly and easily. It's a great choice for small-business and departmental use. The Standard Edition supports file and printer sharing, offers secure Internet connectivity, and enables centralized desktop application deployment. For more information, see "Standard Edition" later in this chapter.

- **Windows Server 2003, Enterprise Edition,** is built for the general-purpose needs of businesses of all sizes. It's an ideal platform for applications, Web services, and infrastructure, delivering high reliability, performance, and excellent business value. The Enterprise Edition is a full-function server operating system that supports up to eight processors, provides enterprise-class features such as eight-node clustering, and provides support for up to 32 GB of memory. It's available for Intel Itanium–based computers and will soon be available for 64-bit computing platforms capable of supporting eight processors and 64 GB of memory. For more information, see "Enterprise Edition" later in this chapter.

- **Windows Server 2003, Datacenter Edition,** is built for mission-critical applications that require the highest levels of scalability and availability. Microsoft believes that the Datacenter Edition is the most powerful and functional server operating system that the company has ever produced. It supports up to 32-way symmetric multiprocessing (SMP) and 64 GB of memory. It provides both eight-node clustering and load-balancing services as standard features. It will soon be available for 64-bit computing platforms capable of supporting 32 processors and 128 GB of memory. For more information, see "Datacenter Edition" later in this chapter.

- **Windows Server 2003, Web Edition,** is a new addition to the Windows family of server operating systems. Microsoft provides the Web Edition for building and hosting Web applications, Web pages, and XML Web services. Microsoft designed it for use primarily as an Internet Information Services (IIS) 6.0 Web server. It provides a platform for rapidly developing and deploying XML Web services and applications that use ASP.NET technology, which is a key part of the .NET Framework. For more information, see "Web Edition" later in this chapter.

The sections following this describe each edition of Windows Server 2003 in more detail. They begin with the Standard Edition. The Enterprise Edition and the Datacenter Edition include all of the great features and enhancements in the Standard Edition. All three editions include the functionality you find in the Web Edition.

Standard Edition

Designed for use by departments and small organizations, Windows Server 2003, Standard Edition, extends Microsoft Windows 2000 Server technologies by making them easier to deploy, manage, and use. The result is an operating system that is secure, reliable, and ready to use out of the box, with features that provide robust availability and scalability. At a high level, the Standard Edition supports the following:

- Four-way SMP
- Four GB of memory
- Advanced networking features such as Internet Authentication Service (IAS), Network Bridge, and Internet Connection Sharing (ICS)

Key features in the Standard Edition include the following:

- **Internet Information Services.** IIS 6.0 is the Web server in Windows Server 2003 that makes it easy to share information among partners, customers, and employees over an intranet, the Internet, or an extranet. IIS 6.0 provides an updated architecture that meets the most demanding needs in the areas of dependability, versatility, and manageability.

- **IIS Securitys.** IIS 6.0 security settings are locked down during setup by default to ensure that only required services are running. This change from earlier versions significantly reduces initial security risks. Using the IIS Security Lockdown Wizard, administrators can enable or disable server functionality based on their business requirements.

- **Directory services.** The Microsoft Active Directory service is a central component of the Windows platform, providing the means to manage the identities and relationships that make up network environments.

- **Update management.** Auto Update provides the ability to systematically download critical operating system updates, such as security fixes and security patches. Administrators choose when to install these critical operating system updates.

- **Internet firewall.** Connecting to the Internet is more secure than ever before with the built-in Internet Connection Firewall. The integration of an Internet firewall in the operating system also reduces capital costs necessary to connect to the Internet.

- **Remote access.**   Dial-up users can be quarantined by administrator policy. They can be prevented from accessing the network until their systems are verified to have administrator-specified software such as virus-detection updates.

- **Server hardware support.**   Driver verifiers check new device drivers to help keep the server up and running.

- **Application verification.**   Applications running on Windows Server 2003 can be tested and verified using the Application Verifier tool. This tool focuses on subtle issues such as software heap corruptions and compatibility issues.

- **File services.**   Windows Server 2003 file system performance has improved since Microsoft Windows NT Server 4.0 and Windows 2000 Server.

- **Assisted support.**   Microsoft incident submission and management allow users to submit electronic support incidents to Microsoft, collaborate with support engineers, and manage submitted incidents from Windows Server 2003.

- **Server event tracking.**   Administrators can report an accurate record of uptime using the new server shutdown tracker. It writes Windows events for server shutdowns to a log file.

- **Configure Your Server Wizard.**   The Configure Your Server Wizard is an easy-to-use wizard that steps administrators through the process of setting up various server roles such as file server, print server, remote access server, and other roles to ensure that components are installed and configured correctly the first time.

- **Manage Your Server Wizard.**   The Manage Your Server Wizard provides an easy-to-use interface for ongoing management of the server, making it easy to perform such common tasks as adding new users and creating file shares.

- **Remote server administration.**   With Remote Desktop for Administration (formerly known as Terminal Services in Remote Administration mode), administrators can manage a computer from almost any other computer on the network. Remote Desktop for Administration is specifically designed for server management.

- **Remote assistance.**   Administrators can use Remote Assistance to control a remote desktop computer. If the administrator or help-desk staff has an invitation from the remote user, Remote Assistance is a convenient way to connect to a remote computer from a computer running Microsoft Windows XP or any edition of Windows Server 2003. After connecting to the remote computer, the person giving assistance can view the remote computer's screen and chat in real time with the system user. If the person requesting assistance allows it, the assisting person can even control the remote computer's mouse and keyboard.

- **Shadow copy.**   This feature provides consistent, point-in-time versions of files in network shares. Administrators can view network folder contents as they existed at points of time in the past. End users can recover accidentally deleted files or folders on network shares without requiring system administrator intervention.

- **Terminal Server.**   When using Terminal Server, a user can access programs running on the server from a variety of older devices. For example, a user can access a virtual Windows XP Professional desktop and x86-based applications for Windows from hardware that cannot run the software locally. Terminal Server provides this capability for both Windows-based and non-Windows-based client devices.

- **Web application server role.**   Windows Server 2003 is also a full Web application server. It integrates the .NET Framework with core server resources to help users develop, deploy, and manage applications and XML Web services. The .NET Framework provides a fully managed, protected, and feature-rich application execution environment, simplified development and deployment, and seamless integration with a wide variety of programming languages.

- **Windows Media Services.**   Windows Server 2003, Standard Edition, includes Windows Media Services for distributing streaming audio and video over corporate intranets and the Internet.

- **Wireless LAN support.**   This feature provides security and performance improvements for wireless local area networks (LANs), such as automatic key management, user authentication, and authorization prior to LAN access. Windows Server 2003, Standard Edition, makes it much easier than ever before to use and deploy wireless services.

Enterprise Edition

Windows Server 2003, Enterprise Edition, is for medium to large businesses. It's the operating system that Microsoft recommends for servers running applications such as networking, messaging, inventory and customer service systems, databases, and e-commerce Web sites. The Enterprise Edition delivers high reliability, performance, and business value superior to those of any earlier versions of Windows. It will soon be available in both 32-bit and 64-bit editions. It includes everything that the Standard Edition includes but adds support for high-performance servers and the ability to cluster servers to handle larger loads. These capabilities provide reliability that lets you make sure your systems are available regardless of system failure and no matter how large an application becomes. At a high level, Windows Server 2003 Enterprise Edition supports the following:

- Eight-way SMP
- Eight-node clustering
- 32 GB of memory in 32-bit editions; 64 GB in 64-bit editions

Windows Server 2003, Enterprise Edition, scales both ways: up and out. First, it lets you increase server performance and capacity by adding processors and memory. This approach to increasing your network capacity is known as *scaling up*. Enhanced SMP support in the Enterprise Edition supports multiprocessor servers. The operating system also supports enhanced memory capabilities that let you increase the memory available for server processing to as much as 8 GB. In addition to scaling up, the Enterprise Edition lets you add servers to a load-balancing cluster. This approach is known as *scaling out*. Windows Server 2003, Enterprise Edition, is the most dependable, enterprise-ready server operating system Microsoft has ever created. The enhancements include improvements to key technologies introduced in Windows 2000 Server, such as Network Load Balancing (NLB), server clusters, and the Microsoft Active Directory directory service.

The Enterprise Edition supports 64-bit computing on certified hardware platforms, allowing faster completion of processor-intensive and memory-intensive applications. This includes support for the Intel Itanium and Itanium 2 processors.

In addition to including all the features in the Standard Edition, the Enterprise Edition adds several important features that enhance availability, scalability, and dependability. (These features are also in Windows Server 2003, Datacenter Edition.)

■ **Cluster Service.** Server clusters provide high availability and disaster tolerance for mission-critical database management, file sharing, intranet data sharing, messaging, and general business applications. With Windows Server 2003 Enterprise Edition and Windows Server 2003 Datacenter Edition, cluster service supports up to eight-node clusters. This provides increased flexibility for adding and removing hardware in a geographically dispersed cluster environment, as well as providing improved scaling options for applications. The Enterprise Edition allows server clusters to be deployed in a variety of different configurations, in particular single-cluster configurations with dedicated storage, multiple clusters on a storage area network, and clusters spanning multiple sites.

■ **64-bit support.** Windows Server 2003, Enterprise Edition, is available in a 32-bit edition and will soon be available in a 64-bit edition. The 64-bit edition will be optimized for memory-intensive and computational-intensive tasks such as mechanical design, computer-aided design (CAD), professional graphics, high-end database systems, and scientific applications. The 64-bit edition includes support for both the Intel Itanium and Itanium 2 processors.

■ **Multiprocessor support.** Windows Server 2003 scales from single-processor solutions all the way up to 32-way systems. Windows Server 2003, Enterprise Edition, supports servers with up to eight processors, while Windows Server 2003, Datacenter Edition, supports up to 32 processors.

■ **Metadirectory Services support.** Microsoft Metadirectory Services (MMS) helps companies to integrate identity information from multiple directories, databases, and files with Active Directory. MMS provides an organization with a unified view of identity information, enables the integration of business processes with MMS, and helps synchronize identity information across an organization.

■ **Hot-add memory.** Hot-add memory allows ranges of memory to be added to a computer and made available to the operating system and applications as part of the normal memory pool. This does not require rebooting the computer and involves no downtime. This feature currently will operate only on servers that have hardware support for adding memory while the server is operating. For these servers, the act of installing memory will automatically invoke the Hot-Add Memory feature.

- **Server 2003Non-Uniform Memory Access (NUMA) support.** System firmware can create a table called the Static Resource Affinity Table that describes the NUMA topology of the system. Windows Server 2003, Enterprise Edition, uses this table to apply NUMA awareness to application processes, default affinity settings, thread scheduling, and memory management features. Additionally, the topology information is made available to applications using a set of NUMA application programming interfaces.

- **Terminal Services Session Directory.**   This is a load-balancing feature that allows users to easily reconnect to a disconnected session on a server farm running Terminal Services. Session Directory is compatible with the Windows Server 2003 load-balancing service and is supported by third-party external load-balancer products.

Windows Server 2003, Enterprise Edition, lets you deploy highly available and scalable applications on industry-standard PC hardware. Common examples of applications suitable for the Enterprise Edition include database, messaging, and file and print servers. Regardless of the size of your organization, the Enterprise Edition is a good choice for running applications that must be available at all times. It also gives growing organizations the ability to ensure the availability of critical applications while allowing them to scale those applications both up and out to meet increased demand.

Datacenter Edition

Windows Server 2003, Datacenter Edition, is for businesses that demand the highest levels of scalability, availability, and reliability. It lets you deliver mission-critical solutions for databases, software for planning enterprise resources, high-volume real-time transaction processing, and server consolidation. The Datacenter Edition will soon be available in both 32-bit and 64-bit editions. It includes all of the features in Windows Server 2003Server 2003, Enterprise Edition, and includes support for more powerful multiple processing and greater memory. Windows Server 2003, Datacenter Edition, is available only through the Windows Datacenter Program, which provides an integrated hardware, software, and service offering delivered by Microsoft and qualified server vendors, such as original equipment manufacturers (OEMs). At a high level, Windows Server 2003, Datacenter Edition, supports the following:

- 32-way SMP
- Eight-node clustering
- 64 GB of memory in 32-bit editions; 128 GB in 64-bit editions

Microsoft developed the Windows Datacenter Program to provide customers with a list of qualified servers that have been thoroughly tested and proven to be highly reliable. The Windows Datacenter Program provides the support you need to ensure maximum uptime for your applications. Only Microsoft certifies OEMs who have succeeded in passing their hardware through rigorous compatibility tests in order to gain permission to license and support Windows Server 2003, Datacenter Edition. The Datacenter Edition is unique because the operating system is available only already loaded onto OEM systems; the software cannot be acquired separately. The Windows Datacenter Program offers these benefits:

■ A single point of contact for support, provided by a joint support team comprising both OEM and Microsoft personnel

■ Rigorous system testing and qualification of hardware and software to ensure that they perform optimally together

■ Coordinated maintenance and change control for hardware and software updates

■ Strict reliability assurance through new Microsoft Certified Support Center (MCSC) requirements designed for this program

Unlike proprietary systems offered by some vendors, Windows Server 2003, Datacenter Edition, is available from a wide choice of vendors that sell high-end Intel-based systems able to run your organization's existing applications. Customers can choose from a range of platforms and services from these suppliers and pick the best provider for their specific requirements. The Windows Datacenter Program includes a qualification process and the Datacenter Hardware Compatibility List, which extends and enhances the current hardware compatibility requirements from Microsoft. This ensures that all server components are tested together in a high-stress environment, assuring that the overall system will operate without hardware or software conflicts among components of the configuration.

Windows Hardware Quality Labs (WHQL) exists to ensure that OEMs produce quality hardware and software that interacts well with Microsoft products and technologies. OEM products must pass the appropriate Hardware Compatibility Test. If successful, they are placed on the Hardware Compatibility List and receive the "Designed for Windows" logo. The Windows logo on hardware and software products lets customers know the products meet Microsoft standards for compatibility with Windows operating systems. Hardware intended for use with Windows Server 2003, Datacenter Edition, must be designed to the specifications of the Hardware Design Guide.

Customers who receive servers validated by the Windows Datacenter Program know they are receiving a complete configuration that has been rigorously tested with all hardware components and kernel-level software products. Windows Server 2003, Datacenter Edition, can be sold only by OEMs who are willing to do this extra testing and configuration control. The result is a highly reliable and dependable server. The testing that OEMs must undertake helps ensure that the following components will work together smoothly on servers running Windows Server 2003, Datacenter Edition:

- All hardware components

- All hardware drivers

- All software that works at the kernel level, including virus software, disk and tape management, backup software, and similar types of software

The Joint Support Queue for Windows Server 2003, Datacenter Edition, is staffed with both OEM and Microsoft support personnel to ensure tight collaboration between the hardware vendor and Microsoft. This creates a single point of contact for supporting business-critical solutions. The Datacenter Joint Support Queue has access to all OEM Datacenter Hardware Compatibility List hardware configurations and Windows Server 2003, Datacenter Edition, source code to enable rapid problem reproduction, isolation, and resolution.

In addition to the features included in Windows Server 2003, Standard Edition, and Windows Server 2003, Enterprise Edition, Windows Server 2003, Datacenter Edition, offers the following extra features and capabilities:

- **Expanded physical memory space.**   On 32-bit Intel platforms, Windows Server 2003, Datacenter Edition, supports Physical Address Extension (PAE), which extends system memory capability to 64 GB of physical RAM. On 64-bit Intel platforms, the memory support increases to an architectural maximum of 16 terabytes.

- **Intel Hyper-Threading support.**   Hyper-Threading technology allows a single physical processor to execute multiple threads (instruction streams) simultaneously, potentially providing greater throughput and improved performance.

- **Windows Sockets: Direct Access for SANs.**   This feature enables Windows Sockets applications that use Transmission Control Protocol/Internet Protocol (TCP/IP) to obtain the performance benefits of storage area networks (SANs) without making application modifications.

The fundamental component of this technology is a Windows Sockets Server 2003layered service provider that emulates TCP/IP semantics over native SAN service providers.

Windows Server 2003, Datacenter Edition, offers significant reliability, scalability, and manageability improvements compared with Windows 2000 Datacenter Server and is capable of supporting mission-critical workloads in enterprise data centers. The key element distinguishing Windows Server 2003, Datacenter Edition, from the other editions of the Windows Server 2003 family is its strong community of OEMs, independent hardware vendors, and independent software vendors. These companies are actively involved with Windows Server 2003, Datacenter Edition, customers and are committed to partnering with them over the lifetime of their systems, making Windows Server 2003, Datacenter Edition, unlike any other platform solution available today.

Web Edition

Designed for building and hosting Web applications, Web pages, and XML Web services, Windows Server 2003, Web Edition, delivers a single-purpose solution for Internet service providers (ISPs), application developers, and others wanting to use or deploy specific Web functionality only. The Web Edition takes advantage of improvements in IIS 6.0, Microsoft ASP.NET, and the Microsoft .NET Framework. (For more information about the features and capabilities of IIS 6.0, see Chapter 8, "Internet Information Services.") It will be obtainable only through selected partner channels and will not be available for retail. Service providers should visit the Microsoft Service Providers Web site, *http://www.microsoft.com/serviceproviders*, for more information. At a high level, the Web Edition provides support for the following:

- Two-way SMP

- Two GB of memory

- Advanced Web application development and hosting features, including ASP.NET and the .NET Framework, which is integrated into the operating system

Like every other member of the Windows Server 2003 family, Windows Server 2003, Web Edition, is built on industry standards that allow organizations to extend existing applications and quickly develop new ones. Developers can build directly on the application server, using XML Web services and managed code, and then run these applications on any Web application platform. This level of easy application development encourages business-process innovation and increases business opportunities both internally and externally.

Windows Server 2003, Web Edition, is designed to be used specifically as a Web server. Although computers running the Web Edition can be members of an Active Directory domain, organizations cannot run Active Directory on the Web Edition. Therefore, the Web Edition alone cannot be used to perform powerful management features such as Group Policy, Software Restriction Policies, Remote Installation Services (RIS), Microsoft Metadirectory Services, Internet Authentication Service (IAS), and so on. Likewise, organizations cannot deploy enterprise Universal Description, Discovery, and Integration (UDDI) services, an essential part of enabling discovery and reuse of XML Web services. In addition, scalability features designed for enterprise functionality aren't available.

Designed to be used specifically as a Web server, Windows Server 2003, Web Edition, delivers the next generation of Web infrastructure capabilities in the Windows server operating systems. ISPs and others desiring stand-alone Web functionality will benefit from this low-cost operating system, which is easy to deploy and manage. Integrated with ASP.NET and the .NET Framework, the Web Edition lets developers rapidly build and deploy XML Web services and applications.

For enterprise capabilities or more advanced management features such as Microsoft Active Directory service, organizations should consider obtaining one of the more fully featured editions of Windows Server 2003: Standard Edition, Enterprise Edition, or Datacenter Edition. All of the features in Windows Server 2003, Web Edition, including IIS 6.0 and Microsoft ASP.NET, are also included in these other members of the Windows Server 2003 family.

Compare the Features

Table 1-1 compares the features available in each edition of Windows Server 2003. You see the following symbols in this table:

- ⬤—feature included

- ◒—feature partially included

- ◯—feature not included

Table 1-1   **Feature Comparison**

Feature	Standard	Enterprise	Datacenter	Web
.NET Application Services				
.NET Framework	●	●	●	●
Internet Information Services (IIS) 6.0	●	●	●	●
ASP.NET	●	●	●	●
Enterprise UDDI services	●	●	●	○
Clustering Technologies				
Network load balancing	●	●	●	●
Cluster service	○	●	●	○
Communications and Networking Services				
Virtual Private Network (VPN) support	●	●	●	◑
Internet Authentication Service (IAS)	●	●	●	○
Network bridge	●	●	●	○
Internet Connection Sharing (ICS)	●	●	○	◑
IPv6	●	●	●	●
Directory Services				
Active Directory	●	●	●	◑
Metadirectory Services (MMS) support	○	●	●	○
File and Print Services				
Distributed File System (DFS)	●	●	●	●
Encrypting File System (EFS)	●	●	●	●

(continued)

Table 1-1 Feature Comparison *(continued)*

Feature	Standard	Enterprise	Datacenter	Web
File and Print Services *(continued)*				
Shadow Copy Restore	●	●	●	●
Removable and remote storage	●	●	●	○
Fax service	●	●	●	○
Services for Macintosh	●	●	●	○
Management Services				
IntelliMirror	●	●	●	●
Resultant Set of Policy (RSoP)	●	●	●	●
Windows Management Instrumentation (WMI) command line	●	●	●	●
Remote operating system installation	●	●	●	●
Remote Installation Services (RIS)	●	●	●	○
Multimedia Services				
Windows Media Services	●	●	●	○
Scalability				
64-bit support for Intel Itanium–based computers	○	●	●	○
Hot-add memory	○	●	●	○
Non-Uniform Memory Access (NUMA)	○	●	●	○
Datacenter Program	○	○	●	○

Table 1-1   Feature Comparison   *(continued)*

Feature	Standard	Enterprise	Datacenter	Web
Security Services				
Internet Connection Firewall	●	●	○	○
Public key infrastructure, certificate services, and smart cards	◐	●	●	◐
Terminal Services				
Remote Desktop for Administration	●	●	●	●
Terminal Server	●	●	●	◐
Terminal Server Session Directory	○	●	●	○

The .NET Framework and ASP.NET aren't supported in the 64-bit versions of Windows Server 2003. Windows Media Services is likewise not supported in the 64-bit versions. Also, hot-add memory and Non-Uniform Memory Access (NUMA) might be limited by lack of support from OEM hardware.

Check the Requirements

Table 1-2 describes the hardware requirements for Windows Server 2003.

Table 1-2   Hardware Requirements

Requirement	Standard	Enterprise	Datacenter	Web
Minimum CPU speed	133 MHz	■ 133 MHz for x86-based computers ■ 733 MHz for Itanium-based computers	■ 400 MHz for x86-based computers ■ 733 MHz for Itanium-based computers	133 MHz
Recommended CPU speed	550 MHz	733 MHz	733 MHz	550 MHz
Minimum RAM	128 MB	128 MB	512 MB	128 MB

(continued)

Table 1-2   Hardware Requirements   *(continued)*

Requirement	Standard	Enterprise	Datacenter	Web
Recommended minimum RAM	256 MB	256 MB	1 GB	256 MB
Maximum RAM	4 GB	■ 32 GB for x86-based computers ■ 64 GB for Itanium-based computers	■ 64 GB for x86-based computers ■ 128 GB for Itanium-based computers	2 GB
Multiprocessor support	1 or 2	Up to 8	■ Minimum 8 ■ Maximum 32	1 or 2
Disk space for setup	1.5 GB	■ 1.5 GB for x86-based computers ■ 2.0 GB for Itanium-based computers	■ 1.5 GB for x86-based computers ■ 2.0 GB for Itanium-based computers	1.5 GB

The 64-bit versions of Windows Server 2003, Enterprise Edition, and Windows Server 2003, Datacenter Edition, are compatible only with 64-bit Intel Itanium–based systems. They cannot be successfully installed on 32-bit systems.

For More Information

See the following resources for more information:

■ Windows Server 2003 home page at *http://www.microsoft.com/windowsserver2003/*

■ Product Overviews at *http://www.microsoft.com/windowsserver2003/evaluation/overview/*

■ System Requirements at *http://www.microsoft.com/windowsserver2003/evaluation/sysreqs/systemrequirements.mspx*

2

Business Evaluation

This chapter kicks off your evaluation process by describing the benefits of Microsoft Windows Server 2003. With the company's latest server operating system, Microsoft has focused on dependability, productivity, connectivity, and economics. In this chapter, you learn how Windows Server 2003 improves all four areas.

The first section, "Windows Server 2003 Benefits," describes the features that make the operating system enterpriseworthy. The last two sections describe why you should consider upgrading to Windows Server 2003. The section "Upgrading from Windows NT Server" describes the advantages of upgrading from Microsoft Windows NT 4.0. The section "Upgrading from Windows 2000 Server" describes what you pick up when you upgrade from Microsoft Windows 2000 Server. This chapter wraps up by pointing out tools you can use to objectively evaluate Windows Server 2003 and calculate a potential return on investment.

Windows Server 2003 Benefits

Windows Server 2003 improves over Windows 2000 Server in four areas:

■ **Dependability.** Windows Server 2003 is the fastest, most reliable, most secure Windows server operating system Microsoft has ever offered. Windows Server 2003 delivers dependability. It provides an integrated infrastructure that helps you ensure that your business information is secure. It provides reliability, availability, and scalability so that you can provide the network infrastructure that users demand.

- **Productivity.** Windows Server 2003 provides tools that let you deploy, manage, and use your network infrastructure. These flexible tools help match your design and deployment to your organizational and network needs. The operating system helps you manage your network by enforcing policy, automating tasks, and simplifying updates. Also, it helps you lower support overhead by letting users do more on their own.

- **Connectivity.** Windows Server 2003 can help you create the business solutions infrastructure to better connect employees, partners, systems, and customers. The operating system does this by providing an integrated Web server and streaming media server that helps you quickly, easily, and securely create dynamic intranet and Internet Web sites. It also provides an integrated application server that helps you easily develop, deploy, and manage XML Web services.

- **Best Economics.** Windows Server 2003, when combined with products and services from Microsoft's many hardware, software, and channel partners, provides choices that help you get a greater return on your infrastructure investments. Windows Server 2003 does this by providing ease-of-use and prescriptive guidance for complete solutions that let you quickly put technology to work. It helps you consolidate servers by taking advantage of the latest hardware, software, and methodologies to optimize your server deployments. The result is a lower total cost of ownership (TCO) and a fast return on investment.

Dependability

Microsoft built Windows Server 2003 for dependability. It improves on many technologies introduced in Windows 2000 Server, such as support for smart cards, bandwidth throttling, and Plug and Play support. New technologies, such as the common language runtime, strengthen security to help safeguard networks from malicious or poorly designed code. In addition, improvements to Internet Information Services (IIS) 6.0, public key infrastructure (PKI), and Kerberos make it easier to secure Windows Server 2003. The Microsoft Active Directory directory service is now faster and more robust over unreliable wide area network connections, thanks to more efficient synchronization, replication, and credential caching in branch office domain controllers.

Key features for dependability include these:

- **Availability.**   Windows Server 2003 provides improved availability through enhanced clustering support. Clustering services have become essential for organizations deploying business-critical, e-commerce, and line-of-business applications because they provide significant improvements in availability, scalability, and manageability. Clustering installation and setup are easier and more robust in Windows Server 2003 than in earlier versions of Windows, while enhanced network features in the product provide greater failover capabilities and high system uptime.

  The Windows Server 2003 family supports server clusters of up to eight nodes. If one of the nodes in a cluster becomes unavailable because of failure or maintenance, another node immediately begins providing service, a process known as *failover*. Windows Server 2003 also supports network load balancing (NLB), which balances incoming Internet Protocol (IP) traffic across nodes in a cluster.

- **Scalability.**   Windows Server 2003 provides scalability through scale-up, enabled by symmetric multiprocessing (SMP), and scale-out, enabled by clustering. Microsoft's own tests indicate that, compared with Windows 2000 Server, Windows Server 2003 delivers up to 140 percent better performance in the file system and significantly better performance in various other features, including Active Directory, Web server, and Terminal Server components as well as networking services. Windows Server 2003 scales from single-processor solutions all the way up to 32-way systems. It supports both 32-bit and 64-bit processors.

- **Security.**   Businesses have extended the traditional local area network (LAN) by combining intranets, extranets, and Internet sites. As a result, increased system security is now more critical than ever before. As part of Microsoft's commitment to reliable, secure, and dependable computing, the company has intensively reviewed the Windows Server 2003 family to identify possible failure points and exploitable weaknesses.

Windows Server 2003 provides many important new security features and improvements, including the following:

❑ **The common language runtime.** This software engine is a key element of Windows Server 2003 that improves reliability and helps ensure a safe computing environment. It reduces the number of bugs and security holes caused by common programming mistakes. As a result, there are fewer vulnerabilities for attackers to exploit. The common language runtime also verifies that applications can run without error and checks for appropriate security permissions, making sure that code performs only appropriate operations.

❑ **Internet Information Services 6.0.** To increase Web server security, IIS 6.0 is configured for maximum security out of the box—its default installation is locked down. Advanced security features in IIS 6.0 include selectable cryptographic services, advanced digest authentication, and configurable access control of processes. These are among the many new security features in IIS 6.0 that enable you to conduct business securely on the Web.

Productivity

Productivity is also a high priority for Windows Server 2003, which the product achieves through enhanced capabilities in system management and storage. The new task-based design in Windows Server 2003 makes it easier to discover how to carry out common tasks. Improvements to the Microsoft Management Console (MMC) and Active Directory boost performance and make management easier.

Some of the new management and administration features in the Windows Server 2003 family include Domain Rename, cross-domain and cross-forest management, and Resultant Set of Policy (RSoP). Enhanced Windows Management Instrumentation (WMI) providers and command-line tools give administrators greater granular control of server tasks.

Key productivity features include the following:

■ **File and print services.** At the heart of any IT organization is the ability to efficiently manage file and print resources while keeping them available and secure for users. As the network expands with more users located on site, in remote locations, or even at partner companies, IT administrators face an increasingly heavy burden. The

Windows Server 2003 family delivers intelligent file and print services with increased performance and functionality, allowing you to reduce TCO.

- **Active Directory.** Active Directory stores information about objects on the network and makes this information easy for administrators and users to find, providing a logical, hierarchical organization of directory information. Windows Server 2003 brings many improvements to Active Directory, making it more versatile, dependable, and economical to use. In Windows Server 2003, Active Directory provides increased performance and scalability. It also allows you greater flexibility to design, deploy, and manage your organization's directory.

- **Management services.** Even as computing has proliferated on desktops, laptops, and portable devices, the real cost of maintaining a distributed personal computer network has grown significantly. Reducing day-to-day maintenance through automation is key to reducing operating costs. Windows Server 2003 contains several important new automated management tools, including Microsoft Software Update Services (SUS) and server configuration wizards, to help automate deployment. Managing Group Policy is made easier with the new Group Policy Management Console (GPMC), enabling more organizations to better utilize the Active Directory service and take advantage of its powerful management features. In addition, command-line tools let administrators perform most tasks from the command console. GPMC is planned to be available as a separate component by the time Windows Server 2003 is launched.

- **Storage management.** Windows Server 2003 introduces new and enhanced features for storage management, making it easier and more reliable to manage and maintain disks and volumes, back up and restore data, and connect to storage area networks (SANs).

- **Terminal Services.** The Terminal Services component of Microsoft Windows Server 2003 builds on the application server mode in Windows 2000 Terminal Services. Terminal Services let you deliver Windows-based applications, or the Windows desktop itself, to virtually any computing device—including those that cannot run Windows.

Windows Server 2003 also makes storage and backup easier while significantly reducing the demands on system administrators. Among the new and improved file services that make this possible is the Volume Shadow Copy service, which provides point-in-time backups of network shares. The benefits of this unique technology extend to users, who can now retrieve old copies of files or deleted files by using the Shadow Copy Restore feature right from their Windows desktops. Also, file and print services are improved with the addition of the Web-Based Distributed Authoring and Versioning (WebDAV) remote document sharing technology. And enhancements to the Distributed File System (DFS) and Encrypting File System (EFS) allow for powerful, flexible file sharing and storage.

Connectivity

Networking improvements and new features in the Windows Server 2003 family extend the versatility, manageability, and dependability of network infrastructures. Windows Server 2003 makes it easier than ever for users to stay connected to their centralized systems from anywhere and on any device. Microsoft has built significant networking enhancements into Windows Server 2003, including Internet Protocol version 6 (IPv6), Point-to-Point Protocol over Ethernet (PPoE), and Internet Protocol Security (IPSec) over Network Address Translation (NAT).

Key connectivity improvements include the following:

- **XML Web services.**   IIS 6.0 is an important component of the Windows Server 2003 family. Administrators and Web application developers demand a fast, reliable Web platform that is both scalable and secure. Significant architectural improvements in IIS include a new process model that greatly improves reliability, scalability, and performance. IIS is installed by default in a locked-down state. Security is increased because the system administrator enables or disables system features based on application requirements. In addition, direct editing support of the XML metabase improves management.

- **Networking and communications.**   Networking and communications have never been more critical for organizations faced with the challenge of competing in the global marketplace. Employees need to connect to the network wherever they are and from any device. Partners, vendors, and others outside the network need to interact efficiently with key resources, and security is more important than ever. Networking improvements and new features in the Windows Server 2003 family extend the versatility, manageability, and dependability of network infrastructures.

- **Enterprise UDDI services.** Windows Server 2003 includes Enterprise UDDI services, a dynamic and flexible infrastructure for XML Web services. This standards-based solution enables companies to run their own internal UDDI service for intranet or extranet use. Developers can easily and quickly find and reuse the Web services available within the organization. IT administrators can catalog and manage the programmable resources in their network. With Enterprise UDDI services, companies can build and deploy smarter, more reliable applications.

- **Windows Media Services.** Windows Server 2003 includes the industry's most powerful digital streaming media services. These services are part of the next version of the Microsoft Windows Media technologies platform that also includes new versions of Windows Media Player, Windows Media Encoder, audio/video codecs, and the Windows Media Software Development Kit.

Perhaps most important, though, with optimized, native support of Microsoft .NET and XML, Windows Server 2003 represents a revolutionary step forward as the ideal platform to develop, distribute, and host XML Web services created with .NET. Microsoft .NET is deeply integrated into the Windows Server 2003 family. It enables an unprecedented level of software integration using XML Web services: discrete building-block applications that connect to one another—as well as to other, larger applications—via the Internet. Infused into the products that make up the Microsoft platform, .NET provides the ability to quickly and reliably build, host, deploy, and use secure and connected solutions through XML Web services.

The Microsoft platform provides a suite of developer tools, client applications, XML Web services, and servers necessary to participate in this connected world. These XML Web services provide reusable components built on industry standards that invoke capabilities from other applications independent of the way the applications were built, their operating system or platform, or the devices used to access them. With XML Web services, developers can integrate applications inside enterprises and across network boundaries with partners and customers. This advance in computing—opening the door to federated collaboration and more efficient business-to-business and business-to-consumer services—can have a significant potential impact on revenue. Millions of others can use these components in varied combinations to produce highly personal, intelligent computing experiences.

Best Economics

Microsoft designed Windows Server 2003 to help companies build the value of their businesses while keeping costs down. The high reliability of Windows Server 2003 helps control costs by reducing outages and downtime. Windows Server 2003 has the flexibility to scale up and out in response to demand.

Powerful management and configuration tools in Windows Server 2003 allow businesses to deploy and manage systems as easily and efficiently as possible. Compatibility with legacy applications and third-party products means organizations will not lose their investment in existing infrastructure. With the Windows Server 2003 family, organizations benefit from a powerful, robust platform that helps build business value now and into the future.

Upgrading from Windows NT Server

In addition to Microsoft's commitment to provide the fastest, most reliable, and most secure Windows Server ever, Windows Server 2003 integrates a powerful application environment to develop innovative XML Web services and business solutions that dramatically improve process efficiency. Here are the major new features and improvements for organizations considering upgrading from Microsoft Windows NT Server 4.0:

- **Active Directory.** The Microsoft Active Directory directory service simplifies the administration of complex network directories and makes it easy for users to locate resources on even the largest networks. This enterprise-class directory service is scalable, built from the ground up using Internet-standard technologies, and fully integrated at the operating-system level in Windows Server 2003, Standard Edition; Windows Server 2003, Enterprise Edition; and Windows Server 2003, Datacenter Edition. Windows Server 2003 provides numerous ease-of-use improvements to Active Directory and new features, including cross-forest trusts, the ability to rename domains, and the ability to deactivate attributes and classes in the schema so that their definitions can be changed.

- **Group Policy: Group Policy Management Console.** Administrators can use Group Policy to define the settings and allowed actions for users and computers. In contrast with local policy, administrators can use Group Policy to set policies that apply across a given site, domain, or organizational unit in Active Directory. Policy-based management simplifies such tasks as system update operation, application installation, user profiles, and desktop-system lockdown. Expected to be available as an add-in component to Windows Server 2003, GPMC provides the new framework for managing Group Policy. With GPMC, Group Policy becomes much easier to use, a benefit that will enable more organizations to better use Active Directory and take advantage of its powerful management features.

- **Server performance.** In internal tests, Windows Server 2003 shows dramatic performance gains over previous versions of Windows server operating systems. For example, file and Web server performance is two times faster than that of Windows NT Server 4.0. While your organization's performance gains may vary because of unique network and computer settings, Microsoft is confident that the improved performance of Windows Server 2003 will help you deliver faster service for your network solutions.

- **Volume Shadow Copy Restore.** As part of the Volume Shadow Copy service, this feature enables administrators to configure point-in-time copies of critical data volumes without service interruption. These copies can then be used for service restoration or archival purposes. Users can retrieve archived versions of their documents that are invisibly maintained on the server. Productivity is improved by the ability to better recover documents.

- **Internet Information Services 6.0 and the Microsoft .NET Framework.** IIS 6.0 is a full-featured Web server that enables Web applications and XML Web services. IIS 6.0 has been completely re-architected with a new fault-tolerant process model that greatly boosts the reliability of Web sites and applications. Now IIS can isolate an individual Web application or multiple sites in a self-contained process (called an application pool) that communicates directly with the operating-system kernel. This feature increases throughput and capacity of applications while offering more headroom on servers, effectively reducing hardware needs. These self-contained application pools prevent one application or site from disrupting the XML Web services or other Web applications on the server. IIS also provides health monitoring capabilities to discover, recover from, and prevent Web application failures. On Windows Server 2003, Microsoft ASP.NET natively uses the new IIS process model. These advanced application health and detection features are also available to existing applications running under Internet Information Server 4.0 and IIS 5.0, with the vast majority of applications not needing any modification.

The .NET Framework provides the programming model for building, deploying, and running Web-based applications and XML Web services on this highly stable platform. It provides a productive standards-based, multilanguage environment for integrating existing investments with next-generation applications and services as well as the agility to solve the challenges of deployment and operation of Internet-scale applications. Existing applications can be easily repackaged as XML Web services, and UNIX applications can be integrated or even migrated into a solution with less work than in the past.

- **Terminal Services.**   Terminal Services lets administrators deliver Windows-based applications, or the Windows desktop itself, to virtually any computing device—including those that cannot run Windows. When users run an application on Terminal Services, the application execution takes place on the server, and only keyboard, mouse, and display information is transmitted over the network. Users see only their own individual sessions, which are managed transparently by the server operating system and remain independent of any other client session.

  Remote Desktop for Administration builds on the remote administration mode of Windows 2000 Terminal Services. In addition to the two virtual sessions that are available in Windows 2000 Terminal Services remote administration mode, an administrator can also remotely connect to the real console of a server. Terminal Services can enhance an enterprise's software deployment capabilities for a variety of scenarios that remain difficult to solve using traditional application distribution technologies.

- **Clustering (eight-node support).**   Available only in Windows Server 2003, Enterprise Edition, and Windows Server 2003, Datacenter Edition, this service provides high availability and scalability for mission-critical applications such as databases, messaging systems, and file and print services. Clustering works by enabling multiple servers (nodes) to remain in constant communication. If one of the nodes in a cluster becomes unavailable as a result of failure or maintenance, another node immediately begins providing service, a process known as failover. Users who are accessing the service continue their activities, unaware that service is now being provided from a different server (node). Both Windows Server 2003, Enterprise Edition, and Windows Server 2003, Datacenter Edition, support server cluster configurations of up to eight nodes.

■   **Integrated PKI support using Kerberos version 5.**   Using Certificate Services and certificate management tools, organizations can
deploy their own public key infrastructure (PKI). With PKI, administrators can implement standards-based technologies, such as smart
card logon capabilities, client authentication (through Secure Sockets
Layer and Transport Layer Security), secure e-mail, digital signatures,
and secure connectivity using Internet Protocol security (IPSec).
Using Certificate Services, administrators can set up and manage certification authorities that issue and revoke X.509 V3 certificates. This
means that organizations do not have to depend on commercial client
authentication services, although commercial client authentication
can be integrated into an organization's public key infrastructure.

Kerberos version 5 is a mature industry-standard network
authentication protocol. With Kerberos version 5 support, a fast, sin-
gle-logon process gives users the access they need to enterprise
resources, as well as to other environments that support this protocol. Support for Kerberos version 5 includes additional benefits, such
as mutual authentication (client and server must both provide
authentication) and delegated authentication (user credentials are
tracked end to end).

■   **Command-line management.**   The Windows Server 2003 family
provides a significantly enhanced command-line infrastructure, letting
administrators perform most management tasks without using a graphical user interface. Of special importance is the ability to perform a
wide range of tasks by accessing the information store enabled by
Windows Management Instrumentation (WMI). This WMI command-
line (WMIC) feature provides a simple command-line interface that
interoperates with existing shells and utility commands and can be
easily extended by scripts or other administration-oriented applications. Overall, the greater command-line functionality in the Windows
Server 2003 family, combined with ready-to-use scripts, rivals the
power of other operating systems often associated with higher cost of
ownership. Administrators accustomed to using the command line to
manage UNIX or Linux systems can continue managing from the command line in the Windows Server 2003 family.

■ **Intelligent file services: Encrypting File System, Distributed File System, and File Replication Service.**   EFS lets users encrypt and decrypt files to protect them from intruders who might gain unauthorized physical access to their sensitive stored data (for example, by stealing a laptop or an external disk drive). Encryption is transparent: users work with encrypted files and folders just as they do with any other files and folders. If the EFS user is the same person who encrypted the file or folder, the system automatically decrypts the file or folder when the user accesses it later.

DFS simplifies the task of managing shared-disk resources across a network. Administrators can assign logical names to the shared drives on a network rather than require users to know the physical name assigned to each server they need to access. FRS is a significant improvement over the directory replication feature in Windows NT Server 4.0. For example, FRS provides multimaster file replication for designated directory trees between designated servers. FRS is also used by DFS to automatically synchronize content between assigned replicas and by Active Directory to automatically synchronize content from the system volume information across domain controllers.

Upgrading from Windows 2000 Server

Built on the reliable Windows 2000 Server family, Windows Server 2003 integrates a powerful application environment to develop innovative XML Web services and improved applications that dramatically improve process efficiency. Here are the major new features and improvements for organizations considering upgrading to Windows Server 2003 from Windows 2000 Server:

■ **Active Directory improvements.**   Introduced in Windows 2000, Active Directory simplifies the administration of complex network directories and makes it easy for users to locate resources on even the largest networks. This enterprise-class directory service is scalable, built from the ground up using Internet-standard technologies, and fully integrated at the operating-system level in Windows Server 2003, Standard Edition; Windows Server 2003, Enterprise Edition; and Windows Server 2003, Datacenter Edition. Windows Server 2003 provides numerous ease-of-use improvements to Active Directory and new features including cross-forest trusts, the ability to rename domains, and the ability to deactivate attributes and classes in the schema so that their definitions can be changed.

- **Group Policy Management Console.** Administrators can use Group Policy to define the settings and allowed actions for users and computers. In contrast with local policy, organizations can use Group Policy to set policies that apply across a given site, domain, or organizational unit in Active Directory. Policy-based management simplifies such tasks as system update operation, application installation, user profiles, and desktop-system lockdown. Expected to be available as an add-in component to Windows Server 2003, GPMC provides the new framework for managing Group Policy. With GPMC, Group Policy becomes much easier to use, a benefit that will enable more organizations to better utilize Active Directory and take advantage of its powerful management features.

- **Resultant Set of Policy.** The RSoP tool allows administrators to see the effect of Group Policy on a targeted user or computer. With RSoP, organizations have a powerful and flexible base-level tool to plan, monitor, and troubleshoot Group Policy. RSoP is an infrastructure provided as a set of Microsoft Management Console (MMC) snap-ins that let administrators determine and analyze the current set of policies in two modes: logging mode and planning mode. In logging mode, administrators can assess what has applied to a particular target. In planning mode, they can see how policies would be applied to a target and then examine the results before deploying a change to Group Policy.

- **Volume Shadow Copy Restore.** As part of the Volume Shadow Copy service, this feature lets administrators configure point-in-time copies of critical data volumes without interrupting service. These copies can then be used for service restoration or archival purposes. Users can retrieve archived versions of their documents that are invisibly maintained on the server.

- **Internet Information Services 6.0.** IIS 6.0 is a full-featured Web server that enables Web applications and XML Web services. IIS 6.0 has been completely re-architected with a new fault-tolerant process model that greatly boosts the reliability of Web sites and applications. Now IIS can isolate an individual Web application or multiple sites in a self-contained process (called an application pool) that communicates directly with the operating-system kernel. This feature increases throughput and capacity of applications while offering more headroom on servers, effectively reducing hardware needs. These self-contained application pools prevent one application or site from disrupting the XML Web services or other Web applications on the server. IIS also provides health monitoring capabilities to discover, recover from, and prevent Web application failures. On Windows Server 2003, Microsoft ASP.NET natively uses the new IIS process model. These advanced application health and detection features are also available to existing applications running under Internet Information Server 4.0 and IIS 5.0, with the vast majority of applications not needing any modification.

- **Integrated .NET Framework.** The Microsoft .NET Framework is the programming model of Microsoft .NET connected software and technologies for building, deploying, and running Web applications, smart client applications, and XML Web services that expose their functionality programmatically over a network using standard protocols such as SOAP, XML, and HTTP. The .NET Framework provides a highly productive standards-based environment for integrating existing investments with next-generation applications and services. In addition, it helps organizations solve the challenges of deployment and operation of Internet-scale applications. With the .NET Framework fully integrated into the Windows Server 2003 operating system, developers are freed from writing "plumbing" code and can instead focus their efforts on delivering real business value. The .NET Framework takes care of the integration and management details, reducing code complexity and increasing coherence.

- **Command-line management.** The Windows Server 2003 family provides a significantly enhanced command-line infrastructure, letting administrators perform most management tasks without using a graphical user interface. Of special importance is the ability to perform a wide range of tasks by accessing the information store enabled by Windows Management Instrumentation (WMI). This WMI command-line (WMIC) feature provides a simple command-line interface that interoperates with existing shells and utility commands and can be easily extended by scripts or other administration-oriented applications. Overall, the greater command-line functionality in the Windows Server 2003 family, combined with ready-to-use scripts, rivals the power of other operating systems often associated with higher cost of ownership. Administrators accustomed to using the command line to manage UNIX or Linux systems can continue managing from the command line in the Windows Server 2003 family.

■   **Clustering (eight-node support).** Available only in Windows Server 2003, Enterprise Edition, and Windows Server 2003, Datacenter Edition, this service provides high availability and scalability for mission-critical applications such as databases, messaging systems, and file and print services. Clustering works by enabling multiple servers (nodes) to remain in constant communication. If one of the nodes in a cluster becomes unavailable as a result of failure or maintenance, another node immediately begins providing service, a process known as failover. Users who are accessing the service continue their activities, unaware that service is now being provided from a different server (node). Both Windows Server 2003, Enterprise Edition, and Windows Server 2003, Datacenter Edition, support server cluster configurations of up to eight nodes.

■   **Secure wireless LAN (802.1X).**   Companies can move to a security model that ensures that all physical access is authenticated and encrypted, based on the 802.1X support in the Windows Server 2003 family. Using 802.1X-based wireless access points or switches, companies can be sure that only trusted systems are allowed to connect and exchange packets with secured networks. Because 802.1X provides dynamic key determination, 802.1X wireless network encryption is dramatically improved by addressing many of the known issues associated with Wired Equivalent Privacy (WEP) used by IEEE 802.11 networks. This feature provides security and performance improvements for wireless local area networks (LANs), such as automatic key management, user authentication, and authorization prior to LAN access. It also provides access control for Ethernet networks when wired Ethernet is used in public locations.

■   **Emergency management services: headless server support.** "Headless server" capabilities allow IT administrators to install and manage a computer without a monitor, VGA display adapter, keyboard, or mouse. Emergency Management Services is a new feature allowing IT administrators to perform remote-management and system recovery tasks when the server is unavailable through the network or through other standard remote-administration tools and mechanisms.

For More Information

See the following resources for more information:

- Windows Server 2003 home page at *http://www.microsoft.com/windowsserver2003/*

- What's New in Windows Server 2003 at *http://www.microsoft.com/windowsserver2003/evaluation/overview/technologies/*

- Windows Server 2003 features at *http://www.microsoft.com/windowsserver2003/evaluation/features/*

- Feature Highlights Sorter at *http://www.microsoft.com/windowsserver2003/evaluation/features/featuresorter.aspx*

- Business Value of Microsoft Solutions at *http://www.microsoft.com/business/solutions/value/valuehome.asp*

Part II

What's New!

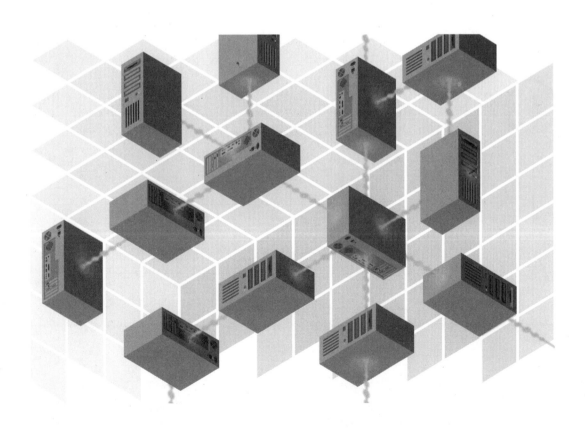

3

Active Directory

The Microsoft Active Directory directory service is a central component of the Windows platform, providing the means to manage the identities and relationships that make up network environments.

Expanding on the foundation of the Microsoft Windows 2000 operating system, the Microsoft Windows Server 2003 family improves the manageability of Active Directory and eases migration and deployment. Application developers and independent software vendors (ISVs), in particular, will also find that Active Directory in Windows Server 2003 is their best choice for developing directory-enabled applications.

Active Directory has been enhanced to reduce total cost of ownership (TCO) and operation within the enterprise. New features and enhancements have been provided at all levels of the product to extend versatility, simplify management, and increase dependability. With Windows Server 2003, organizations can benefit from further reductions in cost while increasing the efficiency with which they share and manage the various elements of the enterprise.

This chapter is for IT professionals and network system architects who want to understand the major improvements and new features of Active Directory in Windows Server 2003. This chapter begins with an overview of basic concepts in Active Directory and then addresses new features of and improvements to Active Directory in the Windows Server 2003 family.

Active Directory Basics

Active Directory is the directory service for the Windows Server 2003 family of products. (Active Directory cannot run on Windows Server 2003, Web Edition, but it can manage any computer running Web Edition.)

Active Directory stores information about objects on the network and makes this information easy for administrators and users to find and use. Active Directory uses a structured data store as the basis for a logical, hierarchical organization of directory information. The sections following this one describe the directory data store and other concepts that are important when evaluating Active Directory and Windows Server 2003.

Directory Data Store

The directory data store is often simply referred to as the *directory*. The directory contains information about objects such as users, groups, computers, domains, organizational units (OUs), and security policies. This information can be published for users and administrators.

The directory is stored on servers known as *domain controllers* and can be accessed by network applications or services. A domain can have one or more domain controllers. Each domain controller has a writable copy of the directory for the domain in which it is located. Changes made to the directory are replicated from the originating domain controller to other domain controllers in the domain, domain tree, or forest. Because the directory is replicated, and because each domain controller has a writable copy of the directory, the directory is highly available to users and administrators throughout the domain.

Directory data is stored in the Ntds.dit file on the domain controller. This file should preferably be stored on an NTFS partition. Some data is stored in the directory database file, and some data (such as logon scripts or Group Policies) is stored in a replicated file system. Three categories of directory data are replicated between domain controllers:

- **Domain data.** The domain data contains information about objects within a domain. This is the information typically thought of as directory information, such as e-mail contacts, user and computer account attributes, and published resources that are of interest to administrators and users. For example, when a user account is added to your network, a user account object and attribute data are stored in the domain data. When changes to your organization's directory objects occur, such as object creation, object deletion, or attribute modification, this data is stored in the domain data.

- **Configuration data.** The configuration data describes the topology of the directory. This configuration data includes a list of all domains, trees, and forests and the locations of the domain controllers and global catalogs.

- **Schema data.** The schema is the formal definition of all object and attribute data that can be stored in the directory. Windows Server 2003 includes a default schema that defines many object types, such as user and computer accounts, groups, domains, organizational units, and security policies. Administrators and programmers can extend the schema by defining new object types and attributes or by adding new attributes for existing objects. Schema objects are protected by access control lists (ACLs), ensuring that only authorized users can alter the schema.

Active Directory and Security

Security is integrated with Active Directory through logon authentication and access control to objects in the directory. With a single network logon, administrators can manage directory data and organization throughout their network, and authorized network users can access resources anywhere on the network. Policy-based administration eases the management of even the most complex network.

Active Directory provides protected storage of user account and group information by using access control on objects and user credentials. Because Active Directory stores not only user credentials but also access control information, users who log on to the network obtain both authentication and authorization to access system resources. For example, when a user logs on to the network, the security system authenticates the user with information stored in Active Directory. Then, when the user attempts to access a service on the network, the system checks the properties defined in the discretionary access control list (DACL) for that service.

Because Active Directory allows administrators to create group accounts, administrators can manage system security more efficiently. For example, by adjusting a file's properties, an administrator can permit all users in a group to read that file. In this way, access to objects in Active Directory is based on group membership.

Active Directory Schema

The Active Directory Schema is the set of definitions that defines the kinds of objects—and the types of information about those objects—that can be stored in Active Directory. Because the definitions are themselves stored as objects, Active Directory can manage the schema objects with the same object management operations used for managing the rest of the objects in the directory. There are two types of definitions in the schema: attributes and classes.

Attributes and classes (also referred to as schema objects or metadata) can be described as follows:

- **Classes.**   Classes, also referred to as *object classes*, describe the possible directory objects that can be created. Each class is a collection of attributes. When you create an object, the attributes store the information that describes the object. The *User* class, for example, is composed of many attributes, including *Network Address*, *Home Directory*, and so on. Every object in Active Directory is an instance of an object class.

- **Attributes.**   Attributes are defined separately from classes. Each attribute is defined only once and can be used in multiple classes. For example, the *Description* attribute is used in many classes but is defined once in the schema, ensuring consistency.

   Attributes describe objects. Each attribute has its own definition describing the type of information that can be specified for that attribute. Each attribute in the schema is specified in the *Attribute-Schema* class, which determines the information that each attribute definition must contain. The list of attributes that can be applied to a particular object is determined by the class of which the object is an instance and by any superclasses of that object's class. Attributes are defined only once and are potentially used many times. This ensures consistency across all classes that share a particular attribute.

- **Multivalued Attributes.**   Attributes can be single-valued or multivalued. The schema definition of an attribute specifies whether an instance of the attribute can have multiple values. An instance of a single-valued attribute can be empty, or it can contain a single value. An instance of a multivalued attribute can be empty, or it can contain a single value or multiple values. Each value of a multivalued attribute must be unique.

- **Indexing Attributes.**   Indexes apply to attributes, not to classes. Indexing an attribute can help queries more quickly find objects having that attribute. When you mark an attribute as indexed, all instances of the attribute are added to the index, not just the instances that are members of a particular class. Adding indexed attributes can affect Active Directory replication time, available memory, and database size. Because the database is larger, it takes longer to replicate.

Multivalued attributes can also be indexed. Indexing multivalued attributes increases the size of Active Directory and object creation time more than does indexing single-valued properties. When choosing attributes to be indexed, make sure that they will be commonly used and balance the cost versus performance.

An indexed schema attribute can also be searched by the container in which the attribute is stored rather than by the entire Active Directory database. This will improve search time and cut down on the amount of resources used during the search.

Experienced developers and network administrators can dynamically extend the schema by defining new classes and new attributes for existing classes. The domain controller that holds the schema operations master role controls the content of the schema. A copy of the schema is replicated to all domain controllers in the forest. The use of this common schema ensures data integrity and consistency throughout the forest. You can also extend the schema by using the Active Directory Schema snap-in. To modify the schema, you must satisfy the both of the following requirements: be a member of the Schema Administrators group (or have the rights to modify the schema master delegated to you by an administrator) and install the Active Directory Schema snap-in on the computer holding the schema operations master role. When considering changes to the schema, you should keep three key points in mind:

- **Schema extensions are global.**   When you extend the schema, you extend it for the entire forest because any changes to the schema are replicated to every domain controller in every domain in the forest.

- **Schema classes related to the system cannot be modified.**   You cannot modify default system classes within the Active Directory schema; however, applications that are used to modify the schema might add optional system classes, which you can change.

- **Schema extensions can be reversible.**   Some properties of attributes or classes can be modified after creation. Once a new class or attribute has been added to the schema, it can be deactivated, but it cannot be removed. However, you can mark definitions as defunct and reuse object identifiers (OIDs) or display names, which allows you to reverse a schema definition.

For more information about modifying the schema, see the Microsoft Windows Resource Kits at *http://www.microsoft.com/reskit/*. Active Directory does not support deletion of schema objects; however, objects can be marked as deactivated, providing many of the benefits of deletion.

The Global Catalog

A *global catalog* is a domain controller that stores a copy of all Active Directory objects in a forest. In addition, the global catalog stores each object's most common searchable attributes. The global catalog stores a full copy of all objects in the directory for its host domain and a partial copy of all objects for all other domains in the forest, thus providing efficient searches without unnecessary referrals to domain controllers.

A global catalog is created automatically on the initial domain controller in the forest. You can add global catalog functionality to other domain controllers or change the default location of the global catalog to another domain controller. A global catalog performs the following directory roles:

- **Finds objects.** A global catalog enables user searches for directory information throughout all domains in a forest, regardless of where the data is stored. Searches within a forest are performed with maximum speed and minimum network traffic. When you search for people or printers from the Start menu or choose the Entire Directory option within a query, you are searching a global catalog. Once you enter your search request, it is routed to the default global catalog port and sent to a global catalog for resolution.

- **Supplies user principal name authentication.** A global catalog resolves user principal names when the authenticating domain controller does not have knowledge of the account. For example, if a user's account is located in *example1.microsoft.com* and the user decides to log on with the user principal name *user1@example1.microsoft.com* from a computer located in *example2.microsoft.com*, the domain controller in *example2.microsoft.com* will be unable to find the user's account and will then contact a global catalog server to complete the logon process.

- **Supplies universal group membership information in a multiple-domain environment.** Unlike global group memberships, which are stored in each domain, universal group memberships are stored only in a global catalog. For example, when a user who belongs to a universal group logs on to a domain that is set to the Windows 2000 native domain functional level or higher, the global catalog provides universal group membership information for the user's account. If a global catalog is not available when a user logs on to a domain running in Windows 2000 native or higher, the computer will use cached credentials to log on the user if the user has logged on to the domain previously. If the user has not logged on to the domain previously, the user can log on to only the local computer.

> **Note**   Members of the Domain Administrators group are able to log on to the network even when a global catalog is not available.

Finding Directory Information

As explained earlier, Active Directory is designed to provide information to queries about directory objects from both users and programs. Administrators and users can easily search for and find information in the directory by using the Search command on the Start menu. Client programs can access information in Active Directory by using Active Directory Services Interface (ADSI).

One of the principal benefits of Active Directory is its rich store of information about network objects. Information published in Active Directory about users, computers, files, and printers is available to network users. This availability is controlled by security permissions.

Everyday tasks on a network involve communication with other users and connection to published resources. These tasks require finding names and addresses to send mail or connect to shared resources. In this respect, Active Directory functions as a shared address book for the enterprise. For example, you can find a user by first name, last name, e-mail name, office location, or other properties of that person's user account. Finding information is optimized by use of the global catalog, as explained earlier.

Administrators can use the Advanced Find dialog boxes in the Active Directory Users And Computers snap-in to perform management tasks with greater efficiency and to easily customize and filter data retrieved from the directory. In addition, administrators can add objects to groups quickly and with minimal network impact by utilizing browseless queries to help find likely members.

Active Directory Replication

Replication provides information availability, fault tolerance, load balancing, and performance benefits for the directory. Active Directory uses multimaster replication, which lets you update the directory at any domain controller, rather than at a single, primary domain controller. The multimaster model has the benefit of greater fault tolerance because, with multiple domain controllers, replication continues, even if any single domain controller stops working. A domain controller stores and replicates the following types of information:

■ **Schema information.**   This defines the objects that can be created in the directory and the attributes those objects can have. This information is common to all domains in the forest. Schema data is replicated to all domain controllers in the forest.

■ **Configuration information.**   This describes the logical structure of your deployment, containing information such as domain structure or replication topology. This information is common to all domains in the forest. Configuration data is replicated to all domain controllers in the forest.

■ **Domain information.**   This describes all of the objects in a domain. This data is domain-specific and is not distributed to any other domains. For the purpose of finding information throughout the domain tree or forest, a subset of the properties for all objects in all domains is stored in the global catalog. Domain data is replicated to all domain controllers in the domain.

■ **Application information.**   Information stored in the application directory partition is intended to satisfy cases in which information needs to be replicated, but not necessarily on a global scale. Application data can be explicitly rerouted to administrator-specified domain controllers within a forest to prevent unnecessary replication traffic, or it can be set to replicate to all domain controllers in the domain.

Sites streamline replication of directory information. Directory schema and configuration information is replicated throughout the forest, and domain data is replicated among all domain controllers in the domain and partially replicated to global catalogs. By strategically reducing replication, you can similarly reduce the strain on your network. Domain controllers use sites and replication change control to optimize replication in the following ways:

■ By occasionally reevaluating which connections are used, Active Directory uses the most efficient network connections.

■ Active Directory uses multiple routes to replicate changes, providing fault tolerance.

■ Replication costs are minimized because only changed information is replicated.

If a deployment is not organized into sites, information exchange among domain controllers and clients can be chaotic. Sites improve the efficiency of network usage. Active Directory replicates directory information within a site more frequently than among sites. This way, the best-connected domain controllers—those most likely to need particular directory information—receive replications first. The domain controllers at other sites receive all changes to the directory, but less frequently, reducing network bandwidth consumption. And because data is compressed when replicated between sites, bandwidth consumption is further reduced. For the sake of efficiency, updates are limited only to times when new directory information has been added or current directory information has been changed.

If directory updates are constantly distributed to all other domain controllers in the domain, they will consume network resources. Although you can manually add or configure connections or force replication over a particular connection, replication is automatically optimized by the Active Directory Knowledge Consistency Checker (KCC) based on information that you provide in the Active Directory Sites And Services administration tool. The KCC is responsible for constructing and maintaining the replication topology for Active Directory. In particular, the KCC decides when replication will occur and the set of servers that each server must replicate with.

Active Directory Clients

With the Active Directory client, many of the Active Directory features available on Windows 2000 Professional or Microsoft Windows XP Professional are available to computers running Microsoft Windows 95, Microsoft Windows 98, and Microsoft Windows NT 4 operating systems:

- **Site awareness.**   You can log on to the domain controller that is closest to the client in the network.

- **Active Directory Services Interface.**   You can use scripting to Active Directory. ADSI also provides a common programming API to Active Directory programmers.

- **Distributed File System (DFS) fault tolerance client.**   You can access Windows 2000 and servers running Windows .NET DFS fault-tolerant and failover file shares specified in Active Directory.

- **NTLM version 2 authentication.**   You can use the improved authentication features in Windows NT Challenge/Response Authentication (NTLM) version 2. For more information about enabling NTLM version 2, see article Q239869, "How to Enable NTLM 2

Authentication," in the Microsoft Knowledge Base at *http://support.microsoft.com/*.

- **Active Directory Windows Address Book (WAB) property pages.** You can change properties, such as phone number and address, on user object pages.

- **Active Directory search capability.** From the Start button, you can locate printers and people in a Windows 2000 Server or Windows .NET domain. For information about publishing printers in Active Directory, see article Q234619, "Publishing a Printer in Windows Active Directory," in the Microsoft Knowledge Base at *http://support.microsoft.com/*.

Windows 2000 Professional and Windows XP Professional provide functionality not included in the Active Directory client on Windows 95, Windows 98, and Windows NT 4, including Kerberos version 5 support, Group Policy or IntelliMirror management technologies support, and service principal name or mutual authentication. You can take advantage of these additional features by upgrading to Windows 2000 Professional or Windows XP Professional. For more information, see the following resources:

- Upgrading to Windows 2000 at *http://www.microsoft.com/windows2000/professional/howtobuy/upgrading/*

- Windows XP Professional Upgrade Center at *http://www.microsoft.com/windowsxp/pro/howtobuy/upgrading/*

- Active Directory client page at *http://www.microsoft.com/windows-2000/server/evaluation/news/bulletins/adextension.asp*

Integration and Productivity

As the principal means to manage enterprise identities, objects, and relationships, the interfaces in Active Directory (both programmatic and user interfaces) have been improved to increase administration efficiency and integration capabilities.

Managing Active Directory

Active Directory contains many enhancements that make it easier to use, such as improvements to Microsoft Management Console (MMC) snap-ins and the object picker component. MMC plug-ins will be able to facilitate management of multiple objects. For example, administrators can do the following tasks:

■ **Edit multiple user objects.**   Select and edit multiple object properties at once.

■ **Save queries.**   Save queries against the Active Directory service for future use. Results are exportable in XML.

■ **Quickly select objects using the improved object picker component.**   The component has been redesigned and enhanced to improve workflow, increase efficiency in finding objects in a large directory, and provide a more flexible query capability. It is used by numerous user interfaces and is available for use by third-party developers.

More Productivity Features

Additional productivity features of Active Directory include the following:

■ **ACL user interface changes.**   The ACL user interface has been enhanced to improve usability as well as improve inherited versus specific object permissions.

■ **Extensibility enhancements.**   An administrator who has an independent software vendor (ISV) or OEM device that uses Active Directory has enhanced management capabilities and can add any class of object to be a member of a group.

■ **User objects from other Lightweight Directory Access Protocol (LDAP) directories.**   User objects defined in LDAP directories that use the *inetOrgPerson* class as defined in RFC 2798 (such as those developed by Novell and Netscape) can be defined using the Active Directory User Interfaces. The user interface that works with Active Directory user objects will work with *inetOrgPerson* objects. Now any application or customer that needs to use the *inetOrgPerson* class can do so easily.

■ **Passport integration (via IIS).**   Passport authentication is now available for Internet Information Services (IIS) 6.0 and enables Active Directory user objects to be mapped to their corresponding Passport identification (if it exists). A token is created by the Local Security Authority (LSA) for the user and is set by IIS 6.0 for the HTTP request. Internet users who have a corresponding Passport identification can now use their Passport to access resources as if they were using their Active Directory credentials.

- **Terminal Server usage with ADSI.** Terminal Server user-specific properties can be scripted using the Active Directory Services Interface (ADSI). User properties can be scripted with ADSI in addition to being set manually through the directory, a benefit that makes it easy to implement bulk or programmatic changes through ADSI.

- **Replication-monitoring and trust-monitoring WMI providers.** Windows Management Instrumentation (WMI) classes can monitor whether domain controllers are successfully replicating Active Directory information among themselves. Because many Windows 2000 components, such as Active Directory replication, rely on interdomain trust, this feature also provides a method to verify that trusts are functioning correctly. Administrators or operations staff can be easily alerted to replication problems through WMI now.

- **MSMQ distribution lists.** Message Queuing (MSMQ) adds support for sending messages to distribution lists that are hosted in Active Directory. MSMQ users can easily manage distribution lists from within Active Directory.

Performance and Scalability

Major changes have been made in the way Windows Server 2003 manages the replication and synchronization of Active Directory information. New features have also been added for installation, migration, and maintenance to make Active Directory more flexible, robust, and efficient.

Branch Office Performance

A branch office deployment usually consists of numerous remote offices, each with its own domain controllers—but with slow links to a corporate hub or data center. Windows Server 2003 improves the logon process for branch offices by no longer requiring access to the central global catalog server each time a user wants to log on. Now organizations do not have to deploy a global catalog server in branch offices where the network is unreliable.

Instead of contacting a global catalog each time a user logs on to a domain controller, the domain controller caches the universal group membership of users who have previously logged on from this site or from off-site global catalog servers when the network was available. Users are then allowed to log on without the need for the domain controller to contact a global catalog server at logon time, which reduces the demand on slow or unreliable networks. This improvement also provides added reliability if a global catalog is unavailable to process logon requests for users.

More Performance Improvements

Additional performance improvements to Active Directory include the following:

- **Disabling compression of intersite replication traffic.** Replication-traffic compression between domain controllers residing in different sites can be disabled. This can reduce the CPU demand on the domain controllers, thereby increasing performance if needed.

- **Clustered virtual server support.** A computer object is now defined for clustered servers. Cluster-aware and Active Directory–aware applications can associate their own configuration information with a well-defined object.

- **Concurrent LDAP binds.** Multiple Lightweight Directory Access Protocol (LDAP) binds can be performed on the same connection for the purposes of authenticating users. This feature, when utilized by the application developer, vastly improves the performance of LDAP binds and authentication requests against Active Directory.

- **Domain controller overload prevention.** This feature prevents overloading a first Active Directory domain controller introduced in a domain that already contains a large number of upgraded Windows 2000 and Windows Server 2003 domain members.

  A Windows NT Server 4 domain contains Windows 2000 and Windows Server 2003 domain members, including both clients and servers. When a primary domain controller (PDC) is upgraded to Windows 2000 Service Pack 2 (SP2) or upgraded to Windows Server 2003, it can be configured to emulate the Windows NT 4 domain controller behavior. The Windows 2000 and Windows Server 2003 domain members will not distinguish between upgraded domain controllers and Windows NT 4 domain controllers.

  To accommodate special needs of administrators, domain members running either Windows 2000 SP2 or Windows Server 2003 can be configured to inform domain controllers running Windows 2000 SP2 or Windows Server 2003 not to emulate Windows NT 4 domain controller behavior when responding to such domain members.

■ **Global catalog replication tuning.** In Windows Server 2003 domains with global catalog replication, tuning in the global catalog synchronization state is preserved rather than reset, minimizing the work generated as a result of a Partial Attribute Set (PAS) extension by transmitting only attributes that were added. The overall benefit is a reduction in replication traffic and more efficient PAS updates.

■ **Group membership replication improvements.** When a forest is advanced to Windows Server 2003 Forest Native Mode, group membership is changed to store and replicate values for individual members instead of the entire membership as a single unit. This results in lower network bandwidth and processor usage during replication and virtually eliminates the possibility of lost updates during simultaneous updates.

■ **LDAP support for Time to Live (TTL) values for dynamic entries.** Active Directory can store dynamic entries. These entries specify a TTL value. The user can modify the TTL value, causing the entry to remain longer than its current remaining life. The LDAP C-language API was extended to support this new capability. This provides application developers with the ability to store information in the directory that does not need to persist for long periods of time and will automatically be deleted by Active Directory once the TTL expires.

■ **Support for 64-bit deployment.** Group Policy settings are now provided to help manage 64-bit software deployment. Options in the Application Deployment Editor (ADE) aid in determining whether 32-bit applications should be deployed to 64-bit clients. Group Policy can be used to ensure that only the appropriate applications are deployed to 64-bit clients.

Administration and Configuration Management

Windows Server 2003 enhances the administrator's ability to efficiently configure and manage Active Directory, even in very large enterprises with multiple forests, domains, and sites.

New Setup Wizards

The new Configure Your Server Wizard eases the process of setting up Active Directory and provides predefined settings for specific server roles, a benefit that helps administrators standardize the way servers are initially deployed. Administrators are assisted during server setup to make the process easier by helping users finish installing optional components that they choose during the Windows setup. They can use the Configure Your Server Wizard to perform the following:

■   Set up the first server on a network by automatically configuring DHCP, DNS, and Active Directory using basic default settings.

■   Help users configure member servers on a network by pointing to the features they need to set up a file server, a print server, a Web and media server, an application server, Remote Access Service (RAS) and routing, or an IP address management server.

An administrator can use this feature for disaster recovery, replicating a server configuration to multiple computers, finishing setup, configuring server roles, or setting up the configuration of the first or primary server on a network.

More Administrative Improvements

Additional administrative improvements to Active Directory include the following:

■   **Automatic creation of DNS zones.**   Domain Name System (DNS) zones and servers can be automatically created and configured when running one of the Windows Server 2003 family operating systems. They are created through the enterprise to host the new zone. They can significantly reduce the time needed to manually configure every DNS server.

■   **Improved intersite replication topology generation.** The Inter-Site Topology Generator (ISTG) has been updated to use improved algorithms and will scale to support forests with a greater number of sites than in Windows 2000. Because all domain controllers in the forest running the ISTG role must agree on the intersite replication topology, the new algorithms are not activated until the forest has advanced to Windows Server 2003 Forest Native Mode. The new ISTG algorithms provide improved replication performance across forests.

■   **DNS configuration enhancements.** This feature simplifies debugging and reporting of an incorrect DNS configuration and helps to properly configure the DNS infrastructure required for Active Directory deployment.

An example of the benefits of this feature is that if a domain controller is promoted in an existing forest, the Active Directory Installation Wizard contacts an existing domain controller to update the directory and replicate the required portions of the directory from the domain controller. If the wizard fails to locate a domain controller because of an incorrect configuration of DNS or if the domain controller is not available, it performs debugging and reports the cause of the failure and indicates how to fix the problem.

To be located on a network, every domain controller must register domain controller locator DNS records. The Active Directory Installation Wizard verifies that the DNS infrastructure is properly configured to allow the new domain controller to perform a dynamic update of its domain controller locator DNS records. If this check discovers the incorrectly configured DNS infrastructure, it is reported with an explanation of how to fix the problem.

- **Install replica from media.**   Instead of replicating a complete copy of the Active Directory database over the network, this feature allows an administrator to source initial replication from files created when backing up an existing domain controller or global catalog server. The backup files, generated by any Active Directory–aware backup utility, can be transported to the candidate domain controller using media such as tape, CD, DVD, or file copy over a network.

- **Migration Tool Enhancements.**   The Active Directory Migration Tool (ADMT) is enhanced in Windows Server 2003 to provide the following features:

  - ❏ **Password migration.**   ADMT version 2 will allow migrating passwords from Windows NT 4 to Windows 2000 or Windows Server 2003 domains as well as migrating passwords from Windows 2000 to Windows Server 2003 domains.

  - ❏ **New scripting interface.**   For the most commonly used migration tasks, such as migration of users, groups, and computers, a new scripting interface is provided. ADMT can now be driven from any language—such as Microsoft Visual Basic Scripting Edition (VBScript), Microsoft Visual Basic, and Microsoft Visual C++—and it supports COM interfaces.

  - ❏ **Command-line support.**   The scripting interface has also been extended to provide command-line support. All scriptable tasks can be executed directly from a command line or through batch files.

❏ **Security translation improvements.** The security translation, such as redoing resources within ACLs, is extended in a way that the source domain can be decommissioned when security translation runs. ADMT will now also allow specifying a mapping file that can be used as input for security translations. ADMT version 2 makes it easier to migrate to Active Directory and provides more options to automate migration.

■ **Application directory partitions.** Active Directory services allows the creation of a new type of naming context, or partition, referred to as *application partition*. This naming context can contain a hierarchy of any type of object except security principals (users, groups, and computers) and can be configured to replicate to any set of domain controllers in the forest, not necessarily all in the same domain.

This feature provides the capability of hosting dynamic data in Active Directory without significantly affecting network performance by providing the ability to control the scope of replication and placement of replicas.

■ **Integrated DNS zones stored in application partitions.** DNS zones in Active Directory can be stored and replicated in the application partition. Using application partitions to store the DNS data results in a reduced number of objects stored in the global catalog. In addition, when DNS zone data is stored in an application partition, it is replicated to only that subset of domain controllers in the domain that is specified in the application partition. By default, DNS-specific application partitions contain only those domain controllers that run the DNS server. In addition, storing the DNS zone in an application partition enables replication of the DNS zone to the DNS servers running on the domain controllers in different domains of an Active Directory forest. By integrating DNS zones in an application partition, it is possible to limit the replication of this information and decrease overall replication bandwidth requirements.

■ **DirSync control improvements.** This feature improves Active Directory support for LDAP control, called DirSync control, to retrieve changed information from the directory. The DirSync control can access checks similar to those performed on normal LDAP searches.

■ **Functionality levels.** Similar to native mode in Windows 2000, this feature provides a versioning mechanism that can be used by Active Directory core components to determine which features are available on each domain controller in a domain and in a forest. It is also used to prevent pre–Windows Server 2003 domain controllers from joining a forest that has the Windows Server 2003–only Active Directory feature activated.

■   **Deactivation of schema attributes and classes.**   Active Directory has been enhanced to allow the deactivation of attributes and class definitions in the Active Directory schema. Attributes and classes can be redefined if an error was made in the original definition.

Deactivation provides the ability to supersede the definition of an attribute or a class after it has been added to the schema if an error was made in setting an immutable property. It is a reversible operation, allowing administrators to undo an accidental deactivation without side effects. Administrators now have greater flexibility with respect to their Active Directory schema management.

■   **Domain rename.**   This feature supports changing the DNS and NetBIOS names of existing domains in a forest while ensuring that the resulting forest is still *well formed*. The identity of a renamed domain represented by its domain globally unique identifier (GUID) and its domain security identifier (SID) will not change. In addition, a computer's domain membership does not change as a result of the holding domain being renamed.

This feature does not include changing which domain is the forest root domain. Although a forest root domain can be renamed, a different domain cannot be designated to become the new forest root.

Domain rename will cause a service interruption, requiring every domain controller to be rebooted. Domain rename will also require every member computer of the renamed domain to be rebooted twice. Although this feature provides a supported means to rename a domain, it is not viewed as nor is it intended to be a routine IT operation.

■   **Upgrading forest and domains.**   Active Directory has added improvements in security and application support. Before the first domain controller running the Windows Server 2003 operating system can be upgraded in an existing forest or domain, the forest and domains have to be prepared for these new features. Adprep is a new tool to aid forest and domain upgrades. The Adprep tool is not needed when upgrading from Windows NT 4 or when Active Directory is clean-installed on servers running Windows Server 2003.

- **Replication and trust monitoring.** This allows administrators to monitor whether domain controllers are successfully replicating Active Directory information among themselves. Because many Windows .NET components, such as Active Directory replication, rely on interdomain trust, this feature also provides a method to verify that trusts are functioning correctly.

Group Policy Management

The Microsoft Group Policy Management Console (GPMC) is the new solution for Group Policy management that helps you manage your enterprise more cost-effectively. It consists of a new Microsoft Management Console (MMC) snap-in and a set of scriptable interfaces for managing Group Policy. GPMC is planned to be available as a separate component by the time Windows Server 2003 is launched. GPMC is designed to do the following:

- Simplify the management of Group Policy by providing a single place for managing core aspects of Group Policy. You can think of GPMC as a one-stop location for managing Group Policy.

- Address top Group Policy deployment requirements, as requested by customers, by providing

    - A user interface (UI) that makes Group Policy much easier to use

    - Backup/restore of Group Policy objects (GPOs)

    - Import/export and copy/paste of GPOs and Windows Management Instrumentation (WMI) filters

    - Simplified management of Group Policy–related security

    - HTML reporting for GPO settings

    - HTML reporting for Group Policy Results and Group Policy Modeling data (formerly known as Resultant Set of Policy)

    - Scripting of GPO operations that are exposed within this tool—but not scripting of settings with a GPO

Prior to GPMC, administrators were required to use several Microsoft tools to manage Group Policy. GPMC integrates the existing Group Policy functionality exposed in these tools into a single, unified console, along with the new capabilities just listed.

Managing Domains

GPMC will be able to manage both Windows 2000 and Windows Server 2003–based domains with the Active Directory service. In either case, the administrative computer on which the tool itself runs must be running one of the following:

- Windows Server 2003

- Windows XP Professional with Service Pack 1 (SP1), plus an additional post-SP1 hot fix, and the Microsoft .NET Framework

More Group Policy Improvements

Additional Group Policy improvements to Active Directory include the following:

- **Redirecting default user and computer containers.**   Windows Server 2003 includes tools to automatically redirect new user and computer objects into specified organizational units where Group Policy can be applied.

  This helps administrators avoid a situation in which new user and computer objects are left in default containers at the domain root level. Such containers were not designed to hold Group Policy links, and clients were not designed to read and apply Group Policy from these containers. This forced many customers who used these containers to introduce domain-level policy, which can be unwieldy in many cases.

  Instead, Microsoft recommends creating a logical hierarchy of organizational units to hold newly created user and computer objects. Administrators can use two new Resource Kit tools—RedirUsr and ReDirComp—to specify an alternative default for the three legacy APIs: *NetUserAdd*, *NetGroupAdd*, and *NetJoinDomain*. This will allow administrators to redirect the default locations to suitable organizational units and then apply Group Policy directly to these new organizational units.

- **Group Policy Results.**   Group Policy Results enables administrators to determine and analyze the current set of policies applied to a particular target. With Group Policy Results, administrators can review existing policy settings on targeted computers. Group Policy Results was formerly known as the logging mode of Resultant Set of Policy.

- **Group Policy Modeling.** Group Policy Modeling is designed to help administrators plan for growth and reorganization. It allows administrators to poll standing policy settings, applications, and security for what-if scenarios. Once an administrator decides that a change is necessary or inevitable, a series of tests can be run to see what would happen to a user or group of users if they were moved to another location, another security group, or even another computer. This includes which policy settings would be applied and which files would be automatically loaded after the change took effect. Group Policy Modeling greatly benefits administrators by providing the means to fully test policy changes before implementing them throughout their networks.

New Policy Settings

Windows Server 2003 includes more than 150 new policy settings. These policy settings provide the capability to customize and control the behavior of the operating system for groups of users. These new policy settings affect functionality such as error reporting, Terminal Server, networking and dial-up connections, DNS, network logon requests, Group Policy, and roaming profiles. The new policy-related features include the following:

- **Web view administrative templates.** This feature enhances the Group Policy Administrative Template extension snap-in, making it possible to view detailed information about the various available policy settings. When a policy setting is selected, information detailing a setting's behavior and additional information about where the setting can be used are displayed in a Web view within the administrative templates user interface. This information is also available from the Explain tab on the property page of each setting.

- **Manage DNS client.** Administrators can configure the DNS client settings on Windows Server 2003 using Group Policy. This simplifies the steps to configure domain members when adjusting DNS client settings such as enabling and disabling dynamic registration of the DNS records by the clients, using devolution of the primary DNS suffix during name resolution, and populating DNS suffix search lists.

- **My Documents folder redirection.** An administrator can use this feature to transition users from a legacy deployment of home directories to the My Documents model while maintaining compatibility with the existing home directory environment.

- **Full installation of user-assigned applications at logon time.** The Application Deployment Editor contains a new option that allows a user-assigned application to be installed completely at logon time instead of on demand. Administrators can ensure that users have the appropriate software automatically installed on their computers.

- **Netlogon.**   This feature provides the capability to configure the Netlogon settings on Windows Server 2003–based computers using Group Policy. This simplifies the steps required to configure domain members when adjusting Netlogon settings such as enabling and disabling dynamic registration of the specific domain controller locator DNS records by the domain controllers, periodicity of refreshing such records, and many other popular Netlogon parameters.

- **Network and dial-up connections.**   Windows Server 2003 networking configuration user interfaces can be made available for (or limited to) specific users via a Group Policy.

- **Distributed eventing policies.**   WMI eventing infrastructure is expanded to operate in a distributed environment. The enhancements consist of components that will enable configuring subscription, filtering, correlation, aggregation, and transport of WMI events. An ISV can enable health monitoring, event logging, notification, autorecovery, and billing with the addition of a user interface and definition of a policy type.

- **Credential Manager disabling.**   A new feature in Windows Server 2003, Credential Manager eases managing user credentials. Group Policy allows you to disable Credential Manager.

- **Support URL for software deployment.**   This feature provides a capability to edit and add a support URL for the package. When the application appears in Add/Remove Programs on target computers, the user can then select the Support Information URL and be directed to a support Web page. This feature can assist in reducing calls to a help desk or support team.

- **WMI Filtering.**   Windows Management Instrumentation (WMI) makes a large amount of data, such as hardware and software inventory, settings, and configuration information, available for a target computer. WMI gathers data from the registry, the drivers, the file system, Active Directory, Simple Network Management Protocol (SNMP), the Windows Installer service, structured query language (SQL), networking, and Exchange Server. WMI Filtering in Windows Server 2003 lets you dynamically determine whether to apply a GPO based on a query of WMI data. These queries (also called WMI filters) determine which users and computers receive the policy settings configured in the GPO where you create the filter. This functionality lets you dynamically target Group Policy based on the properties of the local machine.

For example, a GPO might exist that assigns Office XP to users in a certain organizational unit. However, administrators are uncertain as to whether all of the older desktops in that organizational unit have enough hard disk space to accommodate the software. In this case, a WMI filter can be used with the GPO to assign Office XP only to users who have desktops with more than 400 megabytes (MB) of available hard disk space.

- **Terminal Server.**   An administrator can use Group Policy to manage how a terminal server can be used, such as enforcing redirection capabilities, password access, and wallpaper settings.

Security Enhancements

In the Windows Server 2003 family, Active Directory has been enhanced with some additional security features that make it easier to manage multiple forests and cross-domain trusts. In addition, the new Credential Manager provides a secure store of user credentials and X.509 certificates.

Forest Trust Management

Forest trust is a new type of Windows trust for managing the security relationship between two forests. This feature vastly simplifies cross-forest security administration and enables the trusting forest to enforce constraints on which security principal names it trusts other forests to authenticate. This feature includes the following:

- A new trust type that allows all domains in one forest to (transitively) trust all domains in another forest, via a single trust link between the two forest root domains.

- Forest trust is not transitive at the forest level across three or more forests. If Forest A trusts Forest B, and Forest B trusts Forest C, this does not create any trust relationship between Forest A and Forest C.

- Forest trusts can be one-way or two-way.

- A new wizard simplifies creating all types of trust links, especially forest trust.

- A new property page lets you manage the trusted namespaces associated with forest trusts.

- Trusted namespaces are used to route authentication and authorization requests for security principals whose accounts are maintained in a trusted forest.

- The domain, user principal name (UPN), service principal name (SPN), and security identifier (SID) namespaces that a forest publishes are automatically collected when a forest trust is created and are refreshed by the Active Directory Domains And Trust user interface.

- A forest is trusted to be authoritative for the namespaces it publishes, on a first-come, first-serve basis, as long as they do not collide with trusted namespaces from existing forest trust relationships.

- Overlapping trusted namespaces are automatically prevented. Administrators can also manually disable individual trusted namespaces.

More Security Enhancements

Additional security enhancements to Active Directory include the following:

- **Cross-forest authentication.** Cross-forest authentication enables secure access to resources when the user account is in one forest and the computer account is in another forest. This feature allows users to securely access resources in other forests, using either Kerberos or NTLM, without sacrificing the single-sign-on and administrative benefits of having only one user ID and password maintained in the user's home forest. Cross-forest authentication includes:

  - ❑ **Name resolution.** When Kerberos and NTLM cannot resolve a principal name on the local domain controller, they call a global catalog. When the global catalog cannot resolve the name, it calls a new cross-forest name matching function. The name matching function compares the security principal name with trusted namespaces from all trusted forests. If a match is found, it returns the trusted forest name as a routing hint.

❑   **Request routing.**   Kerberos and NTLM use routing hints to route authentication requests along the trust path from the originating domain to the probable target domain. For Kerberos, Key Distribution Centers (KDCs) generate referrals that follow the trust path, and the client chases them in standard Kerberos fashion. For NTLM, domain controllers chain the request across secure channels that follow the trust path, using pass-through authentication.

❑   **Authentication supported.**   Supported authentication methods include Kerberos and NTLM network logon for remote access to a server in another forest, Kerberos and NTLM interactive logon for physical logon outside the user's home forest, and Kerberos delegation to N-tier application in another forest. UPN credentials are fully supported.

■   **Cross-forest authorization.**   Cross-forest authorization makes it easy for administrators to select users and groups from trusted forests for inclusion in local groups or ACLs. This feature maintains the integrity of the forest security boundary while allowing trust between forests. It enables the trusting forest to enforce constraints on which security identifiers (SIDs) it will accept when users from trusted forests attempt to access protected resources. Here's more information about authorization:

❑   **Group membership and ACL management.**   The object picker has been enhanced to support selection of user or group names from a trusted forest. Names must be typed in completely. Enumeration and wildcard searches are not supported.

❑   **Name-SID translation.**   The object picker and the ACL editor use system APIs to store SIDs in group-member and ACL entries and to translate them back to friendly names for display purposes. Name-SID translation APIs are enhanced to use cross-forest routing hints, and they leverage NTLM's secure channels between domain controllers along the trust path to resolve security principal names or SIDs from trusted forests.

❑   **SID filtering.**   SIDs are filtered when authorization data passes from the root domain of the trusted forest to the root domain of the trusting forest. The trusting forest will accept only SIDs that are relative to domains it trusts the other forest to manage. Any other SIDs are automatically discarded. SID filtering is automatically enforced for Kerberos and NTLM authentication, as well as name-SID translation.

- **Cross-certification enhancements.** The Windows Server 2003 client cross-certification feature is enhanced by enabling the capability for department-level and global-level cross-certifications. For example, WinLogon will now be able to query for cross-certificates and download these into the "enterprise trust/enterprise store." As a chain is built, all cross-certificates will be downloaded.

- **IAS and cross-forest authentication.** If Active Directory forests are in cross-forest mode with two-way trusts, the Internet Authentication Service/Remote Authentication Dial-In User Service (IAS/RADIUS) server can authenticate the user account in the other forest with this feature. This gives administrators the capability to easily integrate new forests with already existing IAS/RADIUS services in their forest.

- **Credential management.** The Credential Manager feature provides a secure store of user credentials, including passwords and X.509 certificates. This will provide a consistent single-sign-on experience for users, including roaming users. For example, when a user accesses a line-of-business application within his or her company's network, the first attempt to access this application requires authentication and the user is prompted to supply a credential. After the user provides this credential, it is associated with the requesting application. In future access to this application, the saved credential is reused without user prompting.

For More Information

See the following resources for more information:

- Microsoft Windows 2000 Active Directory home page at *http://www.microsoft.com/ad/*

- Enterprise Management with the Group Policy Management Console at *http://www.microsoft.com/windowsserver2003/gpmc/*

- Windows DNS overview at *http://www.microsoft.com/windows2000/techinfo/howitworks/communications/nameadrmgmt/dnsover.asp*

4

Management Services

The Microsoft Windows Server 2003 family builds on the foundation of Microsoft Windows 2000, letting you increase the value of your existing investments while lowering overall computing costs. Easier to deploy, configure, and use, Windows Server 2003 provides centralized, customizable management services to reduce total cost of ownership (TCO).

Many resources are available for administrators seeking the skills and knowledge to effectively manage Windows-based networks. The upcoming *Microsoft Windows Server 2003 Resource Kit* (Microsoft Press, 2003) will provide detailed guidance on performing specific tasks across a wide range of areas. And the Help And Support Center available from the Start Menu delivers product documentation as well as links to articles and information about updates.

This chapter provides a technical overview of management services in Windows Server 2003. It shows administrators and decision makers how they can take advantage of the cost saving capabilities of change and configuration management and how they can explore the advanced capabilities afforded by command-line management and other management features.

Managing Configurations

The Windows Server 2003 family offers change and configuration management features that respond to users' needs for reliable operating environments, enabling a more highly managed infrastructure. This has become increasingly important as workers collaborate on complex projects in the enterprise-computing environment, a change that has greatly altered the way work gets done. The distributed office is replacing the traditional corporate model of desktops or terminals as productivity stations.

Within the distributed office, users need a consistent, reliable computing experience, including a well-configured operating system, up-to-date applications, and data that is consistently available—regardless of where they are working. To succeed, an IT department must cost-effectively meet the needs of a variety of users on a corporate network. This requires responding to various factors that require change in an IT environment, including

- New operating system and applications.
- Updates to operating systems and applications.
- New hardware.
- Configuration changes.
- New business requirements.
- New users.
- Security influences.

Managing this change can be viewed as a continuous cycle, as shown in Figure 4-1. Implementing change and configuration management features will help you

- Lower TCO by
  - ❑ Reducing downtime and costs associated with disaster recovery.
  - ❑ Reducing labor costs associated with inefficient client installation and configuration.
  - ❑ Reducing data loss resulting from hardware failure.
- Increase productivity by
  - ❑ Providing data availability, even when network resources are unavailable.
  - ❑ Allowing applications to be remotely installed and upgraded.
  - ❑ Having users' applications, data, and settings available to them regardless of where they work.

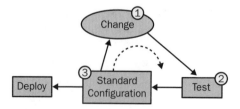

Figure 4-1   This diagram shows the change and configuration management process.

> **Note**   The Software Installation feature of Group Policy is suitable for simple software deployments. However, for software installation scenarios in which scheduling, inventory, reporting, status, and support for installation across a WAN is required, Microsoft recommends using Systems Management Server 2.0 (SMS). For more information, see the Systems Management Server Web site at *http://www.microsoft.com/ smsmgmt/*.

Managing Security

The Windows Server 2003 family was designed to make it easier both to manage security and to protect the network from outside threats. Software restriction policies protect your computing environment from untrusted software by allowing you to specify the software that's permitted to run. And when updates are released, a new infrastructure is available for administrators to acquire and centrally manage software updates.

Security Templates

Security templates let you create security policy for your network. A single point of entry where the full range of system security can be taken into account, security templates do not introduce new security parameters; they simply organize all existing security attributes into one place to ease security administration. Importing a security template to a Group Policy object (GPO) eases domain administration by configuring security for a domain or an organizational unit (OU) at once. Security templates can be used to define the following:

- Account policies
- Password policy
- Account lockout policy
- Kerberos policy
- Local policies
- Audit policy
- User rights assignment
- Security options

- Event log: application, system, and security event log settings

- Restricted groups: membership of security-sensitive groups

- System services: startup and permissions for system services

- Registry: permissions for registry keys

- File system: permissions for folders and files

Each template is saved as a text-based .inf file. This enables you to copy, paste, import, or export some or all of the template attributes. With the exceptions of IP Security (IPSec) and public key policies, all security attributes can be contained in a security template. In each Windows Server 2003 family or Windows XP operating system is a set of predefined templates that supply various levels of security to suit your organization. Several predefined templates can help you secure your system based on your needs. These templates are for

- Reapplying default settings.

- Implementing a highly secure environment.

- Implementing a less secure but more compatible environment.

- Securing the system root.

You can create a new security template with your own preferences or use one of the predefined security templates. For example, the security template Setup security.inf allows you to reapply default security settings; this template is created during setup for each computer and must be applied locally. Before making any changes to your security settings, you should understand the implications of those changes by testing them in a lab environment.

Software Restriction Policies

Software restriction policies address the need to regulate unknown or untrusted software. With the rise in the use of networks, the Internet, and e-mail for business computing, users find themselves exposed to new software in a variety of ways. Users must constantly make decisions about running unknown software. Viruses, like Trojan horses, often intentionally misrepresent themselves to trick users into running them. It's difficult for users to make safe choices about which software they should run.

With software restriction policies, you can protect your computing environment from untrusted software by identifying and specifying which software is allowed to run. You can define a default security level of *unrestricted* or *disallowed* for a GPO so that software is either allowed or not allowed to run by default. You can make exceptions to this default security level by creating rules for specific software. For example, if your default security level is set to disallowed, you can create rules that allow specific software to run.

Software restriction policies consist of the default security level and all the rules that are applied to a GPO. Software restriction policies can be applied across a domain, to local computers, or to individual users. Software restriction policies provide a number of ways to identify software, and they provide a policy-based infrastructure to enforce decisions about whether the identified software can run. With software restriction policies, when users execute programs, they must adhere to the guidelines set up by administrators.

With software restriction policies, you can

- Control the ability of programs to run on your system. For example, if you are concerned about users receiving viruses through e-mail, you can apply a policy setting that does not allow certain file types to run in the e-mail attachment directory of your e-mail program.

- Permit users to run only specific files on multiuser computers. For example, if you have multiple users on your computers, you can set up software restriction policies in such a way that users do not have access to any software but those specific files that are necessary for their work.

- Decide who can add trusted publishers to your computer.

- Control whether software restriction policies affect all users or just certain users on a computer.

- Prevent any files from running on your local computer, organizational unit, site, or domain. For example, if your system has a known virus, you can use software restriction policies to stop a computer from opening the file that contains the virus.

> **Note**   Software restriction policies should not be used as a replacement for antivirus software.

Windows Update

Millions of users each week use Windows Update as a way to keep their Windows systems up-to-date. Windows Update allows users to connect to *http:// www.windowsupdate.com*, where their computers are evaluated to determine which updates need to be applied to keep their systems up-to-date, as well as to determine any critical updates that will keep their systems safe and secure.

Windows Update also extends these services with Critical Update Notification and Automatic Updates.

Specifically, Windows Update provides the following:

■ **Microsoft Windows Update Services Catalog site.**   Administrators can download specific patches and drivers for distribution via SMS or other management tools. For more information, see *http:// windowsupdate.microsoft.com/catalog/*.

■ **Windows Update Consumer site.**   Designed primarily for consumers or users in a lightly managed network environment, this Windows Update site delivers updates to individual computers accessing the Web site. This feature can be turned off or managed via Group Policy. For more information, see *http://windowsupdate.microsoft.com/*.

■ **Auto Update.**   Administrators can automatically download and install critical updates such as security patches, high-impact bug fixes, and new drivers when no driver is installed for a device. Auto Update helps IT managers better manage the deployment and installation of critical software updates, and it consolidates multiple reboots into a single one. Compatible with corporate hosted software update servers, as explained in the following section, Auto Update provides administrators with greater control of updates. Automatic updates can be configured automatically over the Internet or administered in-house.

■ **Dynamic Update.**   Dynamic Update is designed to deliver emergency fixes to address any issues at setup time, such as new drivers that are required but not available on the CD.

■ **Driver services.**   Windows Server 2003 helps administrators get the latest certified drivers to users through Web sites and enables integration with device manager and Plug and Play services.

Software Update Services

Because many corporations do not want their systems or users going to an external source for updates without first testing the updates, Microsoft is providing a version of Windows Update for installation inside your corporate firewall. Microsoft Software Update Services (SUS) allows customers to install a service on an internal Windows 2000–based or Windows Server 2003–based server that can download all critical updates as they are posted to Windows Update. Administrators can also receive e-mail notification when new critical updates have been posted.

SUS, which is currently available as an add-on to Windows 2000 Server, allows administrators to quickly and easily deploy the most critical updates to their servers as well as to desktop computers running Windows 2000 Professional or Windows XP Professional. This solution includes the following features:

■ **Microsoft Software Update Services.** This is the server component installed on a computer running Windows 2000 Server or Windows Server 2003 inside your corporate firewall. It synchronizes with the Windows Update site to deliver all critical updates for Windows 2000 and Windows XP. The synchronization can be automatic or completed manually by the administrator. When the updates are downloaded, you can test the updates in your environment and then decide which updates to approve for installation throughout your organization.

■ **Automatic Updates client.** This is the client component for installation on all of your Windows 2000–based or Windows Server 2003–based servers as well as computers running Windows 2000 Professional or Windows XP Professional. This enables your servers and client computers to connect to a server running SUS and receive any updates. You can control which server each client should connect to as well as schedule when the client should perform all installations of critical updates—either manually or via Group Policy and Active Directory.

■ **Staged deployment.** This is achieved by having multiple servers run SUS. You can have one server in your test lab, where you can publish the updates. If these clients install the updates correctly, you can configure your other servers running SUS to publish their updates. In this way, you can ensure that new changes do not break your standard desktop operating environment.

■ **Server-to-server synchronization.** Because you might need multiple servers running SUS inside your corporation in order to bring the updates closer to your desktops and servers for downloading, SUS allows you to point to another server running SUS instead of Windows Update, allowing these critical software updates to be distributed around your enterprise.

SUS is focused on getting critical updates for Windows 2000, Windows XP, and Windows Server 2003 inside your corporate firewall as quickly as possible. Many customers today can keep their systems secure by using electronic software distribution solutions—such as Systems Management Server (SMS)—for complete software management, including responding to security and virus issues. These customers should continue using these solutions. Security-patch improvements allow SMS customers to know, through inventory, which computers require updates and then deploy those updates quickly and easily.

For more information about Software Update Services, see the Software Update Services Web site at *http://www.microsoft.com/windows2000/windows-update/sus/*.

Improving IntelliMirror

IntelliMirror management technologies is a set of powerful features for change and configuration management. IntelliMirror combines the advantages of centralized computing with the performance and flexibility of distributed computing. IntelliMirror ensures that users' data, software, and personal settings are available when they move between computers and that those settings persist when their computers are connected to the network. Also, administrators can use Remote Installation Services (RIS) to perform remote installations of the operating system. Many IntelliMirror features rely on Group Policy, which in turn requires Active Directory. Active Directory is included with Microsoft Windows 2000 Server and with the Windows Server 2003 family.

Most of the IntelliMirror features in Windows XP and the Windows Server 2003 family are also available in Windows 2000. You can use IntelliMirror in a network that uses all or any of these operating systems. However, improvements in the features that were added for Windows XP and Windows Server 2003 provide greater flexibility in administering computers and user accounts in your network.

The features of IntelliMirror increase the availability of a user's data, personal computer settings, and computing environment by intelligently managing information, settings, and software. Based on policy definitions, IntelliMirror is able to deploy, recover, restore, and replace user data, software, and personal settings in a Windows 2000–based or Windows Server 2003–based environment. Essentially, IntelliMirror provides users with follow-me functionality for their personal computing environment. Users have constant access to all of their information and software, regardless of which computers they are using and whether they are connected to the network, with the assurance that their data is safely maintained and available.

IntelliMirror allows an administrator to set policy definitions once and be confident that the policy will be applied without further administrative intervention. At the core of IntelliMirror are four features:

- **Policy management.**   You use this feature to manage computer and user settings. You can configure settings in Group Policy and have confidence that those settings will be applied to the target computers and users. For example, you can configure password policies for computers and know that Windows will apply those settings without requiring the computer to restart or the user to log off.

- **User data management.**   You use this feature to manage files, documents, spreadsheets, workbooks, and other information that people create and use to perform their jobs. By redirecting specific user data folders, such as the My Documents folder, to a network location and then making this location available to users for offline use, users can access their data at any location on or off the network.

- **User settings management.**   You use this feature to centrally define the computing environment for various groups of users and computers. You can also easily restore user settings in case of computer failure. User settings include both personal preferences and centrally defined customizations of the operating system desktop environment and applications. Settings can include language settings, desktop layout, and other user preferences. Users' customized settings can be made available wherever they log on.

- **Software installation and maintenance.**   You use this feature to install, configure, repair, or remove applications, Service Packs, and operating system upgrades. You can assign or publish software to users or computers. Assigning or publishing to a user provides the applications to that user regardless of where the user logs on to the network. Assigning to computers makes the application available to all users of the targeted computer. The latter is useful for common applications that all users will need, such as productivity and antivirus software. When assigning an application, you can choose to have the application installed in full when the user logs on or on demand—when the user invokes the applications or specific parts of them. If the application is configured for installation on demand, it appears installed to the user; however, the software is not actually installed until the first time the user selects it. Using this option can significantly reduce the time it takes to deploy desktop configurations to multiple users, many of whom do not need to use all the possible features included in a particular program. On the other hand, the full-installation option, available in Windows Server 2003, is useful for specific groups of users such as frequent travelers who might require all available applications to be fully installed before they travel. When you publish an application, the user can install it on their computer through Add Or Remove Programs in Control Panel. In either case, applications follow users or computers, making the same applications available at any computer that a user logs on to.

IntelliMirror features can be used separately or all together, depending on the business or organizational requirements. Alternatively, you can restrict users' data and settings from being available at all times because of network configuration issues, security concerns, or corporate standards.

From an organizational point of view, overall cost compared with benefits is of great concern. IntelliMirror features are designed to deliver new benefits while reducing system administration. The majority of IntelliMirror features are designed to keep users working productively while enabling centralized administration and thus reducing administrative intervention and associated costs. The new level of centralized management made possible with IntelliMirror allows organizations to accomplish their change and configuration management goals more easily because the entire organization can be viewed and altered from the single view of Active Directory. Both administrators and users benefit, resulting in lowered computing costs with improved productivity.

Policy Management

IntelliMirror contains several important new features that give administrators powerful tools for managing users and computers.

Expected to be available as a free add-on to Windows Server 2003, the Group Policy Management Console (GPMC) will provide the new framework for managing Group Policy. With GPMC, Group Policy becomes much easier to use, a benefit that will enable more organizations to better utilize Active Directory and take advantage of its powerful management features. For example, GPMC enables backup and restore of GPOs, import/export and copy/paste of GPOs, reporting of GPO settings and Resultant Set of Policy (RSoP) data, use of templates for managed configurations, and scriptability for all GPMC operations. In addition, GPMC lets you manage Group Policy for multiple domains and sites within a given forest, all in a simplified user interface with drag-and-drop support. And with cross-forest trust, you can manage Group Policy across multiple forests from the same console. GPMC can manage Group Policy for Windows 2000 or Windows .NET domains.

While Group Policy objects can be linked only to sites, domains, or organizational units (OUs) within a given forest, the cross-forest feature in Windows

.NET Server enables several new scenarios that Group Policy supports. For example, it's possible for a user in forest A to log on to a computer in forest B, each with their own sets of policy. Alternatively, settings within a GPO can reference servers in external forests, such as software distribution points. Windows Server 2003 Group Policy successfully supports these interoperability scenarios.

The RSoP tool in Windows Server 2003 allows you to see the effect of Group Policy on a targeted user or computer. With RSoP, you have a powerful and flexible base-level tool to plan, monitor, and troubleshoot Group Policy. RSoP is an infrastructure and tool in the form of MMC snap-ins enabling you to determine and analyze the current set of policies in two modes: logging mode and planning mode. In logging mode, you can assess what has applied to a particular target. In planning mode, you can see how policies would be applied to a target and then examine the results before deploying a change to Group Policy.

RSoP is enabled by WMI by leveraging WMI's capability to gather data from a variety of sources. An MMC-based tool hosts snap-in extensions displaying results based on a given target. A targeting wizard sets the scope used by the RSoP tool. The wizard guides an administrator through the steps necessary to create an appropriate target, generate RSoP data, and start the RSoP tool to use that data.

WMI makes available a large amount of data for a target computer, such as hardware and software inventory, settings, and configuration information. WMI gathers data from the registry, drivers, the file system, Active Directory, Simple Network Management Protocol (SNMP), the Windows Installer service, structured query language (SQL), networking, and Exchange Server. WMI filtering in Windows Server 2003 allows you to dynamically determine whether to apply a GPO based on a query of WMI data. These queries (also called WMI filters) determine which users and computers receive the policy settings configured in the GPO where you create the filter. This functionality lets you dynamically target Group Policy based on the properties of the local machine. Here are some sample properties you might use when constructing WMI filters:

■ **Services**   Computers where Dynamic Host Configuration Protocol (DHCP) is turned on

■ **Registry**   Computers that have a given registry key populated

■ **Hardware inventory**   Computers with a Pentium III processor

■ **Software inventory**   Computers with Visual Studio .NET installed

■ **Hardware configuration**   Computers with network interface cards (NICs) on interrupt level 3

- **Software configuration**   Computers with multicasting turned on

- **Associations**   Computers that have any service dependent on systems network architecture (SNA) service

- **Ping**   Computers that can ping a specific server in less than 100 milliseconds

Policy settings are more easily understood, managed, and verified with Web-view integration in the Group Policy Object Editor. Clicking on a policy instantly shows the text explaining its function and supported environments such as Windows XP–only or Windows 2000. This makes it easier for you to click through various policies and better assess how to achieve a Group Policy goal. This explanatory text has been expanded in the Windows Server 2003 family to include help text for categories of policies such as Start Menu and Taskbar.

The Windows Server 2003 family includes more than 160 new policies. These new policies allow you to control the behavior of numerous features, including

- Terminal Server

- Application compatibility

- Networking such as SNMP, quality of service (QoS), firewall, and dial-up connections

- DNS logon

- Roaming user profiles and Group Policy

- Control Panel

- Windows Media Player

Distinguishing whether policies work on Windows 2000, a particular service pack, or Windows Server 2003 is made easy with the *supported* keyword included in the administrative template (.adm) file for each policy. Administrators or users can search for policies based on these keywords and see only those policies that work on a specific version of the operating system. Explanations of each policy begin with a statement verifying which version of the operating system supports the policy.

User Data Management

Data availability is a leading concern for most organizations. What happens to user data when a hard disk fails? Who ensures that users back up their files on a timely basis? Too often, user data backups are not performed, and important files are lost if a user's hard disk fails. Other data availability concerns include whether users have access to their data if they move to different computers on the network or are only intermittently connected to the network. With IntelliMirror user data management features, you can ensure that users can access their data from any computer wherever they log on, whether on line or off line. You can back up user data centrally and provide fast computer replacement in disaster recovery situations.

When you implement IntelliMirror user data management, users can access their data from any computer running Windows 2000 Professional (or a later operating system) on the corporate network. The user's data follows the user because the data is stored in specified network locations. You can manually configure which files and folders are available or configure them through Group Policy. In addition, if a user takes network-based resources off line, any changes made while off line are synchronized when the user reconnects to the network.

With user data management, you can ensure that users' data is always available to them in the following ways:

■ Administrators can provide improved protection of user data by ensuring that local data is also redirected or copied to a network share, providing a central location for administrator-managed backups. This capability helps to enforce corporate directives such as placing all-important data on servers.

■ Administrators can ensure that the most up-to-date versions of a user's data reside on both the local computer and on the server. Because local caching maintains data on the local computer even when it is disconnected from the network, data is readily available to the user, even when working off line.

■ Data can follow a person when the person roams to another computer on the network. This provides increased accessibility because people can use any computer on the network to access their data.

> **Note**   Through Group Policy, you can redirect a user's My Documents folder to the user's home directory. This aids in transitioning users from a legacy deployment of home directories to the My Documents model while maintaining compatibility with the existing home directory environment.

Implementing user data management relies on some or all of the following technologies:

- Active Directory
- Group Policy
- RSoP
- Roaming user profiles
- Folder redirection
- Offline Files
- Synchronization manager
- Distributed File System (DFS)
- Encrypting File System (EFS)
- Disk quotas

User Settings Management

In most organizations, new users and existing employees who change computers often need help from the IT department to initially configure their computers. With IntelliMirror user settings management, administrators can centrally define computing environments for groups of users and computers so that users automatically get the correct configurations for their jobs. Also, administrators can restore user settings if a computer fails as well as ensure that users' desktop settings follow them if they roam to another computer. With user settings management, you can

- Reduce support calls by providing a preconfigured desktop environment appropriate for the user's job.
- Save time and costs of computer replacement.
- Help users be more efficient by automatically providing their desktop environment, no matter where they work.

The settings you can manage include desktop configurations, security settings, language settings, application settings, and scripts (computer startup and shutdown, and user logon and logoff). These configurations and settings make up a user's profile. This information is stored on every local computer for each user who has logged on to that computer. You can also redirect any of the special folders in a user profile to a network share. Then the same user profiles are available wherever a user logs on.

User settings, like user data, can follow the user, regardless of where that user logs on. You use Group Policy settings to customize and control users' computing environments and to grant or deny the users the ability to customize their own computing environments. These settings can be applied to both users and computers. When users have permission, they often customize the style and default settings of their computing environment to suit their needs and work habits. Settings contain three basic types of information: user and administrative information, temporary information, and data specific to the local computer. Temporary and local computer information typically should not roam with a user; moving such information can cause unnecessary overhead, and differences between computers can disrupt the roaming function. When you use roaming user profiles to manage user settings, Group Policy ensures that only vital user and administrative settings information is retained, while temporary and local computer settings are dynamically and appropriately regenerated as required. This minimizes the amount of information that must be stored and transferred across the network while still allowing users to have a similar experience on any computer that they log on to.

You use the following technologies to implement user settings management:

- Active Directory

- Group Policy

- Offline Files

- Synchronization manager

- DFS

- Folder redirection

- Roaming user profiles

> **Note**   The Windows Server 2003 family includes several new policies to allow more flexible configuration of user profiles, including polices to disable user profiles on a per-machine basis and the ability to configure read-only profiles.

Software Management

There are a number of challenges in providing software to users. Some of these are as follows:

- Users need a wide variety of applications to perform their jobs. Different users require different applications. As a result, many large organizations support hundreds, often thousands, of software applications. Administrators must efficiently deploy these applications to the users who need them.

- An organization's software application needs evolve over time. New applications and new versions of applications become available, offering features and functionality that were not available before. Enhancements such as new user templates, or service packs that become available between full version upgrades, also must be deployed from time to time.

- Users are promoted or change jobs and need several new applications. At the same time, they no longer need some of the applications that were required to do their old jobs. Or users move to a computer in another location and expect to have their key applications available to them. Administrators have to support and manage these rapidly changing software requirements as well.

User productivity is enhanced when users have all of the software applications that will enable them to perform their jobs efficiently. It is also important for administrators to track applications that are no longer being used or are out-of-date, and to make sure they are phased out. The IT department has to determine when to stop supporting software that is no longer useful. You can ask users to stop using certain applications and remove applications that are outdated. In some cases, the best solution is to remove the obsolete application rather than incur the compatibility issues and other problems that can result from its continued use. All of these application management tasks can be extremely labor intensive, which is why many organizations want to automate them for large groups or even for all client computers at one time.

You can use the software installation and maintenance feature of IntelliMirror to install software applications at computer startup, at user logon, or on demand. You can also use this feature to upgrade deployed applications, remove earlier applications that are no longer required, and deploy service packs and operating system upgrades. It can ensure that a person cannot install any software from local media, such as a CD-ROM or a floppy disk. This feature also provides for the following situations:

■ If a user inadvertently deletes files from an application, it will repair itself.

■ If a user moves from one computer to another, their software will always be available to them.

■ If a user does not have an application installed on their computer and they try to open a document associated with that application, the application will automatically be installed and the document will open.

You use Group Policy to define software installation options that specify which applications are to be deployed, upgraded, or removed from a computer. You can apply software installation policies to groups of users or to groups of computers, depending on your organization's needs. There are two methods by which you can install applications on users' computers—assigning and publishing:

■ **Assigning.**   You can assign applications to either a user or a computer using Group Policy. When you assign applications to a computer, the application is automatically installed the next time the computer is started. When you assign applications to a user with Group Policy, the administrator can choose to have the application installed either on demand when the user selects the application or in full when the user next logs on:

❑ **On demand.**   If the application is installed on demand, the user's computer is set up with a Start menu shortcut, and the appropriate file associations are created in the registry. To the user, it looks and feels as if the application is already present. However, the application is not fully installed until the user needs the application. When the user attempts to open the application or a file associated with that application, Windows Installer checks to make sure that all the files and parameters of the application are present for the application to properly execute. If they are not present, Windows Installer retrieves and installs them from a predetermined distribution point. Once in place, the application opens.

❑ **Full installation.**   The full-installation option is useful for specific groups of users such as frequent travelers who might require all available applications to be fully installed before they travel. With full installation, a user's applications are installed at logon.

Assigning applications makes them resilient—they are available no matter what the user does; for example, if the user removes an application, it will automatically be reinstalled on demand.

■ **Publishing.**   When you publish an application, it appears in Add Or Remove Programs in Control Panel. Users can choose to install published applications. Installation can also be configured to occur automatically when a user attempts to open a file that requires a specific published application. You publish applications when the software is not absolutely necessary for users to perform their jobs.

To obtain the full benefits of publishing technology, all published applications should be authored for installation using the Windows Installer service. Although you can still publish non–Windows Installer service applications using .zap files, you won't get the benefits of elevated privileges as explained in the following paragraph, and of course, you won't get the benefits of using Windows Installer either.

> **Note**   A .zap file is a text file that provides a pointer to the setup package, which enables the application to be listed in Add Or Remove Programs.

Deploying software through Group Policy requires applications to use the Windows Installer service, which provides much more than just the capability to install applications. It also protects the integrity of the application against inadvertent mishaps with local files. For example, if a user attempts to use a copy of Microsoft Word that's missing some essential files, the Windows Installer service reinstalls the files from the installation point the next time the application is launched. In addition, Windows Installer–based applications that are deployed using Group Policy can install with elevated privileges, meaning that users don't have to be administrators on their local machines to install software that you, as a network administrator, want them to have. Application repair follows the same logic as on-demand installation. Whenever an application authored by Windows Installer is invoked, the Windows Installer service checks to ensure that the appropriate files are available; if required, files or settings are repaired automatically.

Windows Server 2003 makes other improvements to software deployment:

■ **Full installation at logon of user-assigned applications.**   Available from Software Settings in the Group Policy Object Editor snap-in, the Group Policy Software Installation extension (formerly the Application Deployment Editor) is updated for Windows Server 2003 with the new full-installation option. Full installation allows a user-assigned application to be installed completely at logon, instead of on demand. This is useful for certain groups such as mobile users who need to have all parts of a program installed while traveling away from the network.

■ **64-bit software deployment support.**   This feature provides support for 64-bit software deployment with Group Policy. New options in Group Policy Software Installation aid in determining whether 32-bit applications should be deployed to 64-bit clients. Software Installation also allows existing deployments of Windows 2000 to be managed with the same level of functionality provided by the Windows Server 2003 family. This is useful if an administrator is planning to deploy a 32-bit Windows Installer package to a group of users with 64-bit systems. The administrator knows that the 32-bit package works correctly on 64-bit computers and uses the new Make 32-bit x86 Windows Installer Application Available To IA64 Machines option in Group Policy Software Installation to deploy the package to all users.

Implementing software installation and maintenance uses some or all of the following Windows technologies:

■ Active Directory

■ Group Policy

■ Windows Installer

■ Add Or Remove Programs

■ DFS

■ File Replication service (FRS)

Computer Setup Process

When a user needs a new computer—whether the person is new to the organization, the existing computer has failed, or it's simply time for a hardware upgrade—IT departments have had to spend a great deal of time preparing and installing the operating system and basic applications. This often involves a lengthy in-person support call to the user's office. To support the computer setup process, administrators need a way to

■ Return users to productive work quickly.

■ Significantly reduce the frequency and length of related support calls—or even eliminate those service calls altogether.

Remote Installation helps you significantly reduce the amount of labor required to deploy a new operating system on a computer. The entire process is policy-based and can be accomplished without on-site technical support. You can use the Remote Installation feature to perform a new installation of Windows on Pre-Boot eXecution Environment (PXE) remote boot-enabled client computers throughout your organization. An administrator does not have to visit the new computer to install a new operating system and core applications. You can provide a customized, fully automated installation process from a remote source. When the computer is turned on, the user presses F12 to initiate the operating system installation process. The computer then starts from a network server that supports RIS. After the user logs on, RIS can install either of the following:

- The network equivalent of a CD-based installation of Windows

- An operating system image (referred to as an RIPrep image) that can include preconfigured applications such as word processing and e-mail

You use the following technologies to implement Remote Installation:

- Active Directory

- Group Policy

- DNS

- DHCP

- RIS

Using Command-Line Tools

Windows Server 2003 includes improved command-line management tools that allow you to complete most tasks without having to use a graphical user interface. This can increase efficiency for administrators desiring to use command-line functionality to automate common tasks. More than 60 new command-line tools are available in the Windows Server 2003 family. These include tools to manage key features such as print servers, Internet Information Services (IIS) 6.0, and Active Directory. Command-line management in Windows Server 2003 provides the following benefits:

- **Readiness for use.**   Solutions are ready to use out of the box with little or no extra coding required. All tools have a consistent, standard syntax with easy access to command-line documentation (/? Help text) as well as a comprehensive HTML Help file, ntcmds.chm (available from the Help and Support Center).

- **Support for remote management.**   All new tools support remote server operation via the */S* parameter (remote system name—for example, */S MyServer*), and they run under Telnet and Terminal Services, enabling fully remotable command-line management.

- **Scriptability.**   You can use batch files or scripts at the command line to create customized management solutions and automate common tool usage.

Command Shell

The command shell is a separate software program that provides direct communication between the user and the operating system. The nongraphical command shell user interface provides the environment in which you run character-based applications and utilities. The command shell executes programs and displays their output on the screen by using individual characters, much like the MS-DOS command interpreter Command.com. The Windows Server 2003 operating system command shell uses the command interpreter Cmd.exe, which loads applications and directs the flow of information between applications to translate user input into a form that the operating system understands.

The command shell provides many advantages that improve management efficiency. For example, you can

- Use the command shell to create and edit batch files (also called scripts) to automate routine tasks. For example, you can use scripts to automate the management of user accounts or nightly backups.

- Use the command-line version of Windows Script Host, CScript, to run more sophisticated scripts in the command shell.

- Perform operations more efficiently by using batch files instead of the user interface. Batch files accept all commands that are available at the command line.

- Customize the command prompt window for easier viewing to increase control over how you run programs.

Command-Line Tools

The following list shows the updated and new Windows Server 2003 family command-line tools:

- **Adprep.**   Prepares Windows 2000 domains and forests for upgrade to Windows Server 2003, Standard Edition, Enterprise Edition, or Datacenter Edition.

- **bootcfg.** Configures, queries, or changes Boot.ini file settings.

- **choice.** Prompts the user to make a choice by displaying a prompt and pausing, waiting for the user to choose from a set of options before continuing.

- **clip.** Redirects command output from the command line to the Clipboard.

- **cmdkey.** Creates, lists, and deletes stored user names and passwords or credentials.

- **defrag.** Locates and consolidates fragmented boot files, data files, and folders on local volumes.

- **diskpart.** Manages disks, partitions, or volumes.

- **driverquery.** Queries for a list of drivers and driver properties.

- **dsadd.** Adds a computer, contact, group, organizational unit, or user to a directory.

- **dsget.** Displays selected attributes of a computer, contact, group, organizational unit, server, or user in a directory.

- **dsmod.** Modifies an existing user, computer, contact, group, or organizational unit in a directory.

- **dsmove.** Moves any object from its current location in the directory to a new location (as long as the move can be accommodated within a single domain controller) and renames an object without moving it in the directory tree.

- **dsquery.** Queries and finds a list of computers, groups, organizational units, servers, or users in the directory using specified search criteria.

- **dsrm.** Deletes an object of a specific type or any general object from the directory.

- **eventcreate.** Enables an administrator to create a custom event in a specified event log.

- **eventquery.** Lists the events and event properties from one or more event logs.

- **eventtriggers.** Displays and configures event triggers on local or remote machines.

- **forfiles.** Selects files in a folder or tree for batch processing.

- **freedisk.**   Checks for available disk space before continuing with an installation process.

- **fsutil.**   Manages reparse points and sparse files; dismounts or extends a volume.

- **getmac.**   Obtains the media access control (MAC) address and list of network protocols.

- **gettype.**   Sets the system environment variable *%ERRORLEVEL%* to the value associated with the specified information about the Windows operating system.

- **gpresult.**   Displays Group Policy settings and RSoP for a user or a computer.

- **helpctr.**   Starts the Help and Support Center.

- **inuse.**   Replaces locked operating system files.

- **iisback.**   Creates and manages backup copies of the IIS configuration (metabase and schema) of a remote or local computer.

- **iiscnfg.**   Imports and exports all or selected parts of the configuration of IIS on a local or remote computer.

- **iisftp.**   Creates, deletes, and lists FTP sites on servers that are running IIS 6.0. Also starts, stops, pauses, and continues FTP sites.

- **iisftpdr.**   Creates and deletes virtual directories of FTP sites on servers that are running IIS 6.0 or later.

- **iisvdir.**   Creates and deletes virtual directories of Web sites on servers that are running IIS 6.0 or later.

- **iisweb.**   Creates, deletes, and lists Web sites on servers that are running IIS 6.0. Also starts, stops, pauses, and continues the Web sites.

- **logman.**   Manages and schedules performance counter and event trace log collections on local and remote systems.

- **nlb.**   Replaces wlbs.exe for managing and controlling network load balancing operations.

- **nlbmgr.**   Configures and manages network load balancing clusters and all cluster hosts from a single computer.

- **openfiles.**   Queries, displays, or disconnects open files.

- **pagefileconfig.**   Displays and configures the paging file virtual memory settings of a system.

- **perfmon.**   Enables you to open a Performance console configured with settings files from the Windows NT 4.0 version of Performance Monitor.

- **prncnfg.**   Configures or displays configuration information about a printer.

- **prndrvr.**   Adds, deletes, and lists printer drivers from local or remote print servers.

- **prnjobs.**   Pauses, resumes, cancels, and lists print jobs.

- **prnmngr.**   Adds, deletes, and lists printers or printer connections, in addition to setting and displaying the default printer.

- **prnport.**   Creates, deletes, and lists standard TCP/IP printer ports, in addition to displaying and changing port configuration.

- **prnqctl.**   Prints a test page, pauses or resumes a printer, and clears a printer queue.

- **relog.**   Extracts performance counters from performance counter logs into other formats, such as text-TSV (for tab-delimited text), text-CSV (for comma-delimited text), binary-BIN, or SQL.

- **rss.**   Enables Remote Storage, which is used for extending server disk space.

- **sc.**   Retrieves and sets information about services. Tests and debugs service programs.

- **schtasks.**   Schedules commands and programs to run periodically or at a specific time. Adds and removes tasks from the schedule, starts and stops tasks on demand, and displays and changes scheduled tasks.

- **setx.**   Sets environment variables in the local or system environment, without requiring programming or scripting.

- **shutdown.**   Shuts down or restarts a local or remote computer.

- **systeminfo.**   Queries the system for basic system configuration information.

- **takeown.**   Allows an administrator to recover access to a file by making the administrator the owner of the file.

- **taskkill.**   Ends one or more tasks or processes.

- **tasklist.**   Displays a list of applications, services, and the Process Identifier (PID) currently running on either a local or a remote computer.

- **timeout.**   Pauses the command processor for the specified number of seconds.

- **tracerpt.**   Processes event trace logs or real-time data from instrumented event trace providers and allows you to generate trace analysis reports and CSV (comma-delimited) files for the events generated.

- **tsecimp.**   Imports assignment information from an XML file into the TAPI server security file (tsec.ini).

- **typeperf.**   Writes performance counter data to the command window or to a supported log file format.

- **waitfor.**   Uses signals to synchronize multiple computers across a network.

- **where.**   Locates and displays all files that match the given parameter.

- **whoami.**   Returns domain or computer name, user name, group names, logon identifier, and privileges for the currently logged-on user.

- **WMIC.**   Eases the use of WMI and systems managed through WMI.

WMI Command Line

The WMI Command Line (WMIC) utility provides a simple command-line interface to WMI. WMIC lets you take advantage of WMI to manage computers running Windows. WMIC interoperates with existing shells and utility commands and can be easily extended by scripts or other administration-oriented applications. WMIC allows you to

- Browse the WMI schemas and query their classes and instances, as well as call and execute methods, usually using aliases (friendly names), which make WMI more intuitive.

- Work with the local computer, remote computers, or multiple computers in a single command.

- Customize aliases and output formats to suit your needs.

- Create and execute scripts based on WMIC.

WMI providers are available to allow WMI to manage a wide variety of hardware components, operating system subsystems, and application systems. WMIC can be used with all the schemas implemented by those WMI providers. WMIC can be used from any computer running Windows XP Professional or a member of the Windows Server 2003 family to remotely manage any computer with WMI that is a Windows domain member. WMIC does not have to be available on the remotely managed computer to manage it.

Here are some examples of using WMIC to ease tasks:

- **Local management of a computer.**   You are at the computer and use the WMIC command to manage it.

- **Remote management of a computer.**   You are at one computer and use WMIC to manage another computer.

- **Remote management of multiple computers.**   You are at one computer and use WMIC to manage multiple computers with a single command.

- **Remote management of a computer (using a remote session).**   You use a remote sessioning technology (such as Telnet or Terminal Services) to connect to a remote computer and manage it with WMIC.

- **Automated management using administrative scripting.**   You use WMIC to write a simple management script (batch files) to automate the management of one or more computers (local or remote).

The WMI infrastructure is accessible to you as you use WMIC through intermediate facilitators called *aliases*. Aliases are friendly names used to capture the features of a WMI class that are relevant to some specific task, such as disk or network administration. Aliases can be used to provide better names for WMI classes, properties, and methods or to arrange properties in useful output formats. The output formats can include specific property values or can be formatted in a manner appropriate to some specific presentation strategy or function. For example, an alias might have a brief format that will list only property values essential for the identification of the objects visible through the alias. Management data is retrieved in XML format and processed by built-in or custom XSL output formats.

Understanding the Deployment Tools

Improvements in the Windows Server 2003 family make it easier to manage deployment and migration. Remote Installation Services (RIS) has been extended to give you greater flexibility and precision in deploying specific configurations across the network. User state migration is more powerful, giving you the ability to efficiently migrate files and settings for large numbers of users. Windows Installer eases the process of customizing installations, updating and upgrading applications, and resolving configuration problems.

Remote Installation

The Remote Installation Services feature simplifies the task of installing an operating system on computers throughout an organization. It provides a mechanism for computers to connect to a network server during the initial boot process, while the server controls a local installation of any of the following operating systems:

- Windows XP Professional
- Windows Server 2003, Web Edition
- Windows Server 2003, Standard Edition
- Windows Server 2003, Enterprise Edition
- 64-bit version of Windows Server 2003, Enterprise Edition (RISetup only)
- Windows 2000 Professional
- Windows 2000 Server
- Windows 2000 Advanced Server

Computers without any resident operating system can connect to a networked server during initial startup, and the server performs a local installation of the operating system. It uses RIS during initial startup before the resident operating system, if any, loads. RIS can be used either to install the correct configuration of the operating system on a new computer or to restore a failed computer to a known operating system configuration. With RIS, computer hardware connected through a LAN finds a networked RIS server and requests installation of a new copy of the operating system appropriately configured for the user and computer.

User State Migration

Migrating files and settings for multiple users in a corporate environment is made easier with the User State Migration Tool (USMT). USMT gives you command-line precision in customizing specific settings such as unique modifications to the registry.

USMT is designed for administrators only; individual users do not need to use USMT. In addition, USMT requires a client computer that is connected to a domain controller running Windows 2000 Server or later. USMT reduces the cost of deploying the operating system by addressing each of the following areas:

- Migration technician costs
- Employee downtime repersonalizing the desktop

- Employee downtime finding missing work files
- Help-desk calls assisting employees with repersonalizing their desktop
- Employee ramp-up time on the new operating system
- Employee satisfaction with the migration experience

USMT consists of two executable files (ScanState.exe and LoadState.exe) and four migration rule information files (Migapp.inf, Migsys.inf, Miguser.inf, and Sysfiles.inf). ScanState.exe collects user data and settings based on the information contained in Migapp.inf, Migsys.inf, Miguser.inf, and Sysfiles.inf. LoadState.exe deposits this user-state data on a computer running a fresh (not upgraded) installation of Windows XP Professional. USMT is driven by a shared set of .inf files that can be modified by administrators or OEMs. In virtually all cases, when using USMT for automated migration, administrators will want to modify the .inf files to better handle their unique environment and needs. Additional .inf files can be created for additional migration requirements. With no modification of default settings, USMT migrates the following:

- Internet Explorer settings
- Outlook Express settings and store
- Outlook settings and store
- Dial-up connections
- Phone and modem options
- Accessibility
- Classic desktop
- Screen-saver selection
- Fonts
- Folder options
- Taskbar settings
- Mouse and keyboard settings
- Sound settings
- Regional options
- Office settings
- Network drives and printers
- Desktop folder

- My Documents folder

- My Pictures folder

- Favorites folder

- Cookies folder

- Common Office file types

It's easy to modify what's included in the state that ScanState.exe collects. The tool can be instructed to collect or leave specified files, folders, registry entries, or registry subtrees.

Windows Installer

Managing software applications in a corporate environment has traditionally burdened organizations with high costs. With Windows Installer, you can greatly simplify the process of customizing installations, updating and upgrading applications, and resolving configuration problems. Windows Installer manages shared resources, enforces consistent file version rules, and diagnoses and repairs applications at run time. The result is significantly lower TCO for managing applications.

Before the development of Windows Installer, software applications used various setup technologies, each of which contained unique installation rules for each application. At times, the applications did the wrong things at setup time. For example, an earlier version of a particular file might be installed over a newer version. Utilizing multiple setup technologies makes it difficult to maintain accurate reference counts on shared components for the many applications installed on a computer. As a result, installing or removing applications might break other applications.

Using Windows Installer, the operating system implements all of the proper installation rules. To adhere to those rules and to avoid the problems described in the preceding paragraph, an application needs only to describe itself in a Windows Installer package. Windows Installer then performs the installation tasks for each application, which can help you prevent or minimize common installation problems.

Windows Server 2003 introduces new features that can increase the security of information in your organization and enhance the usability and manageability of Windows Installer.

- **64-bit support.** Windows Installer is implemented as a native 64-bit service in 64-bit editions of Windows Server 2003, Enterprise Edition, and Windows Server 2003, Datacenter Edition. This service handles the installation of both 32-bit and 64-bit applications. Applications that are 64-bit are packaged in specially marked 64-bit Windows Installer packages. These packages enable installation of both 32-bit and 64-bit components.

■ **Software restriction policies.**   The increased role of the Internet in business increases security threats to your network from viruses. Using software restriction policies, you can protect your computer environment from suspect code by identifying and specifying the applications that are allowed to run. The system identifies each application by using a hash rule, a certificate rule, a path rule, or an Internet zone rule.

Windows Installer packages, patches, and transforms are affected by software restriction policies. The levels established for configuring whether to allow users to run a piece of code are either unrestricted or restricted. In particular, Windows Installer runs only those packages that you set at the unrestricted level. If any transforms or patches are involved in an installation, you must set them to run at the unrestricted level for the installation to succeed.

If you configure a software restriction policy to run a package at a level other than unrestricted, Windows Installer displays an error message explaining that a policy is in place that prevents this application from being installed. Windows Installer also logs an event in the application event log.

The system evaluates the software restriction policy when you first install an application, when you apply a new patch, or when Windows Installer needs to recache the installation package for an application. You can apply software restriction policy to all Windows Installer packages for administrators and nonadministrators.

Using Remote Administration

Windows Server 2003 operating systems architectures include additional remote management capabilities such as Remote Desktop for Administration (part of Terminal Services), Microsoft Management Console (MMC), Active Directory Services Interface (ADSI), Telnet service, and WMI. These are grouped under two major modalities for remote management tools and features. First are the tools intrinsic to Windows Server 2003 operating systems. These include Active Directory, Group Policy, Event Manager, Services, and many others. The second modality involves connections to computers remotely using the Remote Desktop snap-in and the Remote Desktop connection.

Systems employing Windows Server 2003 operating systems can be run in a "lights-out" environment. In this environment, a server can be administered remotely without any local interaction, such as from a local keyboard, mouse, or video card and monitor. The administrator can manage and monitor multiple sites remotely from one central location, diagnosing and resolving most problems efficiently without visiting each site individually. With the exception of adding or replacing hardware, you can set up your system so that you can perform all administrative tasks remotely from anywhere on the network using remote management capabilities.

Third-Party Administration Tools

An extensive number of remote management tools are available through other independent software vendors. An example of a type of tool provided by other vendors that you might find useful is an event management tool that aggregates large numbers of events from multiple systems. Other types of tools available include performance monitoring and capacity planning tools, which notify you when additional hardware is needed; and security monitoring tools, which can reduce the risk of unauthorized access to your system.

Remote Desktop for Administration

Remote Desktop for Administration (formerly known as Terminal Services in Remote Administration mode) provides remote access to the desktop of computers running any Windows Server 2003 operating system, allowing you to administer your server from virtually any computer on your network. Remote administration of servers with Remote Desktop for Administration is available on any computer running a member of the Windows Server 2003 family. A simpler version of Remote Desktop is also available on Windows XP Professional.

Using Remote Desktop for Administration can greatly reduce administrative overhead. Enabled by Terminal Services technology, Remote Desktop for Administration is specifically designed for server management. It does not install the application sharing and multiuser capabilities or the process scheduling of the full Terminal Server component (formerly called Terminal Services in Application Server mode). As a result, Remote Desktop for Administration can be used on an already-busy server without creating noticeable CPU impact. This makes Remote Desktop for Administration a convenient and efficient service for remote management.

Remote Desktop for Administration does not require you to purchase special licenses for client computers that access the server. It isn't necessary to install Terminal Server Licensing when using Remote Desktop for Administration. You can also fully administer Windows Server 2003 operating systems from computers running earlier versions of Windows by installing Remote Desktop Connection.

For More Information

See the following resources for further information:

- What's New in Management Services at *http://www.microsoft.com/ windowsserver2003/evaluation/overview/technologies/ mgmtsrvcs.mspx*

- Windows 2000 Management Services at *http://www.microsoft.com/ windows2000/technologies/management/*

- Using SMS 2.0 to Deploy Windows XP and Windows .NET Server at *http://www.microsoft.com/smserver/techinfo/deployment/20/ deployosapps/deploywinxp.asp*

- Application Deployment Using Microsoft Management Technologies at *http://www.microsoft.com/windows2000/techinfo/howitworks/man- agement/apdplymgt.asp*

- Microsoft Management Web site at *http://www.microsoft.com/ management/*

- Software Update Services Web site at *http://www.microsoft.com/ windows2000/windowsupdate/sus/*

5

Security Services

Businesses have extended the traditional local area network (LAN) by combining intranets, extranets, and Internet sites; as a result, increased system security is now more critical than ever before. To provide a secure computing environment, the Microsoft Windows Server 2003 family includes many important new security features and improves on the security features originally included in Microsoft Windows 2000 Server.

Viruses exist, and software security is an ongoing challenge. To address these facts, Microsoft has made Trustworthy Computing a key initiative for all its products. Trustworthy Computing is a framework for developing devices powered by computers and software that are as secure and trustworthy as the everyday devices and appliances you use at home. While no Trustworthy Computing platform exists today, the basic redesign of Windows Server 2003 is a solid step toward making this vision a reality.

The common language runtime (CLR) software engine is a key element of Windows Server 2003 that improves reliability and helps ensure a safe computing environment. It reduces the number of bugs and security holes caused by common programming mistakes—as a result, there are fewer vulnerabilities for attackers to exploit. The CLR verifies that applications can run without error and checks for appropriate security permissions, making sure that code performs appropriate operations exclusively. It does this by checking where the code was downloaded or installed from, whether it has a digital signature from a trusted developer, whether it has been altered since it was digitally signed, and so forth.

As part of its commitment to reliable, secure, and dependable computing, Microsoft has reviewed every line of code underlying its Windows Server 2003 family as part of an enhanced effort to identify possible fail points and exploitable weaknesses.

This chapter discusses the tools and processes that deliver important security benefits to organizations deploying Windows Server 2003. These include authentication, access control, security policy, auditing, Active Directory, data protection, network data protection, public key infrastructure (PKI), and trusts.

Security Benefits

Windows Server 2003 will provide a more secure and economical platform for doing business than earlier versions of Windows.

- **Lower costs.**   Lower costs result from simplified security management processes such as access control lists, Credential Manager, and PKI.

- **Implementation of open standards.**   The IEEE 802.1X protocol makes it easy to secure wireless LANs from the threat of eavesdropping within your business environment. For more information about other supported standards, see RFCs 3280, 2797, 2527, and 2459 and public key cryptography standards (PKCS) 1, 5, 8, 10, and 12.

- **Protection for mobile computers and other new devices.** Security features such as Encrypting File System (EFS), certificate services, and automatic smart card enrollment make it easier to secure a full range of devices. EFS is the core technology for encrypting and decrypting files stored on NTFS volumes. Only the user who encrypts a protected file can open the file and work with it. Certificate Services is the part of the core operating system that allows a business to act as its own certification authority (CA) and issue and manage digital certificates. Automatic certificate enrollment and self-registration authority features provide enhanced security for enterprise users by adding another layer of authentication; this is in addition to simplified security processes for security-conscious organizations.

Authentication

Authentication is the process of verifying that a person, an entity, or an object is who or what he, she, or it claims to be. Examples include confirming the source and integrity of information, such as verifying a digital signature or verifying the identity of a user or computer.

Authentication is a fundamental aspect of system security. It confirms the identity of any user trying to log on to a domain or access network resources. Windows Server 2003 family authentication enables single sign-on to all network resources. With single sign-on, a user can log on to the domain once, using a single password or smart card, and authenticate to any computer in the domain.

Authentication Types

In attempting to authenticate a user, several industry-standard types of authentication can be used, depending on a variety of factors. The types of authentication that the Windows Server 2003 family supports are as follows:

■ **Kerberos V5 authentication.**   This protocol is used with either a password or a smart card for interactive logon. It is also the default method of network authentication for services.

■ **Secure Sockets Layer/Transport Layer Security (SSL/TLS) authentication.**   This protocol is used when a user attempts to access a secure Web server.

■ **NTLM authentication.**   This protocol is used when either the client or the server uses a previous version of Windows.

■ **Digest authentication.**   Digest authentication transmits credentials across the network as an MD5 hash or message digest.

■ **Passport authentication.**   Passport authentication is a user-authentication service that offers single-sign-on service.

Internet Information Services Security

When you use Internet Information Services (IIS), authentication is critical to security. IIS 6.0 is a full-featured Web server that provides the foundation for the Microsoft .NET Framework and existing Web applications and Web services. IIS 6.0 has been optimized to run Web applications and Web services in a hosting environment. Many new features have been included in IIS to enhance security, reliability, manageability, and performance.

Using IIS, you can isolate an individual Web application or multiple sites into a self-contained Web service process that communicates directly with the kernel. These self-contained Web service processes prevent one application or site from disrupting the Web services of other Web applications on the server. IIS also provides health monitoring capabilities to discover, recover, and prevent Web application failures.

Because security is an important consideration for a Web server, you can use IIS to protect your Web server from real-world attacks. IIS is a robust platform that provides the tools and features necessary to easily manage a secure server. For more information about security features in IIS 6.0, see Chapter 8, "Internet Information Services."

Interactive Logon

Interactive logon confirms the user's identification to the user's local computer or Active Directory account. For more information about Active Directory and security, see Chapter 3, "Active Directory."

Network Authentication

Network authentication confirms the user's identification to any network service that the user is attempting to access. To provide this type of authentication, the security system includes these authentication mechanisms:

- Kerberos V5
- Public key certificates
- Secure Sockets Layer/Transport Layer Security (SSL/TLS) Digest
- NTLM (for compatibility with Windows NT 4.0–based systems)

Single Sign-On

Single sign-on makes it possible for users to access resources over the network without having to repeatedly supply their credentials. For the Windows Server 2003 family, users need to authenticate only once to access network resources; subsequent authentication is transparent to the user.

Two-Factor Authentication

Authentication in the Windows Server 2003 family also includes two-factor authentication, such as smart cards. Smart cards are a tamper-resistant and portable way to provide security solutions for tasks such as client authentication, logging on to a Windows Server 2003 family domain, code signing, and securing e-mail. Support for cryptographic smart cards is a key feature of the public key infrastructure (PKI) that Microsoft has integrated into Windows XP and the Windows Server 2003 family. Smart cards provide the following:

- Tamper-resistant storage for protecting private keys and other forms of personal information.

- Isolation of security-critical computations involving authentication, digital signatures, and key exchange from other parts of the computer that do not have a need to know. These operations are all performed on the smart card.

- Portability of credentials and other private information between computers at work, at home, or on the road.

Logging on to a network with a smart card provides a strong form of authentication because it uses cryptography-based identification and proof of possession when authenticating a user to a domain. For example, if a malicious person obtains a user's password, that person can assume the user's identity on the network simply through use of the password. Many people choose passwords they can remember easily, which makes passwords inherently weak and open to attack.

In the case of smart cards, that same malicious person would have to obtain both the user's smart card and the personal identification number (PIN) to impersonate the user. This combination is obviously more difficult to attack because an additional layer of information is needed to impersonate a user. An additional benefit is that, after a small number of unsuccessful PIN inputs occur consecutively, a smart card is locked, making a dictionary attack against a smart card extremely difficult. (Note that a PIN does not have to be a series of numbers; it can also use other alphanumeric characters.) Smart cards are also resistant to undetected attacks because the card needs to be obtained by the malicious person, which is relatively easy for a user to know about.

To log on to a domain with a smart card, users do not need to press Ctrl+Alt+Del. They simply insert the smart card into the smart card reader, and the computer prompts them for their personal identification number (PIN) instead of their user name and password.

Object-Based Access Control

Along with user authentication, administrators are allowed to control access to resources or objects on the network. To do this, administrators assign security descriptors to objects that are stored in Active Directory. A security descriptor lists the users and groups that are granted access to an object and the specific permissions assigned to those users and groups. A security descriptor also specifies the various access events to be audited for an object. Examples of objects include users, computers, and organizational units (OUs). By managing properties on objects, administrators can set permissions, assign ownership, and monitor user access.

Not only can administrators control access to a specific object, they can also control access to a specific attribute of that object. For example, through proper configuration of an object's security descriptor, a user can be allowed to access only a subset of information, such as employees' names and telephone numbers but not their home addresses. To secure a computer and its resources, you must take into consideration the rights that users will have:

- You can secure a computer or multiple computers by granting users or groups specific user rights.

- You can secure an object, such as a file or folder, by assigning permissions to allow users or groups to perform specific actions on that object.

Access Control Concepts

Permissions define the type of access granted to a user or group for an object or object property. For example, the Finance group can be granted Read and Write permissions for a file named Payroll.dat. Permissions are applied to any secured objects such as files, Active Directory objects, or registry objects. Permissions can be granted to any user, group, or computer. (It's good practice to assign permissions to groups.) The permissions attached to an object depend on the type of object. For example, the permissions that can be attached to a file are different from those that can be attached to a registry key. You can assign permissions for objects to the following:

- Groups, users, and special identities in the domain

- Groups and users in that domain and any trusted domains

- Local groups and users on the computer where the object resides

When you set up permissions, you specify the level of access for groups and users. For example, you can let one user read the contents of a file, let another user make changes to the file, and prevent all other users from accessing the file. You can set similar permissions on printers so that certain users can configure the printer and other users can only print from it. If you need to change the permissions on an individual object, you can start the appropriate tool and change the properties for that object. For example, to change the permissions on a file, you can run Windows Explorer, right-click the filename, and click Properties. On the Security tab, you can change permissions on the file.

An owner is assigned to an object when that object is created. By default, the owner is the creator of the object. No matter which permissions are set on an object, the owner of the object can always change the permissions on an object.

Inheritance allows administrators to easily assign and manage permissions. This feature automatically causes objects within a container to inherit all the inheritable permissions of that container. For example, the files within a folder, when created, inherit the permissions of the folder. Only permissions marked to be inherited are inherited.

Effective Permissions

The Effective Permissions tab is a new, advanced option in Windows Server 2003. It lets you see all of the permissions that apply to a security principal for a given object, including the permissions derived from memberships in security groups. The Effective Permissions tab is shown in Figure 5-1.

Figure 5-1   The Effective Permissions tab is new with Windows Server 2003.

To view the effective permissions for a user or group, perform the following steps:

1. On the Effective Permissions tab, click the Select button to open the Select User Or Group dialog box.

2. In the Name box, type the name of the built-in security principal, group, or user for which you would like to view Effective Permissions.

3. Optionally, click the Object Types button, and then select Built-In Security Principals, Groups, or Users.

4. Click OK.

> **Note**   If the security principal is network based, you can click Locations and select a target, or you can type in the domain name together with the group name, such as reskit\users. It's important to specify the correct object types and the locations for your search. Failure to do so will result in an error message and the suggestion that you refine your search before searching again.

User Rights

User rights grant specific privileges and logon rights to users and groups in your computing environment.

Object Auditing

You can audit users' access to objects. You can then view these security-related events in the security log with the Event Viewer.

Security Policy

You can control security on your local computer, or on multiple computers, by controlling the following: password policies, account lockout policies, Kerberos policies, auditing policies, user rights, and other policies.

To create a systemwide policy, you can use security templates; apply templates using the Security Configuration and Analysis snap-in; or edit policies on the local computer, organizational unit, or domain.

Security Configuration Manager

The Security Configuration Manager tool set lets you create, apply, and edit security variables for your local computer, organizational unit, or domain. The following list describes the components of the Security Configuration Manager tool set:

- **Security Templates.**   Defines a security policy in a template. These templates can be applied to Group Policy or to your local computer.

- **Security Settings Extension to Group Policy.**   Edits individual security settings on a domain, a site, or an organizational unit.

- **Local Security Policy.**   Edits individual security settings on your local computer.

- **Secedit Commands.**   Automates security configuration tasks at a command prompt.

Security Configuration and Analysis

Security Configuration and Analysis is a Microsoft Management Console (MMC) snap-in for analyzing and configuring local system security.

Security Analysis

The state of the operating system and applications on a computer is dynamic. For example, you might need to temporarily change security levels so that you can immediately resolve an administration or network issue. However, this change can often go unreversed. This means that a computer might no longer meet the requirements for enterprise security.

Regular analysis enables an administrator to track and ensure an adequate level of security on each computer as part of an enterprise risk management program. An administrator can tune the security levels and, most important, detect any security flaws that might occur in the system over time.

Security Configuration and Analysis lets you quickly review security analysis results. It presents recommendations alongside current system settings and uses visual flags or remarks to highlight any areas where the current settings do not match the proposed level of security. Security Configuration and Analysis also offers the ability to resolve any discrepancies that that analysis reveals.

Security Configuration

Security Configuration and Analysis can be used to directly configure local system security. Through its use of personal databases, you can import security templates that have been created with Security Templates and apply those templates to the local computer. This immediately configures the system security with the levels specified in the template.

Auditing

Auditing gives you a way to track potential security problems, helps to ensure user accountability, and provides evidence in the event of a security breach. To audit effectively, you need to establish an audit policy. This requires you to determine which categories of events, which objects, and which accesses you want to audit.

Establish a Strategy

Your policy should be based on a strategy. For instance, you might decide that you are interested in a record of who accessed the system or specific data on the system, or that you are interested in detecting unauthorized attempts to tamper with the operating system.

Common Events to Be Audited

The most common types of events to be audited are the following:

- Users logging on to and logging off the system

- Management of user accounts and groups

- Accesses of objects, such as files and folders

Implementing Auditing Policy

When you implement auditing policy, keep the following points in mind:

- Develop your audit strategy. Decide which behaviors you want to audit.

- Select the audit categories that correspond to your auditing strategy, and no more.

- Select an appropriate size and retention policy for the security log. You can view the security log and set the log size and retention policy with Event Viewer, as shown in Figure 5-2.

- If you have decided to audit directory service access or object access, determine which objects must be monitored as part of your strategy. Also determine the minimum number of accesses you need to audit to fulfill the goals of your strategy. You shouldn't audit any more objects or accesses than necessary because a too-broad audit selection could cause audit logs to fill very rapidly on a busy machine.

- Deploy your policy. You can do this with the Local Security Policy tool on a stand-alone machine or with Group Policy on a domain.

- Review your security logs regularly. There's no point in auditing if you're never going to look at your logs. An event log collection system can help make this a manageable task.

- Fine-tune your policy as necessary. This might include adding or removing objects or accesses to your audit policy, or enabling or disabling audit categories. After reviewing your logs, you might find that you have collected more or less information than you want.

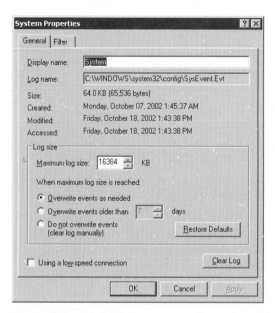

Figure 5-2   Administrators can easily configure the event log's size and retention policy.

Active Directory and Security

The Active Directory directory service ensures that administrators can manage user authentication and access control easily and efficiently. See Chapter 3, "Active Directory," for more information about security and Active Directory.

Active Directory provides protected storage of user account and group information by using access control on objects and user credentials. Because Active Directory stores not only user credentials but also access-control information, users who log on to the network obtain both authentication and authorization to access system resources. For example, when a user logs on to the network, the security system authenticates the user with information stored in Active Directory. Then, when the user attempts to access a service on the network, the system checks the properties defined in the discretionary access control list (DACL) for that service.

Because Active Directory allows administrators to create group accounts, administrators can manage system security more efficiently than ever before. For example, by adjusting a file's properties, an administrator can permit all users in a group to read that file. In this way, access to objects in Active Directory is based on group membership.

Data Protection

Stored data (on line or off line) can be protected by using Encrypting File System (EFS) and digital signatures. Stored data security refers to the ability to store data on disk in an encrypted form.

Encrypting File System

With EFS, data can be encrypted as it is stored on disk. EFS uses public key encryption to encrypt local NTFS data. Once a user has encrypted a file, the file automatically remains encrypted whenever the file is stored on disk. And once a user has decrypted a file, the file remains decrypted whenever the file is stored on disk. EFS provides the following features:

- Users can encrypt their files when storing them on disk. Encryption is as easy as selecting a check box in the file's Advanced Attributes dialog box (accessed via the file's Properties dialog box), as shown in Figure 5-3.

- Accessing encrypted files is fast and easy. Users see their data in plain text when accessing the data from disk.

- Encryption of data is accomplished automatically and is completely transparent to the user.

- Users can actively decrypt a file by clearing the Encrypt Contents check box in the file's Advanced Attributes dialog box.

- Administrators can recover data that was encrypted by another user. This ensures that data is accessible if the user who encrypted the data is no longer available or has lost his or her private key.

Figure 5-3   Encrypting files is as easy as selecting the Encrypt Contents check box.

Note   EFS encrypts data only when it is stored on disk. To encrypt data as it is transported over a TCP/IP network, two optional features are available—Internet Protocol security (IPSec) and PPTP encryption.

The default configuration of EFS requires no administrative effort—users can begin encrypting files immediately. EFS generates an encryption key pair for a user if one does not exist. EFS can use either the expanded Data Encryption Standard (DESX) or Triple-DES (3DES) as the encryption algorithm. Encryption services are available from Windows Explorer. Users can also encrypt a file or folder using the command-line utility *cipher*. For more information about the *cipher* command, type **cipher /?** at a command-line prompt. Users encrypt a file or folder by setting the encryption property for files and folders just as you set any other attribute, such as read-only, compressed, or hidden. If a user encrypts a folder, all files and subfolders created in or added to the encrypted folder are automatically encrypted. It is recommended that users encrypt at the folder level. Files or folders that are compressed cannot also be encrypted. If the user marks a compressed file or folder for encryption, that file or folder will be uncompressed. Also, folders that are marked for encryption are not actually encrypted. Only the files within the folder are encrypted, as well as any new files created or moved into the folder. Once decrypted, a file remains decrypted until you encrypt the file again. There is no automatic reencryption of a file, even if it exists in a directory marked as encrypted.

Data recovery refers to the process of decrypting a file without having the private key of the user who encrypted the file. You might need to recover data with a recovery agent if a user leaves the company, a user loses the private key, or a law enforcement agency makes a request. To recover a file, the recovery agent does the following:

1. Backs up the encrypted files

2. Moves the backup copies to a secure system

3. Imports their recovery certificate and private key on that system

4. Restores the backup files

5. Decrypts the files, using Windows Explorer or the EFS *cipher* command

You can use the Group Policy snap-in to define a data recovery policy for domain member servers, or for stand-alone or workgroup servers. You can either request a recovery certificate or export and import your recovery certificates. You might want to delegate administration of the recovery policy to a designated administrator. Although you should limit who is authorized to recover encrypted data, allowing multiple administrators to act as recovery agents provides you with an alternative source if recovery is necessary.

Digital Signatures

A digital signature is a way to ensure the integrity and origin of data. A digital signature provides strong evidence that the data has not been altered since it was signed and confirms the identity of the person or entity that signed the data. This enables the important security features of integrity and nonrepudiation, which are essential for secure electronic commerce transactions.

Digital signatures are typically used when data is distributed in clear text, or unencrypted form. In these cases, while the sensitivity of the message itself might not warrant encryption, there could be a compelling reason to ensure that the data is in its original form and has not been sent by an impostor because, in a distributed computing environment, clear text can conceivably be read or altered by anyone on the network with the proper access, whether authorized or not.

CAPICOM

Windows Server 2003 includes support for CAPICOM 2.0. This support enables application developers to take advantage of the robust certificate and cryptography features available in CryptoAPI by employing an easy-to-use COM interface. Using this functionality, application developers can easily incorporate digital signing and encryption functionality into their applications. Because CAPICOM is based on COM, application developers can access this functionality in a number of programming environments, such as the Visual C# development tool, the Visual Basic .NET development system, Visual Basic, Visual Basic Scripting Edition, JScript development software, and others.

CAPICOM allows you to do the following:

- Digitally sign and verify arbitrary data with a smart card or software key

- Digitally sign and verify executables with Authenticode technology

- Hash arbitrary data

- Graphically display certificate selection and detailed information

- Manage and search CryptoAPI certificate stores

- Encrypt and decrypt data with a password, or with public keys and certificates

Network Data Protection

Network data within your site (local network and subnets) is secured by the authentication protocol. For an additional level of security, you can also choose to encrypt network data within a site. Using Internet Protocol security, you can encrypt all network communication for specific clients or for all clients in a domain. Network data passing in and out of your site (across intranets, extranets, or an Internet gateway) can be secured by using the following utilities:

- **Internet Protocol Security (IPSec)**   Comprises a suite of cryptography-based protection services and security protocols

- **Routing and Remote Access**   Configures remote access protocols and routing

- **Internet Authentication Service (IAS)**   Provides security and authentication for dial-in users

Internet Protocol Security

The long-term direction for secure networking, IPSec is a suite of cryptography-based protection services and security protocols. Because it requires no changes to applications or protocols, you can easily deploy IPSec for existing networks.

IPSec provides computer-level authentication, as well as data encryption, for virtual private network (VPN) connections that use the Layer 2 Tunneling Protocol (L2TP). IPSec is negotiated between your computer and a L2TP-based VPN server before an L2TP connection is established. This negotiation secures both passwords and data. L2TP uses standard PPP-based authentication protocols, such as Extensible Authentication Protocol (EAP), Microsoft Challenge Handshake Authentication Protocol (MS-CHAP), MS-CHAP version 2, CHAP, Shiva Password Authentication Protocol (SPAP), and Password Authentication Protocol (PAP) with IPSec.

Encryption is determined by the IPSec Security Association (SA). A security association is a combination of a destination address; a security protocol; and a unique identification value, called a Security Parameters Index (SPI). The available encryptions include

- Data Encryption Standard (DES), which uses a 56-bit key
- Triple DES (3DES), which uses three 56-bit keys and is designed for high-security environments

Routing and Remote Access

The Routing and Remote Access service for the Windows Server 2003 family is a full-featured software router and is an open platform for routing and internetworking. It offers routing services to businesses in LAN and WAN environments or over the Internet by using secure VPN connections.

An advantage of the Routing and Remote Access service is integration with the Windows Server 2003 family. The Routing and Remote Access service delivers many cost-saving features, and it works with a wide variety of hardware platforms and hundreds of network adapters. The Routing and Remote Access service is extensible with application programming interfaces (APIs) that developers can use to create custom networking solutions and that new vendors can use to participate in the growing business of open internetworking.

Internet Authentication Service

Internet Authentication Service (IAS) in the Standard Edition, Enterprise Edition, and Datacenter Edition of Windows Server 2003 is the Microsoft implementation of a Remote Authentication Dial-In User Service (RADIUS) server and proxy:

- As a RADIUS server, IAS performs centralized connection authentication, authorization, and accounting for many types of network access, including wireless, authenticating switch, remote access dial-up, and VPN connections.

- As a RADIUS proxy, IAS forwards authentication and accounting messages to other RADIUS servers. RADIUS is an Internet Engineering Task Force (IETF) standard.

Public Key Infrastructure

Computer networks are no longer closed systems in which a user's mere presence on the network can serve as proof of identity. In this age of information interconnection, an organization's network can consist of intranets, Internet sites, and extranets—all of which are potentially susceptible to access by unauthorized individuals who intend to maliciously view or alter an organization's digital information assets.

There are many potential opportunities for unauthorized access to information on networks. A person can attempt to monitor or alter information streams such as e-mail, electronic commerce transactions, and file transfers. Your organization might work with partners on projects of limited scope and duration having employees about whom you know nothing but who, nonetheless, must be given access to some of your information resources. If your users have a multitude of passwords to remember for accessing different secure systems, they might choose weak or common passwords to more easily remember them. This provides an intruder with not only a password that is easy to crack but also one that will provide access to multiple secure systems and stored data.

How can a system administrator be sure of the identity of a person accessing information, and given that identity, control which information that person has access to? Additionally, how can a system administrator easily and securely distribute and manage identification credentials across an organization? These are issues that can be addressed with a well-planned public key infrastructure. A public key infrastructure (PKI) is a system of digital certificates, certification authorities (CAs), and other registration authorities (RAs) that verify and authenticate the validity of each party that is involved in an electronic transaction through the use of public key cryptography. Standards for PKIs are still evolving, even as they are being widely implemented as a necessary element of electronic commerce.

An organization might choose to deploy a PKI using Windows for a number of reasons:

■ **Strong security.**   You can have strong authentication with smart cards. You can also maintain the confidentiality and integrity of transmitted data on public networks by using IPSec, and you can protect the confidentiality of your stored data using EFS.

■ **Simplified administration.**   Your organization can issue certificates and, in conjunction with other technologies, eliminate the use of passwords. You can revoke certificates as necessary and publish certificate revocation lists (CRLs). There is the ability to use certificates to scale trust relationships across an enterprise. You can also take advantage of Certificate Services integration with Active Directory and policy. The capability to map certificates to user accounts is also available.

■ **Additional opportunities for PKI.**   You can exchange files and data securely over public networks, such as the Internet. You have the ability to implement secure e-mail using Secure Multipurpose Internet Mail Extensions (S/MIME) and secure Web connections using Secure Sockets Layer (SSL) or Transport Layer Security (TLS). You can also implement security enhancements to wireless networking.

The following sections describe the features in the Windows Server 2003 family that can help your organization implement a public key infrastructure.

Certificates

A certificate is basically a digital statement issued by an authority that vouches for the identity of the certificate holder. A certificate binds a public key to the identity of the person, computer, or service that holds the corresponding private key. Certificates are used by a variety of public key security services and applications that provide authentication, data integrity, and secure communication across networks such as the Internet.

The standard certificate format used by Windows certificate–based processes is X.509v3. An X.509 certificate includes information about the person to whom or the entity to which the certificate is issued, information about the certificate, and optional information about the certification authority issuing the certificate. Subject information can include the entity's name, the public key, and the public key algorithm. The entity receiving the certificate is the subject of the certificate. The issuer and signer of the certificate is a certification authority.

Users can manage certificates using the MMC snap-in for certificates, as shown in Figure 5-4. Users can also allow certificate autoenrollment to manage their certificates automatically.

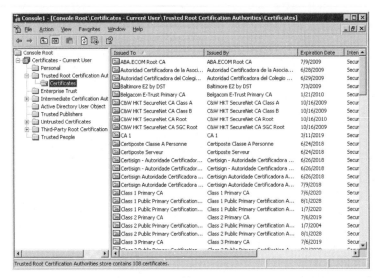

Figure 5-4   You manage certificates using Microsoft Management Console.

Certificates can be issued for a variety of functions, such as Web user authentication, Web server authentication, secure e-mail (S/MIME), IPSec, TLS, and code signing. Certificates are also issued from one CA to another in order to establish a certification hierarchy. Typically, certificates contain the following information:

■   The subject's public key value

■   The subject's identifier information, such as name and e-mail address

■   The validity period (the length of time that the certificate is considered valid)

■   Issuer identifier information

■   The digital signature of the issuer, which attests to the validity of the binding between the subject's public key and the subject's identifier information

A certificate is valid only for the period of time specified within it; every certificate contains Valid From and Valid To dates, which set the boundaries of the validity period. Once a certificate's validity period has passed, the subject of the now-expired certificate must request a new certificate.

In instances in which it becomes necessary to undo the binding that is asserted in a certificate, the issuer can revoke the certificate. Each issuer maintains a certificate revocation list that can be used by programs when checking the validity of any given certificate.

One of the main benefits of certificates is that hosts no longer have to maintain a set of passwords for individual subjects who need to be authenticated as a prerequisite for access. Instead, the host merely establishes trust in a certificate issuer. When a host, such as a secure Web server, designates an issuer as a trusted root authority, the host implicitly trusts the policies that the issuer has used to establish the bindings of certificates it issues. In effect, the host trusts that the issuer has verified the identity of the certificate subject. A host designates an issuer as a trusted root authority by placing the issuer's self-signed certificate, which contains the issuer's public key, into the trusted root certification authority certificate store of the host computer. Intermediate or subordinate certification authorities are trusted only if they have a valid certification path from a trusted root certification authority.

Certificate Services

Certificate Services is the component in the Windows Server 2003 family that is used to create and manage CAs. A CA is responsible for establishing and vouching for the identity of certificate holders. A CA also revokes certificates if they should no longer be considered valid and publishes CRLs to be used by certificate verifiers.

The simplest PKI design has only one root CA. In practice, however, a majority of organizations deploying a PKI will use a number of CAs, organized into certification hierarchies. Administrators can manage Certificate Services by using the Certification Authority MMC snap-in.

Certificate Templates

Certificates are issued by the CA based on information provided in the certificate request and on settings contained in a certificate template. A certificate template is the set of rules and settings that are applied against incoming certificate requests. For each type of certificate that an enterprise CA can issue, a certificate template must be configured.

Certificate templates are customizable in Windows Server 2003, Enterprise Server, and Windows Server 2003, Datacenter Server, enterprise CAs, and they are stored in Active Directory for use by all CAs in the forest. This allows the administrator to choose one or more of the default templates installed with Certificate Services or to create templates that are customized for specific tasks or roles.

Certificate Autoenrollment

Autoenrollment enables the administrator to configure subjects to automatically enroll for certificates, retrieve issued certificates, and renew expiring certificates without requiring subject interaction. Such configuration requires no knowledge by the subject of any certificate operations—unless the certificate template is configured to interact with the subject or the cryptographic service provider (CSP) requires interaction (such as with a smart card CSP). This greatly simplifies the experience of the client with certificates and minimizes administrative tasks. Administrators can configure autoenrollment through configuration of Certificate Templates and CA settings.

Web Enrollment Pages

Web enrollment pages are a separate component of Certificate Services. These Web pages are installed by default when you set up a CA and allow certificate requesters to submit certificate requests using a Web browser.

Additionally, the CA Web pages can be installed on servers running Windows that do not have a CA installed. In this case, the Web pages are used to direct certificate requests to a CA that, for whatever reason, you do not want requesters to directly access.

If you choose to create custom Web pages for your organization to access a CA, the Web pages provided with Windows Server 2003 can be used as samples. Refer to the Microsoft Platform Software Development Kit for information about customizing Certificate Services and CA Web pages.

Smart Card Support

Windows supports logon via certificates on smart cards, as well as the use of smart cards to store certificates and private keys. Smart cards can be used for Web authentication, secure e-mail, wireless networking, and other activities related to public key cryptography.

Public Key Policies

You can use Group Policy in Windows to distribute certificates to subjects automatically, establish common trusted certification authorities, and manage recovery policies for EFS.

Trusts

The Windows Server 2003 family supports domain trusts and forest trusts. Domain trust allows a user to authenticate to resources in another domain. To establish and manage domain trust relationships, you must take into consideration trust direction.

Trust Direction

The trust type and its assigned direction will have a substantial impact on the trust path used for authentication. A trust path is a series of trust relationships that authentication requests must follow between domains.

Before a user can access a resource in another domain, the security system on domain controllers running Windows Server 2003 must determine whether the trusting domain (the domain containing the resource the user is trying to access) has a trust relationship with the trusted domain (the user's logon domain). To determine this, the security system computes the trust path between a domain controller in the trusting domain and a domain controller in the trusted domain. In Figure 5-5, trust paths are indicated by arrows showing the direction of the trust.

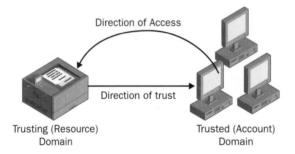

Figure 5-5   This diagram shows trust paths and the direction of each trust.

All domain trust relationships have only two domains in the relationship: the trusting domain and the trusted domain.

Trust Types

Communication between domains occurs through trusts. Trusts are authentication pipelines that must be present for users in one domain to access resources in another domain.

- **One-way trust.**   A one-way trust is a unidirectional authentication path created between two domains. This means that in a one-way trust between domain A and domain B, users in domain A can access resources in domain B. However, users in domain B cannot access resources in domain A. Some one-way relationships can be nontransitive or transitive depending on the type of trust being created:

  - A transitive trust flows throughout a set of domains, such as a domain tree, and forms a relationship between a domain and all domains that trust that domain. For example, if domain A trusts domain B and domain B trusts domain C, domain A trusts domain C. Transitive trusts can be one-way or two-way, and they are required for Kerberos-based authentication and Active Directory replication.

  - A nontransitive trust is restricted to two domains in a trust relationship. For example, even if domain A trusts domain B and domain B trusts domain C, there is no trust relationship between domain A and domain C. Nontransitive trusts can be one-way or two-way.

- **Two-way trust.**   All domain trusts in a Windows .NET forest are two-way transitive trusts. When a new child domain is created, a two-way transitive trust is automatically created between the new child domain and the parent domain. In a two-way trust, domain A trusts domain B and domain B trusts domain A. This means that authentication requests can be passed between the two domains in both directions. Some two-way relationships can be nontransitive or transitive depending on the type of trust being created.

Trust Relationships

A Windows .NET domain can establish a one-way or two-way trust with

- Windows .NET domains in the same forest.

- Windows .NET domains in a different forest.

- Windows NT 4.0 domains.

- Kerberos V5 realms.

Forest Trusts

In a Windows Server 2003 forest, administrators can create a forest trust to extend two-way transitivity beyond the scope of a single forest to a second Windows Server 2003 forest. In other words, with forest trusts you can link two disjoined Windows Server 2003 forests to form a two-way transitive trust relationship between every domain in both forests. Forest trusts provide the following benefits:

- Simplified management of resources across two Windows Server 2003 forests. Forest trusts reduce the number of external trusts needed to share resources with a second forest.

- Complete two-way trust relationships with every domain in each forest.

- Wider scope of UPN authentications. User principal name authentications can be used across two forests.

- Greater trustworthiness of authorization data. Both the Kerberos and NTLM authentication protocols can be used to help improve the trustworthiness of authorization data transferred between forests.

- Flexibility of administration. Administrators can choose to split collaborative delegation efforts with other administrators into forest-wide administrative units.

- Isolation of directory replication within each forest. Schema changes, configuration changes, and the addition of new domains to a forest have forestwide impact only within that forest, not on a trusting forest.

Forest trusts can be created only between two forests and therefore will not be implicitly extended to a third forest. This means that if a forest trust is created between Forest1 and Forest2, and a forest trust is also created between Forest2 and Forest3, Forest1 will not have an implicit trust with Forest3.

> **Note** In Windows 2000, if users in one forest needed access to resources in a second forest, an administrator could create an external trust relationship between the two domains. External trusts are one-way and nontransitive and therefore limit the ability for trust paths to extend to other domains only when explicitly configured.

For More Information

See the following resources for more information:

- What's New in Internet Information Services 6.0 at *http://www.microsoft.com/windowsserver2003/evaluation/overview/technologies/iis.mspx*

- Windows 2000 Security Services at *http://www.microsoft.com/windows2000/technologies/security/*

- What's New in Security for Windows XP at *http://www.microsoft.com/windowsxp/pro/techinfo/planning/security/whatsnew/*

- PKI Enhancements in Windows XP Professional and Windows .NET Server at *http://www.microsoft.com/windowsxp/pro/techinfo/planning/pkiwinxp/*

- Data protection and recovery in Windows XP at *http://www.microsoft.com/windowsxp/pro/techinfo/administration/recovery/*

- Securing Mobile Computers with Windows XP Professional at *http://www.microsoft.com/windowsxp/pro/techinfo/administration/mobile/*

- Wireless 802.11 Security with Windows XP at *http://www.microsoft.com/WindowsXP/pro/techinfo/administration/wirelesssecurity/*

- Institute of Electrical and Electronics Engineers at *http://www.ieee.org/*

6

Communications

This chapter is a technical description of the networking and communications enhancements in the Windows Server 2003 family—improvements that make networks easier to set up, configure, and deploy. It explains how you can take advantage of improved network connectivity, changes to protocols, and better network device support. For example, mobile users in particular have new options for connecting to the network, such as being able to use the Windows Server 2003 family to gain secure Internet access via wireless or Ethernet connections while waiting in an airport. And now infrared-enabled cellular phones can be used just like any other modem to create a network connection.

With Windows Server 2003, IT professionals have more options, and more flexible options, for managing networking infrastructure, through new capabilities such as configuring secure access to a wireless LAN, specifying Group Policy settings to control networking features for certain types of users, and creating a Connection Manager profile that lets traveling users select the optimal VPN server, depending on their location. These are just .a few of the many new capabilities described in this chapter.

Easier Setup, Configuration, and Deployment

The following sections describe the enhancements that make Windows Server 2003 easier to set up, configure, and deploy:

- Network Diagnostics Features
- Network Location Awareness
- Wireless LAN Enhancements

- Routing and Remote Access Service Enhancements
- Connection Manager Enhancements

Network Diagnostics Features

Network diagnostics features were added to the Windows Server 2003 family to support diagnosing network problems, as follows:

- **Network Diagnostics Web page.**   The Network Diagnostics Web page can be viewed from the Tools section of Help and Support or from the Help and Support detailed information section on either troubleshooting or networking. This Web page makes it easy to retrieve important information about the local computer and the network it's connected to. The Web page also includes various tests for troubleshooting network problems.

- **Netsh Diag commands.**   A new Netsh helper DLL provides commands in the Netsh Diag context to enable you to view extensive network diagnostic information and perform diagnostic functions from the command line. To run Netsh diagnostic commands, type **netsh -c diag** at the command prompt.

- **Repair menu option for network connections.**   Sometimes a computer's network configuration can be in a state that prohibits network communication, but the configuration can still be repaired through a set of common procedures, such as renewing the IP address configuration and Domain Name System (DNS) name registrations. To avoid having to take these steps by hand, a Repair option is available on each network connection's shortcut menu. Choosing this option causes a series of steps to be taken that are likely to solve communication problems and are known not to cause worse problems.

- **Support tab for network connections.**   The Status dialog box for each network connection in the Network Connections folder now includes a Support tab. From this tab, TCP/IP configuration information is displayed. The Support tab includes a Repair button, which is equivalent to the Repair context menu option on the network connection.

- **Networking tab for Task Manager.**   Task Manager now includes a Networking tab, shown in Figure 6-1, that displays real-time networking metrics for each network adapter in the system. This tab can provide a quick look at how the network is performing.

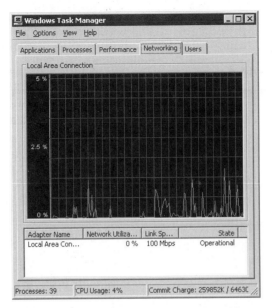

Figure 6-1   The Networking tab in Task Manager is new in Microsoft Windows XP and Windows Server 2003.

- **Updated Netdiag.exe command-line network diagnostics tool.**   The support tools provided on the Windows Server 2003 family product CD-ROM include Netdiag.exe, an enhanced version of the diagnostics tool provided in the Microsoft Windows 2000 Resource Kit. To install the support tools, run the file Support.msi from the Support\Tools folder on the Windows Server 2003 family product CD-ROM.

- **Menu option to enable remote access logging.**   A new Diagnostics tab has been added to the Remote Access Preferences dialog box in the Network Connections folder to globally enable, view, and clear logging for remote access connections. To view the Remote Access Preferences dialog box, choose Remote Access Preferences from the Advanced menu in the Network Connections folder.

Network Location Awareness

Network location awareness allows computers running the Windows Server 2003 family to detect information about the network to which the computer is attached. This allows for seamless configuration of the network stack for that location. This information is also made available through a Windows Sockets

API, allowing applications to retrieve information about the current network or be notified when network information changes.

Components in the Windows Server 2003 family also use the network location to provide appropriate services. For example, the new Group Policy settings to enable or disable the Internet Connection Sharing (ICS), Internet Connection Firewall (ICF), and Network Bridge features are network location–aware; they apply to the computer only when it's connected to the network on which the settings were obtained. For example, if a laptop computer receives a Group Policy setting to disable these features while connected to a corporate network, when the computer is connected to a home network, the Group Policy settings do not apply and the features can be used.

Wireless LAN Enhancements

Several features and enhancements have been added to the Windows Server 2003 family to improve the experience in deploying wireless LANs, including automatic key management and user authentication and authorization prior to LAN access. These enhancements include the following:

- **Enhanced Ethernet and wireless security (IEEE 802.1X Support).** Previously, wireless networking lacked an easy-to-deploy security solution with a key management system. Microsoft and several wireless LAN and PC vendors worked with the IEEE to define IEEE 802.1X, a standard for port-based network access control that applies to both Ethernet and wireless LANs. Microsoft implemented IEEE 802.1X support in Windows XP and worked with wireless LAN vendors to support the standard in their access points.

- **Wireless zero configuration.** In conjunction with the wireless network adapter, the Windows Server 2003 family can choose from available wireless networks to configure connections to preferred networks without user intervention. Settings for a specific wireless network can be saved and automatically used the next time that wireless network is accessed. In the absence of an infrastructure network, the Windows Server 2003 family can configure the wireless adapter to use ad hoc mode.

- **Wireless roaming support.** Windows 2000 included enhancements for detecting the availability of a network and acting appropriately. These enhancements have been extended and supplemented in the Windows Server 2003 family to support the transitional nature of a wireless network. Features added in the Windows Server 2003 family include renewing the DHCP configuration upon reassociation, reauthentication when necessary, and choosing from multiple configuration options based on the network to which the computer is connected.

■ **Wireless Monitor snap-in.** The Windows Server 2003 family includes a new Wireless Monitor snap-in, which can be used to view wireless access point (AP) or wireless client configuration and statistical information.

■ **Password-based authentication for secure wireless connections.** The Windows Server 2003 family includes support for Protected Extensible Authentication Protocol (PEAP) for wireless network connections. With PEAP, you can use a password-based authentication method to securely authenticate wireless connections. PEAP creates an encrypted channel before the authentication process occurs. Therefore, password-based authentication exchanges are not subject to offline dictionary attacks. The Microsoft Challenge Handshake Authentication Protocol version 2 (MS-CHAP v2) is now available as an EAP authentication type. PEAP with the EAP version of MS-CHAP v2 allows you to have secure wireless authentication without having to deploy a certificate infrastructure, also known as a public key infrastructure (PKI), and without having to install certificates on each wireless client. The Windows Server 2003 family Remote Authentication Dial-In User Service (RADIUS) server, known as the Internet Authentication Service (IAS), has also been enhanced to support PEAP.

■ **Group Policy extension for wireless network policies.** A new Wireless Network (IEEE 802.11) Policies Group Policy extension allows you to configure wireless network settings that are part of Group Policy for Computer Configuration. Wireless network settings include the list of preferred networks, Wired Equivalent Privacy (WEP) settings, and IEEE 802.1X settings. These settings are downloaded to domain members, making it much easier than in Windows 2000 Server to deploy a specific configuration for secure wireless connections to wireless client computers. You can configure wireless policies from the Computer Configuration/Windows Settings/Security Settings/Wireless Network (IEEE 802.11) Policies node in the Group Policy snap-in.

■ **Unauthenticated access for wireless LAN connections.** Both the Windows Server 2003 family wireless client and IAS support unauthenticated wireless connections. In this case, Extensible Authentication Protocol with Transport Level Security (EAP-TLS) is used to perform one-way authentication of the IAS server certificate, and the wireless client does not send a user name or user credentials. To enable unauthenticated access for wireless clients, select Authenticate As Guest When User Or Computer Information Is Available on the Authentication tab from the properties of a wireless connection in the Network Connections folder. To enable unauthenticated access for the IAS server, the guest account is enabled and a remote access policy is configured that allows unauthenticated access for EAP-TLS connections using a group containing the guest account. The remote access policy can also specify a virtual LAN (VLAN) ID that corresponds to a temporary network segment for unauthenticated users.

With these enhancements, the following scenarios are possible:

❑ A mobile user is in an airport and can gain secure Internet access via wireless or Ethernet connectivity.

❑ An administrator can use these enhancements to configure secure access to a wireless LAN. The administrator might also require certificates deployed via autoenrollment and authorization based on remote access policies used by IAS.

❑ An administrator can use these features to configure authenticated and authorized access to wire-based Ethernet LANs without requiring data encryption.

Routing and Remote Access Service Enhancements

The following enhancements to the Routing and Remote Access service have been made in the Windows Server 2003 family:

■ **Snap-in and Setup Wizard enhancements.** The Routing And Remote Access Server Setup Wizard has been modified to make it easier to initially configure the Routing and Remote Access service (see Figure 6-2). The Routing And Remote Access snap-in has been modified to make it easier to configure server settings after the initial configuration.

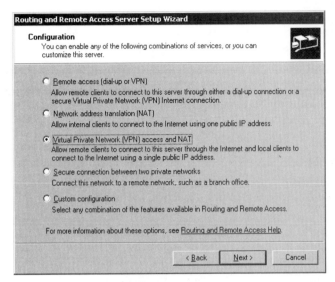

Figure 6-2 The Routing And Remote Access Server Setup Wizard makes configuring different types of remote access much easier.

- **Improved configuration for EAP-TLS properties.** The Smart Card Or Other Certificate Properties dialog box has been improved to allow the configuration of multiple RADIUS servers and multiple root certification authorities. This provides seamless connectivity with multiple wired or wireless networks or large networks that use multiple RADIUS servers. You can access the Smart Card Or Other Certificate Properties dialog box by selecting the Smart Card Or Other Certificate EAP type on the Authentication tab from the properties of a LAN connection in the Network Connections folder and then clicking Properties.

- **NetBIOS over TCP/IP name resolution proxy.** A new NetBIOS over TCP/IP (NetBT) proxy is built into the Routing and Remote Access service to allow remote access clients connecting to a network consisting of one or multiple subnets with a single router (the remote access computer running a member of the Windows Server 2003 family) to resolve names without having to use a Domain Name System (DNS) or Windows Internet Name Service (WINS) server. This new feature allows a small business to configure a remote access or VPN server so that its employees can work from home. With the NetBT proxy enabled, clients connecting remotely are able to resolve the names of computers on the small-business network without requiring the deployment of a DNS or WINS server.

- **Manage Your Server and Routing and Remote Access service integration.** This feature provides an integrated method to configure the NAT/Basic Firewall component of the Routing and Remote Access service using Manage Your Server. With this feature, an IT administrator can configure a Windows .NET family server and the Routing and Remote Access service NAT/Basic Firewall component during the same setup procedure.

- **Ability to enable the Routing and Remote Access service internal interface as a Network Address Translation private interface.** For a computer running Windows 2000 Server that is providing remote access to a private intranet and is acting as a Network Address Translator (NAT) to provide access to the Internet, there is no way to provide Internet access to connected remote access clients. Computers running a member of the Windows Server 2003 family now allow you to add the Internal interface as a private interface to the Network Address Translation component of the Routing and Remote Access service. This allows connected remote access clients to access the Internet.

- **Demand-dial connections can now use PPPoE.** This feature provides the ability to use the Point-to-Point Protocol over Ethernet (PPPoE) for demand-dial connections (also known as dial-on-demand connections). Demand-dial connections are used by the Routing and Remote Access service to make point-to-point connections between LANs over which packets are routed. You can access this feature by selecting the Connect Using PPP Over Ethernet (PPPoE) option in the Connection Type dialog box of the Demand-Dial Interface Wizard. By allowing PPPoE as a connection type for demand-dial connections, a small business can use the NAT/Basic Firewall component of the Routing and Remote Access service and the business's broadband Internet connection to connect its office to the Internet.

- **Improvements in default behavior for Internal and Internet interfaces.** To prevent possible problems with resolving the name of the VPN server and accessing services running on the VPN server, the Routing and Remote Access service by default disables dynamic DNS registration for the Internal interface and disables both dynamic DNS and NetBT for the interface identified in the Routing And Remote Access Server Setup Wizard as the Internet interface.

- **VPN connection limit for Windows Server 2003, Web Edition.**
For the Web Edition, the number of allowed VPN connections is one
VPN connection (either PPTP-based or Layer 2 Tunneling Protocol
[L2TP]–based). This is the same limitation that exists for Windows XP
Professional and Windows XP Home Edition. To support more than
one VPN connection, you must use Windows Server 2003, Standard
Edition; Windows Server 2003, Enterprise Edition; or Windows
Server 2003, Datacenter Edition.

- **NAT and firewall integration.**   The NAT/Basic Firewall component of the Routing and Remote Access service has been enhanced
to support a basic firewall using the same technology as that used by
the Internet Connection Firewall feature provided with Windows XP.
This feature allows you to protect the public interface of a computer
running a member of the Windows Server 2003 family that is using a
NAT to enable access to the Internet. By using a NAT, the computers
on the private network are protected because the NAT computer
does not forward traffic from the Internet unless a private network
client requested it. However, the NAT computer itself can be vulner-
able to attack. By enabling the basic firewall on the public interface
of the NAT computer, all packets that are received on the Internet
interface that do not correspond to traffic requested by the NAT computer (either for itself or for private intranet clients) are discarded.
You can enable this new functionality from the NAT/Basic Firewall
tab on the properties of a private interface configured to use the
NAT/Basic Firewall IP routing protocol component of the Routing
and Remote Access service.

- **L2TP/IPSec NAT traversal.**   With Windows 2000, Internet Key
Exchange (IKE) and Encapsulating Security Payload (ESP) traffic is
not able to traverse a NAT, because if the NAT translates the IP
addresses or ports of the packet, it invalidates the security of the
packets. This means that you cannot create an L2TP/IPSec connection from behind a NAT and must use the Point-to-Point Tunneling
Protocol (PPTP) for VPN connections. The Windows Server 2003
family now supports User Datagram Protocol (UDP) encapsulation
of Internet Protocol security (IPSec) packets to allow IKE and ESP
traffic to pass through a NAT. This allows L2TP/IPSec connections
to be created from Windows XP–based or Windows 2000 Professional–based computers and server computers running a member
of the Windows Server 2003 family that are located behind one or
multiple NATs.

- **NLB support for L2TP/IPSec traffic.**   In Windows 2000, the Network Load Balancing (NLB) service did not have the capability to manage IPSec security associations (SAs) among multiple servers. If a server in the cluster became unavailable, the SAs managed by that cluster were orphaned and eventually timed out. This meant that you could not cluster L2TP/IPSec VPN servers. You could use DNS round robin for load distribution across multiple L2TP/IPSec VPN servers, but this approach offered no fault tolerance. In the Windows Server 2003 family, the NLB service has been enhanced to provide clustering support for IPSec SAs. This means that you can create a cluster of L2TP/IPSec VPN servers, and the NLB service will provide both load balancing and fault tolerance for L2TP/IPSec traffic. This feature is provided only with the 32-bit and 64-bit versions of Enterprise Edition and Datacenter Edition.

- **Preshared key configuration for L2TP/IPSec connections.** The Windows Server 2003 family supports both computer certificates and a preshared key as authentication methods to establish an IP Security (IPSec) security association for L2TP connections. A preshared key is a string of text that is configured on both the VPN client and the VPN server. Preshared key is a relatively weak authentication method; therefore, use of preshared key authentication is recommended only in the interim when your PKI is being deployed to obtain computer certificates or when VPN clients require the use of preshared key authentication. You can enable the use of a preshared key for L2TP connections and specify the preshared key from the Security tab on the properties of a server in the Routing And Remote Access snap-in.

  Windows XP and the Windows Server 2003 family remote access VPN clients also support preshared key authentication. You can enable preshared key authentication and configure a preshared key from IPSec settings on the Security tab on the properties of a VPN connection in Network Connections. Preshared key authentication is also supported for Windows Server 2003 family router-to-router VPN connections. You can enable preshared key authentication and configure a preshared key for demand-dial interfaces from IPSec settings on the Security tab from the properties of a demand-dial interface in the Routing And Remote Access snap-in.

Connection Manager Enhancements

The following enhancements to Connection Manager and the Connection Manager Administrator Kit have been made in the Windows Server 2003 family:

- **Connection Manager Favorites.**   The Connection Manager Favorites feature lets users eliminate repetitive configuration of Connection Manager properties when switching between common dialing locations. This feature provides a method for storing and easily accessing settings and is used in the following scenario:

  A user travels frequently between a company's office and a business partner's site. The user configures Connection Manager settings for each location, including the nearest access telephone number, area code, and dialing rules, and gives each a unique name. The user then chooses from among saved settings to quickly set up network connections from each location.

- **Automatic Proxy Configuration.**   The Automatic Proxy Configuration feature provides the ability to create a Connection Manager profile to ensure that the user's computer has appropriate access to both internal and external resources during a connection to a corporate network. This feature requires the use of Internet Explorer 4.0 or later. For example, a business user's home computer is configured to browse the Internet without any proxy settings. This configuration can cause a problem when the user connects to a corporate network. An IT administrator can create a Connection Manager profile that provides the appropriate proxy settings for use whenever the user is connected to the corporate network.

- **Client log files.**   This feature provides the ability to turn on log files to quickly and accurately troubleshoot problems with Connection Manager connections. For example, a user experiences problems connecting to a network using a Connection Manager profile issued by an IT administrator. A log file is generated on the user's computer, which the user can send to the IT administrator to streamline the troubleshooting process.

- **Support for VPN server selection.**   With the enhanced Connection Manager Administration Kit provided with the Windows Server 2003 family, a Connection Manager profile can be created that allows users to select a Virtual Private Network (VPN) server to use when connecting to the corporation's network. This enables VPN connectivity in the following scenarios:

❑   A company has offices worldwide with VPN servers in many of these locations. An IT administrator can create a Connection Manager profile that allows a traveling user to select the VPN server that best meets their connection needs at the time of the connection attempt.

❑   A corporate VPN server is taken off line for maintenance. During this time frame, users can select a different VPN server with which to connect.

■   **Connection Manager Administration Kit Wizard improvements.** The Connection Manager Administration Kit (CMAK) has expanded the wizard functionality, including improved dialog boxes and the ability to perform most advanced customization tasks before building user profiles. The improvements streamline the process of building custom client connection packages and reduce the need to edit .cms or .cmp files for most advanced customization needs. A greater variety of custom actions are available and configurable from within the CMAK Wizard, including custom actions designed specifically for VPN connections. For example, an IT administrator can configure a single profile to accommodate security settings for a variety of client operating systems or configure a profile to take advantage of remote access server features such as callback and the use of Terminal Services.

■   **Preshared key configuration.**   This feature allows an IT administrator to create a connection manager profile using CMAK that contains the preshared key of the VPN server for use in authenticating L2TP/IPSec connections.

■   **Route management for simultaneous intranet and Internet access for VPN connections.**   Before Windows XP and the Windows Server 2003 family, a Microsoft VPN client automatically created a default route that sent all default route traffic through the VPN tunnel. Although this allows a VPN client to access its organization's intranet, the client can access Internet resources only while the VPN connection is active if Internet access is available through the VPN connection to the organization's intranet. The new Connection Manager support in Windows XP and the Windows Server 2003 family allows for the following:

When the VPN connection is made, the default route isn't changed; instead, specific routes for organization intranet locations are added to the routing table of the VPN client. This allows simultaneous access to intranet (using the specific routes) and Internet (using the default route) resources without having to pass Internet traffic through the organization's intranet. The Connection Manager Administration Kit allows you to configure specific routes as part of the connection manager profile distributed to VPN users. You can also specify a URL that contains the current set of organization intranet routes or additional routes beyond those configured in the profile.

Internet Connectivity Improvements

The following sections describe enhancements to Internet connectivity that have been made in the Windows Server 2003 family:

■   Internet Connection Firewall

■   Network Connection Enhancements

Internet Connection Firewall

When a computer is connected to the Internet or to another pathway to the outside world, it faces threats of unauthorized attempts to access it and its data. Whether the computer connecting to the external network is a stand-alone computer or is acting as a gateway for a network behind the computer (for example, when the Internet Connection Sharing feature is used), a firewall can guard your home network against the threat of unsafe network traffic while allowing appropriate network traffic to pass.

The Windows Server 2003 family includes the Internet Connection Firewall (ICF) for protecting your computers and home networks that are connected in such a manner. ICF is enabled automatically for dial-up and broadband connections when the New Connection Wizard is run, setting up your firewall with default settings that will work for most networks. The firewall can also be enabled or disabled manually for a connection through the Network Connections folder.

ICF monitors communications that were initiated from inside the firewall to determine what traffic should be allowed from the external network. Traffic initiating from the external network is not allowed through the firewall by default. When you host services or programs (such as a Web server) behind the firewall, ICF settings can be changed to suit your needs. ICF can be used to protect a remote access connection when dialing directly into an Internet service provider (ISP) or protect a LAN connection that's connected via a digital subscriber line (DSL) or cable modem.

This feature is provided only with the 32-bit versions of Standard Edition, Enterprise Edition, and Web Edition.

Network Connection Enhancements

The following enhancements to network connections have been made in the Windows Server 2003 family:

- **Updated Group Policy for network and dial-up connections.** This feature provides the ability to apply Group Policy to specify the components of networking functionality for specific users with computers running the Windows XP Professional or a member of the Windows Server 2003 family. This feature allows the following scenarios:

    ❑ An IT administrator can make a user a member of the Network Configuration Operators Group, whose members have access to the TCP/IP properties for LAN connections and can configure their own IP addresses.

    ❑ If a user account is a member of the local Administrators group on a computer, the user can enable and configure ICS, ICF, Network Bridge, and properties of network connections. Enabling or reconfiguring these features might impair network connectivity. With this feature, an IT administrator can enable policies that block even a local administrator from configuring these features.

- **Point-to-Point Protocol over Ethernet client for broadband Internet connections.** The Windows Server 2003 family includes the ability to create connections using Point-to-Point Protocol over Ethernet (PPPoE). Using PPPoE and a broadband Internet connection such as DSL or cable modem, users can gain individual authenticated access to high-speed data networks. In previous versions of Windows, users had to install separate software that was supplied by the ISP. Now this support is built into the operating system. PPPoE-client support allows the following scenarios:

    ❑ A home user has a broadband connection that requires a PPPoE login to connect to the Internet. Using the built-in PPPoE client and the New Connection Wizard, a user can now create a fully integrated Internet connection.

❑   An IT administrator can use this feature to make access to the internal network more secure by using PPPoE to authenticate any network access from public areas in their offices, such as conference rooms and lobbies.

Having this ability built into the Windows Server 2003 family allows you to leverage other features such as ICS (to share your broadband connection with other computers) and ICF (to protect the PPPoE connection from Internet attacks). The PPPoE connection can also be selected from Internet Explorer and other Windows-based components and applications.

More Network Access Options

The following sections describe enhancements to network access that have been made in the Windows Server 2003 family:

■   Network Bridge

■   Remote Access Using Credential Manager Key Ring

■   All-User Remote Access Credential

■   Support for Internet Protocol over IEEE 1394 (IP/1394)

Network Bridge

When building a network in a home or small office, you might find that a particular network medium works well in one area of the network but not in another. For example, several computers might be located near telephone jacks, enabling them to be connected using phone line networking devices. Other computers might not be near a phone jack, requiring you to use, for example, a wireless network connection. The Windows Server 2003 family supports many medium types, including Ethernet, phone line, IEEE 802.11b wireless, and IEEE 1394. The set of computers that can communicate using a specific networking technology defines a LAN segment.

Traditionally, connecting these separate LAN segments by using TCP/IP would require configuring multiple subnet addresses and routers to connect the different mediums. The Network Bridge enables a computer running a member of the Windows Server 2003 family to bridge multiple network segments to create a single subnet. Bridging multiple LAN segments on the bridge computer is as easy as selecting multiple connections in the Network Connections folder, right-clicking one of the connections, and then clicking Bridge Connections.

The result of using the Network Bridge is a network configuration consisting of a single, easily configured subnet connecting all network mediums. The bridge computer detects and maintains information about which computers are on which LAN segment and forwards packets between the appropriate LAN segments.

Remote Access Using Credential Manager Key Ring

The Windows Server 2003 family includes a Credential Manager Key Ring feature that maintains a key ring containing multiple sets of different credentials that have been used on the system. This allows you to access multiple networks (with different credentials consisting of a user name and a password) at the same time, without having to continually reenter credentials in response to prompts. Information about the network resource to which you are connecting (such as the server name and the domain name) is used to select the appropriate credential on the key ring. Remote access participates in the key ring by adding a temporary default credential whenever a dial-up or VPN connection is successfully established. This credential contains the username and the password that were used in setting up the connection since these are often the same credentials that will enable access to the resources on that network. This makes the experience of connecting to a remote network and using resources on both that network and your local network seamless.

All-User Remote Access Credential

The all-user remote access credential feature provides the ability to create a connection with a set of credentials, including the username and the password that are available for all users of that computer. For example, if a user has a network connection from his or her home to a local ISP, the user can specify from the New Connection Wizard that this connection is an all-user connection and save the credentials for all users. Other family members can use this connection without having to remember the username or the password to connect to the ISP.

Support for Internet Protocol over IEEE 1394 (IP/1394)

The Windows Server 2003 family supports the sending and receiving of TCP/IP packets over the IEEE 1394 medium, a serial communications bus medium that supports speeds from 100 to 400 Mbps. IEEE 1394 is commonly used to connect audio and video equipment. Support for IEEE 1394 also includes special handling of IEEE 1394 frames for the Network Bridge. For more information, see RFC 2734. No configuration is needed for IEEE 1394 links. They are automatically detected and configured.

Changes to Protocols

There are numerous protocol changes in Windows Server 2003, and the following sections describe them:

- TCP/IP Changes and Enhancements
- IPv6 Protocol Stack
- Kernel-Mode Processing of Web Traffic
- Quality of Service Enhancements

TCP/IP Changes and Enhancements

The following changes and enhancements have been made to the TCP/IP protocol for the Windows Server 2003 family:

- **TCP/IP Protocol cannot be removed.**   The TCP/IP protocol—called Internet Protocol (TCP/IP) in the properties of a connection in the Network Connections folder—is installed by default and cannot be removed. One step in troubleshooting a possible TCP/IP configuration problem has been to remove the TCP/IP protocol and reinstall it. This is no longer possible in the Windows Server 2003 family. Instead, you can use a new Netsh command to reset the TCP/IP configuration to installation defaults. For more information, see the upcoming item "Netsh command to reset TCP/IP defaults."

- **Automatic alternate configuration for multiple networks connectivity.**   Alternate configuration allows you to manually configure static TCP/IP settings that are configured when the computer is a Dynamic Host Configuration Protocol (DHCP) client and no DHCP server is found when the computer starts. For computers running Windows 2000, Windows 98, and Windows Me, if the computer configured as a DHCP client does not find a DHCP server, Automatic Private IP Addressing (APIPA) assigns a unique address from the 169.254.0.0.16 address space. Although APIPA allows TCP/IP to start, it does not assign a default gateway address, a Domain Name System (DNS) server IP address, or other settings essential for communication on an intranet or the Internet. Alternate configuration is useful in situations in which the computer is used on more than one network, one of those networks does not have a DHCP server, and an APIPA addressing configuration is not desired.

For example, a user has a laptop computer that is used at the office and at home. While at the office, the computer uses a DHCP-allocated TCP/IP configuration. While at home, where no DHCP server is present, the laptop computer automatically uses the alternate configuration, which provides easy access to home network computers and the Internet. With alternate configuration, you do not have to manually reconfigure TCP/IP settings when the laptop computer is connected to either the office or the home network.

You can configure the TCP/IP alternate configuration on the Alternate Configuration tab from the properties of the Internet Protocol (TCP/IP) protocol in the properties of a LAN connection in the Network Connections folder.

■ **Netsh command to reset TCP/IP defaults.** A new Netsh command has been added to the Windows Server 2003 family to allow you to reset your TCP/IP configuration to its default values. The new Netsh command is **netsh interface ip reset** and is issued at the command prompt.

In earlier versions of Windows, you could remove the Internet Protocol (TCP/IP) protocol and reinstall it with the same effect. With the Windows Server 2003 family, TCP/IP is installed by default and cannot be removed. This feature can be useful for IT administrators who find that the computer user has changed the TCP/IP configuration for a computer to unsupported values.

■ **New Netstat option to display TCP port ownership.** A new option is added to the Netstat tool that allows you to display active TCP connections and that includes the Process Identifier (PID) for each connection. You can find the application based on the PID on the Processes tab in Windows Task Manager. By default, the PID is not displayed in the Windows Task Manager. To configure the Windows Task Manager to display the PID, click View, click Select Columns, click PID (Process Identifier) in the list of columns to display, and then click OK.

■ **IGMP version 3.** IGMPv3 provides source-based multicast group membership reporting. Hosts can request to receive multicast traffic from specified sources or from all but a specific set of sources.

Source-specific reporting prevents multicast-enabled routers from delivering multicast traffic to a subnet where there are no listening hosts for the source of the multicast traffic. IGMPv3 support is enabled by default and requires no configuration.

■ **Autodetermination of routing metrics based on interface speed.**   This feature allows the TCP/IP protocol to automatically determine the routing metric for routes derived from the TCP/IP configuration based on the speed of its associated interface. For example, routes derived from the TCP/IP configuration of 10-Mbps Ethernet network adapters have a routing metric of 30, and routes derived from the TCP/IP configuration of 100-Mbps Ethernet network adapters have a routing metric of 20.

This feature is useful if you have multiple interfaces of different speeds that are configured to use the same default gateway; the fastest interface has the lowest routing metric for its default route and is used to forward traffic to its default gateway. If there are multiple interfaces of the fastest speed, the interface that is listed first in the binding order is used to forward traffic to its default gateway. Automatic determination of the interface metric is enabled by default through the Automatic metric check box on the IP Settings tab and when you manually configure default gateways in Advanced TCP/IP Settings from the properties of the Internet Protocol (TCP/IP) protocol from a connection in the Network Connections folder.

■ **TCP receive window size determined by the local network adapter.**   The window size determines the maximum number of bytes that can be sent without requiring an acknowledgment. On a slower-speed dial-up network connection, the window size is almost equal to the size of the queue on the remote access server. When the queue is filled with TCP segments from one TCP connection, a new TCP connection cannot be established until all these packets are sent. Additionally, the TCP slow-start algorithm on the new connection makes the situation worse. With this feature, the Quality of Service (QoS) Packet Scheduler on a computer with ICS will adjust the advertised window size to match the dial-up network connection speed. This will reduce the queue depth at the remote access server and enable new connections to work better.

In a home network, all the home computers are typically on a high-speed LAN and access the Internet through an ICS computer. The ICS computer is connected to the Internet using a dial-up modem. When one home computer is doing a large file transfer, other home computers might get slow performance when accessing the Internet (for example, when using a Web browser). With this feature, new Internet TCP connections from the other home computers are much more responsive. This feature is enabled by default only when ICS is used and requires no configuration.

IPv6 Protocol Stack

The Windows Server 2003 family includes an IPv6 protocol stack that is designed for production use. The IPv6 protocol for the Windows Server 2003 family includes the following features:

■ **Windows Sockets support.** The Windows Server 2003 family includes support for the new Windows Sockets functions *getaddrinfo* and *getnameinfo* to perform name-to-address and address-to-name resolution for Windows Sockets applications, as described in RFC 2553. Using these functions, rather than *getaddrbyname* and *gethostbyname*, you can make your Windows Sockets applications independent of the version of IP (IPv4 or IPv6) that is running on the computer.

■ **6to4 tunneling.** 6to4 tunneling is a tunneling technique that's described in RFC 3056. A component of the IPv6 protocol for the Windows Server 2003 family, 6to4 allows automatic tunneling and IPv6 connectivity between IPv6/IPv4 hosts across the IPv4 intranet. 6to4 hosts use IPv6 addresses derived from IPv4 public addresses. With 6to4, IPv6 sites and hosts can use 6to4-based addresses and the IPv4 Internet to communicate without having to obtain an IPv6 global address prefix from an ISP and connecting to the IPv6 Internet.

■ **Intrasite Automatic Tunnel Addressing Protocol.** Intrasite Automatic Tunnel Addressing Protocol (ISATAP) is an address assignment and automatic tunneling mechanism that allows IPv6/IPv4 nodes within an IPv4 infrastructure of a site to use IPv6 to communicate with one another and with nodes on an IPv6-enabled network, either within the site or on the IPv6 Internet.

■ **PortProxy.** The PortProxy component facilitates the communication among nodes or applications that cannot connect using a common Internet layer protocol (IPv4 or IPv6). PortProxy allows the proxying of TCP traffic for the following: IPv4 to IPv4, IPv4 to IPv6, Server 2003IPv6 to IPv6, and IPv6 to IPv4. For IPv6/IPv4 coexistence and migration, PortProxy enables the following scenarios:

❑   An IPv4-only node can access an IPv6-only node.

❑   An IPv6-only node can access an IPv4-only node.

❑   An IPv6 node can access an IPv4-only service running on an IPv6/IPv4 node.

This last scenario allows computers running the IPv6 protocol for the Windows Server 2003 family to use IPv6 to access Web pages on a computer running a member of the Windows 2000 Server family and Internet Information Services (IIS). Windows 2000 IIS does not support IPv6. Therefore, the only way to access it is by using IPv4. When PortProxy is configured on a computer running a member of the Windows Server 2003 family, incoming IPv6-based Web requests are proxied to the Windows 2000 IIS server, allowing the IIS server to communicate indirectly with IPv6-enabled Web browsers.

To configure the PortProxy service, use the **netsh interface portproxy add|set|delete v4tov4|v4tov6|v6tov4|v6tov6** commands.

■   **Site Prefixes in Router Advertisements.**   Published on-link prefixes can be configured with a site prefix length. You can use the **netsh interface ipv6 add|set route** commands to include a site prefix length with the address prefix.

When a prefix information option that specifies a site prefix is received, an entry is created in the site prefix table. You can view this table by using the **netsh interface ipv6 siteprefixes** command. The site prefix table is used to remove inappropriate site-local addresses from those that are returned by the *getaddrinfo* Windows Sockets function.

■   **DNS support.**   Processing for Domain Name System (DNS) IPv6 host records (known as AAAA, or quad-A, resource records), as defined in RFC 1886, "DNS Extensions to support IP version 6," and for dynamic registration of AAAA records is supported by the DNS resolver (client) in the Windows Server 2003 family and the DNS Server service in Windows Server 2003 family and Windows 2000. DNS traffic is supported over both IPv6 and IPv4.

■   **IPSec support.**   Processing for the Authentication Header (AH) using the Message Digest 5 (MD5) hash and for the Encapsulating

Security Payload (ESP) using the NULL ESP header and the MD5 hash is supported. There is no support for ESP data encryption or the IKE protocol. IPSec security policies, security associations, and encryption keys must be manually configured using the Ipsec6.exe tool.

- **Operating system component and application support.** System components and applications provided with the Windows Server 2003 family that support the use of IPv6 include Internet Explorer, the Telnet client (Telnet.exe), the FTP client (Ftp.exe), IIS 6.0, file and print sharing (the Server and Workstation services), Windows Media Services, and Network Monitor.

- **RPC support.** RPC functions are used to forward application function calls to a remote system across the network. The RPC components in the Windows Server 2003 family are IPv6-enabled. The RPC components have been modified to use the updated Windows Sockets, which allows RPC to work over both IPv4 and IPv6.

- **IP Helper API support.** Internet Protocol Helper (IP Helper) is an API that assists in the administration of the network configuration of the local computer. You can use IP Helper to programmatically retrieve information about the network configuration of the local computer and to modify that configuration. IP Helper also provides notification mechanisms to ensure that an application is notified when certain aspects of the network configuration change on the local computer. IP Helper in the Windows Server 2003 family has been extended to allow the retrieval of information for IPv6 and its components.

- **Static router support.** A computer running the Windows Server 2003 family can act as a static IPv6 router that forwards IPv6 packets between interfaces based on the contents of the IPv6 routing table. You can configure static routes with the **netsh interface ipv6 add route** command. No IPv6 routing protocols are provided for the Routing and Remote Access service.

    A computer running the Windows Server 2003 family can send router advertisements. The contents of router advertisements are automatically derived from the published routes in the routing table. Nonpublished routes are used for routing but are not sent in router advertisements. Router advertisements always contain a source link-layer address option and a Maximum Transmission Unit (MTU) option. The value for the MTU option is taken from the sending interface's current link MTU. You can change this value with the **netsh interface ipv6 set interface** command. A computer running a member of the Windows Server 2003 family will advertise itself as a default router (by using a router advertisement with a router lifetime other than 0) only if a default route is configured to be published.

Kernel-Mode Processing of Web Traffic

HTTP.sys is a kernel-mode implementation of both the client and server sides of the Hypertext Transfer Protocol (HTTP). It aims to provide a scalable, efficient implementation of HTTP that allows the use of true Win32 asynchronous I/O, including the ability to bind request and response completion to completion ports. The user-mode API for the client side will be exposed via existing APIs such as WinHTTP and the .NET Framework Classes. The server side of HTTP.sys is provided in the Windows Server 2003 family and is used by IIS 6.0. The complete version of HTTP.sys that includes both client and server will be provided in a future version of Windows.

Quality of Service Enhancements

When a home network is connected to a corporate or other network through a slow link, such as a dial-up line, a situation can exist that will increase the delay of traffic traversing the slow link.

If the receiving client is running on a relatively fast network (100-Mbps Ethernet, for example) behind an ICS box and the server with which this receiver is communicating behind the remote access box is using a fast network, a mismatch exists. In this scenario, the receiver's receive window is set to a large value based on the speed of the connection. The sender begins sending at a slow rate, but because packets aren't lost, the sender eventually increases to sending nearly a full window size of packets.

This can affect the performance of other TCP connections that traverse the same network, making their packets wait in this potentially large queue. If packet loss occurs, a full window size has to be retransmitted, further congesting the link. The solution to this is to have the ICS computer on the edge of the network set the receive window to a smaller size appropriate to the slow link, overriding the receiver's specification. This setting will not adversely affect traffic as the window size is being set as it would if the receiver were connected directly to the slow link. The QoS packet scheduler component running on the ICS computer makes this window adjustment.

Additional information about QoS can be found on the Windows 2000 Networking and Communications Services Web site at: *http://www.microsoft.com/windows2000/technologies/communications/*.

Improved Network Device Support

Windows Server 2003 improves support for networking devices. You learn about this improved support in the following sections:

- Permanent Virtual Circuit Encapsulation

- NDIS 5.1 and Remote NDIS

- Improved Network Media Support

- CardBus Wake on LAN

- Device Driver Enhancements

- Wake on LAN: Select Wake Event Improvements

- IrCOMM Modem Driver for IrDA

Permanent Virtual Circuit Encapsulation

The Windows Server 2003 family includes an implementation of RFC 2684. This was added to make DSL simpler for vendors to implement. The implementation is an NDIS intermediate driver that looks like an Ethernet interface but uses a DSL/Asynchronous Transfer Mode (ATM) permanent virtual circuit (PVC) to carry Ethernet (or TCP/IP only) frames. This mechanism is commonly used in the industry by carriers and others deploying DSL. With the Windows Server 2003 family and an ATM miniport driver for a DSL device, a DSL deployment can use the following protocol configurations:

- TCP/IP over PPP over ATM (PPPoA) using a vendor DSL ATM miniport driver

- TCP/IP over RFC 2684 (four encapsulation types) using a vendor DSL ATM miniport driver

- TCP/IP over PPPoE over RFC 2684 (four encapsulation types) using a vendor DSL ATM miniport

In addition, 802.1X authentication can be added to the RFC 2684 Ethernet interface. This variety of options meets the needs of a majority of DSL deployments. For more information, see RFC 2684.

NDIS 5.1 and Remote NDIS

The network cards and their drivers used to make the physical network available to the operating system and protocols have been enhanced in the Windows Server 2003 family. Enhancements include the following:

- **Plug and Play and power event notification.**   Enables network card miniport drivers to be notified of power or Plug and Play events. This results in cleaner system operation during these events.

- **Support for send cancellation.**   Allows network protocols to avoid having to wait lengthy amounts of time for network packet send requests to complete.

- **Increased statistics capacity (64-bit statistic counters).**   This enhancement enables accurate network statistic displays, even on today's high-speed network media.

- **Performance enhancements.**   Several enhancements were made to speed up critical network data paths and avoid unnecessary packet copies.

- **Wake on LAN change.**   A change was made to Wake on LAN to allow you to limit wake-up packets to just magic packets (instead of protocol-registered packet patterns). This is now configurable on the Power Management tab from the properties of a network adapter.

- **Miscellaneous changes.**   Several additional changes have been made to support common needs or requests from driver developers or to improve driver integrity.

Remote NDIS is also included as part of the Windows Server 2003 family. Remote NDIS enables the support of USB-attached network devices without the installation of third-party drivers. Microsoft supplies the drivers required to communicate with the network devices. This results in easier installation and a lessened chance of system failure because of a poorly built or tested driver.

For more information about NDIS 5.1 and Remote NDIS, refer to the Windows Server 2003 family DDK and the following Web pages:

- *http://www.microsoft.com/hwdev/tech/network/NDIS51.htm*

- *http://www.microsoft.com/hwdev/tech/network/rmNDIS.htm*

Improved Network Media Support

Support for some of the newest network devices has been added to the Windows Server 2003 family and is available out of the box. This includes support for many new home-networking devices. Most of the new HomePNA (telephone line) devices are supported. Most USB-connected network devices are supported in the Windows Server 2003 family; some use Remote NDIS, eliminating the need for additional drivers. Support for 802.11 wireless devices has improved. Many of these devices also support wireless zero configuration and roaming features in the Windows Server 2003 family. The modem support in Windows has been extended in the Windows Server 2003 family to include many soft modems.

CardBus Wake on LAN

This feature allows a computer to be resumed from standby by a CardBus LAN card. An IT administrator can use this feature to aid in managing a group of servers.

Device Driver Enhancements

This feature adds network device drivers that are commonly used in home networking and removes legacy device drivers that are no longer relevant. It also improves the quality of networking drivers. Driver categories include the following:

- **LAN network drivers**   These include 10/100 network interface cards (NICs), IEEE 802.11, and Home Phoneline Networking Alliance (HomePNA).

- **Broadband.**   Includes cable modems, Asymmetric Digital Subscriber Line (ADSL), and Integrated Services Digital Network (ISDN).

- **Modems.**   These include driver-based and 56-Kbps V.90 modems.

A home user who upgrades a computer to a member of the Windows Server 2003 family discovers that the network devices he or she currently uses are already supported by this new operating system.

Wake on LAN: Select Wake Event Improvements

Wake on LAN (WOL), introduced in Windows 2000, is a hardware capability of WOL-enabled network adapters whereby the NIC can trigger bus power management wake-up events upon the receipt of certain patterns in network packets. Improvements to this functionality include the following:

- WOL fully enabled, with all packet patterns causing wake-up events
- WOL enabled, with only magic packets causing wake-up events
- WOL fully disabled

  These new features enable the following scenarios:

- A user wants to have her computer go into a low-power standby mode to save power. However, she also wants the computer to come out of standby (wake up) if another computer on the network wants to use services on that computer or perform management functions on the computer.
- An IT administrator wants to control WOL on computers and sets the feature to WOL fully enabled.

IrCOMM Modem Driver for IrDA

The IrCOMM modem driver allows a user to use an infrared-enabled cellular phone as a modem. When the cellular phone is placed next to the infrared port, it is enumerated and an appropriate driver is installed (or a generic driver if the model is not recognized). A mobile phone can then be used just like any other modem to create a network connection.

This driver enables the following scenario: A user has an infrared-enabled mobile telephone with the IrCOMM protocol and wants to use it as a modem to access the Internet. With this feature, a mobile computer will recognize the mobile telephone, enumerate it, and install it as a modem. The user can now dial in to the Internet in the same way as with a built-in modem.

This feature is provided only in Enterprise Edition and Web Edition.

New Network Services Support

The following sections describe improvements to network service support that have been made in the Windows Server 2003 family:

- TAPI 3.1 and TAPI Service Providers
- Real Time Communication Client APIs
- DHCP

- DNS

- WINS

- IAS

- IPSec

TAPI 3.1 and TAPI Service Providers

Previous Windows operating systems shipped with earlier versions of the Telephony API (TAPI), the most recent being Windows 2000 shipping with TAPI 3.0. TAPI enables applications to be created that provide various types of telephony services to users.

Windows XP and Windows Server 2003 include TAPI 3.1. TAPI 3.1 supports the Microsoft Component Object Model (COM) and provides a set of COM objects to the programmer. This enables the use of any COM-compatible programming application and scripting languages for writing telephony applications. Also included in Windows Server 2003 are TAPI service providers (TSPs) that provide functionality for H.323-based IP telephony and IP multicast audio and video conferencing on TCP/IP networks. This is in addition to the TSPs provided with earlier versions of Windows. The H.323 TSP and the media service provider (MSP) provide support for H.323 version 2 functionality. Also provided with TAPI 3.1 are the following:

- **File terminals**   Allow applications to record streaming data (such as speech or video) to a file and play this recorded data back to a stream

- **Pluggable terminals**   Allow a third party to add new terminal objects that can be used by any MSP

- **USB phone TSP**   Allows an application to control a USB phone and use it as a streaming endpoint

- **Autodiscovery of TAPI servers**   Allows clients to discover telephony servers available on the network

Additionally, for H.323, the following supplementary services (richer call-control features) have been implemented:

- Call Hold Service (ITU-T Recommendation H.450-2)

- Call Transfer Service (ITU-T Recommendation H.450-2)

- Call Diversion Services (ITU-T Recommendation H.450-3)

- Call Park and Pickup Service (ITU-T Recommendation H.450-5)

Real Time Communication Client APIs

The Real Time Communication (RTC) Client Application Programming Interfaces feature provides the next-generation communications platform based on the Session Initiation Protocol (SIP). SIP provides the protocol to set up a generic session using an e-mail address without having the need to know the location of the caller; therefore, it provides a more efficient means of communication. RTC enables rapid deployment of Internet applications that are enhanced with converged applications, such as voice, video, and data collaboration applications.

The Windows Server 2003 family now includes the RTC client APIs, which include functionality such as buddy-list management, user activity detection, the ability to create instant messaging sessions as well as audio and video sessions between two clients, telephony calls to any telephone number, application sharing, and whiteboard sessions. The client APIs include firewall tunneling to a SIP server over Secure Sockets Layer (SSL), digest and basic authentication, and NAT logic to enable real-time communications sessions across Universal Plug and Play (UPNP)–enabled NATs. The APIs provide access to a high-performance audio and video media stack. Audio and video quality has been greatly improved by other new features, including the following:

- **AcousticEcho cancellation.**   Headsets are not required to make audio calls, and built-in echo cancellation provides high-quality communications.

- **Quality control.**   This new algorithm dynamically alters the settings for audio and video based on detected changes in network conditions.

- **Forward Error Correction.**   Forward Error Correction (FEC) is used to compensate for packet loss introduced by network congestion.

- **Dynamic jitter buffers.**   Dynamic jitter buffers are used to smooth the received audio to eliminate the impact of variation in delay between received packets.

RTC client APIs enable the following scenarios:

- An ISV that develops games leverages the RTC client APIs to add buddy lists, instant messaging, and audio/video to its new game. Players can instantly message, talk, or see one another during a game session.

■ An IT administrator writes a small application to alert all users of an e-mail server going off line for maintenance.

■ An ISV that sells budget management and payroll applications creates an ActiveX control using the RTC client APIs. It embeds the control in its server Web pages so that department administrators can see the availability of their payroll contact, address budget questions through instant messaging or audio, and jointly analyze budget statements using application sharing.

This feature is not provided with the 32-bit version of Web Edition.

DHCP

The following improvements to Dynamic Host Configuration Protocol (DHCP) have been made in the Windows Server 2003 family:

■ **Backup and restoration with DHCP.**   The DHCP snap-in now provides new menu items for backup and restoration of DHCP databases. When the user chooses either of these menu items, a browser window is displayed, offering the selection of a location; new folders can be created as well. An IT administrator can use this feature to do backups and restores on servers running the Windows Server 2003 family. This feature is not provided with Web Edition.

■ **Classless static route option.**   DHCP clients can request this option to be supplied with a list of routes to add to their routing table. This arrangement allows remote access and VPN clients to perform split tunneling when connecting to remote networks. It also allows LAN clients to obtain additional routing information. For example, an IT administrator can use this feature to allow clients to split-tunnel through a virtual private network (VPN) connection and the Internet. This allows traffic destined for the Internet to avoid going through the VPN connection, while also allowing the user to access his or her organization's private network resources.

■ **DHCP database migrations with Netsh.**   This feature enables an easier migration of a DHCP database from one server to another if it is imported using Netsh. Doing so eliminates most manual configurations, such as manually editing the registry or re-creating scopes. The Netsh command is used to locally configure servers and routers and can also use script files to automate configuration tasks. This feature can be used in the following cases:

❑ An IT administrator notices disk error messages on the DHCP server and decides to move the DHCP service before the disk fails completely.

❑ Because of performance issues on the network segment on which the DHCP server resides, an IT administrator needs to divide its DHCP server. The IT administrator can use this feature to move portions of the DHCP database to another computer or computers.

■ **DHCP lease deletion with Netsh.**   Using the new **netsh dhcp server scope** *scopeaddress* **delete lease** command, you can delete a DHCP lease from the command line instead of using the DHCP snap-in. This feature enables easier management of DHCP server operations using command lines and scripts.

DNS

The following improvements to DNS have been made in the Windows Server 2003 family:

■ **Active Directory integrated DNS zones stored in application partitions.**   This feature enables storage and replication of the Domain Name System (DNS) zones stored in the Active Directory service in the application partition. Using application partitions to store the DNS data results in a reduced number of objects stored in the global catalog. In addition, when DNS zone data is stored in an application partition, it is replicated to only that subset of domain controllers in the domain that is specified in the application partition. By default, DNS-specific application partitions contain only those domain controllers that run the DNS server. In addition, storing DNS zone data in an application partition enables replication of the DNS zone to the DNS servers running on the domain controllers in different domains of an Active Directory forest. An IT administrator can use this feature to store a DNS zone in an application partition. This is recommended in case an Active Directory–integrated DNS zone is hosted by the DNS servers running on a member of the Windows Server 2003 family.

■ **Basic compliance with DNS Security Extensions.**   A DNS server running a member of the Windows Server 2003 family provides basic compliance with the Internet Engineering Task Force (IETF)–standard DNS Security Extensions protocol as defined in RFC 2535. The

DNS server can store the record types (KEY, SIG, and NXT) defined in the IETF standard and include these records when responding to the queries according to RFC 2535. The server does not provide full compliance and does not perform the cryptographic operations specified in RFC 2535 (KEY/SIG record generation, message signing, and signature verification). However, the server can store and use standard KEY and SIG records generated by third-party software. An IT administrator can use a DNS server running a member of the Windows Server 2003 family as a secondary server for the signed zone with the primary copy on the server that fully supports DNS Security Extensions (per RFC 2535).

- **Domain join procedure enhancements to detect incorrectly configured DNS.** This feature simplifies debugging and reporting of an incorrect DNS configuration and helps to properly configure the DNS infrastructure required to enable a computer to join a domain. When a computer attempting to join an Active Directory domain fails to locate a domain controller because DNS is incorrectly configured or the domain controllers are not available, the debugging of the DNS infrastructure is performed. This generates a report explaining the cause of the failure and how to fix the problem. If the DNS infrastructure is properly configured to allow the computer to join the domain, an IT administrator will not notice the presence of this feature. Otherwise, if the DNS infrastructure is incorrectly configured and prevents a computer from locating a domain controller and joining a domain, it will be brought to the IT administrator's attention when the IT administrator attempts to join the computer to a domain.

- **Manage DNS clients using Group Policy.** This feature allows administrators to configure the DNS client settings on computers running a member of the Windows Server 2003 family using Group Policy. This simplifies the steps required to configure domain members when adjusting DNS client settings such as enabling and disabling dynamic registration of the DNS records by the clients, using devolution of the primary DNS suffix during name resolution, and populating DNS suffix search lists. In addition to providing simplified administration, Group Policy support for the DNS suffix search list is an important feature, which is required in a transition to an environment without NetBIOS. An IT administrator can use this Group Policy feature to configure DNS clients.

- **Stub zones and conditional forwarding.** Stub zones and conditional forwarding are two DNS server features that provide the ability to control the routing of DNS traffic on a network. A stub zone allows a DNS server to be aware of the names and addresses of servers that are authoritative for the full copy of a zone, without that server having to hold a complete copy of the zone or having to send queries to the DNS root servers. A DNS server running Windows 2000 can be configured to forward DNS queries to only one set of DNS servers. The conditional forwarding feature in the Windows Server 2003 family provides improved granularity, supporting name-dependent forwarding. For example, a DNS server can be configured to simultaneously

  ❑ Forward queries for names ending in usa.microsoft.com to a first set of DNS servers.

  ❑ Forward queries for names ending in europe.microsoft.com to a second set of DNS servers.

  ❑ Forward all other queries to a third set of DNS servers.

  An IT administrator can use this feature to control the routing of DNS traffic on their network.

- **Support for EDNS0 protocol.** The EDNS0 protocol defined in RFC 2671 allows DNS servers to accept and transmit UDP DNS messages with a payload size greater than 512 octets. This feature is useful for an IT administrator when DNS responses, such as service location (SRV) resource record queries used to locate Active Directory domain controllers, are larger than 512 octets. Prior to the Windows Server 2003 family, these responses required extra round trips to set up and tear down a TCP session. In the Windows Server 2003 family, by using the EDNS0 protocol, many of these responses can be returned in a single UDP round trip without requiring TCP session setup and teardown.

- **Additional enhancements.** The DNS Server service in the Windows Server 2003 family also supports the following additional enhancements:

  ❑ **Round-robin support for all resource record (RR) types.** By default, the DNS Server service will perform round-robin rotation for all RR types.

❑ **Enhanced debug logging.** The enhanced DNS Server service debug logging settings can help troubleshoot DNS problems.

❑ **Automatic Name Server resource record.** DNS Server can now control automatic Name Server (NS) resource record registration on a server and zone basis.

WINS

The following improvements to the Windows Internet Name Service (WINS) have been made in the Windows Server 2003 family:

■ **Filtering records.** Improved filtering and new search functions help you locate records by showing only those records that fit the criteria you specify. These functions are particularly useful in analyzing very large WINS databases. You can use multiple criteria to perform advanced searches for WINS database records. This improved filtering capability allows you to combine filters for customized and precise query results. Available filters include record owner, record type, NetBIOS name, and IP address with or without subnet mask. Because you can now store query results in the cache of the memory on your local computer, the performance of subsequent queries is increased, and network traffic is reduced.

■ **Accepting replication partners.** When determining a replication strategy for your organization, you can define a list that controls the source of incoming name records during pull replication between WINS servers. In addition to blocking name records from specific replication partners, you can also choose to accept only name records owned by specific WINS servers during replication, excluding the name records of all servers that are not on the list.

IAS

The following improvements to IAS have been made in the Windows Server 2003 family. IAS is not available with Web Edition:

■ **Support for IEEE 802.1x authentication for secure wireless and local area networks.** IAS has been enhanced to allow authentication and authorization of users and computers connecting to IEEE 802.11b wireless access points and Ethernet switches using IEEE 802.1X authentication. The remote access policy NAS-Port-Type condition now includes the ability to select wireless and Ethernet connection types.

For secure wireless or Ethernet connections, you should use either certificates (EAP-TLS) or passwords protected with Protected EAP (PEAP) and MS-CHAP v2 authentication. EAP-TLS uses certificates to authenticate credentials and provide encryption key material. EAP-TLS requires a certificate infrastructure to issue certificates to both the IAS servers and the wireless or Ethernet clients. With PEAP and MS-CHAP v2, you can use password-based authentication securely because the MS-CHAP v2 authentication exchange is encrypted with a secure TLS channel, preventing offline dictionary attacks against user passwords. The PEAP authentication exchange also produces encryption key material. PEAP with MS-CHAP v2 requires certificates to be installed only on the IAS servers.

PEAP allows for a resumption of the TLS session created from an initial PEAP authentication. This feature of PEAP, known as *fast reconnect*, causes subsequent authentications based on the TLS session to occur very quickly because most of the messages of a full PEAP authentication are not sent. PEAP fast reconnect minimizes connection and authentication times and does not require a user to resubmit authentication credentials, such as a username or password. For example, wireless clients that roam from one wireless authentication protocol to another have more seamless network connectivity and are not prompted for authentication credentials.

To select PEAP with MS-CHAP v2 on an IAS server, perform the following steps: In the Internet Authentication Service snap-in, click EAP Methods on the Authentication tab of the profile properties of a remote access policy. In the Select EAP Providers dialog box, click Protected Extensible Authentication Protocol (PEAP) and either edit its properties or move it to the top of the list of EAP types.

■ **Session time reflects account restrictions.**   IAS now calculates a session time for a connection as needed that is based on the user or computer account's expiration time and permitted logon hours. For example, a user account is restricted to logon from 9:00 A.M. to 5:00 P.M., Monday through Friday. If a connection is made using the user account at 4:00 P.M. on Friday, IAS will automatically calculate a maximum session time of 1 hour for the connection and send the maximum session time as a RADIUS attribute to the access server. At 5:00 P.M., the access server terminates the connection. This new feature provides network access behavior that is consistent with account date and time restrictions.

- **IAS and cross-forest authentication.** If Active Directory forests are in cross-forest mode with two-way trusts, IAS can authenticate the user account in the other forest. An IT administrator can use this feature to provide authentication and authorization for accounts in other two-way trusted Active Directory forests that are in cross-forest mode.

- **IAS as a RADIUS proxy.** This feature allows IAS to forward RADIUS authentication and accounting messages between access servers and RADIUS servers. This functionality includes the following:

  - Flexible rule-based forwarding

  - Load balance and failover between multiple RADIUS servers and load balancing of RADIUS requests

  - Ability to force an access client to use a compulsory tunnel, with or without user authentication

  - Selective forwarding of authentication and accounting requests to different RADIUS servers

  This feature allows the following scenarios:

  - An IT administrator can create an IAS-based RADIUS proxy located in one domain to authenticate and authorize users in another domain that does not have a trust relationship or has only a one-way trust relationship, or is in another forest.

  - An ISP offering outsourced dial-up, VPN, or wireless services to a corporation can forward user authentication and accounting requests to a corporate RADIUS server.

  - In some network perimeter configurations, an IT administrator can install an IAS proxy in the network perimeter. Requests can be forwarded from the IAS proxy at an ISP to an IAS server in the organization's network.

  - ISPs working with partner ISPs or network infrastructure providers can use an IAS RADIUS proxy in a roaming consortium.

  - IT administrators can use IAS for organization networks that connect with partner networks to forward authentication of users from other companies to their user account database.

- **Logging RADIUS information to a SQL database.** IAS can be configured to send logging information for accounting requests, authentication requests, and periodic status to a Structured Query Language (SQL) server. This allows IT administrators to use SQL queries to obtain historical and real-time information about connection attempts that use RADIUS for authentication. To configure, obtain properties of the SQL Server logging method in the Remote Access Logging folder of the Internet Authentication Service snap-in.

■   **EAP-TLS unauthenticated access.** EAP-TLS unauthenticated access provides a means to grant guest access for a wireless or switch client that does not have a certificate installed. If a network access client does not provide credentials, IAS determines whether unauthenticated access is enabled in the remote access policy that matched the connection attempt. EAP-TLS supports one-way authorization or unauthenticated access where the client does not send credentials.

This feature allows the following scenarios:

❑   An IT administrator can use this feature to allow wireless or switch clients that do not have certificates to connect to a restricted virtual local area network (VLAN) for bootstrap configuration.

❑   An IT administrator can use this feature to allow access to visitors or business partners to the corporation's network to access the Internet. This is done by giving them access to a restricted VLAN or by IP filters that allow traffic to go to the Internet.

❑   A wireless ISP can use this feature to allow access to potential subscribers. The potential subscribers can get access to a restricted VLAN with local information. After the user subscribes for Internet access, the client can connect to the Internet.

■   **RADIUS client configuration supports a range of IP addresses.** To simplify administration of Remote Authentication Dial-In User Service (RADIUS) clients when numerous wireless access points are on the same subnet or within the same IP address space, IAS allows you to configure a range of addresses for a RADIUS client.

The address range for RADIUS clients is expressed in the network prefix length notation $w.x.y.z/p$, where $w.x.y.z$ is the dotted decimal notation of the address prefix and p is the prefix length (the number of high-order bits that define the network prefix). This is also known as Classless Inter-Domain Routing (CIDR) notation. An example is 192.168.21.0/24. To convert from subnet mask notation to network prefix length notation, p is the number of high-order bits set to 1 in the subnet mask.

An IT administrator can use this feature to simplify management of wireless access points.

- **Improvement to negotiating EAP authentication method.** This feature allows you to select multiple EAP types when configuring remote access policies. This allows IAS to negotiate the EAP authentication method with clients from multiple selected EAP methods. An IT administrator can use this feature when network access clients use different EAP authentication methods and can configure the server to specify a list of allowed EAP authentication methods.

- **Object identifier checking for user certificates and smart cards.** To require specific types of user-level certificates for specific types of connections, IAS supports the specification of individual certificate issuance policy object identifiers (OIDs) that must be included in the certificate of the access client as part of the remote access policy profile settings. For example, if an IT administrator wants to ensure that remote access VPN connections use a smart card certificate rather than a locally installed user certificate, the administrator configures the appropriate remote access policy to require the object identifier for the Smart Card Logon certificate issuance policy (1.3.6.1.4.1.311.20.2.2) to be present in the certificate offered by the remote access VPN client. You can configure a list of object identifiers required to be present in the user certificate offered by the access client by using the Allow Certificates With These OIDs attribute on the Advanced tab on the properties of a remote access policy profile. No required object identifiers are specified by default.

- **Load balancing as RADIUS proxy.** This feature provides the ability to balance the load of authentication across multiple RADIUS servers when IAS is used as a RADIUS proxy. This provides the ability to scale up and handle geographic failover. The IAS RADIUS proxy dynamically balances the load of connection and accounting requests across multiple RADIUS servers and increases the processing of large numbers of RADIUS clients and authentications per second. Additionally, the RADIUS proxy can be configured to mark certain RADIUS servers with higher preference. The RADIUS servers with lower preference are not used if higher ones are available.

  This feature enables the following scenarios:

  ❏   An IT administrator can use this feature to scale up wireless, virtual private network (VPN), or dial-up authentication to process a large number of connection requests using multiple RADIUS servers.

❑   An IT administrator can use this feature to ensure that connection requests fail over to nearby RADIUS servers if they are available and to configure RADIUS servers at a remote site as backup RADIUS servers.

■   **Support for ignoring the dial-in properties of accounts.**   You can configure a RADIUS attribute on the profile properties of a remote access policy to ignore the dial-in properties of accounts. The dial-in properties of an account contain the following:

❑   Remote access permission

❑   Caller ID

❑   Callback options

❑   Static IP address

❑   Static routes

To support multiple types of connections for which IAS provides authentication and authorization, it might be necessary to disable the processing of account dial-in properties. This can be done to support scenarios in which specific dial-in properties are not needed. For example, the caller ID, callback, static IP address, and static routes properties are designed for a client that is dialing into a network access server (NAS). These settings are not designed for wireless access points (APs). A wireless AP that receives these settings in the RADIUS message from the IAS server might be unable to process them, which could cause the wireless client to become disconnected. When IAS provides authentication and authorization for users who are both dialing in and accessing the organization network through wireless technology, the dial-in properties must be configured to support either dial-in connections (by setting dial-in properties) or wireless connections (by not setting dial-in properties).

You can use IAS to enable dial-in properties processing for the user account in some scenarios (such as dial-in) and to disable dial-in-properties processing for user account dial-in properties in other scenarios (such as wireless and authenticating switch). This is accomplished by configuring the Ignore-User-Dialin-Properties attribute on the Advanced tab of the profile settings for a remote access policy. The Ignore-User-Dialin-Properties attribute is set to the following:

❑   To enable account dial-in properties processing, delete the Ignore-User-Dialin-Properties attribute or set it to *False*. For example, for a remote access policy that is designed for dial-in connections, no additional configuration is required.

❑   To disable user account dial-in properties processing, set the Ignore-User-Dialin-Properties attribute to *True*. For example, this is set for the remote access policy that is designed for wireless or authenticating switch connections. When the dial-in properties of the user account are ignored, remote access permission is determined by the remote access permission setting for the remote access policy.

You can also use this attribute to manage network access control through groups and the remote access permission on the remote access policy. By setting the Ignore-User-Dialin-Properties attribute to *True*, the remote access permission on the user account is ignored. The disadvantage to using the Ignore-User-Dialin-Properties attribute in this way is that you cannot use the additional dial-in properties of caller-ID, callback, static IP address, and static routes for connections that match the remote access policy.

■   **Support for computer authentication.**   Active Directory and IAS support the authentication of computer accounts by using standard user authentication methods. This allows a computer and its credentials to be authenticated for wireless or authenticating switch access clients.

■   **Support for the Authentication Type remote access policy condition.**   You can create remote access policies using the Authentication Type condition. This new condition allows you to specify connection constraints that are based on the authentication protocol or method that is used to validate the access client.

■   **Enhanced IAS SDK.**   The Windows .NET Platform Software Development Kit (SDK) contains two smaller networking SDKs—the IAS SDK and the EAP SDK. The IAS SDK can be used to return custom attributes to the access server in addition to those returned by IAS, to control the number of user network sessions, to import usage and audit data directly into an Open Database Connectivity (ODBC)–compliant database, to create customized authorization modules, and to create customized authentication modules (non-EAP). The EAP SDK can be used to create EAP types. A developer can use the enhancements to the IAS SDK to modify or delete RADIUS attributes and to convert Access-Rejects to Access-Accepts. An ISV or a value-added reseller (VAR) can use this feature to create enhanced solutions with IAS. An IT administrator can use this feature to create custom solutions for IAS.

■ **Scriptable API to configure IAS.**   This feature makes available, in the IAS Platform SDK, a scriptable API that allows configuration of IAS. An ISV can use this feature to provide value-added services on top of an IAS infrastructure, and an IT administrator can use this feature to integrate their IAS with their own service management infrastructure.

■ **Enhanced EAP configuration for remote access policies.**   In Windows 2000, you can select only a single EAP type for a remote access policy. This means that all connections matching the conditions of the policy must use the single EAP type selected in the policy profile settings. Additionally, the configuration of an EAP type is global to all the remote access policies. These limitations can cause problems when you want to individually configure the properties for EAP types for each policy or when you want to select multiple EAP types for a type of network connection or per group. These limitations are removed for IAS in the Windows Server 2003 family. For example, you might want to select different computer certificates for EAP-TLS authentication for wireless connections versus VPN connections, or you might want to select multiple EAP types for wireless connections because some of your wireless clients use EAP-TLS authentication and others use PEAP with MS-CHAP v2.

■ **Separation of authentication and authorization for IAS proxy.**   The proxy component of IAS in the Windows Server 2003 family supports the ability to separate the authentication and authorization of connection requests from access servers. The IAS proxy can forward the user credentials to an external RADIUS server for authentication and perform its own authorization using a user account in an Active Directory domain and a locally configured remote access policy. With this feature, alternative user authentication databases can be used, but connection authorization and restrictions are determined through local administration.

This feature allows the following scenarios:

❏   A visitor to an organization network can be granted access to a guest LAN by authentication using the visitor's credentials and authorization of the connection using a user account in an untrusted visitors Active Directory domain and a remote access policy configured on the IAS proxy. The visitor's credentials can be the credentials of the user account at the visitor's organization.

❑   A public wireless network can use an alternative user database to authenticate wireless access and authorize logons with local user accounts in an Active Directory domain.

This new capability is configured using the Remote-RADIUS-to-Windows-User-Mapping setting in the advanced properties of a connection request policy.

IPSec

The following improvements to IPSec have been made in the Windows Server 2003 family:

■   **New IP Security Monitor snap-in.**   A new IP Security Monitor snap-in provides detailed IPSec policy configuration and active security state. This replaces the Ipsecmon.exe tool provided with Windows 2000. An IPSec policy consists of a set of main-mode policies, a set of quick-mode policies, a set of main-mode filters that are associated with the set of main-mode policies, and a set of quick-mode filters (both transport-mode and tunnel-mode) that are associated with the set of quick-mode policies. The active security state consists of the active main-mode and quick-mode security associations and statistical information about IPSec-protected traffic. An IT administrator can use this new snap-in for improved IPSec monitoring and troubleshooting.

■   **Command-line management with Netsh.**   Using commands in the Netsh ipsec context, you can configure static or dynamic IPSec main mode settings, quick-mode settings, rules, and configuration parameters. To enter the Netsh ipsec context, type **netsh -c ipsec** at the command prompt. The Netsh ipsec context replaces the Ipsecpol.exe tool provided with the Windows 2000 Server Resource Kits. An IT administrator can use this feature to script and automate IPSec configuration.

■   **IP security and network load balancing integration.**   This feature allows a group of servers using Network Load Balancing (NLB) to provide highly available IPSec-based VPN services. This is also supported by down-level L2TP/IPSec clients. This feature also provides the capability for faster IPSec failover. An IT administrator can use this feature to integrate NLB and IPSec-based VPN services for a more secure and reliable network service. Because the IKE protocol automatically detects the NLB service, no additional configuration is required to use this feature. This feature is provided only with the Enterprise Edition and the Datacenter Edition.

■ **IPSec support for RSoP.**   To enhance IPSec deployment and troubleshooting, IPSec now provides an extension to the Resultant Set Of Policy (RSoP) snap-in. RSoP is an addition to Group Policy that you can use to view existing IPSec policy assignments and to simulate planned IPSec policy assignments for a computer or a user. To view existing policy assignments, you can run an RSoP logging-mode query. To simulate planned IPSec policy assignments, you can run an RSoP planning-mode query.

Logging-mode queries are useful for troubleshooting precedence issues for IPSec policy. The results of logging-mode queries display all of the IPSec policies that are assigned to an IPSec client and the precedence of each policy. Planning-mode queries are useful for deployment planning because they allow you to simulate different IPSec policy settings. By simulating different IPSec policy settings, you can evaluate the impact of changing policy settings and determine the optimum settings, before you implement them. After you run an RSoP logging-mode query or an RSoP planning-mode query, you can view detailed settings (the filter rules, filter actions, authentication methods, tunnel endpoints, and connection type that were specified when the IPSec policy was created) for the IPSec policy that is being applied.

■ **IPSec NAT traversal.**   This feature allows IKE-protected and ESP-protected traffic to traverse a NAT. IKE automatically detects that a NAT is present and uses User Datagram Protocol-Encapsulating Security Payload (UDP-ESP) encapsulation to allow ESP-protected IPSec traffic to pass through the NAT. The Windows Server 2003 family support for IPSec NAT traversal is described in the Internet drafts titled "UDP Encapsulation of IPsec Packets" (draft-ietf-ipsec-udp-encaps-02.txt) and "Negotiation of NAT-Traversal in the IKE" (draft-ietf-ipsec-nat-t-ike-02.txt).

With this support, a corporate employee can use L2TP/IPSec when connected to a private network, such as a hotel or home network. This feature also supports more general IPSec ESP transport and mode security associations across a NAT. An administrator can use this feature to configure gateway-to-gateway IPSec tunnels between two computers running members of the Windows Server

2003 family and the Routing and Remote Access service when one or both are behind a NAT. This will also permit server-to-server IPSec connections, such as a server on the perimeter network that is communicating across a NAT to an internal network server.

■ **Network address translation hardware acceleration.** IPSec now supports NAT hardware acceleration for normal ESP traffic. This feature supports the following scenarios:

❑ An IT administrator can use this feature to scale L2TP/IPSec and normal IPSec connections when IPSec over NAT is used.

❑ An independent hardware vendor (IHV) can use this functionality to build new cards or update older firmware to use the new encapsulation.

The IPSec hardware acceleration interface is documented in the Windows DDK as part of TCP/IP Task Offload.

■ **IPSec policy filters allow logical addresses for local IP configuration.** The IP Security Policies snap-in can now configure source or destination address fields to be interpreted by the local IPSec policy service as the addresses for the DHCP server, the DNS servers, the WINS servers, and default gateway. Therefore, IPSec policy can now automatically accommodate changes in the server's IP configuration, using either DHCP or static IP configurations. Computers running Windows 2000 or Windows XP ignore this extension to the IPSec policy.

■ **Certificate mapping to Active Directory computer account provides access control.** The IP Security Policies snap-in can now be configured to map a computer certificate to the computer account within an Active Directory forest. This takes advantage of the same SChannel certificate mapping that IIS and other PKI-enabled services use. After the certificate is mapped to a domain computer account, access controls can be set using the settings for network logon rights Access This Computer From Network and Deny Access To This Computer From Network. A network administrator can now restrict access to a computer running a member of the Windows Server 2003 family using IPSec to allow access only to computers from a specific domain, computers that have a certificate from a particular issuing certification authority, a specific group of computers, or even a single computer. Computers running Windows 2000 or Windows XP ignore this extension to the IPSec policy.

■ **Stronger Diffie-Hellman group for Internet Key Exchange.** IPSec now supports the use of a 2048-bit Diffie-Hellman key exchange, providing support for the Internet draft titled "More MODP Diffie-Hellman groups for IKE." With a stronger Diffie-Hellman group, the resulting secret key derived from the Diffie-Hellman exchange has greater strength. The IP Security Policies snap-in allows you to configure this new Diffie-Hellman group setting for both the local and the domain-based IPSec policy. Computers running Windows XP and Windows 2000 ignore this setting.

■ **Better denial-of-service protection for IKE.** IKE in the Windows Server 2003 family has been modified to better handle denial-of-service attacks involving IKE traffic. The most common attack is garbage packets sent to UDP port 500. IKE attempts to validate the packets until there are too many incoming packets, at which point IKE starts to drop packets. When the incoming rate subsides, IKE quickly restarts inspection for valid IKE packets. The most difficult attack to prevent is a malicious user sending valid IKE initiation messages to an IKE responder, either using invalid source IP addresses or just rapidly sending from a valid source IP address. This attack is similar to the TCP Synchronize (SYN) attack launched against TCP/IP-based servers. With the new protection, the IKE responder responds to the initial valid IKE message with an IKE message containing a special value in the Responder Cookie field. If the IKE initiator does not send the next message with the Responder Cookie field properly set, the IKE exchange is ignored. When Windows Server 2003 is the IKE initiator, it reinitiates properly. The IPSec IKE module does not maintain any state on the IKE negotiation until after the response containing the properly set Responder Cookie field is received. This maintains interoperability with computers running Windows 2000 or Windows XP and third-party IPSec implementations and improves the chance that a legitimate initiator can successfully negotiate, even when the responder is under a limited attack. It is still possible for an IKE responder to be overwhelmed by a flood of legitimate IKE packets. The IKE responder recovers as fast as possible once the attack has ceased.

Additional New Features

The following sections describe a variety of other new networking features in Windows Server 2003:

■   Changes to the Winsock API

■   Windows Sockets Direct for System Area Networks

■   Removal of Legacy Networking protocols

■   Removal of Obsolete RPC Protocols

■   Command-Line Tools

■   Strong Authentication for Services for Macintosh

Changes to the Winsock API

The following changes to the Windows Sockets API have been made to the Windows Server 2003 family:

■   **Removal of support for AF_NETBIOS (64-bit only).** AF_NETBIOS is not supported on 64-bit versions of the Enterprise Edition and Datacenter Edition. Applications should use TCP or UDP as alternatives. Functionality is preserved for 32-bit third-party applications.

■   **ConnectEx/TransmitPackets and TCP/IP.** The following two functions are Microsoft-specific extensions to the Windows Sockets 2 specification:

❑   The Windows Sockets *ConnectEx* function establishes a connection to another socket application and optionally sends the block of data after the connection is established.

❑   The Windows Sockets *TransmitPackets* function transmits in-memory data or file data over a connected socket (either datagram or stream). The operating system's cache manager is used to retrieve file data and locks memory for the minimum time required to transmit it. This provides high performance and efficiency for file and memory data transfer over sockets.

Windows Sockets Direct for System Area Networks

The Windows Server 2003 family contains substantial performance improvements to Windows Sockets Direct (WSD) for storage area networks (SANs). WSD allows Windows Sockets applications written for SOCK_STREAM to obtain the performance benefits of SANs without having to make application modifications. The fundamental component of this technology is the WinSock switch that emulates TCP/IP semantics over native SAN service providers. For the Windows 2000 Server family, WSD support was available only for Windows 2000 Advanced Server and Windows 2000 Datacenter Server. WSD support is included for all members of the Windows Server 2003 family. For more information about the Windows Sockets API, see the Microsoft Platform SDK.

Removal of Legacy Networking Protocols

The following legacy networking protocols have been removed:

- Data Link Control (DLC)
- NetBIOS Extended User Interface (NetBEUI)

The following legacy networking protocols have been removed from the 64-bit versions of the operating system:

- Internetwork Packet Exchange/Sequenced Packet Exchange (IPX/SPX) and IPX-dependent services
- Infrared Data Association (IrDA)
- Open Shortest Path First (OSPF)

Removal of Obsolete RPC Protocols

The following legacy RPC protocols have been superseded by TCP:

- Remote Procedure Call (RPC) over NetBEUI
- RPC over NetBIOS over TCP/IP (NetBT).
- RPC over NetBIOS over IPX (NBIPX)
- RPC over SPX (64-bit only)
- RPC over AppleTalk (64-bit only)

Legacy protocols superseded by UDP include the following:

- RPC over IPX

- RPC over Message Queuing (MSMQ)

Command-Line Tools

New command-line tools or utilities are provided to improve management and administration of computers. A new and updated command-line help file (A–Z) is included as well to document the Cmd.exe shell and every tool. Command-line tools include the following:

- **Bootcfg.exe**   Used to view or set the properties (such as debug on/ off) of the boot.ini file on a local or remote server (not available in 64-bit versions)

- **DriverQuery.exe**   Used to view the currently loaded device drivers and their memory usage

- **Dsadd.exe**   Used to create an object instance of a specified type in Active Directory

- **Dsget.exe**   Used to get or view selected properties of an existing object in Active Directory when the location of the object to be viewed is specifically known

- **Dsmod.exe**   Used to modify selected attributes of an existing object in Active Directory

- **Dsmove.exe**   Used to move an object from its current location to a new parent location within the same naming context or to rename an object in Active Directory

- **Dsquery.exe**   Used to find objects in Active Directory that match specified search criteria

- **Dsrm.exe**   Used to remove an object or the complete subtree under an object in Active Directory

- **Eventcreate.exe**   Used to write a user-defined event to any of the event logs

- **Eventquery.vbs**   Used to specify the type of events to extract from the event log. The selected events can be displayed on the screen or saved to a file

- **Eventtriggers.exe**   Used to launch a process based on the occurrence of an event written to the event log

- **Gpresult.exe**   Used to get the Resultant Set of Policy (RSoP) and the list of policies that are applied to a computer

- **IIS scripts**   Many new scripts (IISWeb.vbs, IISVdir.vbs, and so on) that provide command-line tools to configure and manage a server running IIS and Active Server Pages (ASP) applications

- **Netsh.exe**   Extensive network configuration tool; now adds the basic network diagnostic features provided by the older NetDiag.exe tool

- **Openfiles.exe**   Used to view the list of connected users and files in use per share on a computer

- **Pagefileconfig.vbs**   Used to get the current paging file size or set a new paging file size

- **Print scripts**   Many new scripts (prncnfg.vbs, prnjobs.vbs, and so on) used to manage printer services, drivers, and queues

- **Reg.exe**   Used to view, set, and edit registry keys

- **SC.exe**   Used to start, stop, and manage Win32 services

- **Schtasks.exe**   Used to get, set, or edit a scheduled task using the existing Win32 scheduling service

- **Systeminfo.exe**   Used to view basic properties of a machine (such as CPU and memory)

- **Taskkill.exe**   Used to kill or stop a running process

- **Tasklist.exe**   Used to view or identify all running processes with PIDs

- **Tsecimp.exe**   Used to import Telephony Application Programming Interface (TAPI) user account properties and access rights

An IT administrator can use command-line tools to automate high-volume or common server administration tasks via Visual Basic scripting or command-line batch files. This eliminates one-off operations that are often imposed by the GUI management tools and can reduce IT administration costs.

Strong Authentication for Services for Macintosh

For computers running Services for Macintosh (SFM) and using the Microsoft user authentication module (MSUAM), a new Require Strong Authentication (NTLMv2) check box is present and enabled by default in the MSUAM interface. Selecting this option allows users to authenticate only to a server that implements

NTLMv2. This excludes Windows NT 4.0 and older servers that cannot authenticate using NTLMv2. The user can clear the Require Strong Authentication (NTLMv2) check box to allow authentication to these older servers.

For More Information

See the following resources for further information:

- Introducing the Windows Server 2003 Family at *http://www.microsoft.com/windowsserver2003/evaluation/overview/*

- What's New in Networking and Communications at *http://www.microsoft.com/windowsserver2003/evaluation/overview/technologies/networking.mspx*

- Microsoft Windows–IPv6 Web Site at *http://www.microsoft.com/ipv6/*

- Microsoft Windows–Wi-Fi Web site at *http://www.microsoft.com/wifi/*

- Microsoft Windows–VPN Web Site at *http://www.microsoft.com/vpn/*

- Microsoft Windows–IAS Web Site at *http://www.microsoft.com/windows2000/technologies/communications/ias/*

- Microsoft Windows–IPSec Web Site at *http://www.microsoft.com/windows2000/technologies/communications/ipsec/*

7

Terminal Services

In Microsoft Windows Server 2003, Terminal Services builds on the solid foundation provided by the application server mode in Windows 2000 Terminal Services and includes the new client and protocol capabilities of Windows XP. Terminal Services lets you deliver Windows-based applications, or the Windows desktop itself, to virtually any computing device—including those that cannot run Windows.

Terminal Services in Windows Server 2003 can enhance an enterprise's software deployment capabilities for a variety of scenarios, allowing substantial flexibility in application and management infrastructure. When a user runs an application on Terminal Server (which is enabled by Terminal Services), the application executes on the server, and only keyboard, mouse, and display information is transmitted over the network. Each user sees only his or her individual session, which is managed transparently by the server operating system and is independent of any other client session.

Terminal Services Benefits

Terminal Services in Windows Server 2003 provides three important benefits:

- **Rapid, centralized application deployment.** Terminal Server is great for rapidly deploying Windows-based applications to computing devices across an enterprise—especially applications that are frequently updated, infrequently used, or hard to manage. When an application is managed on Terminal Server and not on each device, administrators can be certain that users are running the latest version of the application.

- **Low-bandwidth access to data.** Terminal Server considerably reduces the amount of network bandwidth required to access data remotely. Using Terminal Services to run an application over bandwidth-constrained connections, such as dial-up or shared WAN links, is effective for remotely accessing and manipulating large amounts of data because only a screen view of the data is transmitted rather than the data itself.

- **Windows anywhere.** Terminal Server helps users become more productive by enabling access to current applications on any device—including underpowered hardware and non-Windows desktops. And because Terminal Server lets you use Windows anywhere, you can take advantage of extra processing capabilities from newer, lighter-weight devices such as the Pocket PC.

Client Features

Several new client features provide improved management of terminal servers and Windows Server 2003–based computers.

Improved User Interface

Most of these new features provide substantial improvements to the client user interface:

- **Remote Desktop Connection.** The Terminal Services client, called *Remote Desktop Connection* (RDC), provides substantial improvements over previous releases, including greater functionality through a simplified user interface. RDC is the same program that's used to connect to a Windows XP Professional–based computer running Remote Desktop, and it can be used to connect to previous versions of Terminal Services, including Microsoft Windows NT 4.0 Terminal Server Edition and Windows 2000. To use RDC, simply type the name of the remote computer and select Connect, as shown in Figure 7-1.

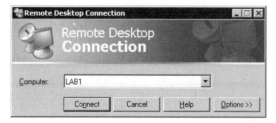

Figure 7-1   Users use Remote Desktop Connection to connect to remote computers.

■ **Moving between a remote session and the desktop.**   By default, a remote session is full screen and high color. The Connection Bar at the top of a full-screen RDC session lets you move easily between the remote session and the local desktop.

■ **Customizing the remote connection.**   If you want to change the various options for configuring the remote connection, a tabbed property sheet allows you to modify settings such as display options, local resources to redirect, and programs to run on connection.

■ **Optimize performance over lower-bandwidth connections.** To optimize performance over lower-bandwidth connections, you can choose your connection speed and strip away unneeded components of the remote session—for example, themes, bitmap caching, and animation. These choices are made using the Experience tab of the Remote Desktop Connection dialog box, as shown in Figure 7-2.

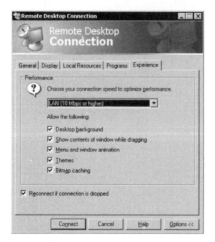

Figure 7-2   You can customize your connection for the bandwidth that's available.

- **No separate Connection Manager.**   Connection Manager is no longer necessary because its functionality has been enhanced and integrated directly into the RDC. This enables users and administrators to save and open connection settings files, which can be used locally or deployed to other users. A password that is saved is securely encrypted and can be decrypted only on the computer on which it was saved.

- **Automatic reconnects.**   To better protect against network dropouts (especially in wireless and dial-up environments), RDC attempts to reconnect to a server when a network interruption causes the session to be lost.

- **Client resource redirection.**   Remote Desktop Connection supports a wide variety of data redirection types. For security reasons, either the client or the server can disable each of these. A security alert is displayed when file system, port, or smart card redirection is requested; the user can cancel the connection or disable the redirection at that time.

Client Resource Redirection Features

Unless specified in the following list, client resource redirection features are available only to clients connecting to the Windows Server 2003 family or to computers running Windows XP Professional. Any computer that can run Remote Desktop Connection can use these new features:

- **File System.**   Client drives, including network drives, are mounted inside the server session. This lets users open or save files on their own computers' disk drives, in addition to opening and saving files on the server.

- **Ports.**   Client serial ports can be mounted on the server. This enables a variety of hardware on the client computer to be accessed by software on the server.

- **Printers.**   All printers installed on the client are visible to the server—including network printers. With Windows 2000 Terminal Services, only locally connected printers were redirected. Redirected printers are given names that are easier to read. For example, users might see *printername on printserver (from clientname) in session 9.* In Windows 2000, they would have seen *_printserver_printername/ clientname/Session 9.* Printer redirection also works when connecting to Windows 2000–based servers.

- **Audio.**   Sounds such as *error* and *new mail* notification events are redirected to the client.

- **Smart card sign-on.**   A smart card that contains Windows logon credentials can provide those credentials to a Windows Server 2003 remote session for logon. This feature requires a client operating system that can recognize the smart card first: Windows 2000, Windows XP, or Windows CE .NET.

- **Windows keys.**   Key combinations such as Alt+Tab and Ctrl+Esc are sent to the remote session by default. The Ctrl+Alt+Del combination is always interpreted at the client computer for security reasons. These key combinations also work when the client is connected to a Windows 2000–based terminal server, but only when the client is using Windows NT–based client operating systems. They do not work with Windows 95–based or Windows 98–based clients.

- **Time zones.**   An RDC client computer can provide its time zone to the server, or users can manually set their own time zones. This lets an administrator use one server for multiple users across different time zones. This feature is also helpful for applications that support features such as calendars. The feature is off by default because it relies on a properly set time zone on the client computer.

- **Virtual Channels.**   Virtual Channels can be used to move various types of data between client and server computers. This feature is available in both Windows Server 2003 and Windows 2000 Server. Information about using Virtual Channels is available from the MSDN developer program at *http://msdn.microsoft.com/*.

Client Deployment Options

Remote Desktop Connection is built into Windows XP and Windows Server 2003. If you want to install RDC on client computers that don't yet have it installed, use one of the following options:

- Use tools such as Microsoft Systems Management Server or Windows 2000 Group Policy to publish/assign the Windows Installer–based RDC.

- Create a client installation share on Windows Server 2003. (This can also be done with Windows 2000 Server.)

- Install directly from the Windows XP or Windows Server 2003 CD, using the Perform Additional Tasks selection from the CD's autoplay menu. (This does not require installing the operating system.)

- Download the RDC from *http://www.microsoft.com/windowsxp/ remotedesktop.*

Note   Remote Desktop Web Connection is an improved safe-for-scripting ActiveX control/COM object. It can be used by application service providers (ASPs) and other organizations that want to deploy Web pages built with Web applications that include Win32 components. Also, a Windows CE version of RDC is included in the Windows CE .NET Platform Builder to give Windows CE hardware vendors the option of including it with their devices.

New Server Features

Several new server features provide improved management of Terminal Services and the Windows Server 2003 family.

Improved Server Management

Most of these features make it easier than ever to manage servers, regardless of whether Terminal Services is installed:

- **Remote Desktop for Administration.**   Remote Desktop for Administration builds on the remote administration mode of Windows 2000 Terminal Services. In addition to the two virtual sessions that are available in Windows 2000 Terminal Services remote administration mode, an administrator can remotely connect to the real console of a server. Tools that would not work in a virtual session before, because they kept interacting with "session 0," will now work remotely.

- **Connecting to the console.**   To connect to the console, administrators can choose one of the following methods:

  ❑ Use the Remote Desktop Microsoft Management Console (MMC) snap-in.

❑   Run the Remote Desktop Connection (mstsc.exe) program with the */console* switch.

❑   Create Remote Desktop Web Connection pages that set the *ConnectToServerConsole* property.

■ **Activating Remote Desktop and Terminal Services.**   Unlike Windows 2000 Server, which had a dual-mode Terminal Services component, Windows Server 2003 separates the remote administration and Terminal Services functionality into separate configurable components. Remote Desktop for Administration is enabled through the System control panel's Remote tab, as shown in Figure 7-3. Terminal Services is enabled by adding the Terminal Server component using the Windows Components portion of the Add/Remove Programs Wizard.

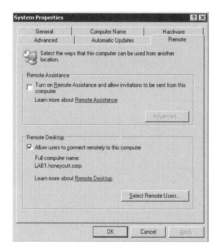

Figure 7-3   Remote Desktop is installed by default and is easily enabled on the Remote tab of the System control panel.

Additional Management Features

The following features enhance the manageability of Terminal Services in Windows Server 2003:

■ **Group Policy.**   Group Policy can be used to control Terminal Services properties. This enables configuration of groups of servers simultaneously, including settings for new features such as per-computer Terminal Services profile path and disabling wallpaper while connected remotely.

- **Windows Management Interface provider.** A full Windows Management Instrumentation (WMI) provider allows for a scripted configuration of Terminal Services settings. A number of WMI aliases are included to provide a simple front end for frequently used WMI tasks.

- **Active Directory Service Interfaces.** An Active Directory Services Interface (ADSI) provider gives programmatic access to per-user Terminal Services profile settings such as Home Directory, Remote Assistance permissions, and others.

- **Printer management.** Printer management has been improved in the following ways:

  - ❑ Printer driver mapping has been enhanced to provide better matching in near-miss cases.

  - ❑ When a driver match can't be made, the Trusted Driver Path lets you specify other standard printer drivers that you sanction on your terminal servers.

  - ❑ The print stream is compressed for better slow-link performance between a server and a client.

- **Terminal Services Manager.** An improved Terminal Services Manager allows for easier management of larger arrays of servers by reducing automatic server enumeration. This gives direct access to arbitrary servers by name and provides for a list of favorite servers.

- **Terminal Server License Manager.** The Terminal Server License Manager has been dramatically improved to make it easier to activate a Terminal Server license server and assign licenses to it.

- **Single-session policy.** Configuring the single-session policy lets an administrator limit users to a single session, regardless of whether it is active—even across a farm of servers.

- **Client error messages.** More than 40 new client error messages make it easier than ever before to diagnose client connection problems.

Enhanced Security

The Terminal Server access model now conforms better than before to Windows Server management paradigms:

- **Remote Desktop Users Group.** Instead of adding users to a list in the Terminal Services Connection Configuration (TSCC) program, you simply make them members of the Remote Desktop Users (RDU) group. For example, the administrator can add the Everyone group to the RDU group to allow everyone to access the terminal server. Using a true Windows NT group also means that access to terminal servers can be controlled through Group Policy across groups of servers. To use per-NIC permissions on multi-NIC servers, administrators must still use TSCC.

■ **Security Policy Editor.**   For additional customization, Terminal Services user rights can be assigned to individual users or groups, using the Security Policy Editor. Doing so will give those users the ability to log on to a terminal server without having to be a member of the Remote Desktop Users group just described.

■ **128-bit encryption.**   By default, connections to terminal servers are secured by 128-bit bidirectional RC4 encryption—when the clients support 128-bit encryption. (RDC is 128-bit by default.) It's possible to connect with older clients using encryption lower than 128 bits unless it's specified that only high-encryption clients be allowed.

■ **Software restriction policies.**   Software restriction policies in Windows Server 2003 enable administrators to use Group Policy to simplify locking down terminal servers (and any other Windows Server 2003–based computer) by allowing only certain programs to be run by specified users. This built-in Windows feature replaces the AppSec (Application Security) tool used in previous versions of Terminal Services.

■ **Session Directory.**   Terminal servers can be organized into farms. This configuration allows clusters of load-balanced computers to appear to their users as a single fault-tolerant service. The new Session Directory feature in Terminal Services allows users to reconnect to the specific disconnected session they've left within a farm, rather than just being directed to the least loaded server when they connect. Session Directory can use the Windows Load Balancing Service or a third-party load balancer, and the service can run on any Windows Server 2003–based computer. However, members of the terminal server farm must be running Windows Server 2003 Enterprise Edition.

For More Information

Log on to the following Web sites for more information:

- What's New in Terminal Server at *http://www.microsoft.com/ windowsserver2003/evaluation/overview/technologies/termi- nalserver.mspx*

- Windows .NET Server Family Overview at *http://www.microsoft.com/ windowsserver2003/evaluation/overview/*

- Windows .NET Server Features Guide at *http://www.microsoft.com/ windowsserver2003/evaluation/features/*

- Introducing the ".NET" in the Windows .NET Server Family at *http:// www.microsoft.com//windows.netserver/evaluation/overview/dotnet/ dotnet.mspx*

- Using Software Restriction Policies to Protect Against Unautho- rized Software at *http://www.microsoft.com/windowsxp/pro/ techinfo/administration/restrictionpolicies/*

- Windows Powered Thin Clients at *http://www.microsoft.com/win- dows/powered/thinclients/*

- Application Deployment Using Microsoft Management Technologies at *http://www.microsoft.com/windows2000/techinfo/howitworks/ management/apdplymgt.asp*

8

Internet Information Services

Administrators and Web application developers demand a fast, reliable Web platform that is both scalable and secure. Internet Information Services (IIS) 6.0 and Microsoft Windows Server 2003 introduce many new features for Web application server management, performance and scalability, availability and reliability, and security. Significant architectural improvements have also been made to meet and exceed customer requirements.

This chapter describes the next generation of Web infrastructure capabilities that are available in the Windows Server 2003 family. It also describes the benefits and new technical features that are available when you deploy IIS 6.0. For example, it covers the IIS architecture, new security and management features, performance improvements, and a host of additional improvements.

Web Application Server Role

Web application server is a new server role for the Windows Server 2003 family of products. This new server role combines some key server technologies into a single entity called the application server. These technologies include the following:

- IIS
- ASP.NET
- ASP
- COM+

- Microsoft Data Engine (MSDE)

- Microsoft Message Queuing (MSMQ)

As a result of the combination of these technologies into a cohesive experience, administrators and Web application developers now have the ability to host dynamic content, such as database-driven ASP.NET applications, without the need to install any other software on the server.

The application server is configurable in two places in Windows Server 2003:

- **Configure Your Server application.** The Configure Your Server (CYS) application, which is a central point for configuring Windows Server 2003 roles, now contains the new Web application server role. This role replaces the existing Web server role. After this new role is installed, management of the role can be accomplished by the Manage Your Server application, which includes the new entry for the application server.

- **Add/Remove Components application.** The application server is also located in the Windows Add/Remove Components application as a top-level optional component. This is the new location where server applications that belong to the application server (IIS, ASP.NET, COM+, and MSMQ) can be installed and have their subcomponents configured. The Windows Add/Remove components method of configuring the application server is the route to take for more granular control over the specific subcomponents that will be installed.

New Request Processing Architecture

Web site and application code is increasingly complex. Custom applications and Web sites hosted in customer environments might contain some imperfect code. Therefore, hosting processes need to be active managers of the run-time environment by automatically detecting memory leaks, access violations, and other errors. When these conditions occur, the underlying architecture needs to be fault tolerant, actively recycle or restart processes as necessary, and continue to queue requests, without interrupting the end user experience.

To provide this robust and actively managed run time, IIS 6.0 provides kernel-level request queuing: this is a new application isolation environment with active process management, known as worker process isolation mode. IIS 5.0 was designed to have one process, Inetinfo.exe, function as the main Web server process, which could farm out requests to one or more out-of-process applications (dllhost.exe). In comparison, IIS 6.0 has been redesigned into two new components that use a new kernel-mode driver. This allows IIS to parse out core Web server code from application-handling code. These two new components are the following:

- **HTTP.sys.**   A kernel-mode HTTP listener
- **WWW Service Administration and Monitoring component.**   A user-mode configuration and process manager

All Web application processing, including loading of Internet Server Application Programming Interface (ISAPI) filters and extensions, as well as authentication and authorization, is done by a new WWW service DLL. This DLL is loaded into one or more host processes called *worker processes*, which service requests for application pools in HTTP.sys. The worker process executable is named w3wp.exe.For more information on how worker processes interact with IIS 6.0, see the upcoming section "Worker Process Isolation Mode." An *application pool* corresponds to one request queue within HTTP.sys and to one or more worker processes. An application pool can serve requests for one or more unique Web applications. These Web applications are assigned to the application pool based on their URLs. Multiple application pools can operate at the same time. For more information about application pools, see the section "Worker Process Isolation Mode."

> **Note**   Preliminary testing has shown a gain of more than 100 percent throughput over previous releases on a benchmark using an eight-processor server. This gain is a result of the new request processing architecture and scalability improvements in the Web application server.

HTTP.sys

In IIS 6.0, HTTP.sys listens for requests and places each request in the appropriate queue. Each request queue corresponds to one application pool. Because no third-party code runs in HTTP.sys, it cannot be affected by failures in user-mode code that normally affect the status of the Web service.

If something causes the user-mode request processing infrastructure to terminate, HTTP.sys continues to accept and queue requests, provided the

WWW service is still up and running. HTTP.sys continues to accept requests and place them in the appropriate queues until no queues are available, no space is left on the queues, or the Web service has been shut down.

Once the WWW service notices the failed worker process, it starts a new worker process if requests for the worker process's application pool are still waiting to be serviced. Thus, while there might be a temporary disruption in user-mode request processing, an end user does not experience the failure because requests continue to be accepted and queued.

WWW Service Administration

Another key portion of the new IIS 6.0 architecture is the functionality in the WWW Service Administration and Monitoring component. The WWW Service Administration and Monitoring component makes up a core portion of the WWW service, where, as in HTTP.sys, critical IIS 6.0 services reside and third-party code is never loaded.

The WWW Service Administration and Monitoring component is responsible for two main areas: configuration and process management. At initialization time, the request process manager portion of WWW service reads metabase information and initializes the HTTP.sys namespace routing table with one entry for each application. Each entry contains information that routes the URLs mapped to an application pool to that specific application pool.

These preregistration steps inform HTTP.sys that there is an application pool that responds to requests in this part of the namespace and that HTTP.sys can request that a worker process be started for the application pool if there is demand. All preregistrations are done before HTTP.sys can begin to route requests to processes. As application pools and new applications are added, the Web service configures HTTP.sys to accept requests for the new URLs, sets up the new request queues for the new application pools, and indicates where the new URLs should be routed.

In the request process management role, the WWW Service Administration and Monitoring component is responsible for controlling the lifetime of the worker processes that process the requests. This includes determining the following:

- When to start a worker process
- When to recycle a worker process
- When to restart a worker process if it is unable to process any more requests (becomes blocked)

Worker Process Isolation Mode

IIS 6.0 introduces worker process isolation mode, which runs all application code in an isolated environment but without the performance penalty of the previous IIS versions. HTTP requests are routed to the correct application pool queue: user-mode worker processes serving an application pool pull the requests directly from HTTP.sys and eliminate the unnecessary process hops encountered when having to send a request to an out-of-process DLL host and back again.

In IIS 6.0, there is no longer any notion of in-process applications: all necessary HTTP application run-time services such as ISAPI extension support are equally available in any application pool. This design prevents a malfunctioning Web application or Web site from disrupting other Web applications (or other Web sites) served from other worker processes on that server. It is now possible to unload in-process components without having to take down the entire Web service. The host worker process can be taken down temporarily without affecting other worker processes serving content. There is also a benefit from being able to leverage other operating system services available at the process level (for example, CPU throttling) per application pool. Additionally, Windows has been re-architected to support many more concurrent processes than ever before.

The IIS 6.0 worker process isolation mode approach is to allow administrators to put different Web applications or Web sites into application pools. For example, a departmental server might have Web-HR in one application pool and Web-Finance in another; an Internet service provider (ISP) might have CustomerX.com in one application pool and CustomerY.com in another.

Worker process isolation mode prevents one application or site from stopping another. In addition, separating applications or sites into separate worker processes simplifies a number of management tasks, such as taking a site or an application on line or off line (independently of all other applications running on the system), changing a component the application uses, debugging the application, monitoring counters for the application, and throttling resources used by the application.

Application Pools

Application pools define a set of Web applications that share one or more worker processes. Each application pool is separated from other application pools by process boundaries. An application that is routed to one application pool is not affected by other application pools, and that application cannot be routed to another application pool while being serviced by the current application pool. Applications can easily be assigned to another application pool while the server is running. Application pools are effectively namespace groups. In HTTP.sys, application pools are represented by a request queue that the user-mode worker processes serving an application pool can grab requests from.

Isolation Improvements

Specifically, worker process isolation mode improves upon its predecessors in the following areas:

- **Robustness.** This architecture prevents different Web applications or Web sites served by IIS 6.0 worker process isolation mode from harming one another or the server as a whole.

- **No reboots.** The user is never forced to reboot the server, or even shut down the entire WWW service. Common operations, such as upgrading content or components, debugging Web applications, and dealing with faulty Web applications, shouldn't affect service to other sites or applications on the server.

- **Self-healing.** IIS 6.0 supports auto-restart of failed applications and periodic restart of leaky/malfunctioning applications or applications with faulty code.

- **Scalable.** IIS 6.0 supports scaling to ISP scenarios, wherein hundreds to thousands of sites might be on a server. IIS 6.0 also supports Web gardens, in which each worker process in a set of equivalent worker processes on a server receives a share of the requests that are normally served by a single worker process. This supports better multiprocessor scalability.

- **Strong application notion.** IIS 6.0 supports the application as the unit of administration. This includes making the application the unit of robustness by enabling application isolation, and also enabling resource throttling and scaling based on the application.

The end result is a Web server that is more reliable and always available, even if applications cause their hosting worker processes to terminate. Worker process isolation mode takes the concept of application isolation, introduced in IIS 4.0, much further. Applications can be completely isolated from one another, such that one application error does not affect another application in a different process. IIS 6.0 worker process isolation mode also allows for better isolation while not incurring a performance penalty for isolation. Requests are pulled directly from the kernel instead of being pulled by a user-mode process from the kernel for the application; they then route accordingly to another user-mode process.

Improved Robustness

Worker process isolation mode contains the following features that improve its robustness without a performance hit:

- **Clean separation between user code and the server.**   All user code is handled by worker processes, which are completely isolated from the core Web server. This improves upon IIS 5.0 in that an ISAPI can be, and often is, hosted in-process to the core Web server. If an ISAPI loaded in a worker process fails or causes an access violation, the only thing taken down is the worker process that hosts the ISAPI. Meanwhile, the WWW service creates a new worker process to replace the failed worker process. The other worker processes are unaffected.

- **Multiple application pools.**   With IIS 5.0, applications can be pooled together out-of-process, but only in one application pool—DLLHOST.EXE. When IIS 6.0 operates in worker process isolation mode, administrators can create multiple application pools, wherein each application pool can have a different configuration.

- **Better support for load balancers.**   With the advent of application pools, IIS has a well-defined physical separation of applications—so much so that it's quite feasible to run hundreds or thousands of sites or applications side by side on one Windows server. In this configuration, it's important that one problematic application not affect other, healthy, applications. It's also desirable to be able to automatically communicate with load balancers and switches to route away only the traffic for a problematic application while still allowing the server to accept requests for the other, healthy, applications. As an example, imagine a server processing requests for applications A and B. If application B fails so often that IIS decides to automatically shut it down (see the upcoming discussion of rapid-fail protection), the server should still be able to receive requests for application A. IIS 6.0 has a built-in extensibility model that can fire events and commands when the WWW service detects a specific application's failure. This configuration ability allows load balancers and switches to be configured to automatically stop routing traffic to problematic applications while still routing traffic to healthy applications.

- **Web gardens.**   IIS 6.0 worker process isolation mode also allows multiple worker processes to be configured to service requests for a given application pool. By default, each application pool has only one worker process. However, an application pool can be configured to have a set of equivalent worker processes share the work. This configuration is known as a *Web garden* because it's similar to a Web farm, the difference being that a Web garden exists within a single server. Requests are distributed by HTTP.sys among the set of worker processes in the group. This distribution is based on matching the queue of incoming requests for an application pool against a queue of *requests for requests* from each set of processes in the Web garden. A benefit of Web gardens is that if one worker process gets bogged down (script engine hangs), other worker processes are available to accept and process requests.

■ **Health monitoring.**   The WWW service is capable of monitoring the health of worker processes by pinging the worker processes periodically to determine whether they are completely blocked. If a worker process is blocked, the WWW service terminates the worker process and creates another worker process for replacement. Furthermore, the WWW service maintains a communication channel to each worker process and can easily tell when a worker process fails by detecting a drop in the communication channel.

■ **Processor affinity.**   Worker processes can have an affinity to specific CPUs to take advantage of more frequent CPU cache (L1 or L2) hits.

■ **Allocating sites and applications to application pools.**   In IIS 6.0, as in IIS 5.0, applications are defined as those namespaces that are labeled in the metabase with the *AppIsolated* property. Sites, by default, are considered to be a simple application—one in which the root namespace (/) is configured as an application. An application pool can be configured to serve anything: from one Web application to multiple applications to multiple sites. Assigning an application to an application pool is as easy as configuring which application pool an application should be routed to in the metabase.

■ **Demand start.**   Application pools get benefits: for example, on-demand starting of the processes that service the namespace group, when the first request for a URL in that part of the namespace arrives at the server. The IIS 6.0 application manager (contained within the WWW service) is the component that does on-demand process starting and generally controls and monitors the life cycles of worker processes.

- **Idle timeout.**   An application pool can be configured to have its worker processes request a shutdown if they are idle for a configurable amount of time. This is done to free up unused resources. Additional worker processes are started when demand exists for that application pool.

- **Rapid-fail protection.**   When a worker process fails, it drops the communication channel with the WWW service. The WWW service detects this failure and takes action, which typically includes logging the event and restarting the worker process. In addition, IIS 6.0 can be configured so that if a particular application pool suffers multiple failures in a row, it can be automatically disabled. This is known as *rapid-fail protection*. Rapid-fail protection places the application pool in out-of-service mode, and HTTP.sys immediately returns a "503–Service Unavailable" out-of-service message to any requests to that portion of the namespace—including requests already queued for that application pool. An administrator can also explicitly put a namespace group in out-of-service mode: for example, if the application is being taken off line because of a serious application problem. The administrator does this by stopping the application pool with either IIS Manager or a script.

- **Orphaning worker processes.**   Worker process isolation mode can be configured to *orphan* any worker process that it deems to be *terminally ill*. If a worker process fails to respond to a ping in a certain amount of time, the WWW service marks that worker process as terminally ill. Normally the WWW service terminates that worker process and starts a replacement. If orphaning is turned on, the WWW service leaves the terminally ill worker process running and starts a new process in its place. Also, the WWW service can be configured to run a command on the worker process (such as attaching a debugger) when it orphans a worker process.

- **Recycling worker processes.**   Today many businesses and organizations have problems with Web applications that leak memory, suffer from poor coding, or have indeterminate problems. This forces administrators to reboot or restart their Web servers periodically. In previous versions of IIS, it was not possible to restart a Web site without an interruption of the entire Web server.

Worker Process Restarts

Worker process isolation mode can be configured to periodically restart worker processes in an application pool to manage faulty applications. Worker processes can be scheduled to restart based on the following criteria:

- Elapsed time

- Number of requests served

- Scheduled times during a 24-hour period

- A liveliness ping, which the process must respond to (See the earlier bullet regarding health monitoring.)

- Virtual memory usage

- Physical memory usage

- On demand

When a worker process restarts, the WWW service tells the existing worker process to shut down and gives a configurable time limit for the worker process to drain its remaining requests. Simultaneously, the WWW service creates a replacement worker process for the same namespace group, and the new worker process is started before the old worker process stops: this approach prevents service interruptions. The old worker process remains in communication with HTTP.sys to complete its outstanding requests and then shuts down normally or is forcefully terminated if it does not shut down after a configurable time limit.

IIS 5.0 Isolation Mode

IIS 6.0 introduces worker process isolation mode in an effort to bring greater reliability, isolation, availability, and performance to Web servers. While worker process isolation mode offers increased isolation, reliability, availability, and performance, some applications might not work in its environment because of compatibility issues, such as session states persisting in process or applications written as read raw data filters. Therefore, IIS 6.0 has the ability to switch to another process model, called IIS 5.0 isolation mode, to ensure compatibility.

IIS 5.0 isolation mode operates similarly to IIS 5.0. Essentially everything above the kernel mode, called user mode, operates in the same fashion as IIS 5.0. Because the same essential user mode processes exist as in IIS 5.0, IIS 5.0 isolation mode is the most compatible way for users to run IIS 6.0. The same methods of application isolation—low, medium (pooled), and high—exist, and Inetinfo.exe is still the master process through which each request must transverse.

Also, IIS 5.0 isolation mode receives the same benefits from HTTP.sys as does worker process isolation mode: kernel-mode request queuing and kernel-mode caching. IIS 6.0 redesigns the way a Web service talks to HTTP.sys.

> **Note**   All other services contained within Inetinfo, such as FTP and SMTP, still work as they did in IIS 5.0, and they are still contained within Inetinfo. Only the WWW service has been changed to pull requests from HTTP.sys.

New Security Features

Experience has taught Microsoft that it's impossible to conceive of every possible attack and proactively address all possible vulnerabilities. Yet patterns have emerged in areas that hackers commonly exploit. As a result, several preventive measures are built into IIS 6.0 to make IIS more secure out of the box. In addition, improvements have been made to IIS to make it easier to further lock down a site and to discover and apply security patches.

Locked-Down Server

IIS ships in a locked-down state, in which only static content (.htm, .jpg, .bmp, and similar files) is served, thereby providing additional protection. IIS provides multiple levels of security, as described in the following list:

- **IIS is not installed by default on Windows Server 2003.**   Security is all about reducing the attack surface of your system. Therefore, IIS is not installed by default on Windows Server 2003. Administrators explicitly select and install IIS.

- **IIS is installed in a locked-down state.**   The default installation of IIS exposes only minimal functionality. Only static files get served, and all other functionality has to be enabled explicitly by the administrator.

- **Disabled on upgrades.**   Accidentally installed IIS servers will be disabled on Windows Server 2003 upgrades.

- **Disabling IIS via Group Policy.**   With Windows Server 2003, domain administrators can prevent users from installing IIS on their computers.

- **Running as a low-privilege account.**   IIS worker processes run in a low-privilege user context. This drastically reduces the effect of potential attacks.

- **Secure ASP.**   All ASP built-in functions always run in a low-privilege account (anonymous user).

- **Recognized file extensions.**   IIS serves requests only to files that have recognized file extensions and rejects requests to file extensions it doesn't recognize.

- **Command-line tools not accessible to Web users.**   Malicious attackers often take advantage of command-line tools that are executable via the Web server. In IIS 6.0, the command-line tools can't be executed by the Web server.

- **Write protection for content.**   Once attackers get access to a server, they often try to deface Web sites. If anonymous Web users are prevented from overwriting Web content, these attacks can be mitigated.

- **Timeouts and limits.**   In IIS 6.0, settings are set to aggressive and secure defaults. This minimizes attacks due to timeouts and limits that were previously too generous.

- **Upload data limitations.**   Administrators can limit the size of data that can be uploaded to a server.

- **Buffer overflow protection.**   A worker process terminates a program if a buffer overflow is detected.

- **File verification.**   The core server verifies that the requested content exists before it gives the request to a request handler (ISAPI extension).

In an effort to reduce the attack surface of your Web server, IIS 6.0 serves only static content after a default installation. Programmatic functionality provided by IIS APIs (ISAPI) or Common Gateway Interfaces (CGI) must be manually enabled by an IIS administrator. ISAPIs and CGIs extend the ability of your Web pages, and for this reason ISAPIs and CGIs are referred to here as Web service extensions. For example, to run Active Server Pages with this version of IIS, the ISAPI asp.dll must be enabled as a new Web service extension.

Using the Web Service Extension node, Web site administrators can enable or disable IIS functionality based on the individual needs of the organization. Therefore, additional functionality such as Active Server Pages or FrontPage

Server extensions will have to be enabled before they work as expected. IIS 6.0 provides programmatic, command-line, and graphical interfaces for enabling Web service extensions.

Worker Process Identity

Running multiple applications or sites on one Web server puts additional requirements on a Web server. If an ISP hosts two companies (who might even be competitors) on one server, it has to guarantee that these two applications run completely isolated from each other. More important, the ISP has to make sure that a malicious administrator for one application can't access the data of the other application.

Complete isolation is a must. IIS 6.0 provides this level of isolation through the configurable worker process identity. Together with other isolation features such as bandwidth and CPU throttling and memory-based recycling, IIS 6.0 provides an environment to host even the fiercest competitors on one Web server. Similarly, IIS 6.0 provides an environment to run multiple applications on one Web server with complete isolation.

IIS Runs as NetworkService

The worker process runs as NetworkService, which is a new built-in account with very few privileges. Running as a low-privilege account is one of the most important security principles. The ability to exploit a security vulnerability can be extremely contained if the worker process has very few rights on the underlying system.

Improvements to SSL

There are three main Secure Sockets Layer (SSL) improvements in IIS 6.0. The following list describes them:

- **Performance.**   IIS 5.0 already provides the fastest software-based SSL implementation on the market. As a result, 50 percent of all SSL Web sites run on IIS. IIS 6.0 will be even faster. Microsoft tuned and streamlined the underlying SSL implementation for even more performance and scalability.

- **Remotable Certification Object.**   In IIS 5.0, administrators cannot manage SSL certificates remotely because the cryptographic service provider (CSP) certificate store is not remotable. Because customers manage hundreds or even thousands of IIS servers with SSL certificates, they need a way to manage certificates remotely.

■ **Selectable cryptographic service provider.** If SSL is enabled, performance drops dramatically because the CPU has to perform a lot of intensive cryptography. There are hardware-based accelerator cards that enable the offloading of these cryptographic computations to hardware. They plug their own Crypto API (CAPI) provider into the system. IIS 6.0 makes it easy to select such a third-party provider.

If authentication answers the question, "Who are you?" authorization answers the question, "What can you do?" So authorization is about allowing or not allowing a user to conduct a certain operation or task. Windows Server 2003 integrates Passport as a supported authentication mechanism for IIS 6.0. IIS 6.0 extends the use of a new authorization framework that comes with the Windows Server 2003 family. Additionally, Web applications can use URL authorization in tandem with Authorization Manager to control access. Constrained, delegated authorization was added in Windows Server 2003 to provide domain administrators with control to allow delegation to particular machines and services only.

Passport Integration

Windows Server 2003 integrates Passport as a supported authentication mechanism for IIS 6.0; this integration provides Passport authentication in the core Web server and uses Passport version 2 interfaces provided by standard Passport components. Administrators can take advantage of the Passport customer base (150,000,000+) without having to deal with account management issues such as password expiration and provisioning.

Once Passport authentication is verified, a Windows Server 2003 Passport user can be mapped to a user of Active Directory through the user's Windows Server 2003 Passport identification—if such a mapping exists. A token is created by the Local Security Authority (LSA) for the user and set by IIS for the HTTP request.

Application developers and Web site administrators can use this security model for authorization based on users of Active Directory. These credentials are also delegatable using the new Constrained Delegation feature, which is supported in Windows Server 2003.

URL Authorization

Today access control lists (ACLs) are used to make authorization decisions. The problem is that the ACL model is very object (file, directory) driven and tries to fulfill the requirements of the resource manager—the NTFS file system. But most Web applications used today are now business applications and are not object driven—they are operation- or task-based. If an application wants to provide an operation- or task-based access control model, it has to create its own. With the new authorization framework in Windows Server 2003, Microsoft provides a way to fulfill the needs of these business applications.

IIS 6.0 extends the use of a new authorization framework that comes with the Windows Server 2003 family by providing gatekeeper authorization to specific URLs. Additionally, Web applications can use URL authorization in tandem with Authorization Manager to control access, from within a single policy store, to URLs that are compromising a Web application and to control application-specific tasks and operations. Maintaining the policy in a single policy store allows administrators to manage access to the URLs and application features from a single point of administration, while leveraging the store-level application groups and user-programmable business rules.

Delegated Authentication

Delegation is the act of allowing a server application to act as a user on a network. An example of this would be a Web service application on an enterprise intranet that accesses information from various other servers in the enterprise as the client and then presents the consolidated data over HTTP to the end user.

Constrained delegation was added in Windows Server 2003 to provide domain administrators with control to allow delegation to particular computers and services only. The following are delegation recommendations:

- Delegation should not allow a server to connect on behalf of the client to any resource in the domain or forest. Only connections to particular services (for example, a back-end SQL database or a remote file store) should be allowed. Otherwise, a malicious server administrator or application can impersonate the client and authenticate against any resource in the domain on behalf of the client.

- Delegation should not require the client to share its credentials with the server. If a malicious server administrator or application has your credentials, it can use them throughout the domain, and not just against the intended back-end data store.

Constrained, delegated authentication is a highly desirable way to design an application suite in the Windows environment because there are many opportunities to leverage high-level protocols, such as Remote Procedure Call (RPC) and Distributed Component Object Model (DCOM). These protocols can be used to transparently carry the user context from server to server, impersonate the user context, and have the user context be authorized against objects as the user by the authorization rules, defined by domain group information, local group information, and discretionary access control lists (DACLs) on resources located on the server.

New Manageability Features

The typical Internet Web site no longer operates on just one server. Web sites now spread across multiple Web servers or across *Web farms*. (Web farms are clusters of servers that are dedicated to delivering content, business logic, and services.) Even intranet sites, especially those delivering Web-enabled line-of-business applications, have increased in number as businesses and organizations are delivering more applications over the Web.

In addition, as remote administration has become more common, there has been an increasing demand for improved API access as well as improvement in direct configuration support. With the Internet and intranet changes over the past few years, managing a Web site is no longer as simple as managing one or a few Web servers from an office but has become an integrated and complex process.

IIS 6.0 introduces new features to improve the administration capabilities for administrators who manage IIS Web sites. IIS 6.0 includes a storage layer replacement of the metabase (configuration store), which allows for direct text editing of the metabase configuration in a robust and recoverable fashion. Furthermore, Windows Management Instrumentation (WMI) support and improved command-line support enable Web site administration without the use of IIS Manager.

XML Metabase

The metabase is a hierarchical store of configuration values used by IIS that incorporates rich functionality such as inheritance, data typing, change notification, and security. The metabase configuration for IIS 4.0 and IIS 5.0 was stored in a proprietary binary file and was not easily readable or editable. IIS 6.0 replaces the proprietary binary file named MetaBase.bin with plain-text XML-formatted files. Here's a brief overview of the XML metabase:

- The benefits of XML-formatted plain-text metabase files are as follows:
    - Improved backup and restore capabilities on machines that experience critical failures
    - Improved troubleshooting and metabase corruption recovery

- ❏ Capability of being edited directly with common text editing tools

- ❏ Exportability and importability of application configuration at user-specified locations

- ❏ Improved performance and scalability

- The new XML metabase allows administrators to easily read and edit configuration values directly without having to use scripts or code to administer the Web server. The XML metabase makes it much easier to do the following:

  - ❏ Diagnose potential metabase corruption

  - ❏ Extend existing metabase schema via XML

  - ❏ View and edit current metabase configuration directly in the metabase file while still being 100 percent compatible with existing public metabase APIs and Active Directory Services Interface (ADSI)

- The new XML metabase also makes strides toward improving performance and scalability. The existing binary metabase will upgrade to the new XML metabase without any problems. The new XML metabase has the following:

  - ❏ Comparable or smaller disk footprint

  - ❏ Faster read times on Web server startup than the IIS 5.0 binary metabase

  - ❏ Write performance equivalent to that of the IIS 5.0 binary metabase

- The new XML metabase addresses manageability concerns by enabling the following scenarios:

  - ❏ Direct metabase configuration troubleshooting and editing in a robust fashion

  - ❏ Reuse of rich-text tools, such as windiff, version control systems, and editing tools

  - ❏ Configuration rollback

  - ❏ Versioned history archives containing copies of the metabase for each change

  - ❏ Web site and application configuration cloning

  - ❏ Server-independent backup and restore

ADSI schema and schema extensibility will continue to be supported. A human-readable, human-editable schema supports ADSI and enhances human readability and editability of the text format. A new IIS 6.0 configuration has been added to the metabase and exposed to ADSI so you can take advantage of new features through existing scripts and tools:

■ **Automatic versioning and history.** The metabase history feature automatically keeps track of changes to the metabase that are written to disk. When the metabase is written to disk, IIS marks the new MetaBase.xml file with a version number and saves a copy of the file in the history folder. Each history file is marked with a unique version number, which is then available for the metabase rollback or restore process. The metabase history feature is enabled by default.

■ **Edit while running.** IIS 6.0 allows the administrator to edit the MetaBase.xml file while IIS is running. New configuration selections can easily be added by opening MetaBase.xml in Notepad, for example, and typing in the new configuration for a new site or virtual directory or editing an existing configuration.

■ **Import and export configuration.** IIS 6.0 introduces two new Admin Base Object (ABO) methods: *Export* and *Import*. These methods allow the configuration from any node level to be exported and imported across servers. Secure data is protected by a user-supplied password similar to the new backup/restore support. These new methods are also available to ADSI and WMI users and through IIS Manager. Using *Export* and *Import*, administrators can complete the following tasks:

❑ Export one node or an entire tree to an XML file from any level of the metabase

❑ Optionally export inherited configuration

❑ Import one node or an entire tree from an XML file

❑ Optionally import inherited configuration

❑ Password-protect secure data

❑ Optionally merge configuration during import with existing configuration

■ **Server-independent backups.** In IIS 6.0, a new Admin Base Object (ABO) API is available for developers to back up and restore the metabase with a password. This allows administrators and developers to create server-independent backups.

The session key is encrypted with an optional user-supplied password during backup and is not based on the machine key. When backing up the metabase, the system encrypts the session key with the password supplied by the user. During the restore operation, the supplied password decrypts the session key, and the session key is reencrypted with the current machine key.

This new restore method can also restore backups made with the old backup method, and it follows the same behavior the old restore method uses when a session key cannot be decrypted. WMI and ADSI support these methods. The existing metabase backup/restore user interface also uses the new backup/restore method.

IIS WMI Provider

Windows 2000 introduced a new means of configuring the server and of gaining access to important pieces of data such as performance counters and system configuration—Windows Management Instrumentation (WMI). To leverage WMI capabilities such as query support and associations between objects, IIS 6.0 now has a WMI provider that provides a rich set of programming interfaces that offer more powerful and flexible ways to administer your Web server. The IIS WMI provider provides functionality similar to that of the IIS ADSI provider for editing the metabase.

The goal of the IIS WMI provider is to provide manageability of IIS at a level of functionality equivalent to the IIS ADSI provider and to support an extensible schema. Specifically, this requires a WMI schema that is congruent with the IIS metabase schema. While they may differ in ways specific to the respective object and data models for ADSI and WMI, the two offer equivalent functionality. In other words, a script written for a task using the ADSI model could also be written using the WMI model. The effects on the metabase would be equivalent. Likewise, any schema extensions done through ADSI are reflected in the WMI provider automatically. If a change is made to the schema in ADSI, that change is pushed into the IIS WMI provider.

Command-Line Administration

IIS 6.0 now ships supported scripts in the Windows\System32 directory that can be used to administer an IIS 6.0 Web server. These scripts, written in Visual Basic scripting language, use the IIS WMI provider to get and set configuration within the metabase. These scripts are designed to do many of the most common tasks facing a Web administrator from the command line without having to use a user interface. IIS 6.0 ships supported command-line administration scripts for the following tasks:

- **Iisweb.vbs.** Create, delete, start, stop, and list Web sites

- **Iisftp.vbs.** Create, delete, start, stop, and list FTP sites

- **Iisvdir.vbs.** Create and delete virtual directories, or display the virtual directories of a given root

- **Iisftpdr.vbs.** Create, delete, or display virtual directories under a given root

- **Iisconfg.vbs.** Export and import IIS configuration to an XML file

- **Iisback.vbs.** Back up and restore IIS configuration

- **Iisapp.vbs.** List process IDs and application pool IDs for currently running worker processes

- **Iisext.vbs.** Configure Web service extensions

Web-Based Administration

Using the Remote Administration (HTML) Tool, administrators are able to remotely administer IIS across the Internet or an intranet through a Web browser.

New Performance Features

A new generation of applications puts a greater demand on performance and scalability attributes of Web servers. Increasing the speed at which HTTP requests can be processed and allowing more applications and sites to run on one server translates directly into fewer servers needed to host a site. It also means that existing hardware investments can be sustained longer while being able to handle greater capacity.

Tip Preliminary testing suggests performance gains in throughput of up to 100 percent higher on an eight-processor server under particular workloads.

Windows Server 2003 introduces a new kernel-mode driver, HTTP.sys, for HTTP parsing and caching. HTTP is specifically tuned to increase Web server throughput and designed to avoid a processor transition to user mode if the content requested is classified as something that can be directly processed in the kernel. This is important to IIS users because IIS 6.0 is built on top of

HTTP.sys. If a user-mode component needs to get involved in the processing of a request, HTTP.sys routes the request to the appropriate user-mode worker process without any other user-mode process getting involved in the routing decision.

IIS 6.0 is also more aware of the processing environment. IIS kernel-mode and user-mode components are written to be aware of processor locality, and they do their best to maintain per-processor internal data locality. This can add to the scalability of a server on multiprocessor systems. Additionally, administrators have the ability to establish affinity between workloads for particular applications or sites and specific processor subsystems. This means that applications can set up virtual application processing silos in one operating system image, as shown in Figure 8-1.

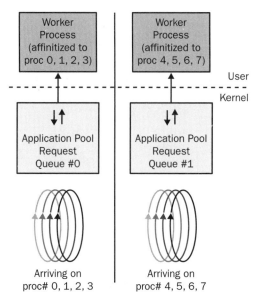

Figure 8-1   This diagram illustrates virtual request processing silos in IIS 6.0.

New Kernel-Mode Driver

The new kernel-mode driver, HTTP.sys, is a single point of contact for all incoming (server-side) HTTP requests. This provides high-performance connectivity for HTTP server applications. The driver sits atop TCP/IP and receives all connection requests from the IP/port combinations it's configured to listen on. HTTP.sys is also responsible for overall connection management, bandwidth throttling, and Web server logging.

> **Note**   Preliminary testing suggests performance gains of 200 percent
> better throughput of static content, and cached responses achieved up
> to 165 percent higher throughput when compared with IIS 5.0.

Caching Policy

IIS 6.0 has advanced heuristics built in to determine the cacheable hot-set of an application or set of sites. Just because an item is cacheable doesn't mean that adding that item to an in-memory cache is sensible, because managing the item and the memory it consumes has a cost. Therefore, IIS 6.0 uses a new heuristic to determine which items should be cached on the basis of the distribution of requests that a particular application receives. This means that the Web server's scalability improves because it makes better use of the resources on the server while sustaining the performance on frequent requests.

IIS 6.0 also has heuristics built in to monitor the overall state of the server and makes decisions to increase or reduce concurrency on that basis. The central idea here is to be efficient in using concurrency. For example, when executing processor-bound requests, starting concurrent work is not always the best approach.

Web Gardens

A Web garden is an application pool that has multiple processes serving the requests routed to that pool. You can configure the worker processes in a Web garden to be bound to a given set of CPUs on a multiprocessor system. Using Web gardens, Web applications have increased scalability because a software lock in one process does not block all the requests going to an application. If there are four processes in the Web garden, a specific software lock blocks roughly a quarter of the requests.

ASP Template Cache

Before Active Server Pages (ASP) code gets executed in IIS 5.0, the ASP engine compiles an ASP file to an ASP template. These ASP templates are stored in process memory. If a site consists of numerous ASP pages, this cache deallocates the oldest templates from memory to free space for new ones. With IIS 6.0, these templates are persisted on disk. If one of these ASP files gets requested again, the ASP engine loads the template instead of loading the ASP file and spending additional CPU time compiling it again.

> **Note**   Preliminary testing suggests performance improvements of greater than 50 percent higher throughput due to persistent on-disk caching.

Large-Memory Support

For workloads that require a great deal of cached data, IIS 6.0 can be configured to cache up to 64 gigabytes (GB) for an x86 system.

Site Scalability

IIS 6.0 has improved the way internal resources are used. The IIS 6.0 approach is much more one of allocating resources as HTTP requests request certain system resources rather than one of preallocating resources at initialization time. This has resulted in the following improvements:

- Many more sites can be hosted on a single IIS 6.0 server.

- A larger number of worker processes can be concurrently active.

- The server can be started and shut down more quickly while hosting sites.

Preliminary testing shows that the number of pooled applications that can be run on IIS 6.0 is an order of magnitude greater than on IIS 5.0. IIS 6.0 is capable of having thousands of isolated applications configured, and each of these applications can run with its own security identity. The number of concurrent isolated applications is a function of system resources. IIS 6.0 can easily have tens of thousands of configured applications per server when applications are configured to execute in a shared application pool.

> **Note**   Preliminary testing of startup times for 20,000 sites has shown that startup takes less than 2 minutes on a two-processor server.

An additional scalability improvement in the new IIS 6.0 architecture is that IIS can listen for requests from a large number of sites without having any worker processes running. (See "New Request Processing Architecture" earlier in this chapter.) Coupling this demand-start feature with the ability to aggressively idle worker processes means that a Web server hosting many sites can be scaled further. This is because IIS 6.0 tunes its resource use to the sites that are actually active. IIS 6.0 will also dynamically trim kernel cached items for these inactive sites.

New Programmatic Features

IIS 6.0 provides several new programmatic features and continues to build on the ISAPI programming model. These new features include the following:

■   ASP.NET and IIS integration

■   Internal redirection (*ExecuteURL* and global interceptors)

■   Buffer and handle send (*VectorSend*)

■   Caching dynamic content

■   ISAPI support for custom errors

■   Worker process recycling

■   Improved ISAPI Unicode support

■   COM+ services in ASP

ASP.NET

Windows Server 2003 offers an improved developer experience with ASP.NET and IIS integration. Building upon IIS 6.0, platform enhancements offer developers very high levels of functionality—for example, rapid application development and a wide variety of languages to choose from. With Windows Server 2003, the experience from using ASP.NET and the .NET Framework is improved as a result of enhanced process model integration in IIS 6.0. IIS 6.0 also offers support for the latest Web standards, including XML, SOAP, and IPv6.

ExecuteURL

The *HSE_REQ_EXEC_URL* server support function now allows an ISAPI extension to easily redirect a request to another URL. It answers growing demand by ISAPI extension developers to chain requests.

ExecuteURL provides functionality to replace almost all read raw data filters. The most common customer scenario for developing read raw data filters is that developers want to examine or modify the request entity body before the target URL processes it. Currently the only way to see the entity body of a request (if you are not the target URL) is through read raw data notifications.

Unfortunately, writing an ISAPI filter to accomplish this goal can be exceedingly difficult, or even impossible in some configurations.

ISAPI extensions, on the other hand, provide functionality for easy retrieval and manipulation of the entity body. *ExecuteURL* allows an ISAPI extension to process the request entity body and pass it to a child request, meeting the needs of nearly all read raw data filter developers.

Global Interceptors

ExecuteURL allows IIS 6.0 to implement ISAPI request interceptors that can intercept, change, redirect, or deny every incoming HTTP request for a specific URL space:

- IIS 5.0 already supports one ISAPI extension that intercepts all requests with a single wildcard (*) script map that's configured by editing the application mappings for an application.

- In IIS 6.0, the single wildcard (*) script map concept is extended to allow a multiple execution of global interceptors.

Accepting all requests for a specific URL was a functionality that was possible only in ISAPI filters. But ISAPI filters have problems. They're global for a Web site. They can't do long running operations (for example, database queries) without starving the IIS thread pool. They can't access the entity body of the request. Because global interceptors are ISAPI extensions, they don't have the limitations of ISAPI filters, and they provide the functionality, together with *ExecuteURL*, to replace almost all read raw data filters.

VectorSend

Today ISAPI developers have only two possibilities if they have multiple buffers that make up a response. They can either call *WriteClient* multiple times or assemble the response in one big buffer.

- The first approach is a performance bottleneck because there is one kernel-mode transition per buffer.

- The second approach costs performance too, and it requires additional memory. *VectorSend* is the IIS 6.0 solution to this problem.

Implemented as a server support function for ISAPIs, *VectorSend* allows developers to put together a list of buffers and file handles to send, in order, and then hand off to IIS 6.0 to compile the final response. HTTP.sys compiles all the buffers and file handles into one response buffer within the kernel and then sends it. This frees the ISAPI from having to construct a buffer or make calls to *WriteClient*.

Caching of Dynamic Content

Another new feature is the implementation of a kernel-mode cache for dynamic content. The benefit of this feature is that many customers have programmatically created content that doesn't change.

In previous versions of IIS, requests had to transition from kernel mode to user mode for every dynamic request, and the responses had to be regenerated. Eliminating this transition and pulling the cached content from the kernel-mode cache results in a marked performance improvement.

ReportUnhealthy

A new ISAPI extension server support function named *HSE_REQ_REPORT_UNHEALTHY* allows an ISAPI extension to call into the IIS 6.0 worker process to request that the worker process be recycled. Developers can use this new server support function to request a recycle if their application ISAPI becomes unstable or enters an unknown state for any reason.

> **Note** To enable recycling after an ISAPI calls *HSE_REQ_REPORT_UNHEALTHY*, health monitoring should be turned on.

When calling *HSE_REQ_REPORT_UNHEALTHY*, the developer can also pass a string representing the reason why the ISAPI is calling *HSE_REQ_REPORT_UNHEALTHY*. This string is then added to the event that the worker process publishes to the Application event log.

Custom Errors

ISAPI developers no longer need to generate their own error messages. Instead, they can plug in to the custom error support built into IIS through a new server support function named *HSE_REQ_SEND_CUSTOM_ERROR*.

Unicode ISAPI

Unicode becomes more and more important in a global economy. Because of the non-Unicode structure of the HTTP protocol, IIS 5.0 limits the developer to the system code page. With UTF-8 encoded URLs, Unicode becomes possible. IIS 6.0 allows customers to get to server variables in Unicode and adds two new server support functions to allow developers to obtain the Unicode representation of a URL. International customers with multilanguage sites benefit from this feature and from an improved development experience.

COM+ Services in ASP

In IIS 4.0 and 5.0, ASP applications are able to use COM+ services by configuring the application's Web Application Manager (WAM) object in the COM+ configuration store to use a set of services. This is because that COM+ services were developed to be used in conjunction with COM components. In IIS 6.0, the IIS and COM+ teams have separated the COM+ services from the components and allowed ASP applications to use a set of COM+ services.

In addition to the services available in COM+ in Windows 2000, a new service called *Fusion* has been added and is supported in ASP. Fusion allows an ASP application to use a specified version of a system run-time DLL or classic COM component. Fusion allows an application developer to specify exact versions of system run-time libraries and classic COM components that work with the developer's application. When the application is loaded and running, it will always receive these versions of the run-time libraries and COM components. Previously, applications had to use whatever version of the system run-time DLL was installed on the system. This could present problems if a newer version were installed and had changed functionality in some way.

Additional COM+ features include the following:

- COM+ partitions allow an administrator to define a different configuration of a single COM+ application for different users. This configuration includes security and versioning information. For more information about COM+ partitions, consult the COM+ documentation.

- When enabled, the COM+ tracker allows administrators to monitor what code is running within the ASP session and when. This information is extremely helpful to debug ASP applications. For more information about the COM+ tracker, consult the COM+ documentation.

■   ASP, through COM+, allows developers to determine which thread-ing model to use when executing the pages in an application. By default, ASP uses the Single Threaded Apartment. However, if the application uses poolable objects, it can be run in the Multi-Threaded Apartment.

Platform Improvements

In addition to the features just described, IIS 6.0 has made a number of improvements to the platform overall. These features make IIS a more compel-ling Web application platform.

64-Bit Support

The complete Windows Server 2003 family code base is compiled for 32-bit and 64-bit platforms. Customers who demand highly scalable applications can take advantage of an operating system that runs and is supported on these two plat-forms.

IPv6.0 Support

Internet Protocol version 6.0 (IPv6.0) is the next-generation IP protocol for the Internet. The Windows Server 2003 family now implements a production-ready IPv6.0 stack. On servers where the IPv6.0 protocol stack is installed, IIS 6.0 will automatically support handling HTTP requests that arrive over IPv6.0.

Granular Compression

On a congested network, it's useful to compress responses. In IIS 5.0, compres-sion was an ISAPI filter and could be enabled only for the entire server. IIS 6.0 allows a much more granular (file-level) configuration.

Quality of Service

Quality of service (QoS) ensures that particular components of the Web server, or specific content served by that server, don't take over all server resources, such as memory and CPU cycles. It allows the administrator to control the resources being used by particular sites, application pools, the WWW service as a whole, and others. QoS also ensures a certain quality of service that other ser-vices, sites, and applications on the system receive. It does this by limiting the resources consumed by particular Web sites and applications or by the WWW service itself. In IIS 6.0, QoS takes the form of the following features:

- Connection limits

- Connection timeouts

- Application pool queue length limits

- Bandwidth throttling

- Process accounting

- Memory-based recycling

Logging Improvements

Logging improvements in IIS 6.0 include the following:

- **UTF-8 logging support.**   With additional Unicode and UTF-8 support, IIS 6.0 now supports writing log files in UTF-8 instead of just ASCII (or the local code page).

- **Binary logging.**   Binary logging allows multiple sites to write to a single log file in a binary, nonformatted manner. This new logging format will offer improved performance over current text-based—World Wide Web Consortium (W3C), IIS, and National Center for Supercomputing Applications (NCSA)—logging formats because the data doesn't have to be formatted in any specific manner.

Additionally, binary logging offers scalability benefits as a result of the dramatic reduction in the number of log file buffers needed to maintain logs for tens of thousands of sites. Tools can then be used to postprocess the log file to extract the log entries. Even homegrown tools can be written to process binary log files because the format of the log entries and file will be published.

IIS 6.0 also supports the ability to log HTTP substatus codes in W3C and binary logging formats. Substatus codes are often helpful in debugging or troubleshooting because IIS returns specific substatus codes for specific types of problems. For example, if a request cannot be served because the application needed has not been unlocked (for example, ASP by default on clean installations), the client will get a generic 404 error code. IIS actually generates a 404.2, which will now be logged to W3C and binary log files.

File Transfer Protocol

Traditionally, ISP/ASP customers have used File Transfer Protocol (FTP) to upload their Web content because of its easy availability and wide adoption. IIS 6.0 allows the isolation of users into their own directories, thus preventing users from viewing or overwriting other users' Web content. The user's top-level directory appears as the root of the FTP service, thus restricting access by disallowing further navigation up the directory tree. Within the user's specific site, the user has the ability to create, modify, or delete files and folders. The FTP implementation is architected across an arbitrary number of front-end and back-end servers, which increases reliability and availability. FTP can be easily scaled based on the addition of virtual directories and servers without affecting the end users.

PASV FTP requires the server to open a data port for the client to make a second connection. This connection is separate from the typical port 21 that's used for the FTP control channel. The port range used for PASV connections is now configurable with IIS 6.0. This feature can reduce the attack surface of IIS 6.0 FTP servers by allowing administrators to have more granular control over the port ranges that are exposed over the Internet.

Improved Patch Management

Windows Server 2003 has greatly improved patch management by offering the following new features:

- **No service interruption while installing patches.**   The new IIS 6.0 architecture includes worker process recycling, which means that an administrator can easily install most IIS hot fixes and most new worker process DLLs without any interruption of service.

- **Auto Update.**   Auto Update version 1.0 provides three options:

  ❑   Notify of patch availability the moment the patch is available

  ❑   Download the patch and notify of its availability

  ❑   Download the patch and install it at a time previously scheduled by the administrator

- **Windows Update Corporate Edition.**   Many IT departments do not allow users to install security patches and other Windows Update packages unless they have been tested in a standard operating environment. Windows Update now lets users run quality assurance tests on patches required by the organization. Once patches have passed the specified tests, they can be placed on the corporate Windows Update server, behind the firewall, where all machines inside the firewall can then pick up the patch.

- **Resource-free DLLs.** Windows has now separated localization resources from the actual implementation. This has improved Microsoft's ability to quickly design fixes for 30 languages.

For More Information

See the following resources for further information:

- What's New in Internet Information Services 6.0 at *http:// www.microsoft.com/windowsserver2003/evaluation/overview/technologies/iis.mspx*

- What's New in Security at *http://www.microsoft.com/ windowsserver2003/evaluation/overview/technologies/security.mspx*

- Technical Overview of Security at *http://www.microsoft.com/ windowsserver2003/techinfo/overview/security.mspx*

- Introducing the ".NET" in the Windows .NET Server Family at *http:// www.microsoft.com/windowsserver2003/evaluation/overview/dotnet/dotnet.mspx*

- Windows 2000 Web and Application Services at *http:// www.microsoft.com/windows2000/technologies/web/*

9

Application Services

The Microsoft Windows Server 2003 family builds on the core strengths of the Windows family of operating systems—security, manageability, reliability, availability, and scalability. Advances in Windows Server 2003 provide many benefits for developing applications, resulting in lower total cost of ownership (TCO) and better performance:

- **Simplified integration and interoperability.** Easily connect with partners and customers, protect and extend existing infrastructure, and build dynamic applications.

- **Improved developer productivity.** Get products to market faster, develop applications that are on time and on budget, and take advantage of quicker and easier build cycles.

- **Increased enterprise efficiency.** Meet customer demands with lowest TCO, improve productivity by using fewer people with better results, and build high-performance applications.

This chapter provides an overview of benefits, new features, and improvements for application services in Windows Server 2003.

Simplified Integration and Interoperability

As the foundation of Microsoft .NET–connected technologies, Windows Server 2003 delivers a revolutionary application environment to build, deploy, and run XML Web services. Integrating support for XML Web services enables applications to take advantage of the loosely coupled principles of Internet computing:

- **Native XML Web services support.**   Windows Server 2003 offers native support for XML Web service standards, including XML; SOAP; Universal Description, Discovery, and Integration (UDDI); and Web Services Description Language (WSDL).

- **Enterprise UDDI.**   Windows Server 2003 includes Enterprise UDDI Services, a dynamic and flexible infrastructure for XML Web services. This service enables companies to run their own internal UDDI services for intranet or extranet use. Developers can easily and quickly find and reuse the Web services available within the organization. IT administrators can catalog and manage the programmable resources in their network. With UDDI Services, companies can build and deploy smarter, more reliable applications.

- **Support for existing services.**   Because XML Web services are deeply integrated into Windows Server 2003, existing services such as COM+ and Microsoft Message Queuing (MSMQ) can readily take advantage of them. Administrators can allow existing COM+ applications to be called using XML/SOAP by simply checking a configuration box. MSMQ can also talk to SOAP and XML as a native format to allow loosely coupled applications to interoperate with a broad range of systems.

- **Federation infrastructure.**   XML Web services deliver the foundation and architecture for application integration. Federation infrastructure is fundamentally about enabling servers and services to interoperate across trust boundaries.

Improved Developer Productivity

The Windows Server 2003 application environment improves the productivity of developers by providing a complete set of integrated application services and industry-leading tool support:

- **Microsoft .NET Framework.**   The .NET Framework incorporates the common language runtime and a unified set of class libraries that include Windows Forms, Microsoft ADO.NET, and Microsoft ASP.NET.

  The .NET Framework provides a fully managed, protected, and feature-rich application execution environment; simplified development and deployment; and seamless integration with a wide variety of programming languages. By integrating the .NET Framework into the Windows Server 2003 application development environment, developers are freed from writing plumbing code and can instead focus their efforts on delivering real business value.

The .NET Framework—which Microsoft Windows XP, Windows 2000 Server and Windows 2000 Professional, Windows 98, Windows Me, and Windows NT 4 all support—lets developers create great Web applications with the help of ASP.NET and other technologies. It can also help them build the same applications they design and develop today. The .NET Framework provides deep cross-programming language integration that boosts productivity by enabling developers to extend one programming language's components within another language by way of cross-language inheritance, debugging, and error handling.

Windows Server 2003 provides the richest set of services available with any development platform, including comprehensive data access, integrated security, interactive user interfaces, a mature component object model, transaction processing monitors, and world-class queuing.

- **ASP.NET: simple Web service creation.**   Using the ASP.NET XML Web services features, developers can write their business logic, and the ASP.NET infrastructure will be responsible for delivering that service via SOAP and other public protocols.

- **Separation of code from content.**   The .NET Framework enables developers and content creators to work in parallel by keeping content separate from application code.

- **Industry-leading tools.**   Microsoft Visual Studio .NET provides an integrated multilanguage tool for building Web applications and XML Web services.

- **Reusable code.**   ASP.NET provides an intelligent architecture that's easy to learn and that allows for improved code reuse.

- **Automatic memory management.**   The .NET Framework runs in the common language runtime, which is a garbage-collected environment. Garbage collection frees applications that are using .NET Framework objects from the need to explicitly destroy those objects, reducing common programming errors dramatically.

- **Server-side Web controls.** The new ASP.NET functionality increases productivity by encapsulating complex interactions in server-side components. Developers can rapidly build scalable Web applications that can service multiple-user interface devices. Web controls are compiled and run on the server for maximum performance and can be inherited and extended for even more functionality.

Increased Enterprise Efficiency

Applications developed in the Windows Server 2003 environment are more responsive and available than those developed in earlier versions of Windows, and because the environment can be managed by fewer people than before, it will deliver lower TCO with better performance, improved scalability and reliability, and more robust security. In addition, Windows Server 2003 eases the burden on IT administrators by making it easier to deploy and manage applications:

- **ASP.NET: integrated with Internet Information Services (IIS) 6.0.** ASP.NET is integrated with the IIS 6.0 process model and leverages support for multiple application pools. This means that individual ASP.NET applications are isolated and talk directly to the kernel-mode HTTP listener. This leads to a reduced number of process hops and allows ASP.NET applications to leverage kernel-mode file caching.

- **ASP.NET: advanced compilation.** The .NET Framework advanced compilation provides increased performance by compiling pages instead of interpreting them. It supports both precompiled applications and on-the-fly-compiled applications. ASP.NET leverages more advanced threading models, which allow it to perform asynchronous I/O, leading to improved performance and scalability. This eliminates the need to convert server-side code before execution and therefore conserves server resources, increasing server performance and scalability.

- **ASP.NET: intelligent caching.** The ASP.NET programming model provides a cache API that enables programmers to activate caching services to improve performance. An output cache saves completely rendered pages, and a fragment cache stores partial pages. Classes are provided so that applications, HTTP modules, and request handlers can store arbitrary objects in the cache as needed.

- **Garbage-collected environment.** The garbage collector in the common language runtime provides an efficient environment for memory management in Web server scenarios. It avoids heap fragmentation issues by using a classic allocation/free model.

Improved Scalability and Reliability

Here are some of the key scalability and reliability features that benefit developers and IT professionals in an application environment:

- **Asynchronous support.** The .NET Framework deeply integrates two asynchronous communication technologies for scalability and reliability: SOAP and MSMQ. This allows developers to build applications that are robust and can handle offline scenarios.

- **Web farm session state.** The process-independent, Web farm–compatible session state increases reliability and scalability by storing session state in a process external to the ASP.NET application; thus, the state can survive application crashes and be referenced from other machines in a Web farm.

- **IIS 6.0 fault-resilient process.** IIS 6.0 provides an architecture that delivers enhanced application isolation. Administrators can create multiple application pools and assign applications to those pools to provide isolation. Application pools can be monitored and automatically recycled to ensure application availability.

- **ADO.NET.** ADO.NET uses a nonpersistent connection and intelligent handling of state. ADO.NET actually sends XML messages between the data source and the application, opening and closing the connection as needed. The result is that applications scale much better with ADO.NET, and ADO.NET can work over many different network transports.

Efficient Deployment and Management

No-touch deployment is enabled by enhanced tools such as Windows Installer services and by new tools such as Fusion. Fusion supports side-by-side versioning for DLLs, while its counterpart, Manifest, tells you exactly which DLLs are required. Windows Installer can contain Fusion manifests and can now describe the application that runs side by side, making it easier to deploy reliable applications.

Additional tools that can shorten the deployment process and ensure greater accuracy include Xcopy deployment and IIS edit while running.

Windows Management Instrumentation (WMI) does in hours what formerly took days, using new tools in Visual Studio .NET. Reliability is improved through command-line tools that are freely available for download via the Internet. Applications and services can easily issue events and define variables.

End-to-End Security

Security in Windows Server 2003 is built on top of a single security model anchored by Active Directory. Security enhancements and innovations new to Windows Server 2003 help reduce the attack surface and make Windows authentication and authorization more secure and powerful via a new application security architecture. Protocol transition capability enables any authentication on the front-end Web server to be transitioned to Kerberos at the back end.

Native integration of Microsoft .NET Passport enables authentication and authorization for any customer or consumer and sets the stage for future federation capabilities. When the front-end server trusts the .NET Passport, the .NET Passport is used for user validation and subsequent logon. The .NET Passport credentials can be mapped to Active Directory for consumers and customers.

For More Information

See the following resources for further information:

- Developing Applications for Windows Server 2003 at *http://www.microsoft.com/windowsserver2003/developers/*

- Windows 2000 Web and Application Services at *http://www.microsoft.com/windows2000/technologies/web/*

- Introducing the ".NET" in the Windows Server 2003 Family at *http://www.microsoft.com/windowsserver2003/evaluation/overview/dotnet/dotnet.mspx*

10

Windows Media Services

Microsoft Windows Media Services 9 Series is the server component of the Windows Media 9 Series platform, and it works in conjunction with Windows Media Encoder and Windows Media Player to deliver audio and video content to clients over the Internet or an intranet. These clients might be other computers or devices that play back the content using a player, such as Windows Media Player, or they might be other computers running Windows Media Services (called *Windows Media servers*) that are providing proxy services, caching data, or redistributing content. Clients can also be custom applications that have been developed by using the Windows Media Software Development Kit (SDK).

Windows Media Services can deliver a live stream or preexisting content, such as a digital media file. If you are planning to stream live content, you'll configure a broadcast publishing point and then connect to encoding software, such as Windows Media Encoder, that is capable of compressing a live stream into a format supported by the server. You can also stream preexisting content that has been encoded by Windows Media Encoder, Microsoft Producer for PowerPoint 2002, Windows Movie Maker, Windows Media Player, or many other third-party encoding programs. You stream preexisting content from an on-demand publishing point. Sample broadcast and on-demand publishing points are provided by default.

This chapter introduces you to the features of Windows Media 9 Series in Windows Server 2003. In it, you learn about Fast Streaming, dynamic content delivery, and more.

Fast Streaming

Fast Streaming refers to a set of features in Windows Media Services that significantly improves the quality of the streaming experience. Fast Streaming is based on the latest technologies and delivers compelling audio and video content over a variety of networks—even when network connections are unreliable. Fast Streaming is possible because of the following four components:

- Fast Start
- Fast Cache
- Fast Recovery
- Fast Reconnect

Fast Start

Fast Start provides an instant-on playback experience with no buffering delay, whether playing a single piece of content or switching between on-demand clips or broadcast channels.

Before it can start playing content, Windows Media Player must buffer a certain amount of data. When streaming to clients who use Windows Media Player for Windows XP or a later version of the player, you can use Fast Start to provide data directly to the buffer at speeds higher than the bit rate of the content requested. This lets users start receiving content more quickly. After the initial buffer requirement is fulfilled, on-demand and broadcast content streams at the bit rate defined by the content stream.

Using Fast Start provides a better experience for users when playing back your content. Users can fast-forward and rewind content without additional delay and rebuffering. A player that connects through broadband networks starts playing the content more quickly, making the experience much more like viewing a television program or listening to a radio broadcast. Content delivered from your server by using server-side playlists switches smoothly and seamlessly between content items. Additionally, the buffering of data makes the player resistant to playback errors resulting from lost packets or other network issues.

Fast Cache

Fast Cache provides an always-on playback experience by streaming content to the Windows Media Player cache as fast as the network will allow, reducing the likelihood of an interruption in play as a result of network issues.

For example, using Fast Cache, the server can transmit a 128-kilobits-per-second (Kbps) stream at 700 Kbps. The stream is still rendered in Windows Media Player at the specified data rate, but the client is able to buffer a much larger portion of the content before rendering it. This allows the client to handle variable network conditions without a perceptible impact on the playback quality of either on-demand or broadcast content. This capability is useful in the following situations:

- The available network bandwidth of the client exceeds the required bandwidth of the content—for example, clients that use a cable modem, a DSL connection, or a corporate intranet.

- The network connectivity is intermittent or has high latency—for example, wireless networks.

- The quality of the content received is of paramount importance—for example, businesses that provide pay-per-view movies.

Fast Recovery

Fast Recovery works in conjunction with Forward Error Correction (FEC) to provide redundant packets of information to clients that are using wireless connections. Providing redundant packets ensures that no data is lost as a result of connectivity disruptions. Because of FEC, Windows Media Player can usually recover lost or damaged data packets without having to request that the data be re-sent by the Windows Media server.

In environments that are subject to latency problems, such as satellite networks and other wireless networks, this process of receiving data is much more efficient. And it's easy to specify the amount of error correction data transmitted per span of data sent using the Windows Media Services user interface.

Fast Reconnect

Fast Reconnect automatically restores live or on-demand player-to-server and server-to-server connections if disconnected during a broadcast. This ensures an uninterrupted viewing experience.

If the client was connected to an on-demand publishing point, the client restarts playback at the point at which the connection was lost by synchronizing itself with the content timeline. If the content includes video, the client estimates the approximate video frame at which the connection was lost. If the content is indexed, this estimate is more accurate. If the client is connected to a broadcast publishing point, the client reconnects to the broadcast in progress. Depending on the content, the user might experience a gap in the broadcast.

Fast Reconnect can be used with clients that connect through any of the default connection protocols: Microsoft Media Server (MMS), Hypertext Transfer Protocol (HTTP), and Real Time Streaming Protocol (RTSP). Fast Reconnect is available for both broadcast and on-demand streaming.

Dynamic Content Delivery

With Windows Media Services 9 Series, you can customize the distribution of your content using server-side playlists and advertisements. Once you've customized your content, it's easy to distribute it to the edge of the Internet by stringing servers together using the latest protocols and cache/proxy solutions.

Server-Side Playlists

The Windows Media server-side playlist is based on the Synchronized Multimedia Integration Language (SMIL) 2.0 standard. It's a robust mechanism for assembling content for playback on personal computers and portable devices. Both broadcast and on-demand publishing points can stream content from a playlist that executes on the server. A server-side playlist can contain live or preexisting content and can be delivered using unicast or multicast transmission.

Windows Media Services fully supports the application of business rules and industry regulations for playlists, including compliance with Recording Industry Association of America (RIAA) and Digital Millennium Copyright Act (DMCA) guidelines.

Here are a few examples of what you can do with server-side playlists:

- Stream an infinite sequence of content, repeat content, or set durations for content.

- Stream content to devices that don't support client-side playlists, such as some handheld personal computers and set-top boxes.

- Insert advertisements, or wrap site branding or sponsor information around your content.

- Interrupt content for ads or emergency announcements.

- Use ASP or CGI scripts to dynamically display ads with each pass through the playlist.

- Switch between live and stored streams with no noticeable delay on the client side.

- Dynamically change and save playlists, or build playlists on the fly based on user profiles or preferences.

- Stream content from a variety of sources, including Windows Media Encoder or another server.

- Nest playlists within one another.

Advertisements

Streaming advertisements is a great way to generate revenue for your Web site. Windows Media Services integrates with third-party ad servers to enable you to use advertising in the following ways:

- Place ads at the beginning and end of your playlist, or at any point within the playlist.

- Dynamically change the ads that you show based on national, regional, local, or other demographic information.

- Personalize ads based on information you gather from cookies or other data gathering tools.

- Overlay ads to comply with rebroadcast requirements, such as those outlined by the American Federation of Television and Radio Artists (AFTRA).

- Log ad data, such as number of ads played in a particular broadcast or number of users who watched the entire ad.

Edge Delivery

To ensure that your content gets where it needs to go when it needs to be there, Windows Media Services provides the following features:

- New cache/proxy support, which enables developers to easily build streaming cache/proxy solutions and control the customization and extension of native cache and proxy policies. Cache/proxy solutions conserve network bandwidth, decrease network-imposed latency, and decrease the load on Windows Media origin servers.

- Improved protocol support between servers, including RTSP and HTTP. Support for new client protocols and standards includes RTSP, HTTP version 1.1, Internet Group Management Protocol (IGMP) version 6, and IP version 6.

- Flexible distribution between servers using User Datagram Protocol/ Transmission Control Protocol (UDP/TCP).

- Interoperability with Windows Media Services version 4.1 for streaming in mixed environments.

Industrial Strength

Windows Media Services 9 Series is more scalable, reliable, and secure than ever, enabling streaming for the largest enterprises and content delivery networks:

- **Built-in security.**   Industrial-strength security is part of Windows Media Services. Authentication and authorization mechanisms ensure secure transfer of data from encoder to server, server to server, and client to server. You'll also find support for HTTP Digest and for digital rights management that ensures on-the-wire and persistent client-side security.

- **Real-time monitoring.**   Real-time monitoring has been improved significantly. Whether you use Windows Performance Monitor or a Simple Network Management Protocol (SNMP) console to keep track of your server's performance, information is available, thanks to 72 performance and SNMP counters that are installed automatically.

- **Administration.**   Administering Windows Media Services has never been easier. With three different administration tools, you can administer your Windows Media Server in virtually any environment:

   ❑ The Windows Media Services snap-in for Microsoft Management Console (MMC) is a brand-new full-featured interface that has been completely redesigned to simplify your server administration tasks. And new wizards ease setup and configuration of common management activities.

   ❑ Windows Media Services Administrator for the Web, an HTML 3.2–based interface, is a brand-new way to administer your server when you're not in the office or when you want to administer Windows Media Services through a firewall or a low-bandwidth network.

   ❑ The command line lets you use scripts to administer your Windows Media server.

Extensible Platform

Windows Media Services is an open platform exposing more than 500 properties and methods on nearly 60 interfaces. You can use the rich set of interfaces to programmatically configure a Windows Media server, monitor both the server and clients connected to it, or access all logging statistics.

Customize the functionality of your Windows Media server using installed plug-ins, or create your own. The Windows Media Services SDK now provides interfaces that let you create the following types of plug-ins:

- Authentication
- Cache/proxy
- Control protocol
- Data writer
- Data source
- Event notification and authorization
- Logging
- Media parser
- Playlist parser

The newly expanded Windows Media Services SDK provides full developer support for all of the interfaces, properties, and methods just listed and is scenario-based. Use C, Visual C++, Visual C#, Visual Basic, Visual Basic Scripting Edition (VBScript), Microsoft JScript, and other scripting languages to create your custom applications.

For More Information

See the following resources for more information:

- Introducing the Windows Server 2003 Family at *http://www.microsoft.com/windowsserver2003/evaluation/overview/family.mspx*
- Windows Media 9 Series at *http://www.microsoft.com/windows/windowsmedia/*
- Upgrading to Windows Media Services 9 Series at *http://www.microsoft.com/windows/windowsmedia/9series/server.asp*

- Compare the Editions of Windows Server 2003 at *http://www.microsoft.com/windowsserver2003/evaluation/features/compareeditions.mspx*

- Introducing the ".NET" in the Windows Server 2003 Family at *http://www.microsoft.com/windowsserver2003/evaluation/overview/dot-net/dotnet.mspx*

- Windows 2000 Streaming Media Services at *http://www.microsoft.com/windows2000/technologies/other/default.asp#section2*

11

File Services

Microsoft Windows Server technologies deliver low total cost of ownership (TCO) and reliable file services that are essential to enterprise computing infrastructures. Windows Server 2003 delivers an exciting set of customer-focused improvements in file services, especially for businesses using Windows NT Server 4.0 to provide file services. This chapter discusses improvements in Windows Server 2003 file services, describing core infrastructure file service innovations, new features, and improved management tools that lower the cost associated with managing file servers.

Microsoft built important improvements to file services in the Windows Server 2003 product family, most of which are the result of customer feedback. These improvements focus on three key areas:

- **Improved infrastructure services.** Improved infrastructure services provide more flexibility with storage options and file delivery. As new storage topologies and applications have become more popular in the past five years (think "storage area networks"), it has been a struggle to get different components of a solution to work well together. New standardized infrastructure services in Windows Server 2003 help streamline the development of core server management and file services.

- **Enhanced end user experience.** Windows Server 2003, used in conjunction with Microsoft Windows XP, delivers seamless access to network data and files. It also strengthens the safety net for end users who save files on network shares, even files from non–Windows XP clients.

- **Lower TCO.** Improved manageability in Windows Server 2003 leads to a lower total cost of ownership. This is accomplished by using improved Web-based management tools, as well as more extensive command-line tools that enable the use of scripts to manage remote or local file servers.

This chapter describes the many new file service features in Windows Server 2003. You learn about local storage improvements, Virtual Disk Service, Volume Shadow Copy Service, and much more. This chapter starts with the benefits to file systems in Windows Server 2003.

File Service Benefits

The Windows Server 2003 family provides the following file service benefits:

- **Increased dependability.** Windows Server 2003 ensures higher reliability with new features such as Automated System Recovery (ASR), making it easier to recover your system, back up your files, and maintain maximum availability.

- **Greater productivity.** Windows Server 2003 delivers an enhanced file system infrastructure, making it easier to use, secure, and store files and other essential resources. Employees benefit by always being able to access the resources they need or quickly recover files without costly assistance from a help desk.

- **Enhanced connectivity.** Windows Server 2003 provides new and enhanced features such as remote document sharing, improving connectivity within and across organizations.

New File Service Features

The Windows Server 2003 family provides many enhancements to the file system infrastructure. The features and descriptions in the following list provide a general overview of what's new and improved in File Services for Windows Server 2003:

- **Remote document sharing (WebDAV).** A new feature in Windows Server 2003, remote document sharing increases connectivity to your business through the WebDAV redirector. With the WebDAV redirector, clients can access files in Web repositories through file system calls.

- **Automated System Recovery (ASR).**   A new feature in Windows Server 2003, ASR improves productivity by enabling one-step restoration of operating system, system state, and hardware configuration in disaster recovery situations.

- **Command-line interface.**   Administrators gain powerful new command-line utilities for many disk management tasks in Windows Server 2003, including performing various disk and RAID configurations, managing shadow copies, and tuning the file system.

- **GUID partition table.**   Windows XP, 64-Bit Edition, and the 64-bit versions of Windows Server 2003, Enterprise Edition and Datacenter Edition, support a new disk partitioning style, the GUID partition table (GPT). In contrast with master boot record (MBR) partitioned disks, data critical to platform operation is located in partitions instead of in unpartitioned or hidden sectors. In addition, GPT partitioned disks have redundant primary and backup partition tables for improved partition data structure integrity.

- **Higher-performance defragmentation tool.**   The Windows Defragmenter tool can increase disk availability and performance by optimizing files on a volume. Defragmentation in Windows Server 2003 is faster and more efficient than it was in Windows 2000. In addition, it supports online defragmentation of the Master File Table (MFT) and can defragment NTFS volumes of any cluster size.

- **Content indexing.**   Content indexing is a fast, easy, and secure way for users to search for information locally or on the network. Users can search in files in different formats and languages, either through the Search command on the Start menu or through HTML pages that they view in a browser.

- **Enhanced Distributed File System.**   Distributed File System (DFS) helps businesses deliver highly available file services at a low total cost of ownership. DFS can be used to create one logical file system out of multiple physical systems, making your environment easier for users to use and more efficient in terms of equipment utilization. With DFS, you can create a single directory tree that includes multiple file servers and file shares in a group, a division, or an enterprise, allowing users to easily find files or folders distributed across the network. With the Active Directory directory service, DFS shares can also be published as Volume Objects and administration can be delegated. In Windows Server 2003, DFS now offers a closest-site selection capability, wherein DFS uses Active Directory site metrics to route a client to the closest available file server for a given path. Plus, a single Windows Server 2003 system can host multiple DFS roots.

- **DFS File Replication Services.** File Replication Services (FRS) enables businesses to achieve a low TCO, just as with DFS, by ensuring that data stays synchronized. FRS works in conjunction with DFS by replicating data on file shares, automatically maintaining synchronization among copies across multiple servers. A new feature in Windows Server 2003, the DFS MMC UI allows configuration of replication topologies. The FRS service itself also has new features—compression of replication traffic and the ability to damp unnecessary replication traffic.

- **Enhanced Encrypting File System.** Windows Server 2003 strengthens the security of your file services with enhanced Encrypting File System (EFS). EFS complements other access controls, providing an added level of protection for your data. EFS runs as an integrated system service, making it easy to manage, difficult to attack, and transparent to use.

- **New support for antivirus products.** Protecting your resources from malicious code delivered by viruses is key to providing secure and reliable file services. Windows Server 2003 enhances the already robust antivirus support for Windows Server by providing new kernel APIs that enable higher performance and reliability from third-party antivirus products. In addition, there is now a Windows Hardware Quality Lab (WHQL) test suite and a driver certification process for antivirus file-system filters.

- **Increased CHKDSK performance.** Because the NTFS file system has always been a true journaled file system, CHKDSK operations are rarely required. In the unlikely event that a disk does need to be checked (less than 1 percent of unplanned outages require such checking), CHKDSK performs twice as fast as it did in Windows 2000.

Improved File System Infrastructure

The Virtual Disk and Volume Shadow Copy services are key elements of the improved file system infrastructure in Windows Server 2003.

Virtual Disk Service

Whereas the Volume Shadow Copy service, described in the next section, provides an important building block for managing data on disks, the Virtual Disk service (VDS) provides an important new set of APIs for managing the disks themselves.

In Windows 2000, each storage area network (SAN) hardware vendor provided its own proprietary set of APIs for managing its hardware. This makes it challenging to develop uniform SAN-management software. Windows Server 2003 addresses this issue with VDS. VDS implements a single uniform interface for managing disks. Each hardware vendor writes a VDS provider that translates the general-purpose VDS APIs into specific instructions for its hardware. With this abstraction layer provided by VDS, Windows Server 2003 gives customers a more robust set of solutions, including greater flexibility for making long-term investment decisions regarding SANs and other storage options.

Management applications no longer need to take into account the specific hardware being targeted. Instead, by developing applications that target VDS, the next generation of Windows disk management applications will be able to manage any hardware that has a VDS provider.

There is an immediate benefit from the VDS architecture: Microsoft has implemented VDS providers for basic and dynamic disks. This brings functionality to basic disks, such as online growth, that formerly applied only to dynamic disks. See Figure 11-1 for an illustration of the Virtual Disk service.

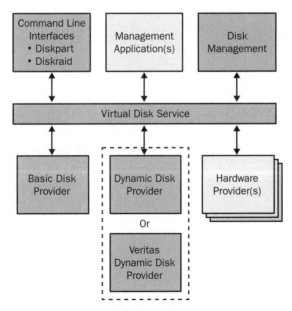

Figure 11-1   Virtual Disk service.

Volume Shadow Copy Service

The Volume Shadow Copy service is a general infrastructure for creating point-in-time copies of data on a volume. The goal of Volume Shadow Copy is to provide an efficient, robust, and useful mechanism for the next generation of data management applications.

Shadow Copy Restore, described later in this chapter, is the most visible application of Volume Shadow Copy in Windows Server 2003. Another set of applications that use Volume Shadow Copy is backup applications. Using Windows 2000 Server, you had to either stop activity on your server during the backup process or live with the side effects of an online backup: inconsistent data and open files that could not be backed up. With Windows Server 2003, you get the best of both worlds: you are able to do an online backup that results in consistent data, and you don't have to worry about open files.

Volume Shadow Copy facilitates online backups that result in consistent data by formalizing the relationship among three important entities in the data management process:

- **Requestors.**   These are applications, such as backup applications, that perform storage management tasks.

- **Writers.**   These are applications that generate data.

- **Providers.**   This is hardware or software that is able to create a point-in-time copy of a disk.

Figure 11-2 shows how requestors, writers, and providers interact.

> **Note**   The built-in Windows shadow copy provider uses a *copy-on-write* algorithm to provide shadow copies in the most space-efficient way possible. For example, if you have 3 GB of data on a volume, Windows Server 2003 does not copy all 3 GB when you create a shadow copy. Instead, Windows Server 2003 simply makes copies of the original data on the volume as applications make changes.

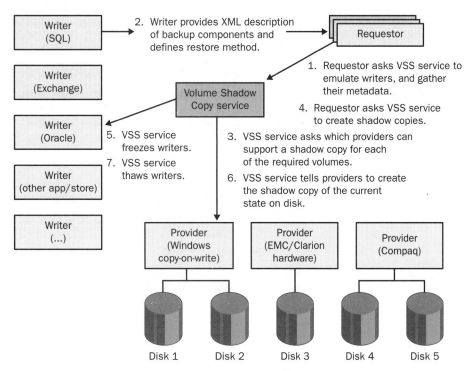

Figure 11-2   Volume Shadow Copy interacts with requesters, writers, and providers.

Distributed File System

Windows Server 2003 contains improvements to the Distributed File System (DFS). DFS is a powerful feature for managing federated file servers. It provides the following capabilities:

■   **Service layer.**   DFS provides a service layer by separating the names that clients use to access files on the network from the names of the servers that actually host the files.

■   **Scalability.**   DFS improves scalability by letting you balance the client workload among multiple servers.

■   **Reliability.**   DFS improves reliability by transparently redirecting client requests to a different server in the event of a failure. DFS uses the File Replication service (FRS) to automatically synchronize replicas.

■ **DFS roots and DFS junctions.** The fundamental concepts of DFS are DFS roots and DFS junctions:

❑ A DFS root is a server, or a set of servers, that clients go to first when trying to access a file.

❑ A DFS junction is a reference from the DFS root to the server, or set of servers (replicas), that can handle the file request.

Windows Server 2003 includes an important reliability enhancement for DFS—the capability of a single server to host multiple DFS roots. In Windows 2000, you could not have multiple DFS roots on a single server. As a consequence, you could have at most one DFS root in a server cluster. If you had more than one DFS root in the cluster, the system would throw an exception if cluster failover required one of the cluster nodes to host both DFS roots at the same time. Because this restriction has been removed in Windows Server 2003, you can use clustering to efficiently improve the reliability of your DFS roots.

Windows Server 2003 improves the manageability of DFS by allowing delegation of administration. In Windows 2000, an administrator for any part of the DFS namespace needs to be an administrator for the entire DFS namespace. This situation presents problems for large corporations that want to build a companywide DFS namespace because Windows 2000 offers no way to assign permissions to administrators in a subsidiary for managing only the DFS namespace affecting that subsidiary.

In Windows Server 2003Server 2003, you can give a principal the rights to administer a specific portion of the DFS namespace.

Windows Server 2003 also improves the behavior of DFS when you set up replicas that span multiple sites. In Windows 2000, DFS would give priority to replicas within the same site as the client, and if no replicas were within the same site, DFS would pick any available replica at any other site for the client's request. This is not the most efficient algorithm.

For example, if your company has sites in Redmond, Washington; Silicon Valley; and Tasmania, and the replica at the Silicon Valley site goes down, DFS in Windows 2000 will send your requests, with equal probability, to either Redmond or Tasmania. Windows Server 2003, on the other hand, uses the site-costing information in Active Directory to choose from among off-site replicas to satisfy a client request. In this example, DFS would see from Active Directory that it is more expensive to communicate from Silicon Valley to Tasmania than from Silicon Valley to Redmond, and it would correspondingly redirect the Silicon Valley client to the Redmond replica.

Other File Serving Improvements

Windows Server 2003 contains many other file serving improvements:

- Improved Common Internet File System (CIFS) throughput (especially on multiprocessor servers)

- Increased scalability for DFS (including a reduced memory footprint and faster startup/configuration)

- Better diagnostic tools for FRS

- Better disk space and network bandwidth management for FRS

Enhanced End User Experience

Shadow Copy Restore and improvements to Offline Files and WebDAV Redirector combine to provide an enhanced user experience.

Shadow Copy Restore

Studies have shown that human error causes more than one-third of all data loss. Windows Server 2003 includes a new feature to address this problem: shadow copies.

A shadow copy is a previous version of a file. Using shadow copies, a Windows. NET Server 2003–based file server will efficiently and transparently maintain a set of previous versions of all files on the file server. Clients use a separate add-on program, which is included on the Windows Server 2003 CD and integrates seamlessly with the client machine, to view the previous versions.

Shadow copies are a low-cost way to recover files from many accidents caused by human error, such as inadvertent editing, corruption, and deletion.

While shadow copies cannot replace your current backup solution—for example, shadow copies cannot protect you from data loss resulting from media failures—shadow copies should reduce the number of times you need to restore data from tape.

Improvements to Offline Files

Windows Server 2003, in conjunction with changes made to the Windows XP client, presents several improvements for file serving. On the client side, Windows XP includes several improvements to Offline Files. This feature, introduced in

Windows 2000, lets client machines cache copies of network files and folders on local machines.

There are two types of caching—caching for documents and caching for programs. The server administrator chooses the type of caching used for a network file share:

- When the client is caching documents, the operating system uses the copy of the document on the file server if the server is available. However, when the file server is not available, Windows XP transparently lets the user work on the cached copy of the document.

- When the client is caching programs and the file server is available, Windows XP simply checks the file server to verify that the cached version of the program is up-to-date. If the program is up-to-date, Windows XP executes the cached copy of the program. This offloads work from the file server to the desktop operating system, improving the scalability of the file server.

Improvements to Offline Files are more robust in Windows XP and Windows Server 2003 than in Windows 2000 for additional reasons. For example, with Windows XP, users can cache files from a DFS namespace—an improvement over Windows 2000. Also, Offline Files in Windows XP works better with the Encrypting File System (EFS).

WebDAV Redirector

The WebDAV Redirector provides an improved file sharing experience on the Windows XP client.

Today you can create Web-based document repositories, and special-purpose Web publishing tools can use the WebDAV protocol to update the documents in those repositories. In Windows XP, the WebDAV Redirector makes those Web repositories accessible to any application. It does this by mapping a drive letter to the WebDAV server. Existing applications can access the files through the new drive letter.

Lower Total Cost of Ownership

IT professionals who are responsible for managing file servers have asked for features that help them deliver services at a reduced cost. Windows Server 2003 includes some important advances that help achieve the objective of lower TCO. These include the following:

■ **Web user interface for server administration.** Windows Server 2003 includes a Web-based management user interface for file servers. You can use this interface to manage your file servers from any browser. This interface allows you to change disk management settings, quota settings, and share settings.

■ **Command-line tools.** In addition to the Web-based interface, Windows Server 2003 adds three important command-line tools for managing local storage:

  ❑ Diskpart.exe manages partitions. It lets you create mirrors and stripe sets, extend volumes, and so on.

  ❑ Fsutil.exe manages advanced NTFS features, such as the USN Journal, hard links, and quotas.

  ❑ Vssadmin.exe manages the Volume Shadow Copy service.

■ **Automated System Recovery.** Another important server management scenario is disaster recovery. Windows Server 2003 includes Automated System Recovery (ASR) to help with disaster recovery scenarios. ASR can help when you are faced with either the physical destruction of your hardware (for example, in an earthquake or a fire) or a catastrophic hardware failure.

In Windows 2000, recovering from a disaster is a long, manual process, which includes

1. Acquiring new hardware

2. Installing a basic version of Windows

3. Manually configuring the storage hardware to match the predisaster configuration

4. Installing your restoration software

5. Restoring the operating system settings

6. Restoring the application settings

7. Restoring the application data

The goal of ASR is to quickly and automatically bring a nonbootable machine to a state in which you can run a restoration program to recover data. ASR will configure the new storage to the same specifications as the predisaster storage; it will also restore the operating system, all applications, and settings. As opposed to the lengthy, manual process faced in recovering from a disaster when using Windows 2000 or an earlier-version Windows operating system, ASR in Windows Server 2003 presents the administrator with an easy solution. The process for recovering a system using ASR in Windows Server 2003 is as follows:

1. Boot from a Windows .NET Server CD, and choose Automated System Recovery.

2. Provide access to the backup medium and a previously prepared ASR floppy disk.

3. Take a long break—you'll come back to a working machine with the operating system and all applications properly configured.

You need to prepare an ASR backup before running this process. An ASR backup is a regular system backup plus the creation of an ASR floppy disk. This disk contains important configuration information about your storage system (for example, the number and size of your partitions), as well as information about how to restore the backup that you just created.

What makes ASR work is a small amount of bootstrap code in the Windows setup program. If you boot from the CD and press the F8 key when prompted, you will enter the ASR bootstrap program. The ASR code in Windows Setup knows how to read the ASR floppy disk to reconfigure the storage system. The ASR version of Windows Setup will then install just enough of the operating system to run a restore program. ASR can then automatically invoke the restore program to restore the rest of the data from your ASR backup.

Microsoft provides a complete ASR solution in Windows Server 2003, which is fully extensible by third-party vendors offering backup solutions.

Better Utilities Improve Availability

Windows Server 2003 contains enhancements to key utilities:

■ **CHKDSK.** Windows Server 2003 includes improvements in CHKDSK performance that began with Windows 2000. Independent testing by eTesting Labs verifies that CHKDSK on Windows Server 2003 is 90 percent faster than on Windows NT Server 4.0 on volumes with millions of files. Beyond these improvements in CHKDSK performance, remember that one of the goals of the NTFS file system is to minimize the number of incidents in which running CHKDSK is required. NTFS is a fully journaled file system: it uses write-ahead logging (the same technique used in most databases) to ensure that its metadata is consistent, even after a crash. CHKDSK is required only when the hardware fails and corrupts the NTFS metadata.

■ **Disk Defragmenter.**   Windows Server 2003 also includes improvements to Disk Defragmenter. Microsoft has improved the defragmentation engine to improve performance. In Windows Server 2003, the disk defragmenter can also defragment the NTFS Master File Table (MFT).

For More Information

Log on to the following Web sites for more information:

■ What's New in File and Print Services for Windows Server 2003 at *http://www.microsoft.com/windowsserver2003/evaluation/overview/technologies/fileandprint.mspx*

■ Introducing the Windows Server 2003 Family at *http://www.microsoft.com/windowsserver2003/evaluation/overview/family.mspx*

■ Windows Server 2003 Family Technical Overviews at *http://www.microsoft.com/windowsserver2003/techinfo/overview/*

■ What's New in Storage Management at *http://www.microsoft.com/windowsserver2003/evaluation/overview/technologies/storage.mspx*

■ Windows 2000 File and Print Services at *http://www.microsoft.com/windows2000/technologies/fileandprint/*

12

Print Services

File and print servers are among the most common types of servers in any size of organization. Microsoft Windows Server 2003 contains enhancements for many of the print features delivered with Microsoft Windows 2000. Microsoft designed these enhancements to ensure enterprise levels of reliability, manageability, security, and agility for print services. This chapter describes the features and benefits provided by print services in Windows Server 2003 and outlines key improvements in print server manageability.

Print Services Benefits

Table 12-1 describes the benefits of the printer enhancements in Windows Server 2003.

Table 12-1   Print Services Benefits

Benefit	Feature
Reliability	Increased reliability with print driver control.
	Performance improvements for spooling on heavily loaded servers.
	Mission-critical applications are highly available and scalable.
	Print cluster driver installation propagates to all nodes automatically.
Best for New Devices	Greater device support—more than 3800 printer devices are supported.
	High-end color printer support (Unidrv color PCL XL minidriver).
	USB 2.0 support.

(continued)

Table 12-1 Print Services Benefits   *(continued)*

Benefit	Feature
Manageability	Enhanced print server setup for clustering.
	Windows Management Instrumentation (WMI) Print Provider.
	More secure Spooler service.
	Universal print driver versioning.
	Kernel-mode driver blocking (on by default).
	Performance improvements for Terminal Server printer redirection.
Internet Enabling	More secure point-and-print for Internet printing.
Availability	Automatic restarting of the Spooler service.
	Customizable to meet individual IT needs.

Print Services Improvements

The Windows Server 2003 family provides many enhancements to the print services. The following list provides a general overview of what's new and improved in print services for Windows Server 2003.

- **Command-line interface.** Windows Server 2003 provides new and expanded command-line functionality for many print management tasks, including extension of printer management and configuration, job and queue control, port management, and driver management.

- **Print cluster support (Enterprise and Datacenter Editions only).** This new feature in Windows Server 2003 improves productivity by making it easier to install printer drivers on server clusters. When a printer driver is installed on a virtual cluster, Windows Server 2003 automatically propagates the driver to all nodes of the cluster.

- **64-bit printing support.** A new feature in Windows Server 2003 is support for 64-bit drivers and applications. *Point-and-print* provides client-server printing support for interoperability of 32-bit to 64-bit clients and servers.

- **Wide range of devices.** Windows Server 2003 improves connectivity, with built-in support for more than 3800 printer drivers.

- **Reliability improvements.** Windows Server 2003 increases the reliability of print servers by providing kernel-mode driver blocking. This gives administrators fine-grain control of driver installation on the server.

- **Active Directory enhancements.** By publishing printers in the Active Directory directory service, you enable users to quickly locate and connect to printers based on criteria such as location, ability to print color, and the speed of the printer.

- **Performance improvements.** Windows Server 2003 improves performance over Windows 2000 by optimizing file spooling (read/write from disk) for management of higher print volumes. Users benefit by getting their documents faster.

- **Plug and Play enhancements.** Windows Server 2003 improves your productivity by recognizing and adapting to hardware configuration changes automatically.

- **Easier printer management.** You can easily monitor the operations of local and remote printers. With System Monitor, you can control counters for a variety of criteria, such as bytes printed per second, job errors, and total pages printed.

- **Increased performance for network printing.** The standard port monitor, Microsoft's primary method for fast and robust printing to network attached printers, has been updated to provide better performance and richer device status.

  Windows Server 2003 also includes wireless (802.1X, Bluetooth) printing support. In addition, print drivers are downloaded automatically when client computers connect to print servers, a benefit that simplifies printing across a network and saves time.

- **Security enhancements.** Two new group policies have been added to provide tighter security control of the print environment. These include a policy to prevent managed clients from connecting to untrusted print servers and a policy that prevents the print spooler from allowing client connections if the server is not providing print services.

- **Broad interoperability.** Using AppleTalk, LPR/LPD, and IPX protocols, Windows print servers can accept jobs from other client operating systems, such as Macintosh, UNIX, Linux, and Novell. Conversely, Windows-based client computers can print to servers running other operating systems.

Print Services Manageability

Key improvements in print server manageability for Windows Server 2003 include

- **Centralized printer configuration.** By providing print services through a Windows print server, administrators can control the availability of print devices by using appropriate change control management, high-availability practices, and so on. Administrators can set default printing behavior to enable users to use the advanced features of print devices without having to understand printer configurations. Additionally, settings such as *duplex by default* represent a cost-saving opportunity for businesses of all sizes.

- **Printer scheduling and access controls.** To manage print device resources, administrators can use printer scheduling and access controls to manage print access, priority, and load distribution. For example, an administrator can create two printers for the same device: configuring one to take print jobs all day and configuring the second printer to accept jobs only during off-peak hours. Large batch print jobs can be set to use the second printer throughout the day (those jobs will simply queue up until they can be printed), with minimal impact on the normal printer requirements of other users.

- **Managing print drivers.** Windows Server 2003 maintains the same blocking functionality for *known-bad* drivers that was introduced with Windows 2000 and adds to that the ability to block known-bad user-mode drivers. A new policy introduced with Windows Server 2003 provides an administrator with the ability to control whether kernel-mode printer drivers can be installed. By default, kernel-mode drivers are set to *disallowed* on Windows Server 2003.

- **Driver distribution.** Windows point-and-print provides seamless distribution of drivers and settings to a wide range of clients. In addition, Windows 2000–based and Windows XP–based clients provide rich support for automatic settings updates, driver version updates, and more.

- **Scripting support.** WMI Print Provider for Windows Server 2003 provides rich scripting support. Printer information can be gathered, manipulated, and used to re-create (or clone) printers and settings on new or existing servers. The Windows Server 2003 Resource Kit contains more information about the Windows Management Instrumentation Command Line (WMIC) console, support, and features. (WMIC is a command-line interface to Windows Management Instrumentation.) Six in-box scripts for command-line/GUI-less management include the following:

- ❑   **Prnqctl.**   Pause, resume, purge, and print test page

- ❑   **Prnport.**   Enumerate, add, and remove tcpmon ports

- ❑   **Prnmngr.**   Add, remove, and list printers and connections

- ❑   **Prnjobs.**   Pause, resume, cancel, and list jobs

- ❑   **Prndrvr.**   Enumerate, add, and remove drivers

- ❑   **Prncnfg.**   Set printer configuration (share, location, name, and so on)

■ **Device support.**   Device support is outstanding in Windows Server 2003. In addition to covering the top Windows 95 drivers, Windows Server 2003 includes additional enterprise printer model drivers and introduces PCL XL color functionality in the core printing engine—Unidrv.

■ **Clustering.**   Installing printers on a cluster is much simpler and faster than ever before with Windows Server 2003. In addition to propagating printer port information, Windows Server 2003 delivers automatic distribution of printer drivers from the cluster spooler resource to all member nodes of the cluster. This reduces new deployment effort by approximately 30 percent. The following are new clustering features in Windows Server 2003:

- ❑   Up to 8 nodes supported

- ❑   Consolidated print driver management (install drivers only once)

- ❑   Majority node set quorum

- ❑   Reduction in shared disk requirements (no quorum partition needed)

- ❑   Terminal Services and printer server clusters now able to coexist on the same nodes

Clustered print servers will still need shared storage for spooler resources. Shared storage is always required for virtual servers. See Chapter 13, "Clustering Services," for more information about the requirements to use clustering.

- **Ease of installation.** The standard TCP/IP port monitor (SPM) brings a new level of ease and efficiency to installing network printer ports. SPM provides a detailed status of printer events through a Web-based interface from any Internet-connected client. In addition to detailed status, SPM allows for more accurate error reporting, such as *paper out*, as compared with the limited print error messages enabled by port monitors such as line printer remote (LPR). The WMI interface in Windows Server 2003 provides powerful capabilities for installing and configuring printers remotely and by means of scripts.

- **Active Directory integration.** The integration of print services with Active Directory means that users can go to a limited set of print servers and browse for a printer that best meets their needs. Using logical and standard server and printer naming conventions will maximize this benefit. Using well-developed standards for printer names, comments, and location entries will provide for a very accessible and efficient printing environment.

- **Searching for printers.** Combining printer location tracking—a feature available in Windows 2000—and Windows Server 2003 Active Directory will allow users to search for printers based on a standard identification for buildings, cities, and other specifications. Active Directory will also let users search for print devices by printer features and capabilities, such as duplex, color, and speed. By using these Active Directory and print services integration features, administrators can simplify troubleshooting if a problem with a particular printer or server occurs.

For More Information

See the following resources for further information:

- What's New in File and Print Services for Windows Server 2003 at *http://www.microsoft.com/windowsserver2003/evaluation/overview/technologies/fileandprint.mspx*

- Windows 2000 File and Print Services at *http://www.microsoft.com/windows2000/technologies/fileandprint/*

- What's New in Storage Management at *http://www.microsoft.com/windowsserver2003/evaluation/overview/technologies/storage.mspx*

13

Clustering Services

First designed for the Microsoft Windows NT Server 4.0 operating system, server clusters and network load balancing clusters are substantially enhanced in Microsoft Windows Server 2003, Enterprise Edition and Datacenter Edition. They provide three principal advantages:

- **Improved availability.**   By enabling services and applications to continue providing service during hardware or software component failure or during planned maintenance

- **Increased scalability.**   By supporting servers that can be expanded with multiple processors (up to a maximum of 8 processors in Windows Server 2003, Enterprise Edition, and 32 processors in the Datacenter Edition) and additional memory (up to a maximum of 8 gigabytes of random access memory in the Enterprise Edition and 64 GB in the Datacenter Edition) and by aggregating several servers into a single cluster platform for hosting applications

- **Improved manageability.**   By enabling administrators to manage devices and resources within the entire cluster as if they were managing a single computer

By combining the Windows clustering technologies in an end-to-end solution, enterprise-class services that are highly scalable and highly available can be deployed on Windows operating systems.

Clustering Overview

High availability and scalability have become increasingly essential for organizations deploying business-critical e-commerce and line-of-business applications. This chapter addresses the needs of IT professionals who currently use Microsoft Windows–based servers in the enterprise, and of those who need information showing how Windows Server 2003 provides clustering solutions that lead to a more effective enterprisewide computing environment.

Microsoft Cluster Technologies

While Microsoft Windows 2000 represents a dramatic improvement over its predecessors in terms of total uptime (availability), reduced system failure (reliability), and ability to add resources and computers to improve performance (scalability), Windows Server 2003 takes the availability, reliability, and scalability of the Windows operating system to the next level by enhancing existing features and providing new options. With Windows 2000 and Windows Server 2003, Microsoft uses a three-part clustering strategy that includes the following:

- **Network Load Balancing.** Available in all versions of the Windows Server 2003 family, this service load-balances incoming IP traffic across clusters. Network Load Balancing (NLB) enhances both the availability and scalability of Internet services such as Web services, streaming media services, and Terminal Services. By acting as the load balancing infrastructure, and by providing control information to management applications built on top of Windows Management Instrumentation (WMI), Network Load Balancing can seamlessly integrate into existing Web server farm infrastructures.

  Component load balancing provides dynamic load balancing of middle-tier application components that use COM+. With component load balancing, COM+ components can be load-balanced over multiple nodes to dramatically enhance the availability and scalability of software applications. Component load balancing is available as part of the Application Center 2000 software suite.

- **Server Clusters.** Available only in Windows Server 2003, Enterprise Edition and Datacenter Edition, server clusters provide high availability and scalability for mission-critical applications such as databases, messaging systems, and file and print services. If one of the nodes in a cluster becomes unavailable as a result of planned downtime for maintenance or unplanned downtime caused by failure, another node takes over to provide the service to the end user—a process known as *failover*. When failover occurs, users who are accessing the Cluster service continue to access the service and are unaware that it is now being provided from a different server (node). Windows Server 2003 supports up to eight-node server clusters in the Enterprise Edition and the Datacenter Edition.

Although component load balancing is a part of the overall availability and scalability story for applications deployed on the Windows platform, it isn't part of the Windows Server 2003 release. The remainder of this document will focus on Network Load Balancing and server clusters. For further information about component load balancing, see the Application Center 2000 documentation.

Protection Against Downtime

Microsoft cluster technologies protect against the following:

- Application or service failure, affecting application software and essential services

- System or hardware failure, affecting hardware components (for example, CPUs, drives, memory, network adapters, power supplies, and others)

- Site failure caused by natural disaster, power outages, or connectivity outages

- Downtime resulting from planned maintenance such as upgrading of applications or the operating system and installation of service packs or hot fixes

Purposes and Requirements

Each technology has a specific purpose and is designed to meet different requirements:

- Network Load Balancing is designed to address scalability and availability issues for front-end Web services and edge servers such as Virtual Private Network (VPN) servers and firewalls.

- Component load balancing is designed to address the unique scalability and availability needs of middle-tier applications.

- Windows Clustering is designed to provide failover support for back-end database services or for long-running services that have state and data associated with them (such as print services).

Organizations can use Microsoft cluster technologies to increase overall availability while minimizing single points of failure and reducing costs by using industry-standard hardware and software.

Windows Clustering

The Windows Clustering technologies have been enhanced to provide additional facilities that enable a wider range of server cluster scenarios and topologies to be deployed.

The many important new and improved features for server clusters cover a wide range of categories: general, installation, resources, network enhancements, storage, operations, support, and troubleshooting.

General Improvements

General improvements in the Cluster service for Windows Server 2003 include the following:

- **Larger cluster sizes.** Windows Server 2003, Enterprise Edition, now supports eight-node clusters (formerly two), and the Datacenter Edition now supports eight-node clusters (formerly four). Larger cluster sizes provide greater flexibility. Being able to use larger cluster sizes provides much more flexibility in how applications can be deployed on a server cluster. Applications that support multiple instances can run more instances across more nodes; multiple applications can be deployed on a single server cluster with much more flexibility and control over the semantics if a node fails or is taken down for maintenance.

- **64-bit support.** The 64-bit versions of Windows Server 2003 support the Cluster service; 64-bit supports large memory needs. SQL Server 2000 Enterprise Edition (64-bit) is one example of an application that can make use of the increased memory space of the 64-bit versions of Windows Server 2003 (up to 4 TB—Windows 2000 Datacenter Server supports up to 64 GB only), while at the same time taking advantage of clustering. This provides an incredibly powerful platform for the most computer-intensive applications while ensuring high availability of those applications.

- **High availability.** Terminal Server directory service can be made highly available through failover.

- **Cluster installation wizard.** The cluster installation wizard provides validation and verification. It allows generic scripting to make applications highly available.

- **Majority node set clusters.** Windows Server 2003 has an optional quorum resource that does not require a disk on a shared bus for the quorum device. This feature is designed to be built into larger end-to-end solutions by OEMs, independent hardware vendors (IHVs), and other software vendors rather than to be deployed by end users specifically—although this is possible for experienced users. Scenarios in which majority node set (MNS) clusters add value include

  - ❏ **Geographically dispersed clusters.** This mechanism provides a single Microsoft-supplied quorum resource that is independent of any storage solution for a geographically dispersed or multisite cluster. There is a separate cluster hardware compatibility list (HCL) for geographic clusters.

  - ❏ **Highly available devices with no shared disks.** These low-cost or appliance-like devices use techniques other than shared disks, such as log shipping or software disk—or file system replication and mirroring—to make data available on multiple nodes in the cluster.

    Windows Server 2003 provides no mechanism to mirror or replicate user data across the nodes of an MNS cluster. So while building clusters with no shared disks at all is possible, making the application data highly available and redundant across machines is an application-specific issue. MNS clusters provide the following benefits:

  - ❏ **Storage abstraction.** Frees up the storage subsystem to manage data replication among multiple sites in the most appropriate way without having to worry about a shared quorum disk; at the same time, the concept of a single virtual cluster is supported.

  - ❏ **No shared disks.** Some scenarios require tightly consistent cluster features yet don't require shared disks—for example, (a) clusters wherein the application keeps data consistent between nodes, such as database log shipping and file replication for relatively static data; and (b) clusters that host applications that have no persistent data but need to cooperate in a tightly coupled way to provide consistent volatile state.

- **Enhanced redundancy.** If the shared quorum disk is corrupted in any way, the entire cluster goes off line. With majority node sets, the corruption of quorum on one node does not bring the entire cluster off line.

Installation

Improvements in the server cluster installation process include the following:

- **Installation by default.** Cluster files are placed on the nodes when Windows Server 2003 is installed. You need only configure a cluster by launching Cluster Administrator or script the configuration with Cluster.exe. In addition, third-party quorum resources can be preinstalled and then selected during server cluster configuration rather than having additional, resource-specific, procedures. All server cluster configurations can be deployed the same way. These features provide the following benefits:

  - **Easier administration.** You no longer need to provide a media CD to install the Cluster service.

  - **No reboot.** You no longer need to reboot after you install or uninstall the Cluster service.

- **Preconfiguration analysis.** The installation process analyzes and verifies hardware and software configuration and identifies potential problems. It provides a comprehensive and easy-to-read report on any potential configuration issues before the server cluster is created. This ensures that any known incompatibilities are detected prior to configuration. For example, Services for Macintosh (SFM), NLB, dynamic disks, and addresses issued using Dynamic Host Configuration Protocol (DHCP) are not supported with the Cluster service.

- **Default values.** Installation creates a server cluster that conforms to best practices using default values and heuristics. Many times, for newly created server clusters, the default values are the most appropriate configuration. Server cluster creation asks many fewer setup questions, data is collected, and the code makes decisions about the configuration. The goal is to get a default server cluster up and running that can then be customized using the server cluster administration tools if required. This allows multiple nodes to be added to a server cluster in a single operation. This makes it quicker and easier to create multinode server clusters.

■ **Extensible architecture.** Extensible architecture allows applications and system components to take part in server cluster configuration. For example, applications can be installed prior to a server being clustered, and the application can participate in (or even block) this node joining the server cluster. This allows applications to set up server cluster resources or change their configuration as part of server cluster installations rather than as a separate postserver cluster installation task.

■ **Remote administration.** Remote administration allows full remote creation and configuration of the server cluster. New server clusters can be created and nodes can be added to an existing server cluster from a remote management station. In addition, drive letter changes and physical disk resource failover are updated to Terminal Server client sessions. This allows for better remote administration via Terminal Services.

■ **Command-line tools.** Server cluster creation and configuration can be scripted through the Cluster.exe command-line tool. This makes it much easier to automate the process of creating a cluster.

■ **Simpler uninstallation.** Uninstalling the Cluster service from a node is now a one-step process of exiting the node. Previous versions required eviction and then uninstallation. Uninstalling the Cluster service is much more efficient than before because you need only to evict the node through Cluster Administrator or Cluster.exe, and the node is unconfigured for Cluster support. Also, a new switch for Cluster.exe will force the uninstallation if getting into Cluster Administrator is problematic.

■ **Local quorum.** If a node isn't attached to a shared disk, it will automatically configure a local quorum resource. It's also possible to create a local quorum resource once the Cluster service is running. It's easy for a user to create a test cluster on his or her local PC for testing out cluster applications or for getting familiar with the Cluster service. You don't need special cluster hardware that has been certified on the Microsoft Cluster HCL to run a test cluster. Local quorum is supported only for one-node clusters. In addition, the use of hardware not certified on the HCL isn't supported for production environments. In the event that you lose all your shared disks, one option for getting a temporary cluster working (for example, while you wait for new hardware) is to use the Cluster.exe */fixquorum* switch to start the cluster. After doing this, create a local quorum resource and set it as your quorum:

❏ For a print cluster, you can point the spool folder to the local disk.

❏ For a file share, you can point the file share resource to the local disk, where backup data has been restored.

■ **Quorum selection.**   You no longer need to select which disk is going to be used as the quorum resource. It's automatically configured on the smallest disk that is larger than 50 MB and formatted using NTFS. The end user no longer has to worry about which disk to use for the quorum. The option to move the quorum resource to another disk is available during setup or after the cluster has been configured.

■ **Active Directory.**   The Cluster service now has much tighter integration with the Active Directory directory service, including a virtual computer object, Kerberos authentication, and a default location for services such as Microsoft Message Queuing (MSMQ) to publish service control points. By publishing a cluster virtual server as a computer object in Active Directory, users can access the virtual server just as they can access any other Windows 2000 server.

The only roles for the virtual server computer object in Windows Server 2003 are to allow Kerberos authentication for services hosted on a virtual server and to allow cluster-aware and Active Directory–aware services (such as MSMQ) to publish service provider information specific to the virtual server they are hosted in. Following are further details of Kerberos authentication and of publishing services:

❏ **Kerberos authentication.**   Kerberos authentication allows a user to be authenticated against a server without ever having to send the user's password. Instead, the user presents a ticket that grants access to the server. This contrasts with NTLM authentication, used by Windows Clustering in Windows 2000, which sends the user's password as a hash over the network. In addition, Kerberos supports mutual authentication of client and server and allows delegation of authentication across multiple machines. To have Kerberos authentication for the virtual server in a mixed-mode cluster—for example, Windows 2000 and Windows Server 2003—you must be running Windows 2000 Enterprise Server SP3 or a later version. Otherwise, NTLM will be used for all authentication.

❑ **Publishing services.**   Now that the Cluster service is Active Directory–aware, it can integrate with other services that publish information about a service in Active Directory. For example, MSMQ 2.0 can publish information about public queues in Active Directory so that users can easily find their nearest queue. Windows Server 2003 now extends this service to allow clustered public queue information to be published in Active Directory. Cluster integration does not make any changes to the Active Directory schema.

> **Caution**   Although the network name server cluster resource publishes a computer object in Active Directory, that computer object should *not* be used for administrative tasks such as applying Group Policy.

Resources

Improvements in server cluster resources include the following:

■ **Printer configuration.**   Windows Clustering now provides a much simpler configuration process for setting up clustered printers. To set up a clustered print server, you need to configure only the spooler resource in Cluster Administrator and then connect to the virtual server to configure the ports and print queues. This is an improvement over previous versions of Windows Clustering, in which you had to repeat the configuration steps on each node in the cluster, including installing printer drivers.

■ **MSDTC configuration.**   The Microsoft Distributed Transaction Coordinator (MSDTC) can now be configured once and replicated to all nodes. In previous versions, the Comclust.exe utility had to be run on each node in order to cluster the MSDTC. It's now possible to configure MSDTC as a resource type, assign it to a resource group, and have it automatically configured on all cluster nodes. Also, once configured, when new nodes are added to the cluster, DTC is set up on the new node automatically.

■ **Scripting.** You can make existing applications server cluster–aware by using scripting (Visual Basic Scripting Edition and JScript) rather than by writing resource DLLs in C or Visual C++. Scripting makes it much simpler to write specific resource plug-ins for applications so that they can be monitored and controlled in a server cluster. Scripting supports resource-specific properties, which enable a resource script to store server cluster–wide configurations that can be used and managed in the same way as any other resource. Adding to the script can also enhance health checking. For example, you can start off with a simple generic script, and you can then add to it later to check whether it's providing the desired service.

■ **MSMQ triggers.** The Cluster service has enhanced the MSMQ resource type to allow multiple instances on the same cluster. MSMQ triggers let you have multiple clustered message queues running at the same time. This provides increased performance (in the case of Active/Active MSMQ clusters) and flexibility. You can have only one MSMQ resource per cluster group.

Network Enhancements

Improvements in network enhancements for Windows Clustering include the following:

■ **Enhanced network failover.** The Cluster service now supports enhanced logic for failover when a complete loss of internal (heartbeat) communication has occurred. The network state for public communication of all nodes is now taken into account. In Windows 2000, if node A owned the quorum disk and lost all network interfaces (for example, public and heartbeat), it would retain control of the cluster, even though no one could communicate with it and another node might have had a working public interface. Windows Server 2003 cluster nodes now take the state of public interfaces into account prior to arbitrating for control of the cluster.

■ **Media sense detection.** When using the Cluster service, if network connectivity is lost, the TCP/IP stack does not get unloaded as it did in Windows 2000 by default. There is no longer the need to set the DisableDHCPMediaSense registry key. In Windows 2000, if network connectivity was lost, the TCP/IP stack was unloaded, which meant that all resources that depended on IP addresses were taken off line. Also, when the networks came back on line, their network role reverted to the default setting—for example, client and private. With Media Sense disabled by default, the network role is preserved and all IP address–dependent resources are kept on line.

- **Multicast heartbeat.** Multicast heartbeats are allowed between nodes in a server cluster. Multicast heartbeat is automatically selected if the cluster is large enough and if the network infrastructure can support multicasting between the cluster nodes. Although the multicast parameters can be controlled manually, a typical configuration requires no administration tasks or tuning to enable this feature. If multicast communication fails for any reason, the internal communications will revert to unicast. All internal communications are signed and secure. Using multicast reduces the amount of traffic in a cluster subnet. This can be particularly beneficial in clusters of more than two nodes or in geographically dispersed clusters.

Storage

Improvements in storage when using Windows Clustering include the following:

- **Resizing of clustered disks.** Clustered disks can be resized dynamically by using the command-line tool DiskPart, provided the underlying storage infrastructure is capable of extending a logical unit dynamically. If you increase the size of a shared disk, the Cluster service will now dynamically adjust to it. This is particularly helpful for storage area networks (SANs), where volume sizes can change easily to avoid disk-full situations.

- **Volume mount points.** Volume mount points are now supported on shared disks (excluding the quorum) and will work properly on failover if configured correctly. Volume mount points (in Windows 2000 or later versions) are directories that point to specified disk volumes in a persistent manner: for example, you can configure C:\Data to point to a disk volume. They alleviate the need to associate each disk volume with a drive letter, thereby overcoming the 26-drive-letter limitation. For example, without volume mount points, you would have to create a G drive to map the data volume to. Now that the Cluster service supports volume mount points, you have much greater flexibility in how you map your shared disk namespace. The directory that hosts the volume mount point must be NTFS because the underlying mechanism uses NTFS reparse points. However, the file system that is being mounted can be file allocation table (FAT), FAT32, NTFS, Compact Disc File System (CDFS), or Universal Disc File System (UDFS).

- **Client-side caching.** Client-side caching (CSC) is now supported for clustered file shares. CSC for clustered file shares enables a client to cache data stored on a clustered share. The client works on a local copy of the data, which is uploaded back to the server cluster when the file is closed. This allows any failure of a server in the server cluster, and subsequent failover of the file share service, to be hidden from the client.

- **Distributed File System.** Distributed File System (DFS) has had a number of improvements, including multiple stand-alone roots, independent root failover, and support for Active-Active configurations. DFS allows multiple file shares on different machines to be aggregated into a common namespace: for example, \\dfsroot\share1 and \\dfsroot\share2 are actually aggregated from \\server1\share1 and \\server2\share2. New clustering benefits include

  ❑ **Multiple stand-alone roots.** Previous versions supported only one clustered stand-alone root. You can now have multiple clustered stand-alone roots, giving you much greater flexibility in planning your distributed file system namespace: for example, multiple DFS roots on the same virtual server or multiple DFS roots on different virtual servers.

  ❑ **Independent failover.** Granular failover control is available for each DFS root. This lets you configure failover settings on an individual basis, which results in faster failover times.

  ❑ **Active/active configurations.** You can now have multiple stand-alone roots running actively on multiple nodes.

- **Encrypting File System.** With Windows Server 2003, the Encrypting File System (EFS) is supported on clustered file shares. This allows data to be stored in an encrypted format on clustered disks.

■ **Storage area networks.**   Clustering has been optimized for SANs, including targeted device resets and shared storage buses:

❑ **Targeted bus resets.**   The server cluster software now issues a special control code when releasing disk drives during arbitration. This control code can be used in conjunction with host bus adapter (HBA) drivers, which support the extended Windows Server 2003 feature set, to selectively reset devices on the SAN rather than perform a full bus reset. This ensures that the server cluster has much lower impact on the SAN fabric.

❑ **Shared storage bus.**   Shared disks can be located on the same storage bus as the boot, page-file, and dump-file disks. This allows a clustered server to have a single storage bus (or a single redundant storage bus).

This feature is disabled by default because of configuration restrictions. It can and should be enabled only by OEMs and IHVs for specific and qualified solutions. This is *not* a general-purpose feature exposed to end users.

Operations

Improvements in operations for Windows Clustering include the following:

■ **Backup and restore.**   You can actively restore the local cluster nodes' cluster configuration, or you can restore the cluster information to all nodes in the cluster. Node restoration is also built into Automated System Recovery (ASR).

❑ **Backup and restore.**   Backup (NTBackup.exe) in Windows Server 2003 has been enhanced to enable seamless backups and restores of the local cluster database and to make it possible to restore the configuration locally and to all nodes in a cluster.

❑ **Automated system recovery.**   ASR can completely restore a cluster in a variety of scenarios, including damaged or missing system files, complete operating system reinstallation as a result of hardware failure, a damaged cluster database, or changed disk signatures (including shared).

■ **Group affinity support.**   Group affinity support allows an application to describe itself as an N+I application. This means that if an application is running actively on N nodes of a server cluster, I spare nodes are available if an active node fails. In the event of failure, the failover manager will try to ensure that the application is failed over to a spare node rather than to a node that is currently running the application. Applications are failed over to spare nodes before active nodes.

- **Node eviction.** Evicting a node from a server cluster no longer requires a reboot to clean up the server cluster state. A node can be moved from one server cluster to another without having to reboot. In the event of a catastrophic failure, the server cluster configuration can be force-cleaned regardless of the server cluster state. The following benefits ensue:

  - ❑ **Increased availability.** No reboots increases the uptime of the system.

  - ❑ **Disaster recovery.** In the event of a node failure, the cluster can be cleaned up easily.

- **Rolling upgrades.** Rolling upgrades allow one node in a cluster to be taken off line for upgrading while other nodes in the cluster continue to function on an older version. Rolling upgrades are supported in Windows 2000 and Windows Server 2003, although there is no support for rolling upgrades from a Microsoft Windows NT 4.0 cluster to a Windows Server 2003 cluster. An upgrade from Windows NT 4.0 is supported, but the cluster will have to be taken off line during the upgrade.

- **Password change.** Using Windows Server 2003, you can change the Cluster service account password on the domain as well as on each local node without having to take the cluster off line. If multiple clusters use the same Cluster service account, you can change them simultaneously. In Microsoft Windows NT 4.0 and Microsoft Windows 2000, to change the Cluster service account password, you have to stop the cluster service on all nodes before you can make the password change.

- **Resource deletion.** Resources can be deleted in Cluster Administrator or with Cluster.exe without taking them off line first. In previous versions, you first had to take a resource off line before you could delete it. Now the Cluster service will take resources off line automatically and then delete them.

- **WMI support.**   Server clusters provide WMI support for

  - ❏ **Cluster control and management functions.** These include starting and stopping resources, creating new resources and dependencies, and other functions.

  - ❏ **Application and cluster state information.** WMI can be used to query whether applications are on line and whether cluster nodes are up and running, as well as to request a variety of other status information.

  - ❏ **Cluster state change events.** Cluster state change events are propagated via WMI to allow applications to subscribe to WMI events that show when an application has failed, when an application is restarted, when a node fails, and other occurrences.

  - ❏ **Better management.** WMI support enables server clusters to be managed as part of an overall WMI environment.

Supporting and Troubleshooting

Improvements in support and troubleshooting when working with Windows Clustering include the following:

- **Offline/failure reason codes.** These codes provide additional information to the resource as to why the application was taken off line or why it failed. Reason codes enable an application to use different semantics if it or one of its dependencies has failed, as opposed to the administrator specifically moving the group to another node in the server cluster.

- **Software tracing.** The Cluster service now has a feature called software tracing that will produce more information to help with troubleshooting cluster issues. This is a new method for debugging that will allow Microsoft to debug the Cluster service without loading checked build versions of the DLLs (symbols).

- **Cluster logs.** A number of improvements have been made to the Cluster service log files, including a setup log, error levels (info, warn, err), local server time entry, and GUID to resource name mapping.

  - ❏ **Setup log.** During configuration of the Cluster service, a separate setup log (%SystemRoot%\system32\Logfiles\Cluster\ClCfg-Srv.log) is created to assist in troubleshooting.

- ❏ **Error levels.** This makes it easy to be able to highlight just the entries that require action—for example, *err*.

- ❏ **Local server time stamp.** This assists in comparing event log entries with cluster logs.

- ■ **Event Log.** Additional events are written to the event log, not only indicating error cases but showing when resources are successfully failed over from one node to another. Improvements to the event log enable event log parsing and management tools to be used to track successful failovers rather than just catastrophic failures.

- ■ **Clusdiag.** A new tool named Clusdiag is available in the Windows Server 2003 Resource Kit. Clusdiag offers the following abilities:

  - ❏ **Better troubleshooting.** Clusdiag makes reading and correlating cluster logs across multiple cluster nodes and debugging of cluster issues more straightforward.

  - ❏ **Validation and testing.** Clusdiag allows users to run stress tests on the server, storage, and clustering infrastructure. As a result, it can be used as a validation and test tool before a cluster is put into production.

- ■ **CHKDSK log.** The Cluster service creates a CHKDSK log whenever CHKDSK is run on a shared disk. This allows a system administrator to find out about and react to any issues that were discovered during the CHKDSK process.

- ■ **Disk corruption.** When disk corruption is suspected, the Cluster service reports the results of CHKDSK in event logs and creates a log in %SystemRoot%\Cluster. Results are logged in the Application event log and in Cluster.log. In addition, Cluster.log references a log file (for example, %windir%\CLUSTER\CHKDSK_DISK2_SIGE9443789.LOG) in which detailed CHKDSK output is recorded.

Network Load Balancing: New Features

Windows Clustering technologies have been enhanced. A wider range of NLB scenarios and topologies can now be deployed.

Network Load Balancing Manager

In Windows 2000, to create an NLB cluster users had to separately configure each machine in the cluster. Not only was this additional work, but it also opened up the possibility of user error because identical cluster parameters and port rules had to be configured on each machine. A new utility in Windows Server 2003 called the Network Load Balancing Manager helps solve some of these problems by providing a single point of configuration and management of NLB clusters. The NLB Manager lets you do the following:

- Create new NLB clusters and automatically propagate cluster parameters and port rules to all hosts in the cluster. You can also propagate host parameters to specific hosts in the cluster.

- Add and remove hosts to and from NLB clusters.

- Automatically add cluster IP addresses to TCP/IP.

- Manage existing clusters by simply connecting to them or by loading their host information from a file and saving this information to a file for later use.

- Configure NLB to load-balance multiple Web sites or applications on the same NLB cluster. This includes adding all cluster IP addresses to TCP/IP and controlling traffic sent to specific applications on specific hosts in the cluster.

- Diagnose improperly configured clusters.

Virtual Clusters

In Windows 2000, users could load-balance multiple Web sites or applications on the same NLB cluster simply by adding the IP addresses corresponding to those Web sites or applications to TCP/IP on each host in the cluster. This is because NLB on each host load-balanced all IP addresses in TCP/IP except the dedicated IP address. The shortcomings of this feature in Windows 2000 were as follows:

- Port rules specified for the cluster were automatically applied to all Web sites or applications load-balanced by the cluster.

- All the hosts in the cluster had to handle traffic for all the Web sites and applications hosted on them.

- To block out traffic for a specific application on a specific host, traffic for all applications on that host had to be blocked.

A new feature in Windows Server 2003 called *virtual clusters* overcomes these deficiencies by providing per-IP port rules capability. This allows the user to

- Configure different port rules for different cluster IP addresses, wherein each cluster IP address corresponds to a Web site or application being hosted on the NLB cluster. This is in contrast to NLB in Windows 2000, wherein port rules were applicable to an entire host and not to specific IP addresses on that host.

- Filter out traffic sent to a specific Web site or application on a specific host in the cluster. This allows individual applications on hosts to be taken off line for upgrades, restarts, and other purposes, without affecting other applications being load-balanced on the rest of the NLB cluster.

- Specify which host in the cluster should service traffic sent to a specific Web site or application being hosted on the cluster. This way, not all hosts in the cluster need to handle traffic for all applications being hosted on that cluster.

Multi-NIC Support

Windows 2000 allowed the user to bind NLB to only one network card in the system. Windows Server 2003 allows the user to bind NLB to multiple network cards, thus removing the limitation. This now enables users to

- Host multiple NLB clusters on the same hosts while leaving them on entirely independent networks. This can be achieved by binding NLB to different network cards in the same system.

- Use NLB for firewall and proxy load balancing in scenarios in which load balancing is required on multiple fronts of a proxy or firewall.

Bidirectional Affinity

The addition of the multi-NIC support feature enabled several other scenarios in which there was a need for load balancing on multiple fronts of an NLB cluster. The most common use of this feature will be to cluster Internet Security and Acceleration (ISA) servers for proxy and firewall load balancing. The two most common scenarios in which NLB will be used together with ISA are

■ **Web publishing.**   In the Web publishing scenario, the ISA cluster typically resides between the Internet and the front-end Web servers. In this scenario, the ISA servers will have NLB bound only to the external interface, so there will be no need to use the bidirectional affinity feature.

■ **Server publishing.**   In the server publishing scenario, the ISA cluster will reside between the Web servers in the front and the published servers in the back. Here NLB will have to be bound to both the external interface (facing the Web servers) and the internal interface (facing the published servers) of each ISA server in the cluster.

This scenario increases the level of complexity: now, when connections from the Web servers are being load-balanced on the external interface of the ISA cluster and then forwarded by one of the ISA servers to a published server, NLB has to ensure that the response from the published server is always routed to the same ISA server that handled the corresponding request from the Web server because this is the only ISA server in the cluster that has the security context for that particular session. So NLB has to make sure that the response from the published server doesn't get load-balanced on the internal interface of the ISA cluster because this interface is also clustered using NLB.

Bidirectional affinity makes multiple instances of NLB on the same host work in tandem to ensure that responses from published servers are routed through the appropriate ISA servers in the cluster.

Limiting Switch Flooding Using IGMP Support

The NLB algorithm requires every host in the NLB cluster to see every incoming packet destined for the cluster. NLB accomplishes this by never allowing the switch to associate the cluster's media access control (MAC) address with a specific port on the switch. However, the unintended side effect of this requirement is that the switch ends up flooding all of its ports with all incoming packets meant for the NLB cluster. This can certainly be a nuisance and a waste of network resources. To arrest this problem, a new feature called *Internet Group Management Protocol support* (IGMP support) has been introduced in Windows Server 2003.

IGMP support helps to limit the flooding to only those ports on the switch that have NLB machines connected to them. This way, non-NLB machines do not see traffic intended only for the NLB cluster, while at the same time all NLB machines see traffic meant for the cluster. This satisfies the requirements of the algorithm. IGMP support can be enabled only when NLB is configured in multicast mode.

Multicast mode has its own drawbacks, which are discussed extensively in knowledge base articles available on Microsoft.com. You should be aware of the shortcomings of multicast mode before deploying IGMP support.

Switch flooding can also be limited when using unicast mode by creating virtual LANs (VLANs) in the switch and putting the NLB cluster on its own VLAN. Unicast mode does not have the same drawbacks as multicast mode does, so limiting switch flooding using this approach might be preferable.

Server Cluster Architecture

Server clusters are based on a shared-nothing model of cluster architecture. This model refers to how servers in a cluster manage and use local and common cluster devices and resources.

Shared-Nothing Cluster

In the shared-nothing cluster, each server owns and manages its local devices. Devices common to the cluster, such as a common disk array and connection media, are selectively owned and managed by a single server at any given time.

The shared-nothing model makes it easier to manage disk devices and standard applications. This model does not require any special cabling or applications and enables server clusters to support standard Windows Server 2003–based and Windows 2000–based applications and disk resources.

Local Storage Devices and Media Connections

Server clusters use the standard Windows Server 2003 and Windows 2000 Server drivers for local storage devices and media connections. Server clusters support several connection media for the external common devices that need to be accessible by all servers in the cluster.

External storage devices that are common to the cluster require small computer system interface (SCSI) devices and support standard PCI-based SCSI connections as well as SCSI over Fibre Channel and SCSI bus with multiple initiators. Fiber connections are SCSI devices, simply hosted on a Fibre Channel bus instead of a SCSI bus. Conceptually, Fibre Channel technology encapsulates

SCSI commands within the Fibre Channel and makes it possible to use the SCSI commands server clusters are designed to support. These SCSI commands are Reserve/Release and Bus Reset and will function the same over standard or nonfiber SCSI interconnect media.

Figure 13-1 illustrates components of a two-node server cluster that can comprise servers running either Windows Server 2003, Enterprise Edition, or Windows 2000 Enterprise Server with shared storage device connections using SCSI or SCSI over Fibre Channel.

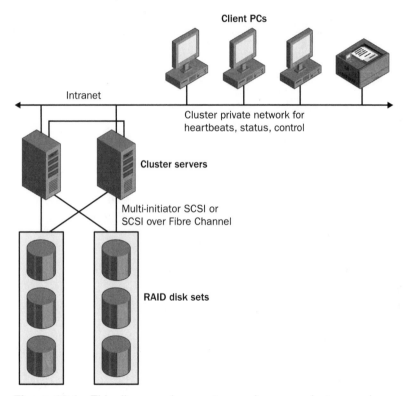

Figure 13-1 This diagram shows a two-node server cluster running Windows Server 2003, Enterprise Edition.

Windows Server 2003, Datacenter Edition, supports from two to eight node clusters and does require device connections using Fibre Channel, as shown in Figure 13-2.

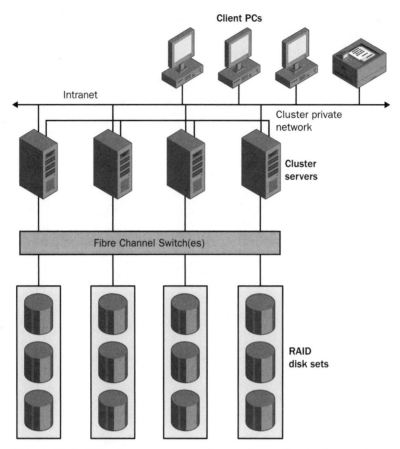

Figure 13-2   This diagram shows a four-node server cluster running Windows Server 2003, Datacenter Edition.

Virtual Servers

One of the benefits of clusters is that applications and services running on a server cluster can be exposed to users and workstations as virtual servers in the following circumstances:

- **Physical view.**   To users and clients, connecting to an application or service running as a clustered virtual server appears to be the same process as connecting to a single physical server. In fact, the connection to a virtual server can be hosted by any node in the cluster. The user or client application will not know which node is actually hosting the virtual server. Services or applications that are not accessed by users or client applications can run on a cluster node without being managed as a virtual server. Multiple virtual servers representing multiple applications can be hosted in a cluster, as illustrated in Figure 13-3.

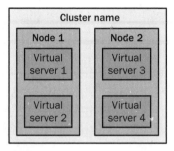

Figure 13-3 This diagram shows a physical view of virtual servers under server clusters.

Figure 13-3 illustrates a two-node cluster with four virtual servers; two virtual servers exist on each node. Server clusters manage the virtual server as a resource group, with each virtual server resource group containing two resources: an IP address and a network name that is mapped to the IP address.

■ **Client view.** Application client connections to a virtual server are made by a client session that knows only the IP address that the cluster service publishes as the address of the virtual server. The client view is simply a view of individual network names and IP addresses. Using the example of a two-node cluster supporting four virtual servers, Figure 13-4 illustrates the client view of the cluster nodes and four virtual servers.

As shown in Figure 13-4, the client sees only the IP addresses and names and does not see information about the physical location of any of the virtual servers. This allows server clusters to provide highly available support for the applications running as virtual servers.

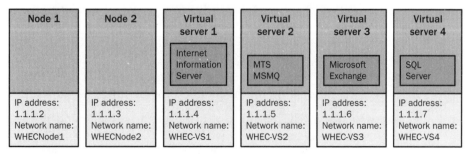

Figure 13-4 This diagram shows a client view of server cluster virtual servers.

- **Application or server failure.**   In the event of an application or server failure, the cluster service moves the entire virtual server resource group to another node in the cluster. When such a failure occurs, the client will detect a failure in its session with the application and attempt to reconnect in exactly the same manner as the original connection. It will be able to do this successfully because the cluster service simply maps the published IP address of the virtual server to a surviving node in the cluster during recovery operations. The client session can reestablish the connection to the application without needing to know that the application is now physically hosted on a different node in the cluster.

    Note that while this provides high availability of the application or service, session state information related to the failed client session is lost unless the application is designed or configured to store client session data on disk for retrieval during application recovery. Server clusters enable high availability but do not provide application fault tolerance unless the application itself supports fault-tolerant transaction behavior.

- **DHCP.**   Microsoft DHCP service is a service that provides an example of an application that stores client data and can recover from failed client sessions. DHCP client IP address reservations are saved in the DHCP database. If the DHCP server resource fails, the DHCP database can be moved to an available node in the cluster and restarted with restored client data from the DHCP database.

Resources

A resource represents a physical object or an instance of running code: a disk, an IP address, an MSMQ queue, a COM object, and so on. From a management perspective, resources can be independently started and stopped and each one can be monitored to ensure that it is healthy. From the cluster service perspective, a resource can be in a number of states, as follows:

- **Off line.**   The resource is shut down or out of service.

- **Started.**   The resource is loaded into memory and is capable of being brought on line as required by the resource manager.

- **On line.**   The resource is functioning correctly and is capable of servicing requests.

- **Failed.**   The resource is no longer functional and could not be restarted.

Resources and Dependencies

As just described, an application actually consists of multiple pieces. Some pieces can be code, and others can be physical resources required by the application. The various pieces of an application are related in various ways: for example, an application that writes to a disk cannot come on line until the disk is available. If the disk fails, then, by definition, the application cannot continue to run because it writes to the disk.

Dependencies can be set up among resources that express various relationships among the resources. In Figure 13-5, the SQL resource has a start order dependency on a disk resource and a network name resource. A network name resource in turn has a dependency on an IP address resource. If the user attempts to bring the SQL resource on line when the IP address and network name resources are off line and the disk resource is on line, the IP address resource is brought on line first, followed by the network name resource, and finally the SQL resource is brought on line. Resources that have no dependencies among them, such as the network name and the disk in Figure 13-5, have no defined startup order. In these cases, the resources can be started in parallel.

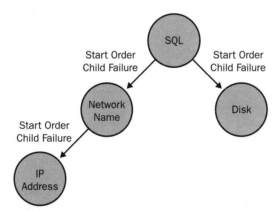

Figure 13-5   This diagram shows dependencies among resources.

A resource group is a collection of one or more resources that are managed and monitored as a single unit. A resource group can be started or stopped. If a resource group is started, each resource in the group is started (taking into account any start order defined by the dependencies among resources in the group). If a resource group is stopped, all the resources in the group are stopped (taking into account any stop order resource dependencies). Dependencies among resources cannot span a group. In other words, the set of resources within a group is an autonomous unit that can be started and stopped independently of any other group. A group is a single indivisible unit, and in a cluster environment it cannot span the nodes of a cluster: it's restricted to a single node. In clusters that support failover applications, the group is the unit of failover. Figure 13-6 represents the SQL resources placed together in a group, called SQL Group.

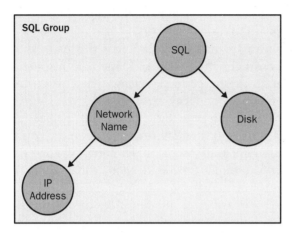

Figure 13-6 This diagram shows resources making up a SQL Group.

Resource groups are logical collections of cluster resources. Typically, a resource group is made up of logically related resources such as applications and their associated peripherals and data. However, resource groups can contain cluster entities that are related only by administrative needs, such as an administrative collection of virtual server names and IP addresses. A resource group can be owned by only one node at a time, and individual resources within a group must exist on the node that currently owns the group. In any given instance, different servers in the cluster cannot own different resources in the same resource group.

Each resource group has an associated clusterwide policy that specifies the server on which the group prefers to run and the server to which the group should move in case of a failure. Each group also has a network service name and address to enable network clients to bind to the services provided by the resource group. In the event of a failure, resource groups can be failed over or moved as atomic units from the failed node to another available node in the cluster.

Each resource in a group might depend on other resources in the cluster. Dependencies are relationships among resources that indicate which resources need to be started and be available before another resource can be started. For example, a database application might depend on the availability of a disk, an IP address, and a network name to be able to start and provide services to other applications and clients. Resource dependencies are identified using cluster resource group properties and enable the Cluster service to control the order in which resources are brought on and off line. The scope of any identified dependency is limited to resources within the same resource group. Cluster-managed dependencies cannot extend beyond the resource group because resource groups can be brought on line and off line and moved independently.

Failover Policies

Failover is the mechanism that single-instance applications and the individual partitions of a partitioned application typically employ for high availability. (The term *pack* has been coined to describe a highly available single-instance application or partition.) In a two-node cluster, defining failover policies is trivial. If one node fails, the only option is to fail over to the remaining node. As the size of a cluster increases, different failover policies are possible, and each one has different characteristics:

■ **Failover pairs.**   In a large cluster, failover policies can be defined such that each application is set to fail over between two nodes. The simple example illustrated in Figure 13-7 shows two applications—App1 and App2—in a four-node cluster.

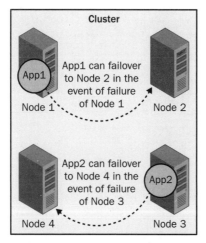

Figure 13-7   This diagram illustrates failover with two applications in a four-node cluster.

This configuration has the following pros and cons:

❑ Good for clusters that are supporting heavyweight applications such as databases. This configuration ensures that in the event of failure, two applications will not be hosted on the same node.

❑   Very easy to plan capacity. Each node is sized based on the application that it will need to host (just like a two-node cluster hosting one application).

❑   Easy to determine effect of a node failure on availability and performance of the system.

❑   Provides the flexibility of a larger cluster. In the event that a node is taken out for maintenance, the *buddy* for a given application can be changed dynamically. (Standby policy might result. See the next main bulleted item for more details of standby policy.)

❑   In simple configurations such as this one, only 50 percent of the capacity of the cluster is in use.

❑   Administrator intervention might be required in the event of multiple failures.

Server clusters support failover pairs on all versions of Windows by limiting the possible owner list for each resource to a given pair of nodes.

■   **Hot standby server.**   To reduce the overhead of failover pairs, the spare node for each pair can be consolidated into a single node. This provides a hot standby server that is capable of picking up the work in the event of a failure, as illustrated in Figure 13-8.

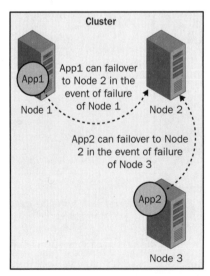

Figure 13-8   This diagram illustrates a failover configuration using a hot standby server.

The standby server configuration has the following pros and cons:

❏   Good for clusters that are supporting heavyweight applications such as databases. This configuration ensures that in the event of a single failure, two applications will not be hosted on the same node.

❏   Easy to plan capacity. Each node is sized based on the application that it will need to host; the spare is sized to be the maximum of the other nodes.

❏   Easy to determine effect of a node failure on availability and performance of the system.

❏   Configuration targeted toward a single point of failure.

❏   Doesn't really handle multiple failures well. This might be an issue during scheduled maintenance, when the spare might be in use.

Windows Clustering supports standby servers today using a combination of the possible owners list and the preferred owners list. The preferred node should be set to the node on which the application will run by default, and the possible owners for a given resource should be set to the preferred node and the spare node.

■   **N+I.**   Standby server works well for four-node clusters in some configurations; however, its ability to handle multiple failures is limited. N+I configurations are an extension of the standby server concept, according to which *N* nodes host applications and *I* nodes are spare, as illustrated in Figure 13-9.

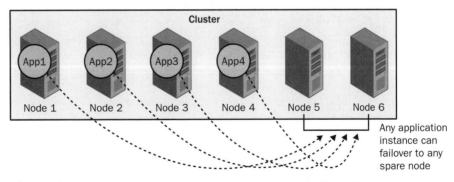

Figure 13-9   This diagram illustrates an N+I spare node configuration.

An N+I configuration has the following pros and cons:

❑   Good for clusters that are supporting heavyweight applications such as databases or Microsoft Exchange. This configuration ensures that in the event of a failure an application instance will fail over to a spare node, not one that is already in use.

❑   Easy to plan capacity. Each node is sized based on the application that it will need to host.

❑   Easy to determine effect of a node failure on availability and performance of the system.

❑   Works well for multiple failures.

❑   Does not really handle multiple applications running in the same cluster well. This policy is best suited to applications running on a dedicated cluster.

Windows Clustering supports N+I scenarios in Windows Server 2003 using a cluster group public property, *AntiAffinityClassName*. This property can contain an arbitrary string of characters. In the event of a failover, if a group being failed over has a nonempty string in the *AntiAffinityClassName* property, the failover manager will check all other nodes.

If any nodes (in the possible owners list for the resource) are *not* hosting a group with the same value in *AntiAffinityClassName*, those nodes are considered a good target for failover. If all nodes in the cluster are hosting groups that contain the same value in the *AntiAffinityClassName* property, the preferred node list is used to select a failover target.

■   **Failover ring.**   Failover rings allow each node in the cluster to run an application instance. In the event of a failure, the application on the failed node is moved to the next node in sequence, as shown in Figure 13-10.

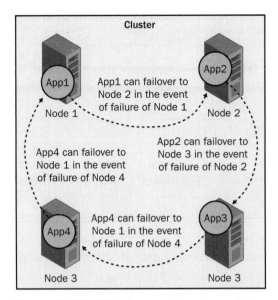

Figure 13-10   This diagram illustrates a failover configuration using a failover ring.

This configuration has the following pros and cons:

❑ Good for clusters that are supporting several small application instances wherein the capacity of any node is large enough to support several at the same time.

❑ Easy to predict effect on performance of a node failure.

❑ Easy to plan capacity for a single failure.

❑ Does not work well for all cases of multiple failures. If node 1 fails, node 2 will host two application instances and nodes 3 and 4 will each host one application instance. If node 2 then fails, node 3 will be hosting three application instances and node 4 will be hosting one instance.

❑ Not well suited to heavyweight applications because multiple instances might end up being hosted on the same node, even if there are lightly loaded nodes.

Failover rings are supported by server clusters using Windows Server 2003. This is done by defining the order of failover for a given group using the preferred owner list. A node order should be chosen, and then the preferred node list should be set up with each group starting at a different node.

■ **Random.**   In large clusters or even four-node clusters that are running several applications, defining specific failover targets or policies for each application instance can be extremely cumbersome and error prone. The best policy in some cases is to allow the target to be chosen at random, with a statistical probability that this will spread the load around the cluster in the event of a failure.

A random failover policy has the following pros and cons:

❑   Good for clusters that are supporting several small application instances wherein the capacity of any node is large enough to support several at the same time.

❑   Does not require an administrator to decide where any given application should fail over to.

❑   As long as there are sufficient applications or the applications are partitioned finely enough, provides a good mechanism to statistically load-balance the applications across the cluster in the event of a failure.

❑   Works well for multiple failures.

❑   Well tuned to handling multiple applications or many instances of the same application running in the same cluster.

❑   Can be difficult to plan capacity. There is no real guarantee that the load will be balanced across the cluster.

❑   Not easy to predict effect on performance of a node failure.

❑   Not well suited to heavyweight applications because multiple instances might end up being hosted on the same node, even if there are lightly loaded nodes.

Windows Clustering in Windows Server 2003 randomizes the failover target in the event of node failure. Each resource group that has an empty preferred owners list will be failed over to a random node in the cluster in the event that the node currently hosting it fails.

- **Customized control.**   In some cases, specific nodes might be preferred for a given application instance. A configuration that ties applications to nodes has the following pros and cons:

  ❑   Administrator has full control over what happens when a failure occurs.

  ❑   Capacity planning is easy since failure scenarios are predictable.

  ❑   With many applications running in a cluster, defining a good policy for failures can be extremely complex.

  ❑   It's very hard to plan for multiple cascaded failures.

Preferred Node List

Windows Clustering provides full control over the order of failover by using the preferred node list feature. The full semantics of the preferred node list can be defined as shown in Table 13-1.

Table 13-1   Preferred Node List

Preferred Node List Item	Move Group to *Best Possible* Initiated via Administrator	Failover Resulting from Node or Group Failure
Contains all nodes in cluster	Group is moved to highest node in preferred node list that is up and running in the cluster.	Group is moved to the next node on the preferred node list.
Contains a subset of the nodes in the cluster	Group is moved to highest node in preferred node list that is up and running in the cluster. If no nodes in the preferred node list are up and running, the group is moved to a random node.	Group is moved to the next node on the preferred node list. If the node that was hosting the group is the last on the list or was not in the preferred node list, the group is moved to a random node.
Empty	Group is moved to a random node.	Group is moved to a random node.

Network Load Balancing Architecture

This section describes the architecture of Network Load Balancing in Windows Server 2003:

■   How Network Load Balancing Works

■   Managing Application State

■   Detailed Architecture

■   Distribution of Cluster Traffic

■   Load Balancing Algorithm

■   Convergence

■   Remote Control

How Network Load Balancing Works

Network Load Balancing scales the performance of a server-based program, such as a Web server, by distributing its client requests across multiple servers within the cluster. With Network Load Balancing, each incoming IP packet is received by each host but accepted only by the intended recipient. The cluster hosts concurrently respond to different client requests, even multiple requests from the same client. For example, a Web browser might obtain the multiple images within a single Web page from different hosts in a Network Load Balancing cluster. This speeds up processing and shortens the response time to clients.

Each Network Load Balancing host can specify the load percentage that it will handle, or the load can be equally distributed across all of the hosts. Network Load Balancing servers use a distributed algorithm to statistically map workload among the hosts of the cluster according to the load percentages. This load balance dynamically changes when hosts enter or leave the cluster.

The load balance does not change in response to varying server loads (such as CPU or memory usage). For applications such as Web servers, which have numerous clients and relatively short-lived client requests, statistical partitioning of the workload efficiently provides excellent load balance and fast response to cluster changes.

Network Load Balancing cluster servers emit a heartbeat to other hosts in the cluster and listen for the heartbeat of other hosts. If a server in a cluster fails, the remaining hosts adjust and redistribute the workload while maintaining continuous service to their clients.

Existing connections to an offline host are lost, but the Internet services remain continuously available. In most cases (for example, with Web servers), client software automatically retries the failed connections, and the clients experience only a few seconds' delay in receiving a response.

Managing Application State

Application state refers to data maintained by a server application on behalf of its clients. If a server application (such as a Web server) maintains state information about a client session that spans multiple TCP connections, it's usually important that all TCP connections for this client be directed to the same cluster host. A shopping cart at an e-commerce site and Secure Sockets Layer (SSL) state information are examples of a client's session state. Network Load Balancing can be used to scale applications that manage session state that spans multiple connections.

When the Network Load Balancing client affinity parameter setting is enabled, Network Load Balancing directs all TCP connections to the same cluster host. This allows session state to be maintained in host memory. If a server or network failure occurs during a client session, a new logon may be required to reauthenticate the client and reestablish session state. Also, adding a new cluster host redirects some client traffic to the new host, which can affect sessions, although ongoing TCP connections are not disturbed.

Client/server applications that manage client state so that it can be retrieved from any cluster host (for example, by embedding state within cookies or pushing it to a back-end database) do not need to use Network Load Balancing client affinity.

To further assist in managing session state, Network Load Balancing provides an optional client affinity setting that directs all client requests from a TCP/IP Class C address range to a single cluster host. This feature enables clients that use multiple proxy servers to have their TCP connections directed to the same cluster host.

The use of multiple proxy servers at the client's site causes requests from a single client to appear to originate from different systems. Assuming that all of the client's proxy servers are located within the same 254-host Class C address range, Network Load Balancing ensures that client sessions are handled by the same host with minimum impact on load distribution among the cluster hosts. Some very large client sites can use multiple proxy servers that span Class C address spaces.

In addition to session state, server applications often maintain persistent server-based state information that's updated by client transactions—for example, merchandise inventory at an e-commerce site.

Network Load Balancing should not be used to directly scale applications that independently update interclient state, such as SQL Server (other than for read-only database access), because updates made on one cluster host will not be visible to other cluster hosts.

To benefit from Network Load Balancing, applications must be designed to permit multiple instances to simultaneously access a shared database server that synchronizes updates. For example, Web servers with Active Server pages need to push client updates to a shared back-end database server.

Detailed Architecture

To maximize throughput and high availability, Network Load Balancing uses a fully distributed software architecture. An identical copy of the Network Load Balancing driver runs in parallel on each cluster host.

The drivers arrange for all cluster hosts on a single subnet to concurrently detect incoming network traffic for the cluster's primary IP address (and for additional IP addresses on multihomed hosts). On each cluster host, the driver acts as a filter between the network adapter's driver and the TCP/IP stack, allowing a portion of the incoming network traffic to be received by the host. By this means, incoming client requests are partitioned and the load balanced among the cluster hosts.

Network Load Balancing runs as a network driver logically beneath higher-level application protocols, such as HTTP and FTP. Figure 13-11 on page 284 shows the implementation of Network Load Balancing as an intermediate driver in the Windows 2000 network stack. The implications of this architecture include the following:

- **Maximizing throughput.** This architecture maximizes throughput by using the broadcast subnet to deliver incoming network traffic to all cluster hosts and by eliminating the need to route incoming packets to individual cluster hosts. Because filtering unwanted packets is faster than routing packets (which involves receiving, examining, rewriting, and resending), Network Load Balancing delivers higher network throughput than do dispatcher-based solutions.

    As network and server speeds grow, the throughput of Network Load Balancing throughput grows proportionally, thus eliminating any dependency on a particular hardware routing implementation. For example, Network Load Balancing has demonstrated 250 megabits per second (Mbps) throughput on gigabit networks.

■   **High availability.**   Another key advantage of Network Load Balancing's fully distributed architecture is enhanced high availability resulting from (N-1)–way failover in a cluster with N hosts. In contrast, dispatcher-based solutions create an inherent single point of failure, which must be eliminated using a redundant dispatcher that provides only one-way failover. This offers a less robust failover solution than does a fully distributed architecture.

■   **Using hub and switch on the subnet.**   The Network Load Balancing architecture takes advantage of the subnet's hub and switch architecture to simultaneously deliver incoming network traffic to all cluster hosts. However, this approach increases the burden on switches by occupying additional port bandwidth.

   This is usually not a concern in most intended applications, such as Web services and streaming media, because the percentage of incoming traffic is a small fraction of total network traffic. However, if the client-side network connections to the switch are significantly faster than the server-side connections, incoming traffic can occupy a prohibitive fraction of the server-side port bandwidth. The same problem arises if multiple clusters are hosted on the same switch and measures are not taken to set up virtual LANs for individual clusters.

■   **NDIS driver.**   During packet reception, Network Load Balancing's fully pipelined implementation overlaps the delivery of incoming packets to TCP/IP and the reception of other packets by the Network Driver Interface Specification (NDIS) driver. This speeds up overall processing and reduces latency because TCP/IP can process a packet while the NDIS driver receives a subsequent packet. It also reduces the overhead required for TCP/IP and the NDIS driver to coordinate their actions, and in many cases, it eliminates an extra memory copy of packet data.

   During packet sending, Network Load Balancing also enhances throughput and reduces latency and overhead by increasing the number of packets that TCP/IP can send with one NDIS call. To achieve these performance enhancements, Network Load Balancing allocates and manages a pool of packet buffers and descriptors that it uses to overlap the actions of TCP/IP and the NDIS driver.

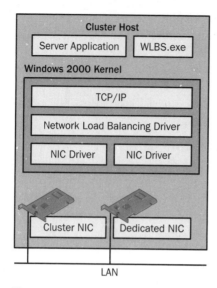

Figure 13-11 This diagram shows Network Load Balancing as an intermediate driver between TCP/IP and a NIC driver.

Distribution of Cluster Traffic

Network Load Balancing uses Layer 2 broadcast or multicast to simultaneously distribute incoming network traffic to all cluster hosts. In its default, unicast, mode of operation, Network Load Balancing reassigns the station address (MAC address) of the network adapter for which it is enabled (called the cluster adapter), and all cluster hosts are assigned the same MAC address. Incoming packets are thereby received by all cluster hosts and passed up to the Network Load Balancing driver for filtering.

To ensure uniqueness, the MAC address is derived from the cluster's primary IP address entered in the Network Load Balancing Properties dialog box. For a primary IP address of 1.2.3.4, the unicast MAC address is set to 02-BF-1-2-3-4. Network Load Balancing automatically modifies the cluster adapter's MAC address by setting a registry entry and then reloading the adapter's driver; the operating system does not have to be restarted.

If the cluster hosts are attached to a switch instead of a hub, the use of a common MAC address will create a conflict because Layer 2 switches expect to see unique source MAC addresses on all switch ports. To avoid this problem, Network Load Balancing uniquely modifies the source MAC address for outgoing packets; a cluster MAC address of 02-BF-1-2-3-4 is set to 02-h-1-2-3-4, where h is the host's priority within the cluster (set in the Network Load Balancing Properties dialog box). This technique prevents the switch from learning the cluster's actual MAC address, and as a result, incoming packets for the cluster are delivered to all switch ports. If the cluster hosts are connected directly to a hub instead of to a switch, Network Load Balancing's masking of the source MAC address in unicast mode can be disabled to avoid flooding upstream switches. This is accomplished by setting the Network Load Balancing registry parameter *MaskSrcMAC* to 0. The use of an upstream level-three switch will also limit switch flooding.

Network Load Balancing's unicast mode has the side effect of disabling communication between cluster hosts using the cluster adapters. Because outgoing packets for another cluster host are sent to the same MAC address as the sender, these packets are looped back within the sender by the network stack and never reach the wire. This limitation can be avoided by adding a second network adapter card to each cluster host. In this configuration, Network Load Balancing is bound to the network adapter on the subnet that receives incoming client requests, and the other adapter is typically placed on a separate, local subnet for communication between cluster hosts and with back-end file and database servers. Network Load Balancing uses only the cluster adapter for its heartbeat and remote control traffic. Communication between cluster hosts and hosts outside the cluster is never affected by Network Load Balancing's unicast mode.

Network traffic for a host's dedicated IP address (on the cluster adapter) is received by all cluster hosts because they all use the same MAC address. Because Network Load Balancing never load-balances traffic for the dedicated IP address, Network Load Balancing immediately delivers this traffic to TCP/IP on the intended host. On other cluster hosts, Network Load Balancing treats this traffic as load balanced traffic (because the target IP address does not match another host's dedicated IP address), and it might deliver it to TCP/IP, which will discard it. Excessive incoming network traffic for dedicated IP addresses can impose a performance penalty when Network Load Balancing operates in unicast mode because of the need for TCP/IP to discard unwanted packets.

Network Load Balancing provides a second mode for distributing incoming network traffic to all cluster hosts. Called multicast mode, this mode assigns a Layer 2 multicast address to the cluster adapter instead of changing the adapter's station address. The multicast MAC address is set to 03-BF-1-2-3-4 for a cluster's primary IP address of 1.2.3.4. Because each cluster host retains a unique station address, this mode alleviates the need for a second network adapter for communication between cluster hosts, and it also removes any performance penalty from the use of dedicated IP addresses. Network Load Balancing's unicast mode induces switch flooding in order to simultaneously deliver incoming network traffic to all cluster hosts. Also, when Network Load

Balancing uses multicast mode, switches often flood all ports by default to deliver multicast traffic. However, Network Load Balancing's multicast mode opens up the opportunity for the system administrator to limit switch flooding by configuring a virtual LAN within the switch for the ports corresponding to the cluster hosts. This can be accomplished by manually programming the switch or by using IGMP or GMRP protocols. The current version of Network Load Balancing does not provide automatic support for IGMP or GMRP.

Network Load Balancing implements the necessary Address Resolution Protocol (ARP) functionality to ensure that the cluster's primary IP address and other virtual IP addresses resolve to the cluster's multicast MAC address. (The dedicated IP address continues to resolve to the cluster adapter's station address.) Experience has shown that Cisco routers currently do not accept an ARP response from the cluster that resolves unicast IP addresses to multicast MAC addresses. This problem can be overcome by adding a static ARP entry to the router for each virtual IP address, and the cluster's multicast MAC address can be obtained from the Network Load Balancing Properties dialog box or from the Wlbs.exe remote control program. The default unicast mode avoids this problem because the cluster's MAC address is a unicast MAC address.

Network Load Balancing does not manage any incoming IP traffic other than TCP, User Datagram Protocol (UDP), and Generic Routing Encapsulation (GRE, as part of PPTP) traffic for specified ports. It does not filter ICMP, IGMP, ARP (except as described earlier), or other IP protocols. All such traffic is passed unchanged to the TCP/IP protocol software on all of the hosts within the cluster. As a result, the cluster can generate duplicate responses from certain point-to-point TCP/IP programs (such as ping) when the cluster IP address is used. Because of the robustness of TCP/IP and its ability to deal with replicated datagrams, other protocols behave correctly in the clustered environment. These programs can use the dedicated IP address for each host to avoid this behavior.

Load Balancing Algorithm

Network Load Balancing employs a fully distributed filtering algorithm to map incoming clients to the cluster hosts. This algorithm was chosen to enable cluster hosts to independently and quickly make a load balancing decision for each incoming packet. It was optimized to deliver statistically even load balance for a large client population making numerous relatively small requests, such as those typically made to Web servers.

When the client population is small or the client connections produce widely varying loads on the server, Network Load Balancing's load balancing algorithm is less effective. However, the simplicity and speed of Network Load

Balancing's algorithm allow it to deliver very high performance, including both high throughput and low response time, in a wide range of useful client/server applications.

Network Load Balancing load-balances incoming client requests so as to direct a selected percentage of new requests to each cluster host; the load percentage is set in the Network Load Balancing Properties dialog box for each port range to be load-balanced. The algorithm does not respond to changes in the load on each cluster host (such as the CPU load or memory usage). However, the mapping is modified when the cluster membership changes, and load percentages are renormalized accordingly.

When inspecting an arriving packet, all hosts simultaneously perform a statistical mapping to quickly determine which host should handle the packet. The mapping uses a randomization function that generates a host priority based on the IP address, port, and other information. The corresponding host forwards the packet up the network stack to TCP/IP, and the other cluster hosts discard it. The mapping remains invariant unless the membership of cluster hosts changes, ensuring that a given client's IP address and port will always map to the same cluster host. However, the particular cluster host to which the client's IP address and port map cannot be predetermined because the randomization function takes into account the current and past cluster's membership to minimize remappings. The load balancing algorithm assumes that client IP addresses and port numbers (when client affinity is not enabled) are statistically independent. This assumption can break down if a server-side firewall is used that proxies client addresses with one IP address and client affinity is enabled. In this case, all client requests will be handled by one cluster host, and load balancing is defeated. However, if client affinity is not enabled, the distribution of client ports within the firewall usually provides good load balance.

In general, the quality of load balance is statistically determined by the number of clients making requests. This behavior is analogous to dice throws, where the number of cluster hosts determines the number of sides of a die, and the number of client requests corresponds to the number of throws. The load distribution improves with the number of client requests just as the fraction of throws of an n-sided die resulting in a given face approaches $1/n$ with an increasing number of throws. As a rule of thumb, with client affinity set, there must be many more clients than cluster hosts to begin to observe even load balance. As the statistical nature of the client population fluctuates, the evenness of load balance can be observed to vary slightly over time. Note that achieving precisely identical load balance on each cluster host imposes a performance penalty (throughput and response time) because of the overhead required to measure and react to load changes. This performance penalty must be weighed against the benefit of maximizing the use of cluster resources (principally CPU and memory). In any case, excess cluster resources must be maintained to absorb the client load in case of failover. Network Load Balancing takes the approach of using a very simple and robust load balancing algorithm that delivers the highest possible performance and availability.

The Network Load Balancing client affinity settings are implemented by modifying the statistical mapping algorithm's input data. When client affinity is selected in the Network Load Balancing Properties dialog box, the client's port information is not used as part of the mapping. Hence, all requests from the same client always map to the same host within the cluster. This constraint has no timeout value (as is often used in dispatcher-based implementations) and persists until there is a change in cluster membership. When single affinity is selected, the mapping algorithm uses the client's full IP address. However, when Class C affinity is selected, the algorithm uses only the Class C portion (upper 24 bits) of the client's IP address. This ensures that all clients within the same Class C address space map to the same cluster host.

In mapping clients to hosts, Network Load Balancing cannot directly track the boundaries of sessions (such as SSL sessions) because it makes its load balancing decisions when TCP connections are established and prior to the arrival of application data within the packets. Also, it cannot track the boundaries of UDP streams because the logical session boundaries are defined by particular applications. Instead, the Network Load Balancing affinity settings are used to assist in preserving client sessions. When a cluster host fails or leaves the cluster, its client connections are always dropped. After a new cluster membership is determined by convergence (described shortly), clients that previously mapped to the failed host are remapped across the surviving hosts. All other client sessions are unaffected by the failure and continue to receive uninterrupted service from the cluster. In this manner, the Network Load Balancing load balancing algorithm minimizes disruption to clients when a failure occurs.

When a new host joins the cluster, it induces convergence, and a new cluster membership is computed. When convergence completes, a minimal portion of the clients will be remapped to the new host. Network Load Balancing tracks TCP connections on each host, and, after their current TCP connection completes, the next connection from the affected clients will be handled by the new cluster host; UDP streams are immediately handled by the new cluster host. This can potentially break some client sessions that span multiple connections or comprise UDP streams. Hence, hosts should be added to the cluster at times that minimize disruption of sessions. To completely avoid this problem, session state must be managed by the server application so that it can be reconstructed or retrieved from any cluster host. For example, session state can be pushed to a back-end database server or kept in client cookies. SSL session state is automatically re-created by reauthenticating the client.

The GRE stream within the Point-to-Point Tunneling Protocol (PPTP) protocol is a special case of a session that is unaffected by adding a cluster host. Because the GRE stream is temporally contained within the duration of its TCP control connection, Network Load Balancing tracks this GRE stream along with its corresponding control connection. This prevents the addition of a cluster host from disrupting the PPTP tunnel.

Convergence

Network Load Balancing hosts periodically exchange multicast or broadcast heartbeat messages within the cluster. This allows them to monitor the status of the cluster. When the state of the cluster changes (such as when hosts fail, leave, or join the cluster), Network Load Balancing invokes a process known as *convergence*, in which the hosts exchange heartbeat messages to determine a new, consistent state of the cluster and to elect the host with the highest host priority as the new default host. When all cluster hosts have reached consensus on the correct new state of the cluster, they record the change in cluster membership upon completion of convergence in the Windows event log.

During convergence, the hosts continue to handle incoming network traffic as usual except that traffic for a failed host does not receive service. Client requests to surviving hosts are unaffected. Convergence terminates when all cluster hosts report a consistent view of the cluster membership for several heartbeat periods. If a host attempts to join the cluster with inconsistent port rules or an overlapping host priority, completion of convergence is inhibited. This prevents an improperly configured host from handling cluster traffic. At the completion of convergence, client traffic for a failed host is redistributed to the remaining hosts. If a host is added to the cluster, convergence allows this host to receive its share of load balanced traffic. Expansion of the cluster does not affect ongoing cluster operations and is achieved transparently to both Internet clients and to server programs. However, it might affect client sessions because clients might be remapped to different cluster hosts between connections, as described in the preceding section.

In unicast mode, each cluster host periodically broadcasts heartbeat messages, and in multicast mode, it multicasts these messages. Each heartbeat message occupies one Ethernet frame and is tagged with the cluster's primary IP address so that multiple clusters can reside on the same subnet. Network Load Balancing heartbeat messages are assigned an ether type value of hexadecimal 886F. The default period between sending heartbeats is 1 second, and this value can be adjusted with the *MsgAlivePeriod* registry parameter. During convergence, the exchange period is reduced by half to expedite completion. Even for large clusters, the bandwidth required for heartbeat messages is very low (for example, 24 KB/second for a 16-way cluster). Network Load Balancing assumes that a host is functioning properly within the cluster as long as it participates in the normal heartbeat exchange among the cluster hosts. If other hosts do not receive a heartbeat message from any member for several periods of message exchange, they initiate convergence. The number of missed heartbeat messages required to initiate convergence is set to 5 by default and can be adjusted using the *NumAliveMsgs* registry parameter.

A cluster host will immediately initiate convergence if it receives a heartbeat message from a new host or if it receives an inconsistent heartbeat message that indicates a problem in the load distribution. When receiving a heartbeat message from a new host, the host determines whether the other host has been handling traffic from the same clients. This problem can arise if the cluster subnet was rejoined after having been partitioned. More likely, the new host was already converged alone in a disjoint subnet and has received no client traffic. This can occur if the switch introduces a lengthy delay in connecting the host to the subnet. If a cluster host detects this problem and the other host has received more client connections since the last convergence, it immediately stops handling client traffic in the affected port range. Because both hosts are exchanging heartbeats, the host that has received more connections continues to handle traffic, while the other host waits for the end of convergence to begin handling its portion of the load. This heuristic algorithm eliminates potential conflicts in load handling when a previously partitioned cluster subnet is rejoined; this event is logged in the event log.

Remote Control

The Network Load Balancing remote control mechanism uses the UDP protocol and is assigned port 2504. Remote control datagrams are sent to the cluster's primary IP address. Because they are handled by the Network Load Balancing driver on each cluster host, these datagrams must be routed to the cluster subnet (instead of to a back-end subnet to which the cluster is attached). When remote control commands are issued from within the cluster, they are broadcast on the local subnet. This ensures that they are received by all cluster hosts, even if the cluster runs in unicast mode.

For More Information

See the following resources for further information:

- What's New in Clustering Services at *http://www.microsoft.com/windowsserver2003/evaluation/overview/technologies/clustering.mspx*

- Windows Server 2003 Product Overviews at *http://www.microsoft.com/windowsserver2003/evaluation/overview/*

- Windows Server 2003 vFeatures guide at *http://www.microsoft.com/windowsserver2003/evaluation/features/*

- Introducing the ".NET" in the Windows Server 2003 Family at *http://www.microsoft.com/windowsserver2003/evaluation/overview/dotnet/dotnet.mspx*

- Windows 2000 Server at *http://www.microsoft.com/windows2000/server/*

- Application Center 2000 at *http://www.microsoft.com/applicationcenter/*

- Windows 2000 Clustering Technologies at *http://www.microsoft.com/windows2000/technologies/clustering/*

- Increasing System Reliability and Availability with Windows 2000 at *http://www.microsoft.com/windows2000/server/evaluation/business/relavail.asp*

- Hardware Compatibility List at *http://www.microsoft.com/hcl/*

- Windows 2000 Server Family: Advanced Scalability at *http://www.microsoft.com/windows2000/advancedserver/evaluation/business/overview/scalable/*

14

Multilingual Support

A truly global enterprise is one that is able to do business seamlessly in multiple languages, providing support for language and cultural differences across regional borders. To achieve this goal, you need powerful and flexible multilingual technologies that are easy to use and deploy. Your users, partners, and customers need access to resources in the language of their choice regardless of where or on what platform they are working. Most of all, you need to be able to provide these services while keeping support and deployment costs under control. Microsoft has a number of technologies that can help make this goal a reality.

Microsoft has devoted years of effort and commitment to supporting multilingual computing. With the Microsoft Windows 2000 platform, Microsoft took a major step forward by converting all operating system elements to the international Unicode standard. Microsoft also introduced the Multilingual User Interface (MUI) pack for Windows 2000. The MUI allowed users to switch the languages of their user interfaces and applications. Microsoft improved this technology with Windows XP by supporting more languages and locales and by making the technology both easier to use and more flexible. With the release of the Windows Server 2003 family, Microsoft has taken this technology to the next level by creating a server platform that can support the multilingual enterprise.

One of the key goals of MUI technology is to enable IT professionals to deliver MUI-based technology in as simple and cost-effective a manner as possible. Microsoft has a number of deployment technologies, including Windows Installer, which makes the Multilingual User Interface one of the most cost-effective ways to provide global computing. The MUI is also fully supported by Microsoft Office and other localizable Unicode applications. Plus developers can utilize the functionality of the MUI through published APIs, allowing line-of-business and third-party applications to use it as well.

Global Business Challenges

A global enterprise is one that can carry out its business in any location in the world, in any language, as seamlessly and efficiently as possible. Microsoft and its partners have years of experience in deploying software in a global environment. Critical areas that must be taken into account to achieve the goal of a truly global enterprise include the following:

- **Accommodating regional differences.**   In today's global market, people and organizations need to work and communicate in a variety of languages. Not only do they need technologies that support the languages of their users, customers and partners, but they also need to be able to deal with local currencies, date and time formats, character sets, and more. User applications and servers must be able to function in this environment. They must support international formats and standards. Users need to be able to open and display documents regardless of the language in which they were created. Your systems need to be able to display and store information regardless of the character set they use.

- **Supporting localized applications.**   Most companies today use customized software applications. These can be line-of-business applications, tools for managing human resources or carrying out analyses, or internal applications used by a single department or division. For these applications to operate in an international enterprise, they need to be localizable. Localizable software is software that can be easily adapted to a global environment without the application being rewritten. Enabling software for multilingual use, however, can entail a costly development effort without an easy and cost-effective way to leverage international standards. Thus, not only do companies need their applications to support multiple languages but they also need a way to standardize this support across the enterprise at a reasonable cost.

- **Providing support for multilanguage users, services, and workstations.**   In a multinational environment, it's becoming increasingly important to support multiple languages within a single office or division. A single user might need access to software in multiple languages. Equipment in one location might be used in more than one language. This situation can become further complicated when mobile or roaming users need access to systems in the language of their choice in more than one location. Supporting and providing services to users who need to work in more than one language has traditionally posed significant challenges and high costs.

■ **Managing deployment across multiple regions.** Deploying software in an international environment poses significant challenges above and beyond those associated with deployment in one location only. Deployment must account for every unique combination of language and operating system, not to mention server and desktop applications. When you add the vast diversity of currencies and localized standards for representing numbers, date and time values, and so on, the complexity of the deployment can become immense. This results in longer deployment and higher costs. The ideal goal is to find a way to simplify the deployment while still meeting the multilingual requirements of your organization.

■ **Deploying patches and hot fixes in a worldwide environment.** Support for patches, hot fixes, and upgrades is an increasingly important consideration as networks grow. The ability to quickly deploy critical changes is crucial not only for reasons of network security but as a cost-saving measure. Regular maintenance and upgrade tasks account for a significant measure of the work that the information technology (IT) department has to do every day. This load increases considerably with the number of configurations they must support. In a multilingual environment, this load can quickly overwhelm an IT department. Every combination of operating system, language, and localization is another potential support case that needs its own tracking, upgrade path, and support plan. In addition, there is the elapsed time involved in getting a crucial fix in every language where it is required. The elapsed time between release of an upgrade or patch for the English version of software and for localized versions can be significant. A key goal in planning for a global enterprise is to find a way to minimize the demands on IT resources by creating a standardized deployment that can be applied internationally. This leads to savings in time and support costs and frees your highly trained IT professionals to work on high-level tasks that help build the value of your business.

One factor, however, runs through this entire discussion: the total cost of ownership (TCO). A business has to keep its eye on the bottom line. A solution that solves all your localization challenges and yet is too expensive to deploy and maintain will ultimately fail. A solution that is cost-effective contributes to the business as a whole by lowering costs.

Enabling a Multinational Enterprise

Microsoft has a number of options available to help you achieve the goal of a truly multilingual and multinational enterprise. Windows Server 2003 will soon be available in a number of localized versions optimized for particular regions of the world. In addition, the English-language version of Windows Server 2003, in conjunction with the Multilingual User Interface, allows you to switch the language of the interface as needed, supporting a wide variety of languages and locales. Each option has its own advantages and disadvantages. Finding the option that fits the needs of your organization is the first step toward a multilingual enterprise.

Multilingual User Interface

The MUI is a product from Microsoft that enables IT professionals to deploy Windows in a multilingual, global environment without creating a unique localized installation for each region that must be supported. The MUI allows the user interface, including the Start Menu, program elements, alerts, and help files on a particular installation to switch among languages as needed.

The MUI runs on top of the English version of the operating system. This means that the IT department does not have to deploy and manage a unique version of software for every language that is required. Instead, they can standardize the deployment to the English-language version of the operating system with the MUI. The MUI also supports desktop applications, including Microsoft Office, as well as server products such as Microsoft SQL Server.

Options for Multinational Enterprises

The English version of Windows Server 2003 is the best choice for organizations that do most of their business in English but occasionally need to work in another language. For example, a company based in the United States has a subsidiary located in Japan. The company does the bulk of its business in English; however, it sometimes needs to read e-mail and documents written in Japanese. It also maintains a Japanese-language Web site. The English-language version of Microsoft Windows Server 2003 is a sufficient server for this company's needs. In addition, the company might use Microsoft Windows XP as the desktop operating system. It might also use Microsoft Office XP to view Japanese documents and read e-mail written in Japanese.

The Multilingual User Interface brings flexible support for multiple languages to the English version of Windows Server 2003. The MUI is the best solution for businesses that need to carry out their business in a number of languages. For example, imagine a company that has numerous offices based worldwide. Users in its various offices need to be able to work in their regional language, and in some locations multiple languages must be supported. The IT department has determined that the only way to support the entire company in a cost-effective manner is to create a standardized deployment that can be rolled out to all regions. Deploying Windows Server 2003 with the Multilingual User Interface allows them to meet these goals. The MUI is also the best choice when a company needs to work either in two or more languages in a single location, particularly where multiple users need to log on to the same computer in different languages, or where there are roaming users. Take a company based in the United States that has branch offices in a number of countries, for example. In these locations, people do their work in a mix of English and the language of their region. By deploying the operating system and Office XP with the MUI, the company is able to achieve this goal.

Microsoft will also ship versions of Windows Server 2003 localized for a single region. Localized versions are optimized for use in a single language other than English. This comes at the cost of some flexibility. A localized version of Windows Server 2003 can support only the language in which it is localized. In addition, deploying and maintaining multiple localized versions is typically more difficult and expensive than supporting a single version. A localized version is the best choice when a company requires only a single language other than English. A company based in Japan, which does its business in Japanese, can use the Japanese-language versions of Windows Server 2003 to do its business.

Multinational Improvements

Windows Server 2003 and Windows XP Professional are the next step in multi-language support. They incorporate a number of important improvements over the previous version of the MUI, including the following:

- **More locales.**   Windows 2000 featured support for a variety of languages, locales, and input methods. This has been expanded in Windows XP and Windows Server 2003 with the addition of nine new locales, bringing the total number of localizations supported to 135.

- **Easier to use.**   The Regional And Language Options control panel has also been improved in Windows XP and Windows Server 2003 to make it easier to carry out language-related tasks, particularly those that are most commonly used. The new task-based design makes it easier to manage and configure language support on desktop computers.

- **Easier to get help.** The Multilanguage Document Consultant in the Windows XP Help and Support Center can help users diagnose and resolve problems encountered in opening, viewing, and editing multilingual documents.

- **Support for multiple languages and scripts.**   One of the three included language collections is installed by default, depending on the language version; the other collections are installed on demand. The Basic Language Collection supports most Western and Central European languages, while the Complex Script Collection supports complex script languages such as Arabic, Hebrew, Indic, and some Asian languages and languages that use right-to-left script. Finally, the East Asian Collection includes support for additional Asian languages.

- **Language for non-Unicode programs.** Windows XP Professional and Windows Server 2003 also allow you to specify a language setting for non-Unicode programs. This setting determines the language to be used by programs that do not support the Unicode standard.

Multilingual User Interface

With Windows 2000 Professional, Microsoft introduced the Multilingual User Interface, a technology that enabled multiple localized interfaces to coexist on the same installation of Windows. Microsoft has continued to improve this technology. The MUI for Windows XP made this technology even more powerful, adding localizations and making the technology easier to use and deploy. The Multilanguage User Interface for Office XP, a related technology, enables user interface switching for Office applications as well as advanced proofreading and editing tools for multiple languages. With Windows Server 2003, Microsoft has taken this technology to the next level, including further improvements to the deployment methodology, support for multilingual Terminal Server sessions, and more.

Other MUI improvements in Windows XP Professional and Windows Server 2003 include the following:

- **Support for Terminal Services.** Terminal Services is a technology from Microsoft that allows users to log on remotely to a central server and create virtual Windows sessions. The MUI for Windows Server 2003 now supports multilingual Terminal Services sessions. A server running the Multilingual User Interface and Windows Server

2003 will now allow users to log on and create terminal sessions in different languages simultaneously on the same Terminal Services server. In the past, a separate localized terminal server was required for each localization that was to be supported. The MUI can drastically reduce the costs involved in creating and supporting terminal sessions in a multilingual environment.

■ **Better deployment options and technologies.** Deployment costs are a major consideration in supporting the large number of possible language and localization combinations. To make deployment easier, the MUI for Windows Server 2003 now supports Microsoft Windows Installer technology. Microsoft Windows Installer is a technology for creating setup packages that can be easily managed and deployed. This means that the MUI is easier to deploy, maintain, and configure, resulting in a considerable savings in deployment costs. Microsoft has a number of deployment technologies that can be used to make your global deployment run more smoothly. For more information, see the section "Deploying a Multilingual Enterprise" later in this chapter.

Supported Software and Platforms

In addition to Windows XP Professional and Windows Server 2003, the MUI supports a number of platforms and applications.

■ **Office XP.** The Multilanguage User Interface for Office XP offers a number of powerful international features, including user interface switching and proofreading and editing tools for multiple languages.

■ **Windows CE.** Developers can use the MUI APIs to create localizable applications for mobile devices running Windows CE.

■ **SQL Server.** Unicode-aware server products such as SQL Server can be run on Windows Server 2003 with the Multilingual User Interface to provide services in a multilingual enterprise. Microsoft SQL Server offers support for multiple languages and character sets. See your SQL Server documentation for details.

■ **Legacy products.** The MUI for Windows Server 2003 uses technologies similar to those of the MUI for Windows 2000 and the MUI for Office 2000. At the time that a Windows 2000 Server is upgraded to Windows Server 2003, the MUI should be updated as well to achieve full functionality.

What the MUI Can Do for You

The Multilingual User Interface pack for Windows Server 2003 is a powerful tool for enabling your global enterprise to meet its goals. The MUI lets you provide flexible multilingual support while keeping costs manageable. In particular, it lets you do the following:

- **Accommodate regional requirements.**   The MUI provides a flexible way to accommodate regional requirements throughout your enterprise. The MUI supports management for a variety of alternative input devices such as keyboards for Asian character sets as well as language switching for the bulk of user interface elements, including the Start Menu, alerts and dialogs, and Help. This enables you to meet your regional software requirements around the globe with a single operating system.

- **Support multilingual desktops and users.**   Windows XP with the MUI is an excellent choice for a multilingual desktop platform. A more flexible multilingual solution means that you can support a wider variety of global scenarios. For example, under the MUI, users who log on to the same computer can use different languages. Without the MUI, this kind of functionality would typically require a cumbersome dual-boot configuration. The MUI can also be configured to support multilingual roaming users. In a fully MUI-enabled environment, users can log on in their language of choice at any computer.

- **Deploy a single-server configuration internationally.**   Deployment of software in a global environment can pose serious challenges. The MUI pack for Microsoft Windows Server 2003 has been designed to help reduce these challenges and make multilingual deployment as simple as possible. Because the MUI is based on the English-language versions of the operating system, IT staff have only one binary version of the operating system to deploy and maintain. This can lead to considerable savings in the deployment effort and in the cost of supporting and maintaining the software down the road. For more information about deploying the Multilingual User Interface, see the upcoming section "Deploying a Multilingual Enterprise."

- **Simplify support and maintenance.**   Deployment is only the beginning of the costs associated with supporting a piece of software. The MUI pack has been designed to offer companies the ability to achieve a lower TCO throughout the lifetime of the software. With the MUI, there is only one binary version of the operating system to be maintained and updated. The MUI makes common maintenance tasks, such as deploying hot fixes and patches, much simpler. Organizations that rely on localized versions of the operating system often experience lag time as hot fixes and updates are localized into various languages. Not only does this mean that fixes and updates are faster under the MUI, but it means that your environment is more secure because fixes are deployed in a timely fashion. The bottom line is a powerful, flexible multilingual enterprise that has a low TCO.

- **Support multiple language with terminal services.**   With Terminal Services, the Multilingual User Interface for Windows Server 2003 can provide terminal support to multiple users in their languages of choice. Terminal sessions can be created on the server in any installed language simultaneously. This gives administrators a cost-effective way to support multiple languages without requiring an additional server for each language supported.

Deploying a Multilingual Enterprise

There are a number of important considerations to weigh in planning any deployment. Deploying worldwide brings additional challenges because of the sheer number of languages and locales that must be supported. A number of common factors must be taken into account when deploying and maintaining a multilingual enterprise:

- **Regional requirements.**   The first step to a smooth international deployment is to determine the language requirements for the regions that your organization spans. You must also consider line-of-business applications that must accommodate multiple languages. For every region in your enterprise, determine exactly which languages, dialects, currencies, and calendar formats must be supported. Also note whether these regions require any alternative input devices. This information will be invaluable as you proceed through the deployment process.

- **Hardware requirements.**   The Multilingual User Interface uses installable modules called *language packs* to supply support for individual localizations. These packages require additional hard disk space. For the complex and right-to-left language pack, which supports Hebrew, Arabic, and other languages, an additional 100 MB of hard disk space is required. The East Asian language pack requires 230 MB. You must also consider hardware requirements for any alternative input devices you are using.

- **Roaming users' needs.** The Microsoft Windows Server 2003 MUI pack allows you to support roaming users in multiple languages. If this is your goal, you must ensure either that the required MUI packs are installed on all desktops that support roaming users or that they are available for installation on demand on those desktops. See the upcoming section "Configuring Desktops" for more information about install-on-demand configurations.

- **Microsoft Office XP multilanguage deployments.** Microsoft Office XP is a premium class, world-ready productivity platform. If you are using Microsoft Office XP in your organization, consider deploying it at the same time you deploy the operating system. Microsoft has a number of powerful tools and technologies that can be used to make deploying Office simpler. Microsoft Office XP is available in localized versions or with the Microsoft Office Multilingual User Interface Pack.

> **More Info**   For more information about Multilanguage Office XP deployment, see "Microsoft Office XP in a Multilingual Environment" at *http://www.microsoft.com/office/evaluation/indepth/multilingual/*.

Configuring Server Platforms

Because the MUI supports Microsoft Windows Installer technology natively, you can use any of the Microsoft tools that use Windows Installer to help you configure and maintain your servers. The MUI packages each supported language as a separate .msi package. These can be installed individually by double-clicking the package or by using Add Or Remove Programs in Control Panel.

- **Command prompt installation.** The MUI can be installed from the command prompt by invoking Msiexec. You can specify a number of switches, including options to install the package for the current user only, for all users on the current machine, or for the default user on the current machine. If you specify the default user, the MUI will be available for all subsequent users created on the same machine.

■ **Unattended installation.** Windows Server 2003 with the MUI supports unattended setup. Use an unattended installation to automate the installation of the MUI either as a part of Windows Server 2003 setup or after Windows setup has completed. Because the MUI comes in several CDs, you need to create a network share containing all the language packages you want to include in your installation and an answer file specifying the configuration you would like to install.

Configuring Desktops

There are a number of considerations to take into account when configuring multilingual desktops for users. Microsoft offers several features that can make this task run much more smoothly:

■ **Default user language settings.** After you have determined the language settings that are required within your organization, you can apply these as the default on your desktop computers. When the default language settings have been defined on a desktop computer, all subsequent users created on that computer will inherit those language settings. User accounts that already exist will not be affected. These settings can be defined through the UI on that computer or by means of an answer file during an unattended installation.

■ **Group Policy.** Users' regional and language options can be centrally managed using Group Policy. An administrator can create a logon script that applies language settings, including default language and input methods, when the user logs on.

■ **Install-on-demand deployment of MUI packages.** Administrators can define user and computer configurations using per-computer assigned installations by means of a Group Policy. This will allow them to install MUI packages on user computers before these users log on. When an administrator is installing MUI packages for East Asian or Complex Script languages, the installation will fail unless the required language packs for these languages are already installed on the user computer or the Windows Server 2003 installation CD is still in the CD drive. MUI packages in the Active Directory directory service are always per-user installations. MUI per-user installations are not recommended, although they work because only the installing user can uninstall the package from Add Or Remove Programs. Other users will be able to use the MUI packages installed in the computer but won't be able to uninstall them.

- **Configuring localized content.**   You can configure your desktops to receive localized content such as news and weather from the Internet, or information from intranet- and extranet-based servers. This is configured by changing the Location setting on the Regional And Language Options control panel.

- **Microsoft Office XP multilanguage support.**   Microsoft Office XP is the productivity suite of choice for a multilingual environment. Office XP is available in localized versions or with the Office XP Multilingual User Interface Pack based on the English-language version of Office XP, which includes proofreading tools for viewing and editing documents in multiple languages. When deploying Microsoft Windows XP in a multilingual environment, you should consider deploying Office XP at the same time. Microsoft has a number of powerful tools and technologies to help you deploy Office XP as simply as possible.

Considerations for Multilingual Applications

Developing localizable applications can have a big payoff in a multilingual environment. The MUI provides public APIs that can be used to develop fully localizable applications. Your applications can support multiple languages and complex scripts when you take these steps to leverage the power of the multilingual support contained in the MUI and the operating system:

- **Make your application Unicode.**   One of the key considerations when developing multinational applications is to utilize Unicode. Unicode is an international standard capable of representing most of the languages in use in the world today. Applications coded to Unicode can easily display user interface elements in any language. This frees you from reliance on code pages for language support. To be localizable, an application must be Unicode enabled.

- **Create a resource DLL for each supported language.**   MUI-enabled applications use separate resource DLLs to store user interface strings for different languages. This method might require additional effort at the outset, but it provides significant advantages in the long run. Not only does this method of coding allow user interface switching, but it's easy to update applications with new languages without making changes to the core binary or other resource DLLs. This makes your application completely localizable.

For More Information

See the following resources for further information:

- Multilingual Features in Microsoft Windows XP Professional at *http:// www.microsoft.com/windowsxp/pro/techinfo/planning/multilingual/*

- Microsoft Office XP in a Multilingual Environment at *http://www.micro- soft.com/office/evaluation/indepth/multilingual/*

- Windows XP and Windows 2000 MUI FAQ at *http://www.micro- soft.com/globaldev/FAQs/Multilang.asp*

- Writing Multilingual User Interface Applications at *http://www.micro- soft.com/globaldev/articles/muiapp.asp*

Part III

Getting Started

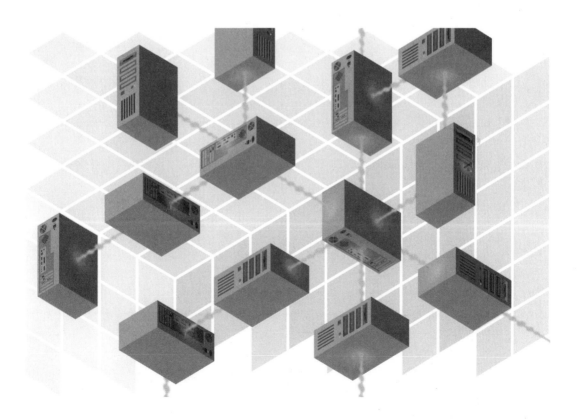

15

Deploying Windows Server 2003

The purpose of this chapter is to help you plan for the installation of Windows Server 2003 in a network environment. This chapter only scratches the surface, though. The *Microsoft Windows Server 2003 Deployment Kit* (Microsoft Press, 2003) contains much more help with planning and deploying Microsoft's latest server operating system. Also, for information about setting up multiple domains with structured relationships, see the deployment kit. You can view the Resource Kits on Microsoft's Web site at *http://www.microsoft.com/windows/reskits/*.

After reading this chapter, you'll be ready to run Windows Server 2003 Setup and, later, use the Configure Your Server Wizard. Together, Setup and the Configure Your Server Wizard help you get your servers up and running quickly. To find out more about Configure Your Server, see Help and Support Center in Windows Server 2003. To open Help and Support Center, after completing Setup, click Start, and then click Help And Support. You can also view Help and Support topics on Microsoft's Web site at *http://www.microsoft.com/windowsserver2003/*.

Upgrades Compared with New Installations

This section compares upgrading with performing a new installation to help you decide whether to perform a new installation. (See Chapter 16, "Upgrading from Windows NT 4.0 Server," and Chapter 17, "Upgrading from Windows 2000 Server," for more information about upgrading.) Upgrading is either replacing Windows NT 4.0 (with Service Pack 5 or later) with a product in the Windows

Server 2003 family or replacing Windows 2000 with a product in the Windows Server 2003Server 2003 family. Installing, in contrast with upgrading, means completely removing the previous operating system or installing a product in the Windows Server 2003 family on a disk or disk partition with no previous operating system.

Upgrade Considerations

The following list contains some points to consider when doing an upgrade:

- With an upgrade, configuration is simpler, and your existing users, settings, groups, rights, and permissions are retained.

- With an upgrade, you do not need to reinstall files and applications. As with any major changes to the hard disk, however, it is recommended that you back up the disk before beginning an upgrade.

- If you want to upgrade and then use the same applications as before, be sure to review application information in Relnotes.htm (in the \Docs folder on the Setup CD). Also, for the most recent information on compatible applications for products in the Windows Server 2003 family, see the software compatibility information in the Windows Catalog at *http://www.microsoft.com/windows/catalog/*.

New Installation Considerations

The following list contains some points to consider when doing clean installations:

- If you reformat your hard disk and then perform a new installation, the efficiency of your disk might improve (compared with not reformatting it). Reformatting also gives you the opportunity to modify the size or number of disk partitions to make them match your requirements more closely.

- If you want to practice careful configuration management, such as on a server where high availability is important, you might want to perform a new installation on that server instead of an upgrade. This is especially true on servers on which the operating system has been upgraded several times in the past.

- It's possible to install Windows Server 2003 and also allow the computer to sometimes run another operating system. Setting up the computer this way, however, presents complexities because of file system issues. For more information, see "Installing Multiple Operating Systems" later in this chapter.

■   If you want to install Windows Server 2003 on a computer that previously ran an operating system released before Windows 2000, note theServer 2003 following:

❏   Do not upgrade to or install Windows Server 2003 on a compressed drive unless the drive was compressed with the NTFS file system compression utility. Uncompress a DriveSpace or DoubleSpace volume before running Setup on it.

❏   If you used Windows NT 4.0 to create a volume set, mirror set, stripe set, or stripe set with parity and you want to run Setup for Windows Server 2003 on that computer, you must prepare the disk set first. For details, see "Working with Volumes, Mirrors, and Stripes" later in this chapter.

System Requirements

To ensure adequate performance, make sure computers on which you install Windows Server 2003 meet the following requirements:

■   One or more processors with a recommended minimum speed of 550 MHz. (The minimum supported speed is 133 MHz.) Processors from the Intel Pentium/Celeron family or AMD K6/Athlon/Duron family or compatible processors are recommended. See Chapter 1, "Product Family," to learn how many processors each edition of Windows Server 2003 supports.

■   256 MB of RAM recommended minimum. (128 MB is the minimum supported.) See Chapter 1, "Product Family," to learn the maximum amount of memory that each edition of Windows Server 2003 supports. For computers with more than 4 GB of RAM, be sure to check the hardware compatibility information in the Windows Catalog at *http://www.microsoft.com/windows/catalog/*.

> **Note**   For Windows Server 2003, Enterprise Edition, running on Itanium-based computers, the requirements are slightly different: one or more processors with a minimum speed of 733 MHz (a maximum of eight processors per computer is supported) and 1 GB of RAM minimum.

- A hard disk partition or volume with enough free space to accommodate the setup process. To ensure that you have flexibility in your later use of the operating system, it is recommended that you allow considerably more space than the minimum required for running Setup, which is approximately 1.25 GB to 2 GB on an x86-based computer and 3 GB to 4 GB on an Itanium-based computer. The larger amount of space is required if you are running Setup across a network instead of from a CD-ROM or if you are installing on a FAT or FAT32 partition. (NTFS is the recommended file system.)

  After Setup is finished, actual hard disk space used for the operating system will be more than the free space required for Setup because of space needed for the paging file, for any optional components you install, and (on domain controllers) for user accounts and other Active Directory information. The usual size for the paging file is 1.5 times the size of the RAM. For information about the paging file, optional components, user accounts, and information stored in Active Directory, see Help and Support Center. To open Help and Support Center, after completing Setup, click Start, and then click Help And Support.

- VGA or higher-resolution monitor (Super VGA 800×600 or higher recommended), keyboard, and (optionally) a mouse or other pointing device.

  As an alternative, for operation without a monitor or keyboard, you can choose a remote diagnostic and support processor that is designed for products in the Windows Server 2003 family. See the hardware compatibility information in the Windows Catalog at *http://www.microsoft.com/windows/catalog/* for more information.

- For CD installation, a CD-ROM or DVD drive.

- For network installation, one or more network adapters and related cables that are designed for products in the Windows Server 2003 family. Also a requirement is a server from which to offer network access for the Setup files.

- Appropriate hardware for the functionality you require. For example, if you plan to support network clients, the servers and clients must have appropriate network adapters and cables. As another example, if you require a server cluster, the entire cluster solution must be listed as compatible with Windows Server 2003. For more details about your hardware, see the hardware compatibility information in the Windows Catalog at *http://www.microsoft.com/windows/catalog/*.

Hardware Compatibility

One of the most important steps to take before installing a server is to confirm that your hardware is compatible with products in the Windows Server 2003 family. You can do this by running a preinstallation compatibility check from the Setup CD or by checking the hardware compatibility information at the Windows Catalog Web site. Also, as part of confirming hardware compatibility, verify that you have obtained updated hardware device drivers and an updated system basic input/output system (BIOS). (For an Itanium-based computer, check for an updated Extensible Firmware Interface.) Regardless of whether you run a preinstallation compatibility check, Setup checks hardware and software compatibility at the beginning of an installation and displays a report if there are incompatibilities.

Running a Preinstallation Compatibility Check

You can run a hardware and software compatibility check from the Setup CD. The compatibility check does not require you to actually begin an installation. You can run the compatibility check in either of two ways:

- Insert the Setup CD in the CD-ROM drive, and, when a display appears, follow the prompts for checking system compatibility. You will be offered the option to download the latest Setup files (through Dynamic Update) when you run the check. If you have Internet connectivity, it is recommended that you allow the download.

- Insert the Setup CD in the CD-ROM drive, open a command prompt, and type *d***:\i386\winnt32 /checkupgradeonly**, where *d* represents the CD-ROM drive.

Checking Drivers and System BIOS

Check that you have obtained updated drivers for your hardware devices and that you have the latest system BIOS (for an x86-based computer) or Extensible Firmware Interface (for an Itanium-based computer). The device manufacturers can help you obtain these items. Finally, if you have devices that do not use Plug and Play, or if you are aware that your Plug and Play devices are not implemented exactly to the standards, consider taking a device inventory of the hardware devices on your computer.

Inventorying Non–Plug and Play Devices

Products in the Windows Server 2003 family include Plug and Play technology so that devices (for example, video and network adapters) can be automatically recognized by the operating system, configuration conflicts are avoided, and you do not have to specify each device's settings by hand. However, if you have devices that do not use Plug and Play, or you are aware that your Plug and Play devices are not implemented exactly to the standards, you might want to take steps to avoid device configuration conflicts. This section describes steps you can take, if you choose, to understand your device configuration before running Setup.

To take an inventory of your devices, if your computer has an existing operating system, use it to obtain the current settings, such as memory address and interrupt request (IRQ), used with your devices. For example, with Windows NT 4.0, you can use Control Panel to view settings. (On the Start menu, point to Settings, click Control Panel, and then double-click icons such as Network and Ports.) You might also choose to view system BIOS information. To do this, watch the screen while starting the computer, and then press the appropriate key when prompted.

At the beginning of an installation, the Setup program automatically takes a device inventory as well. For devices that do not use Plug and Play or that are not implemented exactly to Plug and Play standards, taking your own inventory helps prevent the following difficulties:

■   If two or more adapters share IRQ settings or memory addresses, the Setup program might not be able to resolve the conflict. To prevent this, you can take one of two approaches:

  ❑   You can remove one of the adapters before running Setup and reinstall it afterward. For information about installing and configuring adapters and other hardware devices, see Help and Support Center.

  ❑   As an alternative, you can modify one adapter's IRQ settings and memory addresses before running Setup so that each adapter's settings are unique.

■   If adapters do not respond in a standard way to the attempts by Setup to detect or enumerate them, Setup might receive indecipherable or inaccurate information. In this case, you might need to remove these devices before running Setup and reinstall and configure them afterward. For information about installing and configuring adapters and other hardware devices, see Help and Support Center.

Table 15-1 shows the kinds of information to gather if you have devices that do not use Plug and Play and you decide to take a device inventory before starting Setup.

Table 15-1   Inventorying Device Configurations

Adapter	Information to Gather
Video	Adapter or chip set type and how many video adapters
Network	IRQ, I/O address, direct memory access (DMA) channel (if used), connector type (for example, BNC or twisted pair), and bus type
SCSI controller	Adapter model or chip set, IRQ, and bus type
Mouse	Mouse.type and port (COM1, COM2, or PS/2) or USB
I/O port	IRQ, I/O address, and DMA channel (if used) for each I/O port
Sound adapter	IRQ, I/O address, and DMA channel
Universal serial bus (USB)	Which devices and hubs are attached
PC card	Which adapters are inserted and in which slots
Plug and Play	Whether enabled or disabled in BIOS
BIOS settings	BIOS revision and date
External modem	COM port connections (COM1, COM2, and so on)
Internal modem	COM port connections; for nonstandard configurations, IRQ and I/O address
Advanced Configuration and Power Interface (ACPI); power options	Enabled or disabled; current setting
PCI	Which PCI adapters are inserted and in which slots

Mass Storage Drivers and the Setup Process

If your mass storage controller (such as a SCSI, RAID, or Fibre Channel adapter) is compatible with products in the Windows Server 2003 family but you are aware that the manufacturer has supplied a separate driver file for use with your operating system, obtain the file (on a floppy disk) before you begin Setup. During the early part of Setup, a line at the bottom of the screen will prompt you to press F6. Further prompts will guide you in supplying the driver file to Setup so that it can gain access to the mass storage controller.

If you are not sure whether you must obtain a separate driver file from the manufacturer of your mass storage controller, you can try running Setup. If the controller is not supported by the driver files on the Setup CD and therefore requires a driver file supplied by the hardware manufacturer, Setup stops and displays a message saying that no disk devices can be found or displays an incomplete list of controllers. After you obtain the necessary driver file, restart Setup, and press F6 when prompted.

> **Note**   Don't forget that you can check all compatibility issues in the Windows Catalog at *http://www.microsoft.com/windows/catalog/*.

Using a Custom Hardware Abstraction Layer File

If you have a custom hardware abstraction layer (HAL) file supplied by your computer manufacturer, before you begin Setup, locate the floppy disk or other medium containing the file. During the early part of Setup, a line at the bottom of the screen will prompt you to press F6; at this time, press F5 (not F6) to include your HAL file in the setup process. After you press F5, follow the prompts that are provided.

Understanding the ACPI BIOS for an x86-Based Computer

For an x86-based computer, the BIOS is a set of software through which the operating system (or Setup) communicates with the computer's hardware devices. ACPI is the current standard for the way the BIOS works. Products in the Windows Server 2003 family support not only ACPI-compliant BIOS versions but also some BIOS versions based on older Advanced Power Management (APM) and Plug and Play designs.

Some ACPI-based BIOS versions are not compliant with the standard. The more recent the version of an ACPI BIOS, the more likely that it's compliant. An ACPI-based BIOS that isn't compliant with the ACPI standard might not support workable communication between the operating system (or Setup) and your hardware. If workable communication is not supported, Setup stops and displays instructions for contacting your hardware manufacturer and taking other steps to solve the problem. If this happens, follow the instructions provided.

To learn more about the ACPI compliance of your BIOS:

- For information about your BIOS version, before running Setup, restart the computer and watch the text on the screen. Pay particular attention to blocks of text containing the words *BIOS* or *ACPI BIOS*.

- For information about BIOS versions for your hardware, check your hardware documentation and contact your hardware manufacturer.

Using Dynamic Update for Updated Drivers

If you have a working Internet connection on the computer on which you run Setup, you can choose Dynamic Update during Setup and obtain the most up-to-date Setup files, including drivers and other files. Whenever an important update is made to any crucial Setup file, that update is made available through Dynamic Update functionality built into the Windows Update Web site. Some of the updated files will be replacements (for example, an updated driver or updated Setup file), and some will be additions (for example, a driver not available at the time the Setup CD was created). It's recommended that you use Dynamic Update when running Setup.

Dynamic Update has been carefully designed so that it's reliable and easy to use:

- The files on the Dynamic Update section of the Windows Update Web site have been carefully tested and selected. Only files that are important in ensuring that Setup runs well are made available through Dynamic Update. Files with minor updates that will not significantly affect Setup are not part of Dynamic Update.

- Because Dynamic Update downloads only the files that are required for your computer, the Dynamic Update software briefly examines your computer hardware. No personal information is collected, and no information is saved. The only purpose is to select appropriate drivers for your hardware configuration. This keeps the download as short as possible and ensures that only necessary drivers are down-loaded to your hard disk.

■   You can use Dynamic Update when running a preinstallation com-patibility check from the product CD or when running Setup itself. Either way, you obtain the most up-to-date files for running Setup. For information about running the compatibility check, see "Hard-ware Compatibility" earlier in this chapter.

■   You can use Dynamic Update with unattended Setup. Preparing for this requires several steps. For details about how to use Dynamic Update with unattended Setup (also called automated installation), see the *Microsoft Windows XP Professional Resource Kit* or the *Microsoft Windows Server 2003 Deployment Kit*.

The Windows Update Web site offers a variety of updates that you can use after completing Setup. To learn more, see *http://windowsupdate.microsoft.com/*.

Important Files to Review

At some point in your planning process, before you run Setup, familiarize your-self with the Relnotes.htm file found in the \Docs folder on the CD for Win-dows Server 2003. This file contains important usage information about hardware, networking, applications, and printing. Also familiarize yourself with information about hardware compatibility for products in the Windows Server 2003 family. For more information, see "Hardware Compatibility" earlier in this chapter.

Decisions to Make for a New Installation

This list outlines the basic decisions to make for a new installation:

■   **Which licensing modes to use.**   Products in the Windows Server 2003 family support two licensing modes: *Per Device or Per User* and *Per Server*. Per Device or Per User mode requires a separate Client Access License (CAL) for each computer that accesses a server run-ning a product in the Windows Server 2003 family. Per Server mode requires a separate CAL for each concurrent connection to a server. For more information about licensing, see the next section, "Choos-ing a Licensing Mode."

- **Whether you want to be able to choose between different operating systems each time you start the computer.** You can set up a computer so that each time you restart it, you can choose from several different operating systems. For more information, see "Installing Multiple Operating Systems" later in this chapter.

- **Which file system to use on the installation partition.** You can potentially choose among three file systems for an installation partition: NTFS, FAT, and FAT32. NTFS is strongly recommended in most situations. It's the only file system that supports Active Directory, which includes many important features such as domains and domain-based security. However, it might be necessary to have a FAT or FAT32 partition on a basic disk in an x86-based computer if you must set up the computer so that it sometimes runs Windows Server 2003 and sometimes runs Windows NT 4.0 or an earlier operating system. For more information, see "Choosing a File System" later in this chapter.

- **Which partition or volume you plan to install the operating system on.** If you are performing a new installation, review your disk partitions or volumes before you run Setup. (For an upgrade, you will use existing partitions or volumes.) Both partitions and volumes divide a disk into one or more areas that can be formatted for use by one file system. Different partitions and volumes often have different drive letters (for example, C and D). After you run Setup, you can make adjustments to the disk configuration as long as you do not reformat or change the partition or volume that contains the operating system. For information about planning the partitions or volumes for a new installation, see "Planning Disk Partitions" later in this chapter.

- **How to handle IP addresses and TCP/IP name resolution.** With TCP/IP, you need to make decisions about how to handle IP addressing and name resolution (the translating of IP addresses into names that users recognize). For more information, see "Configuring Networking" later in this chapter.

Choosing a Licensing Mode

Products in the Windows Server 2003 family support two licensing modes: Per Device or Per User and Per Server. If you choose the Per Device or Per User mode, each computer or user that accesses a server running a product in the

Windows Server 2003 family requires a separate CAL. With one CAL, a particular client computer can connect to any number of servers running products in the Windows Server 2003 family. This is the most commonly used licensing method for companies with more than one server running products in the Windows Server 2003 family. Figure 15-1 illustrates this mode.

In contrast, Per Server licensing means that each concurrent connection to this server requires a separate CAL. In other words, this server can support a fixed number of connections at any one time. For example, if you select the Per Server client licensing mode with five licenses, this server can have five concurrent connections. (If each client requires one connection, this is five clients at any one time.) The clients using the connections do not need any additional licenses. The Per Server licensing mode is often preferred by small companies with only one server. It's also useful for Internet or remote access servers, where the client computers might not be licensed as network clients for products in the Windows Server 2003 family. You can specify a maximum number of concurrent server connections and reject any additional logon requests. Figure 15-2 shows Per Server licensing mode.

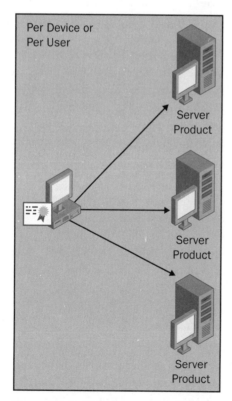

Figure 15-1   This diagram shows Per Device or Per User licensing mode.

If you are unsure which mode to use, choose Ser Server because you can change once from Per Server mode to Per Device or Per User mode at no cost. After you choose Per Server and complete Setup, you can display topics about licensing modes in Help and Support Center. (Click Start, and then click Help and Support.)

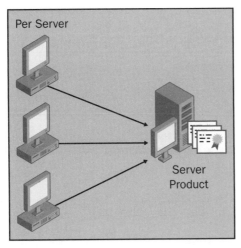

Figure 15-2   This diagram illustrates Per Server licensing mode.

Installing Multiple Operating Systems

On a computer with an appropriate disk configuration (outlined in Table 15-2), you can install more than one operating system and then choose between the operating systems each time you restart the computer.

For example, on an x86-based computer, you can set up a server to run Windows Server 2003 most of the time but allow the server to sometimes run Windows NT Server 4.0, Enterprise Edition, in order to support an older application. (However, to do this you would need to make specific file system choices and would need Service Pack 5 or later, as described in "File System Compatibility" and "Choosing a File System" later in this chapter.) During restarts, a display appears for a specified number of seconds, allowing you to select between the two operating systems. (You can specify a default operating system that will run if no selection is made during the restart process.)

Table 15-2 shows the disk configurations on which you can install more than one operating system. You must follow the requirements in the table. For example, on a basic disk, you must install each operating system, including Windows Server 2003, in a separate partition. This ensures that each operating system does not overwrite crucial files that are needed by another operating system.

Table 15-2 Requirements for Multiple Operating Systems

Disk Configuration	Requirements
Basic disk or disks	You can install multiple operating systems, including Windows NT 4.0 and earlier operating systems, on a basic disk. Each operating system must be on a separate partition or logical drive on the disk. A partition or logical drive is a section of the disk that functions as a separate unit. Different partitions often have different drive letters, for example, C and D.
Single dynamic disk	You can install only one operating system. However, if you used Windows 2000 or Windows XP to change a disk with no partitions directly to a dynamic disk, you must return the disk to basic before you can install an operating system on it. For more information, see the paragraph that follows this table.
Multiple dynamic disks	Each dynamic disk can contain one installation of Windows 2000, Windows XP, or a product in the Windows Server 2Server 2003003 family. No other operating systems can start from a dynamic disk. However, if you used Windows 2000 or Windows XP to change a disk with no partitions directly to a dynamic disk, you must return the disk to basic before you can install an operating system on it. For more information, see the paragraph that follows this table.
Master Boot Record (MBR) disk on an Itanium-based computer	You cannot start operating systems from an MBR disk on an Itanium-based computer. You must use a GPT disk for this purpose.
GUID partition table (GPT) disk on an Itanium-based computer	You can install one or more operating systems on a GPT disk on an Itanium-based computer. The guidelines in this table for basic and dynamic disks apply to GPT disks on Itanium-based computers.

> **Note**   On an Itanium-based computer, the operating systems that you can install include Windows XP, 64-Bit Edition; the 64-bit version of Windows Server 2003, Enterprise Edition; and the 64-bit version of Windows Server 2003, Datacenter Edition. On an Itanium-based computer, you cannot install earlier operating systems such as Windows 2000.

If you used Windows 2000 or Windows XP to change a disk with no partitions directly to a dynamic disk, you must return the disk to basic before you can install an operating system on it. All data will be lost in this process, so back it up first. You can then use Windows 2000 or Windows XP to revert to basic, or you can use Windows Server 2003 Setup. To use Windows 2000 or Windows XP, follow the instructions in Help for your operating system. To use Windows Server 2003 Setup, during the partitioning phase, find the dynamic disk among the list of available partitions and then delete it (which erases all data on all volumes). You will be prompted to confirm your action. After you do this, the disk will contain only unpartitioned space, and you can use Setup to create a new (basic disk) partition on it.

Reasons to Install Only One Operating System

Setting up a computer so that you can choose between two or more operating systems at startup does have an advantage: It allows you to use applications that run only with a particular operating system. However, there are definite reasons to install only one operating system:

- Each operating system uses valuable disk space.

- Compatibility issues such as file system compatibility can be complex. For more information, see "File System Compatibility" later in this chapter.

- On a dynamic disk, you can have only one operating system per disk. Dynamic disks also will not work with some operating systems. For more information, see Table 15-2.

- It's no longer necessary to maintain multiple operating systems as a safeguard against problems with starting the computer. With products in the Windows Server 2003 family, you have other options for system recovery. For example, if you have a problem with a newly installed device driver, you can use safe mode, in which Windows Server 2003 restarts with default settings and the minimum number of drivers.

Requirements for Installing Multiple Operating Systems

Before you decide to set up a computer with more than one operating system, review the following restrictions.

- On computers that contain MS-DOS and Windows Server 2003:

  ❏ Install each operating system on a different partition, and install the applications used with an operating system on the same partition with it. If an application is used with two different operating systems, install it on two partitions.

  ❏ MS-DOS must be installed on a basic disk on a partition formatted with FAT. If MS-DOS is not installed on the system partition, which is almost always the first partition on the disk, the system partition must also be formatted with FAT.

  ❏ Windows Server 2003 must be installed last. Otherwise, important files that are needed for starting Windows Server 2003 might be overwritten.

  ❏ File system compatibility might be an issue. See the upcoming section "File System Compatibility."

- On computers that contain Windows 98 or Windows Me and Windows Server 2003:

  ❏ Install each operating system on a different partition, and install the applications used with an operating system on the same partition with it. If an application is used with two different operating systems, install it on two partitions.

  ❏ Windows 98 or Windows Me must be installed on a basic disk on a partition formatted with FAT or FAT32. If either Windows 98 or Windows Me is not installed on the system partition, which is almost always the first partition on the disk, the system partition must also be formatted with FAT or FAT32.

  ❏ Windows Server 2003 must be installed last. Otherwise, important files that are needed for starting Windows Server 2003 might be overwritten.

❑   File system compatibility might be an issue. See the upcoming section "File System Compatibility."

■   Regarding computers that contain Windows NT 4.0 and Windows Server 2003, see the upcoming sections "File System Compatibility" and "Multibooting with Windows NT 4.0."

■   On computers that contain some combination of Windows Server 2003 with Windows 2000 or Windows XP, or that contain multiple partitions with products in the Windows Server 2003 family:

❑   Install each operating system on a different partition or, for dynamic disks, on a different disk, and install the applications used with an operating system on the same disk or partition with it. If an application is used with two different operating systems, install it in two places.

❑   For an x86-based computer, choose any product in the Windows Server 2003 family for installation on a specific partition. For example, you can install Windows Server 2003, Standard Edition, in one location and Windows Server 2003, Web Edition, in another.

❑   For an Itanium-based computer, you can choose among Windows XP, 64-Bit Edition; the 64-bit version of Windows Server 2003, Enterprise Edition; and the 64-bit version of Windows Server 2003, Datacenter Edition.

❑   If Windows 2000 and Windows Server 2003 are installed, Windows Server 2003 must be installed last. Otherwise, important files that are needed for starting Windows Server 2003 might be overwritten.

❑   If the computer participates in a domain, use a different computer name for each installation. Because a unique security identifier (SID) is used for each installation on a domain, the computer name for each installation must be unique, even for multiple installations on the same computer.

❑   If you want to use the Encrypting File System (EFS), you must take certain steps to ensure that encrypted files will be available from each of the installations. For more information, see "Encrypting File System" later in this chapter.

File System Compatibility

On computers that contain multiple operating systems, compatibility becomes more complex when you consider file system choices. The file systems to choose from are NTFS, FAT, and FAT32. (For more information, see "Choosing a File System" later in this chapter.)

NTFS is normally the recommended file system because it is more efficient and reliable and supports important features, including Active Directory and domain-based security. With NTFS, however, you need to take file system compatibility into account when considering whether to set up a computer to contain more than one operating system because with Windows 2000 and the Windows Server 2003 family, NTFS has new features in addition to those in Windows NT. Files that use any new features will be completely usable or readable only when the computer is started with Windows 2000 or a product in the Windows Server 2003 family. For example, a file that uses the new encryption feature won't be readable when the computer is started with Windows NT Server 4.0 or Windows NT Server 4.0, Enterprise Edition, which were released before the encryption feature existed.

> **Note**   If you want to set up a computer with both Windows NT and Windows Server 2003, and you want to have an NTFS partition, the only appropriate version of Windows NT is version 4.0 with the latest released service pack. Using the latest service pack maximizes compatibility between Windows NT 4.0 and Windows Server 2003. (Specifically, you must have Service Pack 5 or later.) Even the latest service pack, however, does not provide access to files using the new features in NTFS.

Using NTFS as the only file system on a computer that contains both Windows Server 2003 and Windows NT is not recommended. On these computers, a FAT partition containing the Windows NT 4.0 operating system ensures that when started with Windows NT 4.0, the computer will have access to needed files. In addition, if Windows NT is not installed on the system partition, which is almost always the first partition on the disk, it's recommended that the system partition also be formatted with FAT.

If you set up a computer so that it starts with Windows NT 3.51 or earlier on a FAT partition and Windows Server 2003 on an NTFS partition, when that computer starts with Windows NT 3.51, the NTFS partition will not be visible. If you set up a computer this way, and the partition containing Windows NT 3.51 is not the system partition (which is almost always the first partition on the disk), the system partition must also be formatted with FAT.

Multibooting with Windows NT 4.0

If you plan to set up a computer so that it contains Windows NT 4.0 and Windows Server 2003, first review the following precautions:

- If your only concern is ensuring that you can always start the computer, setting up the computer so that you can start it with different operating systems at different times is not necessary.

- Using NTFS as the only file system on a computer that contains both Windows Server 2003 and Windows NT is not recommended.

- Make sure that Windows NT 4.0 has been updated with the latest released service pack.

- Install each operating system on a different partition, and install the applications used with an operating system on the same partition with it. If an application is used with two different operating systems, install it on two partitions.

- Don't install Windows Server 2003 on a compressed drive unless the drive was compressed with the NTFS file system compression feature.

- Windows Server 2003 must be installed last. Otherwise, important files that are needed for starting Windows Server 2003 might be overwritten.

- If the computer participates in a domain, use a different computer name for each installation.

Encrypting File System

If you set up a server so that it contains some combination of Windows Server 2003 and Windows 2000 or Windows XP, or contains multiple partitions with products in the Windows Server 2003 family, and you want to use EFS on the computer, you must take certain steps. These steps make encrypted files readable between the different installations:

- One approach is to ensure that all the installations are in the same domain and that the user of these installations has a roaming profile.

■   Another approach is to export the user's file encryption certificate and associated private key from one installation and import it into the other installations.

For more information about EFS, roaming user profiles, and importing and exporting certificates, see Help and Support Center.

Choosing a File System

You can choose among three file systems for an installation partition: NTFS, FAT, and FAT32. NTFS is strongly recommended in most situations. You can use important features such as Active Directory and domain-based security only by choosing NTFS as your file system.

> **Note**   On GPT disks, which are available only on Itanium-based computers, it's strongly recommended that you use NTFS for the installation partition. However, if you have an Itanium-based computer and you see that it has a small FAT partition of 100 MB or more, do not delete or reformat this partition. The partition is required for the loading of the operating system.

Table 15-3 describes a number of installation scenarios for x86-based computers (the last two scenarios are fairly uncommon) and provides file system guidelines for each one:

Table 15-3   File Systems for Scenarios

Scenario	File System
The computer currently uses NTFS only (no FAT or FAT32).	Continue to use NTFS. No additional information about file systems is needed.
The computer is x86-based and has one or more FAT or FAT32 partitions; and the computer contains only one operating system, or the operating systems on the computer include Windows 2000, Windows XP, or a product in the Windows Server 2003 family but no other operating systems.	If the computer is Itanium-based, see the important note earlier in this section. Consider reformatting or converting partitions so that all partitions use NTFS.

Table 15-3   File Systems for Scenarios   *(continued)*

Scenario	File System
The computer will contain multiple operating systems, one of which is MS-DOS, Windows 95, Windows 98, or Windows Me.	For any partition that must be accessible from MS-DOS, Windows 95, Windows 98, or Windows Me, use FAT (or, when appropriate, FAT32).
The computer will contain multiple operating systems, one of which is Windows NT.	Read "File System Compatibility" earlier in this chapter.

The sections that follow provide information about reformatting or converting a FAT or FAT32 partition to use NTFS, as well as additional background information about NTFS, FAT, and FAT32.

Reformatting or Converting to NTFS

If you have a FAT or FAT32 partition on which you want to install a product in the Windows Server 2003 family, and you want to use NTFS instead, you have two choices:

■ You can convert the FAT or FAT32 partition to NTFS. This leaves files intact, although the partition might have somewhat more fragmentation and slower performance than a partition formatted with NTFS. However, it is still advantageous to use NTFS, regardless of whether the partition was formatted with NTFS or converted.

If you install a product in the Windows Server 2003 family on a FAT or FAT32 partition, you are offered the option to convert the partition to NTFS. You can also convert a FAT or FAT32 partition after Setup by using Convert.exe. For more information about Convert.exe, after completing Setup, type **help convert** at the command prompt.

■ You can reformat the partition with NTFS. This erases all files on the partition but results in less fragmentation and better performance than with a converted partition.

> **Note**   If you have an Itanium-based computer and you see that it has a small FAT partition of 100 MB or more, do not delete or reformat this partition. The partition is required for loading the operating system.

If you format a partition during Setup, the file system choices are listed as NTFS and FAT. Table 15-4 provides information about the relationship between partition size and file system choices during Setup.

Table 15-4   Formatting Partitions during Setup

Partition State	Setup Choices
Unformatted, less than 2 GB.	Setup offers NTFS or FAT. Setup uses the format chosen.
Unformatted, 2 GB or larger, up to a maximum of 32 GB.	Setup offers NTFS or FAT. If FAT is chosen, Setup uses FAT32.
Unformatted, larger than 32 GB.	Setup allows only NTFS.
Previously formatted with FAT32 and larger than 32 GB. (Partition created with Windows 95, Windows 98, or Windows Me.)	No formatting needed, even though an unformatted partition of this size, when formatted during or after Setup for a product in the Windows Server 2003 family, would have to use NTFS. In other words, previously formatted FAT32 partitions of this size continue to be supported by the Windows Server 2003 family.

If you format a partition during Setup, you can choose between a quick format and a full format:

■ **Quick format.**   Quick format creates the file system structure on the disk without verifying the integrity of every sector. Choose this method for any disk that has no bad sectors and no history of file-corruption problems that might be related to bad sectors.

■ **Full format.**   A full format identifies and tracks bad sectors so that they are not used for storing data. Choose this method for any disk that has bad sectors or has a history of file-corruption problems that might be related to bad sectors.

NTFS Compared with FAT and FAT32

NTFS has always been a more powerful file system than FAT and FAT32. Windows 2000, Windows XP, and the Windows Server 2003 family include a new version of NTFS, with support for a variety of features, including Active Directory, which is needed for domains, user accounts, and other important security features.

FAT and FAT32 are similar to each other except that FAT32 is designed for larger disks than FAT. The file system that works most easily with large disks is NTFS. Note that file system choices have no effect on access to files across the network. For example, using NTFS on all partitions on a server does not affect clients connecting across a network to shared folders or shared files on that server, even if those clients run an earlier operating system such as Windows 98 or Windows NT. The following list describes the compatibility and sizes of each file system with various operating systems:

- **NTFS.** A computer running Windows 2000, Windows XP, or a product in the Windows Server 2003 family can access files on a local NTFS partition. A computer running Windows NT 4.0 with Service Pack 5 or later might be able to access some files. Other operating systems allow no local access. The recommended minimum volume size is approximately 10 MB. The maximum volume and partition sizes start at 2 terabytes (TB) and range upward. For example, a dynamic disk formatted with a standard allocation unit size (4 KB) can have partitions of 16 TB minus 4 KB. The maximum file size is potentially 16 TB minus 64 KB, although files cannot be larger than the volume or partition they are located on.

- **FAT.** Access to files on a local partition is available through MS-DOS, all versions of Windows, and OS/2. Volumes can be from floppy-disk size up to 4 GB. The maximum file size is 2 GB.

- **FAT32.** Access to files on a local partition is available only through Windows 95 OSR2, Windows 98, Windows Me, Windows 2000, Windows XP, and products in the Windows Server 2003 family. Volumes from 512 MB to 2 TB can be written to or read using products in the Windows Server 2003 family. Volumes up to 32 GB can be formatted as FAT32 using products in the Windows Server 2003 family. The maximum file size is 4 GB.

> **Note**   On Itanium-based computers with multiple disks, your choices include not only file systems but also partition styles. A partition style determines the way that information about the partition is stored. There are two partition styles. The newer style (used on Itanium-based computers only) stores partition information in the GPT. The older style stores information in the MBR. On Itanium-based computers, you must install Windows Server 2003 on a GPT disk.

Understanding NTFS

This section provides background information about the features available with NTFS. Some of these features are as follows:

- Better scalability to large drives. The maximum partition or volume size for NTFS is much greater than that for FAT, and as volume or partition sizes increase, performance with NTFS doesn't degrade as it does with FAT.

- Active Directory (and domains, which are part of Active Directory). With Active Directory, you can view and control network resources easily. With domains, you can fine-tune security options while keeping administration simple. Domain controllers and Active Directory require NTFS.

- Compression features, including the ability to compress or uncompress a drive, a folder, or a specific file. A file cannot be both compressed and encrypted at the same time.

- File encryption, which greatly enhances security. A file cannot be both compressed and encrypted at the same time.

- Permissions that can be set on individual files rather than just folders.

- Remote Storage, which provides an extension to your disk space by making removable media such as tapes more accessible.

- Recovery logging of disk activities, which allows NTFS to restore information quickly in the event of power failure or other system problems.

- Sparse files. These are very large files created by applications in such a way that only limited disk space is needed. That is, NTFS allocates disk space only to the portions of a file that are written to.

- Disk quotas, which you can use to monitor and control the amount of disk space used by individual users.

This is only a partial list of the features in NTFS in the Windows Server 2003 family. For more information about new features, see Chapter 11, "File Services."

Planning Disk Partitions

You must plan your disk partitions before you run Setup only if both of the following conditions are true:

■   You are performing a new installation, not an upgrade.

■   The disk on which you are installing is a basic disk, not a dynamic disk. Basic disks are the disk type that existed before Windows 2000; most disks are basic disks. Dynamic disks are disks that once were basic but were changed to dynamic using Windows 2000, Windows XP, or a product in the Windows Server 2003 family. If you plan to install to a dynamic disk, you cannot change the volume or partition sizes on the disk during Setup, and therefore no planning is needed regarding partition sizes. Instead, review the guidelines in "Working with Dynamic Disks" later in this chapter.

Disk partitioning is a way of dividing your physical disk so that each section functions as a separate unit. When you create partitions on a basic disk, you divide the disk into one or more areas that can be formatted for use by a file system, such as FAT or NTFS. Different partitions often have different drive letters (for example, C and D). A basic disk can have up to four primary partitions, or three primary partitions and one extended partition. (An extended partition can be subdivided into logical drives, while a primary partition cannot be subdivided.)

> **Note**   If you plan to delete or create partitions on a hard disk, be sure to back up the disk contents beforehand because these actions will destroy any existing data. As with any major change to disk contents, it's recommended that you back up the entire contents of the hard disk before working with partitions, even if you plan to leave one or more of your partitions alone.

Before you run Setup to perform a new installation, determine the size of the partition on which to install. There is no set formula for figuring a partition size. The basic principle is to allow plenty of room for the operating system, applications, and other files that you plan to put on the installation partition. The files for setting up Windows Server 2003 require approximately 1.25 GB to 2 GB on an x86-based computer and 3 GB to 4 GB on an Itanium-based computer, as described in "System Requirements" earlier in this chapter. It's recommended that you allow considerably more disk space than the minimum amount. It's not unreasonable to allow 4 GB to 10 GB on the partition, or more for large installations. This allows space for a variety of items, including optional components, user accounts, Active Directory information, logs, future service packs, the paging file used by the operating system, and other items.

When you perform a new installation, you can specify the partition on which to install. If you specify a partition on which another operating system exists, you will be prompted to confirm your choice.

During Setup, create and size only the partition on which you want to install Windows Server 2003. After installation is complete, you can use Disk Management to manage new and existing disks and volumes. This includes creating new partitions from unpartitioned space; deleting, renaming, and reformatting existing partitions; adding and removing hard disks; and changing a basic disk to the dynamic disk storage type, or changing dynamic to basic.

On Itanium-based computers with more than one disk, you can plan not only the sizes of partitions but also the partition style for each disk. A partition style determines the way that information about the partition is stored. There are two partition styles. The newer style (used on Itanium-based computers only) stores partition information in the GUID partition table (GPT). The older style stores information in the MBR. On Itanium-based computers, you must install Windows Server 2003 on a GPT disk. With GPT, you can create more partitions and larger volumes and take advantage of other benefits. For more information about partition styles on Itanium-based computers, see Help and Support Center and the *Microsoft Windows Server 2003 Resource Kit, Server Management Guide*.

Remote Installation Services

If you plan to use Remote Installation Services on this server so that you can install operating systems on other computers, a separate partition for use by Remote Installation Services is necessary. Plan on using NTFS on this partition: NTFS is required for the Single Instance Store feature of Remote Installation Services.

If you need to create a new partition for Remote Installation Services, plan on doing it after Setup, and leave enough unpartitioned disk space so that you can create it. (At least 4 GB of space is recommended.) As an alternative, for the system disk (not cluster disks), you can plan to make the disk a dynamic disk, which allows more flexibility in the use of the disk space than a basic disk. For more information about Remote Installation Services and about disk and partition choices, see Help and Support Center.

Options When Partitioning a Disk

You can change the partitions on your disk during Setup only if you are performing a new installation, not an upgrade. You can modify the partitioning of the disk after Setup by using Disk Management.

If you are performing a new installation, Setup examines the hard disk to determine its existing configuration and then offers the following options:

- If the hard disk is unpartitioned, you can create and size the partition on which you will install a product in the Windows Server 2003 family.

- If the hard disk is partitioned but has enough unpartitioned disk space, you can create the partition for your Windows Server 2003 family product by using the unpartitioned space.

- If the hard disk has an existing partition that is large enough, you can install a product in the Windows Server 2003 family on that partition, with or without reformatting the partition first. Reformatting a partition erases all data on the partition. If you do not reformat the partition but you do install a Windows Server 2003 family product where there is already an operating system, the operating system will be overwritten, and you must reinstall any applications you want to use with the Windows Server 2003 family product.

- If the hard disk has an existing partition, you can delete it to create more unpartitioned disk space for a partition for a Windows Server 2003 family product. Deleting an existing partition also erases any data on that partition.

Working with Dynamic Disks

A dynamic disk is a disk using the new storage type introduced with Windows 2000. If you changed a disk to dynamic and you want to perform a new installation on the disk, review the following:

- If you used Windows 2000 or Windows XP to change a disk with no partitions directly to a dynamic disk, you must revert the disk to basic before you can install an operating system on it. All data will be lost in the process of returning the disk to basic, so back it up first.

   You can use Windows 2000 or Windows XP to return to basic, or you can use the Setup program for a product in the Windows Server 2003 family. To use Windows 2000 or Windows XP, follow the instructions in Help for your operating system. To use Setup for a product in the Windows Server 2003 family, during the partitioning phase, find the dynamic disk among the list of available partitions and then delete it (which erases all data on all volumes). You will be prompted to confirm your action. After you do this, the disk will contain only unpartitioned space, and you can use Setup to create a new (basic disk) partition on it.

■   If you plan to rerun Setup on a computer on which a product in the Windows Server 2003 family was already installed, and the computer contains dynamic disks, be sure to read about the limitations for installing operating systems on disks that are changed to dynamic using a product in the Windows Server 2003 family. For more information, see topics about dynamic disks and the partition table in Help and Support Center.

Working with Volumes, Mirrors, and Stripes

With the disk management technologies in Windows NT 4.0, you could create volume sets, mirror sets, stripe sets, or stripe sets with parity, each with specific capabilities and limitations. By using the dynamic disk technology introduced with Windows 2000, you can use similar technologies, with the added flexibility of being able to extend disk volumes without repartitioning or reformatting.

This transition from the technologies used in Windows NT 4.0 means that you must make certain choices before running Setup for Windows Server 2003. Any volume sets, mirror sets, stripe sets, or stripe sets with parity that you created with Windows NT 4.0 are not supported in Windows Server 2003, although they were supported to a limited extent in Windows 2000.

If you used Windows NT 4.0 to create a volume set, mirror set, stripe set, or stripe set with parity, and you want to run Setup for Windows Server 2003 on that computer, you must choose one of the following methods:

■   **For a mirror set, break the mirror.**   If you are running Windows NT 4.0 on a computer that has a mirror set and you want to run Setup for Windows Server 2003 on that computer, first back up the data (as a safeguard—the data will not be erased) and then break the mirror. Ensure that you have applied Service Pack 5 or later, required before running Setup for Windows Server 2003. Then run Setup.

■   **For a volume set, stripe set, or stripe set with parity, back up the data and delete the set.**   If you are running Windows NT 4.0 on a computer that has a volume set, stripe set, or stripe set with parity, and you want to run Setup for Windows Server 2003 on that computer, first back up the data. Next delete the set (which will delete the data). Ensure that you have applied Service Pack 5 or later, required before running Setup for Windows Server 2003. Then run Setup. After running Setup for Windows Server 2003, you can make the disk dynamic, restore backed-up data as necessary, and make use of the volume options shown in the next section, "Types of Multidisk Volumes on Dynamic Disks." For more information about dynamic disks, see Help and Support Center.

■ **If necessary, use the Ftonline support tool.** The preceding methods are the recommended methods for preparing to run Setup for Windows Server 2003 on a computer that contains a volume set, mirror set, stripe set, or stripe set with parity created with Windows NT 4.0. However, if you do not use these methods and you must access one of these sets after running Setup for Windows Server 2003, you can use the Ftonline tool. The Ftonline tool is part of the Windows Server 2003 family Support Tools. For more information, see topics on Support Tools and on Ftonline in Help and Support Center.

Types of Multidisk Volumes on Dynamic Disks

The disk sets described in the preceding section have different names in the Windows Server 2003 family than they had in Windows NT 4.0:

■ A *volume set* is now a *spanned volume on a dynamic disk.*

■ A *mirror set* is now a *mirrored volume on a dynamic disk.*

■ A *stripe set* is now a *striped volume on a dynamic disk.*

■ A *stripe set with parity* is now a *RAID-5 volume on a dynamic disk.*

Configuring Networking

TCP/IP is the network protocol that provides Internet access. It's the protocol used by most servers, although you can use additional or different network adapters and their associated protocols on your servers. Setup and the Configure Your Server Wizard are designed to make it easy to configure TCP/IP and the services that support it.

To use TCP/IP, make sure that each server is provided with an IP address, either a dynamic address provided through software or a static address that you obtain and set. You will also have to provide users with names that are easy to use. Name resolution can be accomplished by various methods, primarily Domain Name System (DNS) and Windows Internet Naming Service (WINS). The following sections provide more information.

For detailed information about TCP/IP, Dynamic Host Configuration Protocol (DHCP), DNS, and WINS, see Help and Support Center as well as the Resource Kits for the Windows Server 2003 family. You can also view Help and Support topics on the Web at *http://www.microsoft.com/windowsserver2003/*.

IP Addresses

As described in the preceding section, using TCP/IP requires an IP address to be provided for each computer. There are two basic approaches for providing an IP address for a server you are installing:

- **DHCP.** You can provide IP addresses to the computers on your network by configuring one or more DHCP servers, which provide IP addresses dynamically to other computers. A DHCP server must itself be assigned a static IP address.

    One server or several servers can provide DHCP along with one or more name resolution services, which are called DNS and WINS. The name resolution services are described in the next section, "Name Resolution."

    If you want to run Setup before you have finalized your decisions about which server to use as your DHCP server and what static IP address to assign to that server, you can choose Typical Settings in the Networking Settings dialog box during Setup and complete the network configuration later. If you do this and there is no DHCP server on the network, Setup will use a limited IP addressing option called Automatic Private IP Addressing (APIPA). During the time that a server is using APIPA, it can communicate only with other computers using APIPA on the same network segment. A server that is using APIPA cannot make connections to the Internet (for browsing or e-mail) and cannot be used with DNS or Active Directory (which depends on DNS).

    If you know which server you want to use as your DHCP server, when installing that server, in the Networking Settings dialog box in Setup, choose Custom settings, and specify a static IP address and related network settings. After Setup, use Configure Your Server, along with information in Help and Support Center, to install the DHCP component and complete the configuration of the DHCP server.

- **Static IPs.**   For certain types of servers, you must assign a static IP address and subnet mask during or after Setup. These servers include DHCP servers, DNS servers, WINS servers, and any server providing access to users on the Internet. It is also recommended that you assign a static IP address and subnet mask for each domain controller. If a computer has more than one network adapter, you must assign a separate IP address for each adapter.

    If you want to run Setup on a server before you have finalized your decision about the static IP address you want to assign to that server, you can choose Typical Settings in the Networking Settings dialog box during Setup and configure that server later. In this situation, if a DHCP server is on the network, Setup will obtain an IP address configuration from DHCP. If no DHCP server is on the network, Setup will use APIPA. APIPA is described in the preceding item in this list.

    For more information about static IP addresses, including private IP addresses (which you choose from certain ranges of addresses) and public IP addresses (which you obtain from an Internet service provider), see Help and Support Center.

Name Resolution

After you have formed a plan for IP addressing, the next components to consider are those for name resolution, which is the process of mapping a computer name (something that users can recognize and remember) to the appropriate IP address. Name resolution is a process that provides users with easy-to-remember server names instead of requiring them to use the numeric IP addresses by which servers identify themselves on the TCP/IP network. The name resolution services are DNS and WINS:

- **DNS.**   DNS is a hierarchical naming system used for locating computers on the Internet and private TCP/IP networks. One or more DNS servers are needed in most installations. DNS is required for Internet e-mail, Web browsing, and Active Directory. DNS is often used as a name resolution service in domains with clients running Windows 2000, Windows XP, or products in the Windows Server 2003 family.

    DNS is installed automatically when you create a domain controller (or promote a server to become a domain controller) unless the Windows Server 2003 software detects that a DNS server already exists for that domain. You can also install DNS by using Configure

Your Server or by using Add/Remove Windows Components, which is part of Add Or Remove Programs in Control Panel.

If you plan to install DNS on a server, specify a static IP address on that server and configure that server to use that IP address for its own name resolution. For information about assigning a static IP address, see the preceding section, "IP Addresses." For more information about configuring DNS, see Help and Support Center.

■ **Windows Internet Naming Service.** If you provide support for clients running Windows NT or any earlier Microsoft operating system, you might need to install WINS on one or more servers in the domain. You might also need to install WINS if it's required by your applications. You can install WINS after Setup by using Configure Your Server or by using Add/Remove Windows Components, which is part of Add Or Remove Programs in Control Panel.

If you plan to install WINS on a server, specify a static IP address on that server. For information about assigning a static IP address, see the preceding section, "IP Addresses." For more information about configuring WINS, see Help and Support Center.

Planning for Your Servers

Domains, and the Active Directory directory system of which they are a part, provide many options for making resources easily available to users while maintaining good monitoring and security. For more information about Active Directory, see Chapter 3, "Active Directory."

With Windows Server 2003, servers in a domain can have one of two roles: domain controllers, which contain matching copies of the user accounts and other Active Directory data in a given domain; and member servers, which belong to a domain but do not contain a copy of the Active Directory data. (A server that belongs to a workgroup, not a domain, is called a stand-alone server.) It's possible to change the role of a server from domain controller to member server (or stand-alone server) and back again, even after Setup is complete. However, it's recommended that you plan your domain before running Setup and change server roles (and server names) only when necessary.

Multiple domain controllers provide better support for users, compared with a single domain controller. With multiple domain controllers, you have multiple copies of user account data and other Active Directory data; however, it's still important to perform regular backups, including Automated System Recovery backups, and familiarize yourself with the methods for restoring a domain controller. In addition, multiple domain controllers work together to support domain controller functions, such as carrying out logon validations.

As you manage your Windows Server 2003 family domains, you might want to learn more about operations master roles. Operations master roles are special roles that are assigned to one or more domain controllers in an Active Directory domain. The domain controllers that are assigned these roles perform operations that are single-master (not permitted to occur at different places on a network at the same time). For example, the creation of security identifiers for new resources (such as new computers) must be overseen by a single domain controller to ensure that the identifiers are unique.

The first domain controller installed in a domain is automatically assigned all the operations master roles. You can change the assignment of operations master roles after Setup, but in most cases this is not necessary. You will need to be particularly aware of operations masters roles if problems develop on an operations master or if you plan to take one out of service. For more information about operations master roles, which are part of Active Directory, see Help and Support Center.

For More Information

See the following resource for more information:

■   Microsoft Windows Server 2003 Deployment Kit at *http://www.microsoft.com/technet/prodtechnol/windowsnetserver/evaluate/cpp/reskit/*

16

Upgrading from Windows NT 4.0 Server

The Microsoft Windows Server 2003 family represents a significant advancement over the Microsoft Windows NT 4.0 family of operating systems. The Windows Server 2003 family—which includes Windows Server 2003, Standard Edition; Windows Server 2003, Enterprise Edition; Windows Server 2003, Datacenter Edition; and Windows Server 2003, Web Edition—gives you a platform that is more productive, dependable, and connected than ever before. New and improved file, print, application, Web, and communication services provide a more robust, comprehensive platform for your mission-critical business resources. Integrated features such as the Active Directory directory service and enterprise-class security services allow you to provide secure yet flexible access to all the resources your users need.

Additionally, the Windows Server 2003 family was designed to allow for an easy upgrade from the Windows NT 4.0 Server family. All you need is to be running Service Pack 5 or later, and you can upgrade directly to Windows Server 2003 without having to install Windows 2000. Moving from Windows NT 4.0 to the Windows Server 2003 family provides you with a substantially improved feature set and enhanced performance.

This chapter provides an overview of the upgrade process, including information about some of the basic decisions you will make during the process—whether you're upgrading an existing system or performing a new installation.

Upgrade Paths

You can upgrade to Windows Server 2003, Enterprise Edition, from the following versions of the Windows NT family of operating systems:

- Windows NT Server 4.0 with Service Pack 5 or later

- Windows NT Server 4.0, Terminal Server Edition, with Service Pack 5 or later

- Windows NT Server 4.0, Enterprise Edition, with Service Pack 5 or later

> **Note** If you have a version of Windows NT earlier than 4.0, you cannot upgrade directly to the Enterprise Edition from it. You must first upgrade to Windows NT 4.0 and apply Service Pack 5 or later before upgrading to a product in the Windows Server 2003 family. If you have servers or clients that run Windows NT 3.51, you should install or upgrade to a newer operating system on all these computers, or retire them from operation. If you have more than one domain, this step is necessary for reliable logon validation. In any case, this step strengthens security and reduces the number of version differences between computers, simplifying management and troubleshooting.

The need to upgrade can be seen with even a quick glance at the enhancements, which include the following:

- **Active Directory.** The Active Directory directory service includes improved methods for finding and changing the location or attributes of objects, command-line tools, greater flexibility in working with the schema, application directory partitions, the capability of adding domain controllers to existing domains using backup media, universal group membership caching, and easier management. As directory-enabled applications become more prevalent, organizations can use the capabilities of Active Directory to manage even the most complicated enterprise-network environments.

- **Application services.** Advances in Windows Server 2003 provide many benefits for developing applications, including simplified integration and interoperability, improved developer productivity, and increased enterprise efficiency, all of which result in lower total cost of ownership (TCO) and better performance.

- **Clustering services.**   Installation and setup are easier and more robust in Windows Server 2003 than in earlier versions of Windows, and enhanced network features provide greater failover capabilities and high system uptime. Clustering services have become increasingly essential for organizations deploying business-critical e-commerce and line-of-business applications.

- **File and print services.**   Windows Server 2003 ensures higher reliability with new features such as Automated System Recovery (ASR), making it easier to recover your system, back up your files, and maintain maximum availability. An enhanced file system infrastructure makes it easier to use, secure, and store files and other essential resources. Employees benefit by always being able to access the resources they need or quickly recover files without costly assistance from an IT help desk, and businesses benefit from a reduced TCO.

- **Internet Information Services 6.0.**   With Internet Information Services (IIS) 6.0, Microsoft has completely revised the IIS architecture in the Windows Server 2003 product family to address the demanding needs of enterprise customers, Internet service providers (ISPs) and independent software vendors (ISVs).

- **Management services.**   Windows Server 2003 provides centralized, customizable management services to reduce TCO and is easier to deploy, configure, and use.

- **Networking and communications.**   Networking improvements and new features in Windows Server 2003 extend the versatility, manageability, and dependability of network infrastructures and expand on the foundation established in Windows 2000 Server.

- **Security.**   The Windows Server 2003 operating system provides many important new security features and improves on the security features originally included in Windows 2000 Server, making it easier to secure a full range of devices. New security features include the IEEE 802.1X protocol (which makes it easy to secure wireless LANs from the threat of eavesdropping within your business environment), Encrypting File System (EFS), certificate services, and automatic smart card enrollment.

- **Storage management.** Windows Server 2003 introduces new and enhanced features for storage management, making it easier and more reliable to manage and maintain disks and volumes, back up and restore data, and connect to storage area networks (SANs).

- **Terminal Server.** The Terminal Server component of Windows Server 2003 provides organizations with a more reliable, more scalable, and more manageable server-based computing platform. It offers new options for application deployment and more efficient access to data over low bandwidth, and it enhances the value of legacy and new, lighter-weight devices.

- **Windows Media Services.** Windows Media Services is the server component of Windows Media Technologies used to distribute digital media content over corporate intranets and the Internet. In addition to traditional digital distribution services, such as file and Web services, Windows Media Services delivers the most reliable, scalable, manageable, and economical solutions for distributing streaming audio and video.

Windows Server 2003 also serves as the foundation for Microsoft .NET, a set of Microsoft software technologies for connecting your world of information, people, systems, and devices. Microsoft .NET enables an unprecedented level of software integration through the use of XML Web services: small, discrete, building-block applications that connect to one another—as well as to other, larger, applications—via the Internet.

.NET-connected software from Microsoft includes a comprehensive family of products—clients that power smart devices, services, servers, and tools—designed to support XML and incorporate Internet industry standards. Development becomes easier with Microsoft Visual Studio .NET and the Microsoft .NET Framework, which not only change the way applications can be developed but also make it possible to create new kinds of applications.

All of this combines for a compelling case for migrating from Windows NT Server 4.0 to the Windows Server 2003 family of operating systems.

Verifying System Requirements

Before upgrading to Windows Server 2003, you will want to make sure that the computer you will be upgrading meets the recommended system requirements and that all hardware components are compatible with the operating system. If you have consistently upgraded your hardware for your Windows NT 4.0 Server systems, this might not be an issue. But if your current servers are running on older computers, you might want to consider installing Windows Server 2003 on new computers.

System Requirements

The most significant area of change is recommended processor speed. While Windows 2000 required a 133-MHz or faster processor, Microsoft recommends a 550-MHz or faster processor for the Web Edition and the Standard Edition, and a 733-MHz or faster processor for the Enterprise Edition and the Datacenter Edition. Memory and disk space requirements are much the same. Chapter 1, "Product Family," describes the minimum and recommended hardware requirements for each edition of Windows Server 2003.

Disk Space Considerations

Disk space, and disk partitions, provide another decision point on whether to upgrade or perform a clean installation on a new system. For example, if your servers currently use the file allocation table (FAT) file system, which limits you to 2-gigabyte (GB) hard disk partitions, you can't upgrade to Windows Server 2003 because more than 2 GB of space are required for the upgrading process.

If your servers currently use the NT file system (NTFS), which has a limit of 32 GB per partition, you can upgrade to Windows Server 2003. But if you want to avoid the 32-GB limit, you need to do a clean installation.

Hardware Compatibility

One of the most important steps to take before running Setup on a server is to confirm that your hardware is compatible with products in the Windows Server 2003 family. You can do this by running a preinstallation compatibility check from the Setup CD or by checking the hardware compatibility information available on the Microsoft Web site. Also, as part of confirming hardware compatibility, verify that you have obtained updated hardware device drivers and an updated system BIOS (or, for an Itanium-based computer, an updated Extensible Firmware Interface).

If you have a mass storage controller (such as a SCSI, RAID, or Fibre Channel adapter) for your hard disk, confirm that it's compatible with products in the Windows Server 2003 family by clicking the appropriate link in Support resources.

If your controller is compatible with products in the Windows Server 2003 family, but you are aware that the manufacturer has supplied a separate driver file for use with your operating system, obtain the file (on a floppy disk) before you begin Setup. During the early part of Setup, a line at the bottom of the screen will prompt you to press F6. Further prompts will guide you in supplying the driver file to Setup so that it can gain access to the mass storage controller.

If you are not sure whether you must obtain a separate driver file from the manufacturer of your mass storage controller, you can try running Setup. If the controller is not supported by the driver files on the Setup CD and therefore requires a driver file supplied by the hardware manufacturer, Setup stops and displays a message saying that no disk devices can be found, or it displays an incomplete list of controllers. After you obtain the necessary driver file, restart Setup, and press F6 when prompted.

Regardless of whether you run a preinstallation compatibility check, Setup checks hardware and software compatibility at the beginning of an upgrade or new installation and displays a report if there are incompatibilities.

Service Pack 5 or Later

Windows NT 4.0 must be running Service Pack 5 or later before you can upgrade to Windows Server 2003. Once Service Pack 5 or later has been installed, you can upgrade directly to Windows Server 2003 without having to install Windows 2000. If you are doing a clean installation, there is no need to install the service pack.

Compatibility Resources

For a comprehensive list of hardware and software supported by Windows operating systems, see the Windows Catalog at the Microsoft Web site (*http://www.microsoft.com/*).

Choosing to Upgrade or Refresh

A basic decision is whether to upgrade or to perform a new installation. Upgrading refers to leaving the existing Windows NT 4.0 (with Service Pack 5 or later) operating system on your computer and updating it by installing the new Windows Server 2003 operating system. A new installation means completely removing the previous operating system or installing a product in the Windows .NET Server family on a volume that has no previous operating system.

Reasons to Upgrade

Especially for small organizations, doing an upgrade rather than a new installation can make sense. Generally, with an upgrade, configuration is simpler, and your existing users, settings, groups, rights, and permissions are retained. And with an upgrade, you do not need to reinstall files and applications. As with any major changes to the hard disk, however, you should back up the system before beginning an upgrade.

See the following resources for more information:

- Regarding upgrading, see the Windows Server 2003 online Help and Support Center section "Operating Systems from Which You Can Upgrade" within the topic "Upgrading Compared with Installing."

- If you are upgrading in a domain that includes domain controllers running Windows NT 4.0, see the Help and Support Center topic "Upgrades in a Windows NT 4.0 Domain."

- If you want to upgrade and then use the same applications as before, be sure to review applications information in Relnotes.htm (in the \Docs folder on the Setup CD). Also, for the most recent information about compatible applications for products in the Windows Server 2003 family, see the software compatibility section of the Microsoft Web site (*http://www.microsoft.com/*).

Reasons to Perform a Clean Installation

There are good reasons to perform a clean installation rather than an upgrade—especially when dealing with large organizations. If you reformat your hard disk and then perform a new installation, the efficiency of your disk might improve (compared with not reformatting it). Reformatting also gives you the opportunity to modify the size or number of disk partitions to make them match your requirements more closely.

If you want to practice careful configuration management—for example, for a server where high availability is important—you might want to perform a new installation on a server instead of an upgrade. This is especially true on servers on which the operating system has been upgraded several times in the past.

It's possible to install the Enterprise Edition and also allow the computer to sometimes run another operating system. Setting up the computer this way, however, presents complexities because of file system issues.

> **More Info**   For more information about using multiple operating systems, see the Windows Server 2003 Help and Support Center topic "Deciding Whether a Computer Will Contain More than One Operating System."

Understanding Server Roles

Computers that function as servers within a domain can have one of two roles: member server or domain controller. A server that is not in a domain is a stand-alone server.

Member Servers

A member server is a computer that

- Runs Windows NT 4.0 Server, Windows 2000 Server, or a Windows Server 2003 operating system.

- Belongs to a domain.

- Is not a domain controller.

A member server does not process account logons, participate in Active Directory replication, or store domain security policy information. Member servers typically function as file servers, application servers, database servers, Web servers, certificate servers, firewalls, and remote access servers.

The following security-related features are common to all member servers:

- Member servers adhere to Group Policy settings that are defined for the site, domain, or organizational unit.

- Access control exists for resources that are available on a member server.

- Member server users have assigned user rights.

- Member servers contain a local security account database, the Security Accounts Manager (SAM).

Domain Controllers

A domain controller is a computer that

- Runs Windows NT 4.0 Server, Windows 2000 Server, or a Windows Server 2003 operating system.

- Stores a read/write copy of the domain database.

- Participates in multimaster replication.

- Authenticates users.

Domain controllers store directory data and manage communication between users and domains, including user logon processes, authentication, and directory searches. Domain controllers synchronize directory data using multimaster replication, ensuring consistency of information over time.

Active Directory supports multimaster replication of directory data between all domain controllers in a domain; however, multimaster replication is not appropriate for some directory data replication. In this case, a domain controller, called the operations master, will process data. In an Active Directory forest, there are at least five different operations master roles that are assigned to one or more domain controllers.

As the needs of your computing environment change, you might want to change the role of a server. Using the Active Directory Installation Wizard, you can promote a member server to a domain controller, or you can demote a domain controller to a member server.

Stand-Alone Servers

A stand-alone server is a computer that

- Runs Windows NT 4.0 Server, Windows 2000 Server, or a Windows Server 2003 operating system.

- Is not a member of domain.

If a server is installed as a member of a workgroup, that server is a stand-alone server. Stand-alone servers can share resources with other computers on the network, but they do not receive any of the benefits provided by Active Directory.

For more information, see the Windows Server 2003 Help and Support Center.

Active Directory Considerations

The Active Directory directory service is an essential and inseparable part of the Windows Server 2003 network architecture that provides a directory service designed for distributed networking environments. It offers a single point of management for Windows-based user accounts, clients, servers, and applications. It also helps organizations integrate systems not using Windows with Windows-based applications and Windows-compatible devices, thus consolidating directories and easing management of the entire network operating system.

Companies can also use Active Directory to extend systems securely to the Internet. Active Directory thus increases the value of an organization's existing network investments and lowers the overall costs of computing by making the Windows network operating system more manageable, secure, and interoperable.

The Active Directory directory service uses a structured data store as the basis for a logical, hierarchical organization of directory information. This data store, also known as the directory, contains information about Active Directory objects. These objects typically include shared resources such as servers, volumes, printers, and the network user and computer accounts. The directory is stored on domain controllers and can be accessed by network applications or services. A domain can have one or more domain controllers. Each domain controller has a copy of the directory for the domain in which it is located.

Security is integrated with Active Directory through logon authentication and access control to objects in the directory. With a single network logon, administrators can manage directory data and organization throughout their network. Authorized network users can access resources anywhere on the network. Policy-based administration eases the management of even the most complex network.

The Active Directory directory service also includes

- **Schema.**   Active Directory Schema is the set of definitions that defines the kinds of objects, and the types of information about those objects, that can be stored in Active Directory. The definitions are themselves stored as objects so that Active Directory can manage the schema objects with the same object management operations used for managing the rest of the objects in the directory. There are two types of definitions in the schema: attributes and classes. Attributes and classes are also referred to as schema objects or metadata.

- **Global catalog.**   The global catalog contains information about every object in the directory. This allows users and administrators to find directory information regardless of which domain in the directory actually contains the data. The global catalog is hosted on one or more domain controllers in a forest.

- **Query and index mechanism.**   Active Directory is designed to provide information to queries about directory objects from both users and programs. Administrators and users can easily search for and find information in the directory by using the Search command on the Start menu. Client programs can access information in Active Directory by using Active Directory Services Interface (ADSI).

- **Replication service.**   Except for very small networks, directory data must reside in more than one place on the network to be equally useful to all of your users. Through the automatic process of replication, the Active Directory directory service maintains copies, or replicas, of directory data on each domain controller. Active Directory replication uses a multimaster replication model. With multimaster replication, you can make directory changes at any domain controller, not just at a designated primary domain controller, and your changes will be replicated to all other relevant domain controllers.

- **Client software.**   Computers running Windows 95, Windows 98, and Windows NT 4.0 can access many of the Active Directory features available on Windows 2000 Professional or Windows XP Professional by running the Active Directory client software. To client computers not running Active Directory client software, the directory will appear just like a Windows NT directory.

New Features for Active Directory

Active Directory plays such an important role in managing the network that as you prepare to move to Windows Server 2003, it's helpful to review the new features of the Active Directory service. With the new Active Directory features available in the Standard Edition, Enterprise Edition, and Datacenter Edition, more efficient administration of Active Directory is available to you.

New features can be divided into those available on any domain controller running Windows Server 2003 and those available only when all domain controllers of a domain or forest are running Windows Server 2003. The following list summarizes the Active Directory features that are enabled by default on any domain controller running Windows Server 2003:

- **Multiple selection of user objects.**   Modify common attributes of multiple user objects at one time.

- **Drag-and-drop functionality.** Move Active Directory objects from container to container by dragging and dropping one or more objects to a desired location in the domain hierarchy. You can also add objects to group membership lists by dragging and dropping one or more objects (including other group objects) onto the target group.

- **Efficient search capabilities.** Conduct efficient browseless searches that minimize network traffic associated with browsing objects.

- **Saved queries.** Save commonly used search parameters for reuse in Active Directory Users and Computers.

- **Active Directory command-line tools.** Run new directory service commands for administration scenarios.

- **Selective class creation.** Create instances of specified classes in the base schema of a Windows Server 2003 forest. You can create instances of several common classes, including country or region, person, *organizationalPerson*, *groupOfNames*, device, and *certificationAuthority*.

- *InetOrgPerson* **class.** The *inetOrgPerson* class has been added to the base schema as a security principal and can be used in the same manner as the user class. The *userPassword* attribute can also be used to set the account password.

- **Application directory partitions.** Configure the replication scope for application-specific data among domain controllers running the Standard Edition, Enterprise Edition, and Datacenter Edition. For example, you can control the replication scope of Domain Name System (DNS) zone data stored in Active Directory so that only specific domain controllers in the forest participate in DNS zone replication.

- **Add domain controllers to existing domains by using backup media.** Reduce the time it takes to add a domain controller in an existing domain by using backup media.

- **Universal group membership caching.** Prevent the need to locate a global catalog across a WAN during logons by storing user universal group memberships on an authenticating domain controller.

New domainwide or forestwide Active Directory features can be enabled only when all domain controllers in a domain or forest are running Windows Server 2003 and the domain functionality or forest functionality has been set to Windows Server 2003. The following list summarizes the domainwide and forestwide Active Directory features that can be enabled when either a domain or a forest functional level has been raised to Windows .NET.

- **Domain controller rename tool.** Rename domain controllers without first demoting them.

- **Domain rename.** Rename any domain running Windows Server 2003 domain controllers. You can change the NetBIOS name or DNS name of any child, parent, tree-root, or forest-root domain.

- **Forest trusts.** Create a forest trust to extend two-way transitivity beyond the scope of a single forest to a second forest.

- **Forest restructuring.** Move existing domains to other locations in the domain hierarchy.

- **Defunct schema objects.** Deactivate unnecessary classes or attributes from the schema.

- **Dynamic auxiliary classes.** Dynamically link auxiliary classes to individual objects, not just to entire classes of objects. Auxiliary classes that have been attached to an object instance can subsequently be removed from the instance.

- **Global catalog replication tuning.** Retain the synchronization state of the global catalog when an administrative action results in an extension of the partial attribute set. This minimizes the work generated as a result of a partial attribute set extension by transmitting only attributes that were added.

- **Replication enhancements.** Replicate individual group members across the network instead of having to treat the entire group membership as a single unit of replication.

Compatibility with Windows NT 4.0

The Active Directory directory service is compatible with Windows NT 4.0 Server and supports a mix of operations that support domain controllers running Windows NT 4.0, Windows 2000, and Windows Server 2003. This allows you to upgrade domains and computers at your own pace, based on your organization's needs.

Active Directory supports the NTLM protocol used by Windows NT. This enables authorized users and computers from a Windows NT domain to log on and access resources in Windows 2000 or Windows Server 2003 domains. To clients running Windows 95, Windows 98, or Windows NT that are not running Active Directory client software, a Windows 2000 or Windows Server 2003 domain appears to be a Windows NT 4.0 domain.

The upgrade to Active Directory can be gradual and performed without interrupting operations. If you follow domain upgrade recommendations, it should never be necessary to take a domain off line to upgrade domain controllers, member servers, or workstations. When upgrading a Windows NT domain, you must upgrade the primary domain controller first. You can upgrade member servers and workstations at any time after this.

Active Directory allows upgrading from any Windows NT 4.0 domain model and supports both centralized and decentralized models. The typical master or multiple-master domain model can be easily upgraded to an Active Directory forest.

Upgrading from a Windows NT Domain

The Active Directory Installation Wizard simplifies upgrading a Windows NT domain to Windows Server 2003 Active Directory. The Active Directory Installation Wizard installs and configures domain controllers, which provide network users and computers access to the Active Directory directory service. Any member server (except those with restrictive license agreements) can be promoted to domain controllers using the Active Directory Installation Wizard. When promoting member servers to domain controllers, you will define one of the following roles for the new domain controller:

- New forest (also a new domain)
- New child domain
- New domain tree in an existing forest
- Additional domain controller in an existing domain

  The upgrade process involves the following steps:

- Planning and implementing a namespace and DNS infrastructure
- Determining forest functionality
- Upgrading the Windows NT 4.0 Server or earlier primary domain controller
- Upgrading any remaining backup domain controllers
- Converting groups

- Completing the upgrade of the domain

- Installing Active Directory client software on older client computers

> **More Info**   For additional information on using the Active Directory Installation Wizard, see the Windows Server 2003 Help and Support Center.

Planning and Implementing a Namespace and DNS Infrastructure

Namespace refers to the naming convention that defines a set of unique names for resources in a network, such as Domain Name System (DNS), a hierarchical naming structure that identifies each network resource and its place in the hierarchy of the namespace, and Windows Internet Naming Service (WINS), a flat naming structure that identifies each network resource using a single unique name.

DNS is required for Active Directory. DNS is a hierarchical, distributed database that contains mappings of DNS domain names to various types of data, such as IP addresses. DNS enables the location of computers and services by user-friendly names, and it also enables the discovery of other information stored in the database.

When setting up a namespace, it's recommended that you first choose and register a unique parent DNS domain name that can be used for hosting your organization on the Internet—for example, microsoft.com. Once you have chosen your parent domain name, you can combine this name with a location or organizational name used within your organization to form subdomain names. For example, if a subdomain is added, such as the itg.example.microsoft.com domain tree (for resources used by the information technology group at your organization), additional subdomain names can be formed using this name. For instance, a group of programmers working on electronic data interchange (EDI) in this division can have a subdomain named edi.itg.example.microsoft.com. Likewise, another group of workers providing support in this division might use support.itg.example.microsoft.com.

Prior to beginning the upgrade from Windows NT 4.0 to the Windows Server 2003 Active Directory service, ensure that you have designed DNS and Active Directory namespaces and either have configured DNS servers or are planning to have the Active Directory Installation Wizard automatically install the DNS service on the domain controller.

Active Directory is integrated with DNS in the following ways:

- **Active Directory and DNS have the same hierarchical structure.**   Although separate and implemented differently for different purposes, an organization's namespaces for DNS and Active Directory have an identical structure. For example, microsoft.com is a DNS domain and an Active Directory domain.

- **DNS zones can be stored in Active Directory.**   If you are using the Windows .NET Server DNS service, primary zone files can be stored in Active Directory for replication to other Active Directory domain controllers.

- **Active Directory uses DNS as a locator service, resolving Active Directory domain, site, and service names to IP addresses.**
  To log on to an Active Directory domain, an Active Directory client queries its configured DNS server for the IP address of the Lightweight Directory Access Protocol (LDAP) service running on a domain controller for a specified domain. While Active Directory is integrated with DNS and shares the same namespace structure, it's important to distinguish between them:

  - ❏ **DNS is a name resolution service.**   DNS clients send DNS name queries to their configured DNS server. The DNS server receives the name query and either resolves the name query through locally stored files or consults another DNS server for resolution. DNS does not require Active Directory to function.

  - ❏ **Active Directory is a directory service.**   Active Directory provides an information repository and services to make information available to users and applications. Active Directory clients send queries to Active Directory servers using LDAP. To locate an Active Directory server, an Active Directory client queries DNS. Active Directory requires DNS to function.

More Info   For more information about DNS configuration, see the Windows Server 2003 Help and Support Center.

Determining Forest Functionality

Forest functionality determines the type of Active Directory features that can be enabled within the scope of a single forest. Each forest functional level has a set of specific minimum requirements for the version of operating systems that domain controllers throughout the forest can run. For example, the Windows .NET forest functional level requires all domain controllers to be running Windows Server 2003 operating systems.

In the scenario in which you are upgrading your first Windows NT domain so that it becomes the first domain in a new Windows Server 2003 forest, it's recommended (you will be prompted during the upgrade) to set the forest functional level to Windows .NET interim. This level contains all of the features used in the Windows 2000 forest functional level and also includes two important advanced Active Directory features:

- Improved replication algorithms in the intersite topology generator

- Replication improvements made to group memberships

The Windows .NET interim functional level is an option when upgrading the first Windows NT domain to a new forest and can be manually configured after the upgrade. This functional level supports only domain controllers running Windows .NET and Windows NT, not domain controllers running Windows 2000. Servers running Windows 2000 cannot be promoted to domain controller in a forest in which the forest functional level has been set to Windows .NET interim. For more information about forest functionality, see the section "Raising Domain Functional Levels" later in this chapter.

Upgrading the Windows NT 4.0 or Earlier Primary Domain Controller

The first Windows NT 4.0 and earlier server you must upgrade is the primary domain controller (PDC). Upgrading the Windows NT PDC is required for successful upgrade of the domain. During the upgrade, the Active Directory Installation Wizard requires that you choose to join an existing domain tree or forest or start a new domain tree or forest. If you decide to join an existing domain tree, you must provide a reference to the desired parent domain.

Running the Active Directory Installation Wizard installs all necessary components on the domain controller, such as the directory data store and the Kerberos V5 protocol authentication software. Once the Kerberos V5 protocol is installed, the installation process starts the authentication service and the ticket-granting service, and if this is a new child domain, a transitive trust relationship is established with the parent domain. Eventually, the domain controller from the parent domain copies all schema and configuration information to the new child domain controller. The existing Security Accounts Manager (SAM) objects will be copied from the registry to the new data store. These objects are security principals.

During the upgrade, objects are created to contain the accounts and groups from the Windows NT domain. These container objects are named Users, Computers, and Builtin and are displayed as folders in Active Directory Users And Computers. User accounts and predefined groups are placed in the Users folder. Computer accounts are placed in the Computers folder. Built-in groups are placed in the Builtin folder. Note that these special container objects are not organizational units. They cannot be moved, renamed, or deleted.

Existing Windows NT 4.0 and earlier groups are located in different folders depending on the nature of the group. Windows NT 4.0 and earlier built-in local groups (such as Administrators and Server Operators) are located in the Builtin folder. Windows NT 4.0 and earlier global groups (such as Domain Admins) and any user-created local groups and global groups are located in the Users folder.

The upgraded PDC can synchronize security principal changes to remaining Windows NT 4.0 and earlier backup domain controllers (BDCs). It's recognized as the domain master by the Windows NT Server 4.0 and earlier BDCs.

If a domain controller running Windows Server 2003 goes off line or otherwise becomes unavailable and no other Windows Server 2003 domain controllers exist in the domain, a Windows NT BDC can be promoted to a PDC to fill the role for the off line Windows Server 2003 domain controller.

The upgraded domain controller is a fully functional member of the forest. The new domain is added to the domain and site structure, and all domain controllers receive the notification that a new domain has joined the forest.

> **More Info** For more information, visit the Windows Server 2003 Help and Support Center.

Upgrading Any Remaining Backup Domain Controllers

Once you have upgraded the Windows NT 4.0 and earlier PDC, you can proceed to upgrade all remaining BDCs. During the upgrade process, you might want to remove one BDC from the network to guarantee a backup if any problems develop. This BDC will store a secure copy of your current domain database.

If any problems arise during the upgrade, you can remove all domain controllers running Windows .NET from the production environment and then bring the BDC back into your network and make it the new PDC. This new PDC will then replicate its data throughout the domain so that the domain is returned to its previous state.

The only drawback to this method is that all changes that were made while the safe BDC was off line are lost. To minimize this loss, you can periodically turn the safe BDC on and off again (when the domain is in a stable state) during the upgrade process, to update its safe copy of the directory.

When upgrading Windows NT 4.0 and earlier domains, only one domain controller running Windows Server 2003 can create security principals (users, groups, and computer accounts). This single domain controller is configured as a PDC emulator master. The PDC emulator master emulates a Windows NT 4.0 and earlier PDC.

> **More Info**   For more information about the PDC emulator role, see "Operations Master Roles" in the Windows Server 2003 Help and Support Center.

Converting Groups

When you upgrade a Primary Domain Controller running Windows NT 4.0 Server to a server running Windows Server 2003, existing Windows NT groups are converted in the following ways:

- Windows NT local groups are converted to domain local groups on servers running Windows Server 2003.

- Windows NT global groups are converted to global groups on servers running Windows Server 2003.

Domain member computers running Windows NT can continue to display and access the converted groups. The groups appear to these clients as Windows NT 4.0 local and global groups. However, a Windows NT client cannot display members of groups or modify the member properties when that membership violates Windows NT group rules. For example, when a Windows NT client views the members of a global group on a server running Windows Server 2003, it does not view any other groups that are members of that global group.

Converting Groups and Microsoft Exchange

Microsoft Exchange allows users to arrange e-mail addresses in groups and distribution lists. When Exchange servers are upgraded to Active Directory, the Exchange distribution lists are converted to distribution groups with universal scope. The administrator can convert the group to a security group later if desired by using Active Directory Users And Computers to change the group properties. The Messaging Application Programming Interface (MAPI) enables computers running previous version Exchange clients to view the converted distribution group.

Using Converted Groups with Servers Running Windows Server 2003

Client computers that do not run Active Directory client software identify groups with universal scope on servers running Windows Server 2003 as having global scope instead. When viewing the members of a group with universal scope, the Windows NT client can view and access only those group members that conform to the membership rules of global groups on servers running Windows Server 2003.

In a Windows Server 2003 domain that is set to a domain functional level of Windows 2000 native, all the domain controllers must be servers running Windows Server 2003. However, the domain can contain member servers that run Windows NT Server 4.0. These servers view groups with universal scope as having global scope and can assign groups with universal scope rights and permissions and place them in local groups.

In a Windows Server 2003 domain, a Windows NT Server 4.0 member server running Windows NT administrative tools cannot access domain local groups. However, you can work around this limitation by using a server running Windows Server 2003 and using its Windows Server 2003 Administration Tools Pack administrative tools to access the server running Windows NT Server 4.0. You can use these tools to display the domain local groups and assign to them permissions to resources on the server running Windows NT Server 4.0.

After you have upgraded all existing Windows NT 4.0 and earlier primary and backup domain controllers to Windows Server 2003, and you have no plans to use Windows NT 4.0 and earlier domain controllers, you can raise the domain functional level from Windows 2000 mixed to Windows 2000 native. For more information about how to raise the domain functional level, see the section "Raising Domain Functional Levels" later in this chapter.

Several things happen when you raise the domain functional level to Windows 2000 native:

- Domain controllers no longer support NTLM replication.

- The domain controller that is emulating the PDC operations master cannot synchronize data with a Windows NT 4.0 and earlier BDC.

- Windows NT 4.0 and earlier domain controllers cannot be added to the domain. (You can add new domain controllers running Windows 2000 or Windows Server 2003.)

- Users and computers using previous versions of Windows begin to benefit from the transitive trusts of Active Directory and (with the proper authorization) can access resources anywhere in the forest. Although previous versions of Windows do not support the Kerberos V5 protocol, the pass-through authentication provided by the domain controllers allows users and computers to be authenticated in any domain in the forest. This enables users or computers to access resources in any domain in the forest for which they have the appropriate permissions. Other than the enhanced access to any other domains in the forest, clients will not be aware of any changes in the domain.

Installing Active Directory Client Software on Older Client Computers

Computers running Active Directory client software can use Active Directory features, such as authentication, to access resources in the domain tree or forest and to query the directory. By default, client computers running Windows XP Professional and Windows 2000 Professional have the client software built in and can access Active Directory resources normally.

However, computers running previous versions of Windows (Windows 98, Windows 95, and Windows NT) require installation of the Active Directory client software before access to Active Directory resources is available. Without the client software, previous versions of Windows can access the domain only as if it were a Windows NT 4.0 and earlier domain, finding only those resources available through Windows NT 4.0 and earlier one-way trusts.

When the domain functional level is set to Windows 2000 mixed, the domain controller exposes to clients using previous versions of Windows only resources in domains that have older, established Windows NT 4.0 and earlier explicit trusts. This creates a consistent environment in that the previous-version clients can access only resources in domains with explicit trusts, regardless of whether domain controllers are running Windows Server 2003 or Windows NT 4.0 and earlier.

Raising Domain Functional Levels

Domains can operate at three functional levels: Windows 2000 mixed, the default setting (which includes domain controllers running Windows 2000, Windows NT 4.0, and Windows Server 2003); Windows 2000 native (which includes domain controllers running Windows 2000 and Windows Server 2003); and Windows Server 2003 (which includes only domain controllers running Windows Server 2003).

Once all domain controllers are running on Windows Server 2003, you can raise the domain and forest functionality to Windows Server 2003 by opening Active Directory Domains And Trusts, right-clicking the domain for which you want to raise functionality, and then clicking Raise Domain Functional Level.

Note that once the domain functional level has been raised, domain controllers running earlier operating systems cannot be introduced into the domain. For example, if you raise the domain functional level to Windows Server 2003, domain controllers running Windows 2000 Server cannot be added to that domain.

Table 16-1 describes the domainwide features that are enabled for the corresponding domain functional level.

Table 16-1 Domainwide Features

Domain Feature	Windows 2000 Mixed	Windows 2000 Native	Windows Server 2003
Domain controller rename tool	Disabled	Disabled	Enabled
Update logon time-stamp	Disabled	Disabled	Enabled
Kerberos KDC key version numbers	Disabled	Disabled	Enabled
User password on *InetOrgPerson* object	Disabled	Disabled	Enabled

Table 16-1   Domainwide Features   *(continued)*

Domain Feature	Windows 2000 Mixed	Windows 2000 Native	Windows Server 2003
Universal groups	Enabled for distribution groups. Disabled for security groups.	Enabled Allows both security and distribution groups.	Enabled Allows both security and distribution groups.
Group nesting	Enabled for distribution groups. Disabled for security groups except for domain local security groups that can have global groups as members.	Enabled Allows full group nesting.	Enabled Allows full group nesting.
Converting groups	Disabled No group conversions allowed.	Enabled Allows conversion between security groups and distribution groups.	Enabled Allows conversion between security groups and distribution groups.
SID history	Disabled	Enabled Allows migration of security principals from one domain to another.	Enabled Allows migration of security principals from one domain to another.

Raising Forest Functional Levels

Forest functionality enables features across all the domains within your forest. Two forest functional levels are available: Windows 2000 (which supports domain controllers running Windows NT 4, Windows 2000, and Windows Server 2003) and Windows Server 2003 (which supports only domain controllers running Windows Server 2003). If you are upgrading your first Windows NT domain so that it becomes the first domain in a new Windows Server 2003 forest, you can choose an additional forest functional level (Windows .NET interim).

By default, forests operate at the Windows 2000 functional level. You can raise the forest functional level to Windows Server 2003. Once the forest functional level has been raised, domain controllers running earlier operating systems cannot be introduced into the forest.

Table 16-2 describes the forestwide features that are enabled for the corresponding forest functional levels.

Table 16-2   Forestwide Features

Forest Feature	Windows 2000	Windows Server 2003
Global catalog replication tuning	Disabled	Enabled
Defunct schema objects	Disabled	Enabled
Forest trust	Disabled	Enabled
Linked value replication	Disabled	Enabled
Domain rename	Disabled	Enabled
Improved replication algorithms	Disabled	Enabled
Dynamic auxiliary classes	Disabled	Enabled
InetOrgPerson object class change	Disabled	Enabled

Domain Controllers

The upgrade to Active Directory can be gradual and performed without interrupting operations. If you follow domain upgrade recommendations, it should never be necessary to take a domain off line to upgrade domain controllers, member servers, or workstations.

In Active Directory, a domain is a collection of computer, user, and group objects defined by the administrator. These objects share a common directory database, security policies, and security relationships with other domains. A forest is a collection of one or more Active Directory domains that share the same class and attribute definitions (schema), site and replication information (configuration), and forestwide search capabilities (global catalog). Domains in the same forest are linked with two-way transitive trust relationships.

To prepare for upgrades in a domain containing Windows 2000 domain controllers, it's recommended that you apply Service Pack 2 or later to all domain controllers running Windows 2000.

Before upgrading a domain controller running Windows 2000 to Windows Server 2003 or installing Active Directory on the first domain controller running

Windows Server 2003, ensure that your server, your forest, and your domain are ready.

Two command-line tools are helpful in upgrading domain controllers:

- **Winnt32.** Use Winnt32 to check the upgrade compatibility of the server.

- **Adprep.** Use Adprep on the schema operations master to prepare the forest. Running Adprep on the schema master updates the schema, which in turn replicates to all of the other domain controllers in the forest.

Note that you cannot upgrade domain controllers running Windows 2000 to Windows Server 2003 or add domain controllers running Windows Server 2003 to Windows 2000 domains until you have used Adprep to prepare the forest and the domains within the forest.

> **More Info**   For more information about Windows Server 2003 command-line tools and about upgrading domain controllers, see Windows Server 2003 Help and Support Center.

Working with Remote Installation Services

All editions of Windows Server 2003, with the exception of Web Edition, offer Remote Installation Services (RIS), a change and configuration management feature that was also included with Windows 2000. RIS enables you to set up new client computers remotely, without the need to physically visit each client machine. You can use RIS to install operating systems on remote boot–enabled client computers by connecting the computer to the network, starting the client computer, and logging on with a valid user account.

If your network uses RIS with Windows NT 4.0 Server, you should make the RIS server the first computer that you upgrade to Windows Server 2003. You won't be able to use RIS later unless it is upgraded first because of design changes in the way that Active Directory does authentication. Upgrading the RIS server to Windows Server 2003 gives it the ability to communicate with the remaining Windows NT 4.0 domain controllers, as well as with Windows Server 2003 domain controllers.

Deployment Resources

To deploy domain controllers running Windows Server 2003, it's recommended that you use the Windows Server 2003 Deployment Kit, which is available on line at the Microsoft Windows Deployment and Resource Kits Web site (*http://www.microsoft.com/windows/reskits/*).

The online deployment kit includes case studies and the necessary information for deploying Windows Server 2003 Active Directory in networks that have domain controllers running Windows NT 4.0 or Windows 2000. If your network includes branch offices, see "Designing the Site Topology" in the Microsoft Windows Server 2003 Deployment Kit (Microsoft Press, 2003). This online guide helps you plan Active Directory deployment when branch office sites are connected with slow network links.

Renaming Domain Controllers

The ability to rename domain controllers running Windows Server 2003 provides you with the flexibility to make changes in a Windows Server 2003 domain whenever the need arises. Rename a domain controller to

- Restructure your network for organizational and business needs.

- Make management and administrative control easier.

When you rename a domain controller, you must ensure that there will be no interruption in the ability of clients to locate or authenticate to the renamed domain controller except when the domain controller is restarted.

Another requirement for renaming a domain controller is that the domain functional level must be set to Windows Server 2003. The new name of the domain controller is automatically updated to DNS and Active Directory. Once the new name propagates to DNS and Active Directory, clients are then able to locate and authenticate to the renamed domain controller. DNS and Active Directory replication latency can delay client ability to locate or authenticate to the renamed domain controller. The length of delay depends on specifics of your network and the replication topology of your particular organization.

During replication latency, clients might not be able to access the newly renamed domain controller. This might be acceptable for clients that try to locate and authenticate to a particular domain controller because other domain controllers should be available to process the authentication request.

Working with Domain Trust

All trusts within a Windows 2000 or Windows Server 2003 forest are transitive and two-way. Therefore, both domains in a trust relationship automatically trust each other. This means that if Domain A trusts Domain B and Domain B trusts Domain C, users from Domain C (when assigned the proper permissions) can access resources in Domain A.

Trust Protocols

A domain controller running Windows Server 2003 authenticates users and applications using one of two protocols: Kerberos V5 or NTLM. The Kerberos V5 protocol is the default protocol for computers running Windows 2000, Windows XP Professional, or Windows Server 2003. If any computer involved in a transaction does not support Kerberos V5, the NTLM protocol will be used.

With the Kerberos V5 protocol, the client requests a ticket from a domain controller in its account domain to the server in the trusting domain. This ticket is issued by an intermediary trusted by the client and the server. The client presents this trusted ticket to the server in the trusting domain for authentication.

When a client tries to access resources on a server in another domain using NTLM authentication, the server containing the resource must contact a domain controller in the client's account domain to verify the account credentials.

Trusted Domain Objects

Trusted domain objects (TDOs) are objects that represent each trust relationship within a particular domain. Each time a trust is established, a unique TDO is created and stored (in the System container) in its domain. Attributes such as a trust's transitivity, its type, and its partner domain name are represented in a TDO.

Forest trust TDOs store additional attributes in order to identify all of the trusted namespaces from its partner forest. These attributes include domain tree names, user principal name suffixes, service principal name suffixes, and security identifier namespaces.

Nontransitive Trust and Windows NT 4.0

A nontransitive trust is restricted by the two domains in the trust relationship and does not flow to any other domains in the forest. A nontransitive trust can be a two-way trust or a one-way trust.

Nontransitive trusts are one-way by default, although you can also create a two-way relationship by creating two one-way trusts. Nontransitive domain trusts are the only form of trust relationship possible between

■ A Windows Server 2003 domain and a Windows NT domain.

■ A Windows Server 2003 domain in one forest and a domain in another forest (when not joined by a forest trust).

Using the New Trust Wizard, you can manually create the following non-transitive trusts:

■ **External trust.** A nontransitive trust created between a Windows Server 2003 domain and a Windows NT domain, a Windows 2000 domain, or a Windows Server 2003 domain in another forest. When you upgrade a Windows NT domain to a Windows Server 2003 domain, all existing Windows NT trusts are preserved intact. All trust relationships between Windows Server 2003 domains and Windows NT domains are nontransitive.

■ **Realm trust.** A nontransitive trust between an Active Directory domain and a Kerberos V5 realm.

External Trust and Windows NT 4.0

You can create an external trust to form a one-way nontransitive relationship with domains outside your forest. External trusts are sometimes necessary when users need access to resources located in a Windows NT 4.0 domain or in a domain located within a separate forest that is not joined by a forest trust.

When a trust is established between a domain in a particular forest and a domain outside that forest, security principals from the external domain can access resources in the internal domain. Active Directory creates a *foreign security principal* object in the internal domain to represent each security principal from the trusted external domain. These foreign security principals can become members of domain local groups in the internal domain. Domain local groups can have members from domains outside the forest.

Directory objects for foreign security principals are created by Active Directory and should not be manually modified. You can view foreign security principal objects from Active Directory Users And Computers by enabling Advanced Features.

> **More Info**   For information about enabling Advanced Features, see "To View Advanced Features" in the Windows Server 2003 Help and Support Center.

To create an external trust, you must have Enterprise Admin or Domain Admin privileges for the domain in the Windows Server 2003 forest and Domain Admin privileges for the domain outside the forest. Each trust is assigned a password that must be known to the administrators of both domains in the relationship.

Note that in Windows 2000 mixed domains, external trusts should always be deleted from a Windows Server 2003 domain controller. External trusts to Windows NT 4.0 or 3.51 domains can be deleted by authorized administrators on the Windows NT 4.0 or 3.51 domain controllers. However, only the trusted side of the relationship can be deleted on Windows NT 4.0 or 3.51 domain controllers. The trusting side of the relationship (created in the Windows Server 2003 domain) is not deleted, and although it will not be operational, the trust will continue to appear in Active Directory Domains And Trusts. To remove the trust completely, you will need to delete the trust from a Windows Server 2003 domain controller in the trusting domain. If an external trust is inadvertently deleted from a Windows NT 4.0 or 3.51 domain controller, you will need to re-create the trust from any Windows Server 2003 domain controller in the trusting domain.

How Some Windows NT Tasks Are Performed in Windows Server 2003

Table 16-3 lists common tasks for configuring Active Directory. The user interface for performing these tasks is different in this version of Windows from the way it was in Windows NT 4.0.

Table 16-3   Tasks Then and Now

Task	In Windows NT 4.0, Use...	In Windows Server 2003, Use...
Install a domain controller	Windows Setup	Active Directory Installation Wizard
Manage user accounts	User Manager	Active Directory Users And Computers

(continued)

Table 16-3   Tasks Then and Now   *(continued)*

Task	In Windows NT 4.0, Use...	In Windows Server 2003, Use...
Manage groups	User Manager	Active Directory Users And Computers
Manage computer accounts	Server Manager	Active Directory Users And Computers
Add a computer to a domain	Server Manager	Active Directory Users And Computers
Create or manage trust relationships	User Manager	Active Directory Domains And Trusts
Manage account policy	User Manager	Active Directory Users And Computers
Manage user rights	User Manager	Active Directory Users And Computers
Manage audit policy	User Manager	Active Directory Users And Computers

Support for Existing Applications

On servers running Windows NT 4.0 and earlier, read access for user and group information is assigned to anonymous users so that existing applications, including Microsoft BackOffice, SQL Server, and some non-Microsoft applications, function correctly.

In Windows 2000 and Windows Server 2003, members of the Anonymous Logon group have read access to this information only when the group is added to the Pre-Windows 2000 Compatible Access group.

Using the Active Directory Installation Wizard, you can choose whether you want the Anonymous Logon group and the Everyone security groups to be added to the Pre-Windows 2000 Compatible Access group by choosing the Permissions Compatible With Pre-Windows 2000 Server Operating Systems option. To prevent members of the Anonymous Logon group from gaining read access to user and group information, choose the Permissions Compatible Only With Windows Server 2003 Operating Systems option.

When upgrading a domain controller from Windows 2000 to Windows Server 2003, if the Everyone security group is already a member of the Pre-Windows 2000 Compatible Access security group (indicating backward compatibility settings), the Anonymous Logon security group will be added as a member of the Pre-Windows 2000 Compatible Access security group during the upgrade.

You can manually switch between the backward-compatible and high-security settings on Active Directory objects by adding the Anonymous Logon security group to the Pre-Windows 2000 Compatible Access security group using Active Directory Users And Computers.

Note that if you select the Permissions Compatible Only With Windows Server 2003 Operating Systems option while promoting a domain controller, and you find that your applications are not functioning correctly, try resolving the problem by manually adding the special group Everyone to the Pre-Windows 2000 Compatible Access security group and then restarting the domain controllers in the domain. Once you have upgraded to applications compatible with Windows Server 2003, you should return to the more secure Windows Server 2003 configuration by removing the Everyone group from the Pre-Windows 2000 Compatible Access security group and restarting the domain controllers in the affected domain.

Best Practices for Active Directory

The following is a set of best practices to use when setting up and working with Active Directory:

■   As a security best practice, it's recommended that you do not log on to your computer with administrative credentials. When you are logged on to your computer without administrative credentials, you can use Run As to accomplish administrative tasks.

> **More Info**   For more information, see "Why You Should Not Run Your Computer as an Administrator" and "Using Run As" in the Windows Server 2003 Help and Support Center.

■   To further secure Active Directory, you should implement the following security guidelines:

   ❑   Rename or disable the Administrator account (and the Guest account) in each domain to prevent attacks on your domains. For more information, see "User and Computer Accounts" in the Help and Support Center.

   ❑   Physically secure all domain controllers in a locked room.

❑   Manage the security relationship between two forests, and simplify security administration and authentication across forests.

❑   To provide additional protection for the Active Directory schema, remove all users from the Schema Admins group, and add a user to the group only when schema changes need to be made. Once the changes have been made, remove the user from the group.

❑   Restrict user, group, and computer access to shared resources; filter Group Policy settings.

❑   By default, all traffic on Active Directory administration tools is signed and encrypted while in transit on the network. Do not disable this feature.

❑   Some default user rights assigned to specific default groups might allow members of those groups to gain additional rights in the domain, including administrative rights. Therefore, your organization must equally trust all personnel that are members of the Enterprise Admins, Domain Admins, Account Operators, Server Operators, Print Operators, and Backup Operators groups.

❑   Establish as a site every geographic area that requires fast access to the latest directory information.

More Info   For general security information about Active Directory, see "Security Overview for Active Directory" and "Securing Active Directory" in the Windows .NET Server Help and Support Center.

Establishing areas that require immediate access to up-to-date Active Directory information as separate sites will provide the resources required to meet your needs.

Place at least one domain controller at every site, and make at least one domain controller at each site a global catalog. Sites that do not have their own domain controllers and at least one global catalog are dependent on other sites for directory information and are less efficient than sites that have those resources.

Leave all site links bridged, and leave site link connection schedules unrestricted. Bridging all site links maximizes replication links between sites and prevents the need to create site link bridges manually. Leaving site link connection schedules unrestricted eliminates connection-scheduling conflicts that might prevent replication. By default, all site links are bridged and site link connection schedules are unrestricted.

Establish a preferred bridgehead server if you are using a firewall or if you want to dedicate a computer to intersite replication. A bridgehead server serves as a proxy for communication with other sites outside a firewall. All sites must be associated with at least one subnet and in at least one site link, or they will not be usable.

Perform regular backups of domain controllers to preserve all trust relationships within that domain.

Application Compatibility

The deployment of an operating system in any organization is a very large project. Application compatibility with the new operating system is one of the most critical steps in the testing and planning phases of a successful deployment. This entails verifying that all existing software and any planned software will function correctly on the new operating system at least as well as it did on the old operating system.

The Application Compatibility Toolkit (ACT) contains several tools that make this process easier to manage. The ACT provides tools to test applications both during the development phase and during deployments. It also provides tools that enable you to gather data about the applications installed on every Windows computer in the network and to package the necessary compatibility fixes for each of those computers. Tools included in the ACT include the following:

- **Analyzer.** This tool gathers information about every program installed on your network. The analyzer can be used to automate the process of creating an inventory of software used in your enterprise.

- **Application Verifier.** This tool assists developers when looking for possible compatibility issues with a new application. It's also possible for IT professionals to use this tool to determine whether a proposed software package has any common compatibility issues.

- **Compatibility Administrator.** This tool determines the necessary compatibility fixes to support an application in Windows. The tool can also package the fixes into a custom compatibility database that can then be distributed to computers on the network.

Chapter 18, "Testing for Application Compatibility," describes the ACT in much more detail and shows you how to use it to test the compatibility of applications.

For More Information

See the following resources for further information:

- Using the Application Compatibility Toolkit at *http://www.microsoft.com/windowsserver2003/compatible/appcompat.mspx*

- Top 10 Features of Windows Server 2003 for Organizations Upgrading from Windows NT Server 4.0 at *http://www.microsoft.com/windowsserver2003/evaluation/whyupgrade/top10nt.mspx*

- Top 10 Features for Organizations Upgrading from Windows 2000 Server at *http://www.microsoft.com/windowsserver2003/evaluation/whyupgrade/top10w2k.mspx*

- Microsoft Windows Server 2003 Deployment Guide at *http://www.microsoft.com/technet/prodtechnol/windowsnetserver/evaluate/cpp/reskit/*

17

Upgrading from Windows 2000 Server

Upgrading from Microsoft Windows 2000 to an edition of Microsoft Windows Server 2003 enables you to take advantage of the new Windows Server 2003 features without restructuring your current network configuration. The process is more straightforward than you read about in Chapter 16, "Upgrading from Windows NT 4.0 Server." When you upgrade to Windows Server 2003, the existing structure of your directory service remains in place.

Windows Server 2003 provides many solutions for your environment in the way of new features and functionality, though. Some of the new features available to you after you upgrade to Windows Server 2003 include the following, which you learned about in Chapter 3, "Active Directory":

- Improved group membership replication

- Application directory partitions

- Forest trust relationships

- Universal group caching

- Improved intersite replication topology generator

This chapter is an overview of issues you must consider before upgrading from Windows 2000 Server to Windows Server 2003. The chapter is also based on the *Microsoft Windows Server 2003 Deployment Kit* (Microsoft Press, 2003). You can learn more about this resource kit at *http://www.microsoft.com/reskit/*. This kit and the tools on its companion CD are invaluable for planning and deploying Windows Server 2003.

Getting Ready to Upgrade

If any domain controllers in your environment are running Windows NT version 4.0, you must complete the process for upgrading from Windows NT 4.0 to Windows Server 2003. For information about upgrading from Windows NT 4.0 to Windows Server 2003, see Chapter 16, "Upgrading from Windows NT 4.0."

To successfully upgrade Windows 2000 domains to Windows Server 2003, you must be familiar with Active Directory domain and forest functional levels. You can initiate an upgrade from Windows 2000 to Windows Server 2003 in one of two ways:

- By upgrading an existing Windows 2000–based domain controller to Windows Server 2003.

- By using the Active Directory Installation Wizard to install Active Directory on a Windows .NET–based member server.

Active Directory Preparation Tool

To prepare the Windows 2000 domain for the upgrade to Windows Server 2003, you must use the Active Directory Preparation tool (ADPrep.exe). After the upgrade, you can take advantage of application directory partitions. You can run ADPrep.exe only from a command line.

ADPrep.exe prepares the forest and the domain for an Active Directory upgrade by performing a collection of operations prior to installation of the first Windows Server 2003 domain controller. ADPrep.exe is located on the Microsoft Windows .NET Server operating system CD. ADPrep.exe copies the files 409.csv and dcpromo.csv from the installation CD or from a network installation point to the local computer to prepare the Active Directory forest and domain.

The ADPrep.exe tool merges your current schema with new schema information that the tool provides, preserving previous schema modifications in your environment. You must successfully run *adprep /forestprep* in a forest before you can prepare the domain by using *adprep /domainprep*. Run *adprep /forestprep* on the schema operations master. Within each domain in which you plan to install a Windows .NET domain controller, you must successfully run *adprep /domainprep* on the infrastructure operations master before you upgrade the first domain controller or join a Windows .NET member server or stand-alone server as an additional domain controller. To prepare your Active Directory forest and domain for the upgrade to Windows Server 2003, ADPrep.exe performs the following tasks:

- Updates the Active Directory Schema

- Improves default security descriptors

- Upgrades display specifiers

- Adjusts access control lists on Active Directory objects and on files in the Sysvol shared folder to allow domain controller access

  In versions of Windows earlier than Windows Server 2003, including the Everyone security identifier (SID) in an ACL or group membership allows authenticated users, guest users, and anyone with an anonymous logon to gain access to many resources. Windows 2000 domain controllers also use anonymous access to gain control of some Active Directory objects and files. In Windows Server 2003, the Everyone SID no longer allows access to anonymous users, thus restricting domain controller access to particular objects. ADPrep.exe adjusts the ACLs on these objects so that domain controllers can still access them.

- Creates new objects that are used by applications such as COM+ and Windows Management Instrumentation (WMI)

- Creates new containers in Active Directory that are used to verify that the preparation was successful

Each time it runs, ADPrep.exe creates a log file that can help you troubleshoot errors. The log file documents each step of the forest preparation process. Each ADPrep log file is located in a subfolder within the %SystemRoot%\system32\debug\adprep directory. Each subfolder is stamped with the date and time when ADPrep was run.

When you are upgrading a Windows 2000 domain controller to Windows Server 2003, Winnt32.exe verifies that the forest and domain have been prepared. If you have not prepared the forest and the domain in which the new domain controller will be a member, Winnt32.exe fails, the upgrade terminates, and you are notified that you must run ADPrep.exe. You cannot upgrade Windows 2000 domain controllers to Windows .NET before running ADPrep.exe.

Application Directory Partitions

If at least one domain controller in your forest is running Windows Server 2003, you can take advantage of application directory partitions, which provide storage for nondomain, application-specific data that can be replicated to any arbitrary set of domain controllers. (See Chapter 3, "Active Directory.")

In Windows Server 2003, application directory partitions can be used to store Domain Name System (DNS) data. If the person who initializes the Active Directory installation is a member of the Enterprise Admin group, DNS-specific application directory partitions are created automatically on all existing DNS servers during the Active Directory installation. If application directory partition creation fails during the installation, the DNS service will attempt to create the partitions again when the computer is restarted after Active Directory is installed. You must be a member of the Enterprise Admin group to create DNS-specific application directory partitions.

During the Active Directory installation, two DNS-specific application directory partitions are created: a forestwide application directory partition named ForestDnsZones and a domainwide partition named DomainDnsZones for each domain in the forest. After upgrading all domain controllers in a domain to Windows Server 2003, you can specify the replication scope for each existing Active Directory–integrated zone by moving the zone into the newly created application directory partition. Moving Active Directory–integrated DNS zones into application directory partitions has the following benefits:

- Active Directory–integrated DNS can be used forestwide because the forestwide application directory partition can replicate outside the domain. You do not have to use conventional DNS zone transfer to replicate the zone file information to DNS servers outside the domain.

- Domainwide replication can be targeted to minimize replication traffic. Administrators can specify which of the domain controllers that are running the DNS service receive the DNS zone data.

- Forestwide replication can be targeted to minimize replication traffic because DNS information is no longer replicated to the global catalog.

For more information about using application directory partitions for DNS information, see "Use DNS Application Directory Partitions" later in this chapter.

Supported Upgrade Paths

To determine whether you can upgrade your computers to Windows Server 2003 or must perform a clean operating system installation, you must first identify the versions of Windows 2000 that are running in your environment. Table 17-1 lists the Windows 2000 platforms, indicating platforms that can be upgraded directly to each edition of Windows Server 2003.

Table 17-1   Supported Upgrade Paths to Windows Server 2003

Platform	Upgrade to Windows Server 2003, Standard Edition	Upgrade to Windows Server 2003, Enterprise Edition	Upgrade to Windows Server 2003, Datacenter Edition
Windows 2000 Professional	No	No	No
Windows 2000 Server	Yes	Yes	No
Windows 2000 Advanced Server	No	Yes	No
Windows 2000 Datacenter Server	No	No	Yes

Hardware Requirements

Review and document the existing hardware configuration and operating system of each computer that you plan to upgrade. Use this information to identify the computers that you can upgrade to Windows Server 2003 and the computers that you must decommission or return to member server status. The recommended minimum hardware requirements for a member server running Windows Server 2003, Standard Edition, are as follows:

- 550-MHz processor
- 256 MB of memory
- 1.5 GB of free disk space

On domain controllers, allow more available disk space to support the Active Directory database and log files. Use the following guidelines to determine how much disk space to allot for your Active Directory installation:

- On the drive that will contain the Active Directory database template, NTDS.dit, provide available space equal to 10 percent of your existing database size, or at least 250 MB.

- On the drive containing the Active Directory ESENT transaction log files, provide at least 50 MB of available space.

> **Tip**   For optimum performance, store the Active Directory database, Active Directory log files, and Windows .NET operating system on separate physical hard disks.

Test Tools and Logs

It's important to develop a plan for testing your upgrade procedures throughout the upgrade process. Be sure to test the state of your existing domain controllers before beginning your upgrade to ensure that they are functioning properly and throughout the upgrade process to verify that Active Directory replication is consistent and functioning properly. Table 17-2 lists the tools and logs that you can use to verify that your upgrade procedures are successful.

Table 17-2   Tools and Logs Used to Test Upgrade Procedures

Tool/Log File	Description	Location
Repadmin.exe	Checks replication consistency and monitors both inbound and outbound replication partners. Displays replication status of inbound replication partners and directory partitions.	Windows Server 2003 CD-ROM in the \Support\Tools directory
Dcdiag.exe	Diagnoses the state of domain controllers in a forest or enterprise; tests for successful Active Directory connectivity and functionality; returns the results as passed or failed.	Windows Server 2003 CD-ROM in the \Support\Tools directory
Netdiag.exe	Diagnoses networking and connectivity problems by performing a series of tests to determine the state of your network client and whether it is functional.	Windows Server 2003 CD-ROM in the \Support\Tools directory
Nltest.exe	Queries and checks the status of trusts and can forcibly shut down domain controllers.	Windows Server 2003 CD-ROM in the \Support\Tools directory
Dnscmd.exe	Diagnoses DNS registration and zone issues by allowing an administrator to view the properties of DNS servers, zones, and resource records.	Windows Server 2003 CD-ROM in the \Support\Tools directory
Adprep log	Provides a detailed progress report of the forest and domain preparation process.	%SystemRoot%\system32\debug\adprep directory

Table 17-2   Tools and Logs Used to Test Upgrade Procedures   *(continued)*

Tool/Log File	Description	Location
DcpromoUI.log	Provides a detailed progress report of the Active Directory installation. Includes information regarding replication and services as well as applicable error messages.	%SystemRoot%\debug directory
ADSIEdit.exe	A Microsoft Management Console (MMC) snap-in that acts as a low-level editor for Active Directory and allows you to view, add, delete, and move objects and attributes within the directory.	Windows Server 2003 CD-ROM in the \Support\Tools directory

Running the Upgrade Process

After the forest is prepared, all changes made by the ADPrep.exe tool have replicated throughout the forest, and all applicable domains have been prepared, you can begin the actual upgrade process. The following list shows the process for upgrading Windows 2000 domain controllers to Windows Server 2003, and the upcoming sections provide more details.

1. Install Active Directory on a Windows Server 2003 member server.

2. Upgrade the first domain to Windows Server 2003.

3. Upgrade the remaining domains to Windows Server 2003.

Install Active Directory on a Member Server

Install Active Directory on a Windows Server 2003 member server by using the Active Directory Installation Wizard. When you install Active Directory, the member server becomes a domain controller. You can install Active Directory on any Windows Server 2003 member server that meets the domain controller hardware requirements. The Active Directory Installation Wizard does the following:

- Allows you to create an additional domain controller and join it to the existing domain

- Configures the local server to host the directory service

■ Creates directory partitions and default domain security principals

■ Allows you to install or configure DNS

You can run the Active Directory Installation Wizard from a command line or by using the Configure Your Server Wizard. You must be a member of the Domain Admins group to run the Active Directory Installation Wizard. After installing Active Directory on the Windows .NET–based member server, allow sufficient time for replication to occur and all domain controllers to synchronize with the new server.

> **More Info** For more information about installing and removing Active Directory, see "Installing and Removing Active Directory" in the Directory Services Guide of the *Microsoft Windows Server 2003 Resource Kit* (or see "Installing and Removing Active Directory" on the Web at *http://www.microsoft.com/reskit/*).

Upgrade the First Domain

After allowing enough time for the new Windows Server 2003 domain controller to synchronize with the other domain controllers in the domain, upgrade the Windows 2000–based domain controllers in the domain to Windows Server 2003. To initiate the installation of the operating system on the domain controller, insert the Windows Server 2003 operating system CD on the domain controller or, if the Windows .NET media are shared over the network, run Winnt32.exe.

You can also perform an unattended installation of Windows Server 2003. Instructions for creating an answer file for an Active Directory installation are located in the Deploy.cab file in the Support\Tools folder on the Windows Server 2003 operating system CD. Inside the Deploy.cab file, see Ref.chm to access the Unattend.txt file. Expand Unattend.txt in the left pane, and click DCInstall.

Upgrade the Remaining Domains

After upgrading the first domain, upgrade the remaining domains in the forest. You can upgrade any additional Windows 2000–based domain controllers in the forest that meet the Windows .NET hardware requirements to Windows Server 2003.

Before you attempt to upgrade a domain controller in another domain, remember that you must first run *adprep /domainprep* on the infrastructure master role holder in that domain. Run *adprep /forestprep* only once in the forest root domain, and run *adprep /domainprep* once in each domain in the forest in which you plan to locate a Windows Server 2003 domain controller.

Completing Postupgrade Tasks

After upgrading all domain controllers in the forest to Windows Server 2003, complete the upgrade by raising the domain and forest functional levels to Windows .NET, and use newly created application directory partitions to store DNS information. The following sections give more information about these tasks.

Raise Forest and Domain Functional Levels

After you upgrade the first domain controller in the forest to Windows Server 2003, the forest automatically operates at the Windows 2000 functional level. If all Windows 2000 domains are in Windows 2000 native mode, the domain functional level is automatically raised to Windows 2000 native after you upgrade the first domain controller in the domain to Windows Server 2003. If all domains in a forest are in Windows 2000 native mode, raising the forest functional level to Windows .NET automatically raises the domain functional level of each domain in the forest to Windows .NET.

However, if your organization has a Windows 2000 domain that is operating in mixed mode, the domain operates at the Windows 2000 mixed functional level after you upgrade the first domain controller in that domain. If a forest includes domains that are operating at the Windows 2000 mixed functional level, you must manually raise the domain functional level to Windows 2000 native before you can raise the forest functional level to Windows .NET. To raise forest functionality, you must be a member of the Enterprise Admins group. To raise domain functionality, you must be a member of the Domain Admins group.

For example, assume that an organization with three domains—a forest root domain and two regional domains—upgrades its Windows 2000 environment to Windows Server 2003. The forest functional level of the corporation is Windows 2000. The domain functional level for each domain is as follows:

- Forest root domain: Windows 2000 native

- Regional domain 1: Windows 2000 native

- Regional domain 2: Windows 2000 mixed

Before the corporation can raise the forest functional level, it must raise the domain functional level of regional domain 2 to Windows 2000 native. The domain administrator for regional domain 2 raises the domain functional level to Windows 2000 native, so all domains in the forest are operating at a Windows 2000 native domain functional level. The enterprise administrator then raises the forest functional level to Windows .NET. Because each domain in the forest is already operating at a Windows 2000 native domain functional level, this automatically raises the domain functional level of each domain to Windows .NET. The corporation can now take advantage of all of the features available to a functional Windows .NET forest.

Use DNS Application Directory Partitions

Using application directory partitions for DNS-integrated zones significantly reduces replication traffic and the amount of data stored in the global catalog. After upgrading all Windows 2000 domain controllers to Windows Server 2003, move the Active Directory–integrated DNS zones on all DNS servers from the domain partition to the newly created DNS application directory partitions. Move DNS zones that you want to replicate to all DNS servers in the forest to the forestwide DNS application directory partition, ForestDnsZones. Move all DNS zones that you want to replicate only to all DNS servers in the domain to the domainwide DNS application partition, DomainDnsZones.

For More Information

See the following resource for further information:

■   Microsoft Windows .NET Server Deployment Guide at *http://www.microsoft.com/technet/prodtechnol/windowsnetserver/evaluate/cpp/reskit/*

18

Testing for Application Compatibility

There are many concerns during the deployment of a new operating system. If you are considering deploying the Microsoft Windows Server 2003 family and Microsoft Windows XP, you're probably concerned about how well these operating systems will support the applications that actually run your day-to-day business. Addressing these concerns will occupy much of the planning and testing phases of your deployment project.

The Application Compatibility Toolkit (ACT) contains several tools that make this process easier to manage. You can download this tool from Microsoft's Web site at *http://www.microsoft.com/downloads/release.asp?releaseid=42071*. The ACT provides tools to test applications both during the development phase and during deployments. It also provides tools that allow you to gather data about the applications installed on every Windows computer on the network and to package the necessary compatibility fixes for each of those computers. Those tools include the following:

- **Analyzer.** This tool gathers information about every program installed on your network. The analyzer can be used to automate the process of creating an inventory of the software used in your enterprise.

- **Application Verifier.** This tool assists developers looking for compatibility issues with a new application. It's also possible for information technology (IT) professionals to use this tool to determine whether a proposed software package has any common compatibility issues.

- **Compatibility Administrator.**   This tool determines the necessary compatibility fixes to support an application in Windows. This tool can also package fixes into a custom compatibility database that can then be distributed to computers on the network.

In addition to describing these tools, this chapter describes how to collect an application inventory. It also shows how to test applications for compatibility, how to create fixes for application compatibility, and how to distribute those fixes. Last it includes a checklist you can use during compatibility testing. For more information about the tools mentioned in this chapter, including more detailed documentation, see *http://www.microsoft.com/windowsserver2003/ compatible/appcompat.mspx*.

Collecting an Application Inventory

Before testing for application compatibility can begin, you need to know and understand which applications are present in your environment. Many organizations will miss the vital nature of this inventory by assuming that they already have a list of every application approved for use. This does not take into account limited-use applications for special projects within the organization, nor does it include nonapproved software that is inevitably present. The need for a proper software inventory then becomes clearer.

There are multiple approaches to the problem of creating a software inventory. Many of those methods are beyond the scope of this book. Microsoft currently offers two methods for collecting a software inventory: Systems Management Server (SMS) and the Analyzer that ships as part of the Application Compatibility Toolkit.

The Compatibility Analyzer tool collects application information from computers, along with identifying machine information, and writes it to log files in XML format. Compatibility Analyzer then consolidates the log files into a database in a central location, from where you can analyze the applications for compatibility status as well as review reports. Compatibility Analyzer comprises three distinct parts:

- **Collector.**   Collector is the first part to run. Collector is a command-line tool that runs quietly in the background without interrupting the user while it collects data about every application on the computer. It then records the data in a log file in a specified location. (It defaults to the user's desktop but can be directed to a network share for central collection.)

- **Merger.**   Merger (Merger.exe) combines the various collected log files into a single database file. By default, Merger enters the data in a Microsoft Access database file (.MDB), but the logs can also be sent to a SQL database.

- **Analyzer.**   Analyzer is the graphical workspace for viewing the collected data and generating meaningful reports from the data.

Collecting Information

You collect application information with Compatibility Analyzer by distributing and running a command-line tool (Collector.exe) on the computers where you want to inventory applications. You can configure this tool to define the scope of the inventory: You can specify which drives, either network or local, and which paths to search and whether to collect device information. You can also specify where you want the logs to be saved. You can collect inventory information on the following platforms:

- Windows 98 clients

- Windows Me clients

- Windows NT 4.0 servers and clients

- Windows 2000 servers and clients

- Windows XP clients

- Windows Server 2003 family servers

- Mixed domains of clients, including any of Windows 98, Windows Me, Windows NT 4.0, Windows 2000, or Windows XP

- Mixed domains of servers, including any of Windows NT 4.0, Windows 2000, or Windows Server 2003 family

Collector detects the client operating system when it starts and loads the appropriate support. For example, the native character type on Windows 98 or Windows Me is ANSI, so Collector would load ANSI support to store the log information. On Windows NT or Windows XP, Collector would load Unicode support to store its data.

The most important function of Compatibility Analyzer is the collection of application compatibility information from client computers. In fact, each successive step in the process assumes that you've already gathered this data from at least one client computer into a log file. The performance of Collector can be customized through the use of command-line switches. The following shows the syntax of the Collector command:

```
collector.exe [-o filename] [-f source] [-e department]
             [-n] [-d days] [-a] [-p profile]
```

-o *filename*   Directs Collector to produce output on the specified path. By default, Collector places output file on the user's desktop.

-f *source*   Provides the source path, either a file or a directory, for Collector to gather information from. If a file or directory is not specified, directs Collector to gather information from all drives on the machine.

-e *department*   Provides department information for use in processing collector logs. This data helps to separate collected information into useful categories once the logs are merged later in the process.

-n   Directs Collector not to collect information from mapped (network) drives. By default, network drives are included.

-d *days*   Directs Collector to collect information only if Collector has not run within the number of days specified by the parameter; if the number of days is not specified, Collector will not run if it has already been executed on the machine once.

-a   Collects information from the shell and installed programs and combines it with information from specified drives and paths.

-p *profile*   Directs Collector to use a specified profile (initialization file).

Reporting Information

The analysis component of Compatibility Analyzer runs on the administrator's computer, where all operations are sent and received. From here, you can analyze compatibility information and generate reports. This component consolidates all the logs into a database, combining identical application information into one record. You can use an ODBC SQL database or an Access database.

You can analyze application compatibility and generate reports on the following platforms, all of which must be running Internet Explorer 5.0 or later:

- Windows NT 4.0 servers or clients

- Windows 2000 servers or clients

- Windows XP clients

- Windows Server 2003 family servers

Here's an overview of using Compatibility Analyzer:

1. Install the analysis component on the administrator's computer where you want to review reports.

2. Define the analysis database, either as an ODBC SQL database or as an Access database.

3.   Configure the collection component to define the scope of inventory and the location of the logs.

4.   Distribute the collection component to the computers where inventory information is to be collected, and run it. This component does not need to run under an administrator account. You can distribute the component in the following ways:

   ❑   Floppy disk

   ❑   CD-ROM

   ❑   Logon scripts

   ❑   Group Policy in an Active Directory environment

   ❑   Hyperlink in e-mail

   ❑   Network distribution share

   ❑   SMS

5.   Consolidate the log files into a database.

6.   Analyze the compatibility status.

7.   Review the reports.

   You can review reports by application or by computer, and you can filter and sort the results. When viewing reports by computer, you can see all the applications installed on a specific computer. When viewing reports by application, you can see how many instances of the application are installed on the network.

   As you make your test plan, you will want to focus most of your efforts on the applications that are installed on many computers and the ones that are incompatible or whose compatibility status is unknown.

Testing for Compatibility

Once the software inventory has been created and verified, you can formulate a test plan. A valid software test plan for the deployment of a new operating system must include basic details, such as whether an application will run on the new operating system, as well as more complex testing that includes combinations of the applications found in the organization.

   This section describes the strategies for testing applications during a Windows deployment. It also provides information regarding the tools in the Application Compatibility Toolkit and how they can help during this phase of your deployment.

The applications to be tested for a Windows deployment should include every program being used within your organization, both desktop and server. Organizations that have standardized on a set of approved applications might find this task somewhat easier than those who have no standardization at all. Once you have gathered the information in your software inventory and analyzed the business priority of each application, the test plan should be formulated.

In a perfect world, you would test every application present in the organization for compatibility with the new Windows operating systems being deployed. Very few IT departments have this luxury both in time and in budget. By assigning a priority to each application in the organization, you can make intelligent choices about where to spend your testing time. Priorities for applications should be assigned according to their relevance to daily business functions. A desktop application that is used occasionally would have a much lower priority than a client-server application that manages the main product of your organization. A suggested priority scale is as follows:

1. **Business-critical.**   Applications in this category are absolutely required for business to be performed. Business-critical programs cannot endure downtime without a significant loss in revenue.

2. **Business-function.**   This category includes applications that are used by a majority of users within the organization for their daily work. An example of a business-function application would be Microsoft Word 2002 if most people in the organization use it for daily business. Some downtime or problems can be tolerated, but the core functionality of the application must be ensured.

3. **Specialty.**   An application in this category would be important to a very small segment of the user population within an organization and not tied directly to the continued success of the organization. An example would be an art program used to process photographs for marketing materials, important to a small segment of users but not impossible to live without if there were a serious compatibility issue.

4. **Other.**   Applications in this last category include nonstandard programs that users have installed on their own. Typically, these programs have little or no bearing on the daily business of the organization, and application compatibility issues here will have no impact on the business.

Microsoft provides the "Designed for Windows XP" Application Test Framework document to describe a suggested set of test cases and procedures, including test lab setup, for evaluating whether an application meets the requirements for the Designed for Windows XP logo. While you might not be concerned about logo requirements of an application during a Windows deployment, this document does provide excellent insight into testing procedures that have been designed to test for Windows application compatibility.

The Test Framework assumes that the tester has the skills to create an effective test plan, run the tests, and evaluate the results. These skills include the following:

- Software testing experience and familiarity with creating test plans

- Experience testing Windows-based desktop applications

- Experience installing and configuring computer hardware

- Familiarity with Windows operating systems

- Ability to install and configure Windows XP and Windows Server 2003 options

- Experience monitoring test applications using kernel-mode debuggers

The depth of testing described in the Test Framework is beyond most IT professionals; still, the benefit of this document is in the description of testing environment and techniques.

Gathering Information About Applications

As mentioned earlier in this chapter, the Analyzer can be used to collect a list of the applications in use within your organization. However, it can't tell you the business purpose of each program. To obtain this information, you must conduct interviews with users that represent a wide variety of environments within your organization. As a general rule of thumb, try to involve the following groups when collecting information about the applications in use in your organization:

- **Management.**   Top-level management might have specific input regarding the applications in use. Also, collect data from the management of individual departments in the organization.

- **Information technology.**   The IT department in the organization is in a unique position to understand which applications are actually used on a day-to-day basis within the organization.

- **Users.**   This group is often overlooked or underutilized during the interview phase. Try to gather information from representative groups of users from various parts of the organization to assemble a cross-section view of what is actually useful to them on a daily basis.

It's entirely possible that applications on the list of installed software are not even in current use. These, then, can be safely listed as low priority for compatibility with the new operating system. This is actually the reason for gathering application usage data. It enables you to set priorities for testing and helps to reduce or eliminate concerns about applications that have compatibility issues with the new operating system, if in fact they are not used very much. A suggested priority scale would be the following:

1. **Business-critical.** Applications that are vital to daily business and cannot tolerate any downtime without adversely affecting the organization. An example would be the electronic commerce application for an online merchant. Without the ability to process new orders, the business is down.

2. **Daily-use.** This category describes the applications that are used on a daily basis by a majority of users in the organization but can tolerate some downtime. A failure of an application in this category would be irritating, but business would still be conducted with only minimal interruption.

3. **Minimal-use.** The final category describes applications that are in use but not essential to business. You might find it necessary to divide this category into subcategories to deal with applications that are infrequently used but still quite important to the organization, and those applications that are simply nice to have on your computer.

By carefully reviewing the usage patterns of the users within your organization, you can adjust the time allocation for application testing to focus primarily on those programs that are most important to the organization. You can also reduce or eliminate the time spent testing applications that are not important to the organization.

Using Compatibility Administrator

Compatibility Administrator can be a useful tool during the latter portions of your testing schedule. This tool will not help you to automate your software testing, nor will it find compatibility issues in your programs. What Compatibility Administrator can do is help to identify possible solutions to the compatibility issues raised by your software testing.

As the testing process identifies areas of concern with the current or planned applications in your organization, Compatibility Administrator can be used to identify possible solutions for those issues. Consider the following example:

- **Application.**   MyApp16, a 16-bit Windows-based application used for entering customer service call data and for tracking incidents.

- **Business impact.**   Daily-use application, used by the customer service department and used to handle all of its incoming customer call data. Can tolerate some downtime but is important to the daily workflow.

- **Compatibility Issue.**   MyApp16 was designed to run on Windows 3.1. It performed adequately when the organization upgraded to Windows 95 but does not run at all on Windows XP Professional or Windows Server 2003.

With an example application like MyApp16, you might be tempted to recommend upgrading to a newer, 32-bit, application that would accomplish the same tasks. Imagine that the budget constraints for the planned deployment of Windows XP Professional to all of the desktops in the organization preclude the simultaneous upgrade of the customer service application. The task then becomes finding a solution that will enable the application to function on Windows XP. Compatibility Administrator can be used to test possible solutions for the problems this application encounters on Windows XP.

Creating Compatibility Fixes

Independent software vendors (ISVs) have long made it a practice to write their products to run as well as possible on the customer's computer. To accomplish this end, they have looked for ways to work with the operating system to perform their tasks in the most efficient ways possible. The result is an application that is highly optimized for the version of Windows that it was originally written for. Application compatibility issues can arise when a customer tries to run a favorite program on a newer version of Windows than the application was originally written for. This might be particularly true with the move to Windows XP because it's built upon the foundation of Windows NT and Windows 2000.

Many ISVs have been developing applications for the home user market, and for years that focus has meant supporting Windows. Windows NT and Windows 2000 have been seen as business operating systems, so some application developers have chosen to write their programs solely for Windows 95 and Windows 98. When applications are moved to Windows XP, they will encounter new ways of doing familiar tasks. Some of these differences will be a result of the new features of Windows XP, but some will be a result of the more stringent rules laid down by the Windows NT heritage of Windows XP.

Applications that worked on other versions of Windows might fail to function properly on Windows XP. This applies mostly to applications written for Windows 95 and Windows 98, but applications written for Windows NT or Windows 2000 might also be affected. This can happen for any of the following reasons:

- The application refuses to run when Windows reports new, higher version numbers. Often the application will work well on the new version of Windows if the user can get past this block in the application.

- The application calls older versions of Win32 API functions that return unexpected values on machines with large amounts of resources such as disk free space.

- The application expects older formats of Windows data.

- The application expects user information, such as personal and temporary folders, to be in specific locations or specific formats.

Understanding the Application Compatibility Process

Windows XP and Windows Server 2003 introduced a new level of commitment to application compatibility. There are methods within the user interface to correct application compatibility issues, as well as more advanced tools meant for developers or administrators. All of these technologies depend on compatibility information gleaned from the files on the local computer that are then matched to data in a system-level compatibility database. This matching information is used to uniquely identify an application that might require additional support from the operating system to function correctly.

Three fundamental levels of compatibility can be applied, depending on the scenario:

- **Compatibility fix.**   This level of compatibility support provides a *shim*, or small piece of code that corrects a particular behavior that results in a compatibility issue. Typically, a compatibility fix addresses only one compatibility issue.

- **Compatibility mode.**   A compatibility mode is a collection of several compatibility fixes that are commonly applied together. An example would be the application of the Windows 98 compatibility layer through the user interface. The Windows 98 compatibility layer is a compatibility mode; that is, it comprises multiple compatibility fixes that are required to support most applications written specifically for Windows 98.

- **AppHelp.**   An AppHelp message is the final option when a compatibility issue cannot be completely resolved. Simply put, an AppHelp message is a message that will be triggered whenever you attempt to run an application with a known unresolved compatibility issue. AppHelp messages range from advisory in nature, wherein the user is simply notified that the program might not support all of its features on the operating system, to a full block, wherein the application is completely blocked from running. The blocking AppHelp message is used only in a situation in which running the application would cause damage to the operating system, such as running a disk utility that was not written to handle the current operating system. Frequently the text of an AppHelp message will direct the user to a Web address where more information and possibly a fix can be found.

The compatibility fix technologies used in Windows XP and Windows Server 2003 are dependent on several database files:

- **MigDB.inf**   This file is used to support the migration from the Windows 95, Windows 98, and Windows Me operating systems. It contains the matching information used to flag applications that are incompatible or require user intervention prior to system upgrade. Problematic applications are listed along with hardware compatibility information in the upgrade report generated by Setup. This file was first included as part of Windows 2000 Setup and has now been updated to run as part of the Windows XP and Windows Server 2003 Setup programs.

- **NTCompat.inf**   This database contains the same type of information as MigDB.inf but is used to support upgrades from the Windows NT 4.0 and Windows 2000 operating systems. This file is also included in the Windows XP and Windows Server 2003 Setup programs.

- **SysMain.sdb**   This file contains both matching information and compatibility fixes. SysMain.sdb contains the information used to provide compatibility fixes for applications that require some help to run correctly on Windows XP and Windows Server 2003. It's in the %windir%\AppPatch folder.

- **AppHelp.sdb**   This database stores only the Help messages that prompt users for patches, provide them with a URL from which to download third-party patches, or tell them where to find further information. This file is also found in the %windir%\AppPatch directory.

These database files form the core functionality of the compatibility technologies in Windows XP and Windows Server 2003. The operating system itself contains no code to verify the compatibility of any software but rather depends on a short system check routine to tell the operating system to refer to the database files for compatibility information. This approach has the effect of giving a high level of support for applications while minimizing the performance impact on the operating system itself.

Creating Compatibility Fixes

Once you have identified and tested fixes for your target applications, you can use Compatibility Administrator to create a custom fix database. Figure 18-1 shows what Compatibility Administrator looks like. You can create a custom fix database that contains applications supported by compatibility layers, as well as applications supported by specific compatibility fixes.

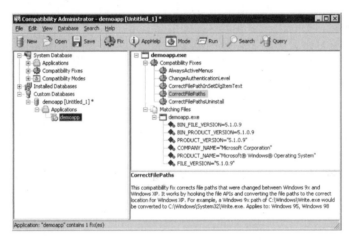

Figure 18-1   Use Compatibility Administrator to build custom fix databases for applications that don't work properly in Windows XP and Windows Server 2003.

To add compatibility fixes to a custom fix database, you click Create New, Application Fix on the Database menu. The program asks you for the name and filename of the program you're fixing. It prompts you for a compatibility mode as well as individual compatibility fixes that you want to apply to the application. Last it asks you for a list of files that identify the application on target computers. Choose files associated with your application that are installed in the same location. For example, choose a .hlp file that resides in the same directory as the .exe file. Try to uniquely identify your application without choosing an unnecessarily high number of matching files.

The application compatibility technology in Windows XP and Windows Server 2003 provides a way to distinguish files with the same or similar names. The operating system does this through the use of file matching information. If you were creating a compatibility fix for a Setup.exe but did not want this compatibility fix used every time you ran a file named Setup.exe, you would specify a group of other files belonging to the application. By gathering data about the specific properties of these files, the operating system can uniquely identify the application requiring the compatibility fix wherever it exists on the computer.

Distributing Compatibility Fixes

Once the compatibility database containing your compatibility fixes has been delivered to the client computers, it must be installed there. There are a few different methods that you can use, and these are described next. Each method relies on the Compatibility Database Installer (Sdbinst.exe) to install and register the compatibility database.

Local Installation

The simplest method of installing a compatibility database is to perform a local installation using Sdbinst.exe. The following shows the syntax of the Sdbinst.exe command:

```
sdbinst.exe [-?] [-q] [-u] [-g] [-n] database | {GUID} | name
```

-?	Displays the help for the command.
-q	Quiet mode; does not display message boxes during the process.
-u	Uninstalls the named database. (The compatibility database to be uninstalled must be identified in some way—as a filename, a GUID, or an internal name.)
-g	Uses the GUID of the compatibility database to identify the information to be uninstalled.
-n *name*	Specifies the internal name of the compatibility database. This is the name assigned internally for the database when it was created in Compatibility Administrator.

Remote Installation

Installing the compatibility database file on a remote computer involves some method of running Sdbinst.exe on the remote computer. Typically, this will be accomplished through a logon script, although other methods such as Remote Desktop Connection (RDC) can be used as well. The benefit of using a logon script to distribute the compatibility database file is that you can use Active Directory to target the users that will need the compatibility database and not install it where it will not be required. Here's how to install a database remotely:

1. Create a shared folder on a server that will be accessible by all client computers requiring the compatibility database. Set permissions to Read for all users that will be receiving the file.

2. Edit the logon script for some level of Active Directory (site, domain, or OU) where the compatibility database will be required, and add a line to install the database:

```
Sdbinst.exe \\servername\sharename\database.sdb -q
```

3. Test the script to verify that it installs the compatibility database correctly.

4. Assign the logon script to the group that requires the database (site, domain, or OU). If you are modifying an existing script, this step will not be required.

Compatibility Testing During Development

During a deployment of Windows within a large organization, there might be concerns about the compatibility of in-house applications. These programs are frequently very important to the flow of normal business and critical in the deployment process. The testing ideas presented in this section are useful for verifying these internal applications, but they can also be used as part of a software evaluation process when considering new programs for the organization.

Testing applications for compatibility with any operating system can be a complicated process. Fortunately, the Application Verifier (AppVerifier) tool developed by the Windows Application and Customer Experience group at Microsoft can assist with this task. AppVerifier encompasses several tools that are specifically designed to test for commonly encountered application compatibility issues and some very subtle kernel issues. These tests can also reveal compatibility issues related to the requirements found in the Designed for Windows XP Application Specification.

AppVerifier is a useful tool for identifying some of the common security issues that applications might create in the Windows operating system, such as writing information to incorrect locations within the registry or the file system, where the information can later be modified by a malicious program. Using the Application Verifier will not prevent every possible security or compatibility issue, but it does provide an easy opportunity to avoid and correct the most commonly identified problems.

Using Application Verifier

Perhaps the first thing to note about AppVerifier is that it is not an automated test program for your applications. AppVerifier will attach to a program and perform its tests whenever you run the program. It's possible to use AppVerifier and an automated test procedure simultaneously. AppVerifier attaches a *stub*, or small piece of code, to the executable program you are testing so that anytime it's run, the AppVerifier tests you have selected will be engaged.

Using AppVerifier to test an application is a relatively simple process. You choose the program files that you want to test. Then choose the tests you want to perform. Some of the tests available to you are the following:

- **Heap corruption detection.**   This test performs regular checks of the heap and adds guard pages at the end of each allocation to catch possible heap overruns.

- **Locks usage checking.**   This test looks for common errors with locks. The output is displayed in a separate debugger application. Note that this test can cause access violations if an error is found.

- **Invalid handle usage detection.**   Checks for common problems with handles. The output is displayed in a separate debugger application. Note that this test can cause access violations if an error is found.

- **Thread stack size checking.**   This test disables stack growth. This will cause a stack overflow exception if the initial allocation was too small.

- **LogStartAndStop.**   This option simply enters log information when the application starts or stops. This helps to make the logs easier to read when reviewing test data.

- **FilePaths.**   This test monitors the application's attempts to obtain file path information to determine whether the program uses hard-coded paths or a nonstandard method of gathering the information. Note that this test can cause the application to crash if an improper method of determining file paths is used.

- **HighVersionLie.** In the past, many applications were written to run on a single version of Windows. This test will return a very high version number when the application attempts to determine which version of Windows it's running in.

- **RegistryChecks.** This test monitors the application's use of the system registry for any inappropriate or dangerous calls. Any problems detected will be logged.

After choosing the tests you want to perform, click Options to configure your tests, as shown in Figure 18-2. Then start the application by clicking the Run button in AppVerifier or by starting the program normally. Exercise the application by trying to use all of the functionality in the program to generate the best data for the AppVerifier logs. After closing the application, view the test results in the AppVerifier log file: click View Logs.

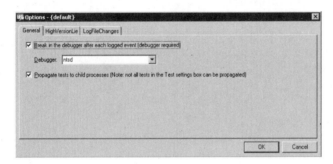

Figure 18-2 Select the options you want to use for testing the application.

The test settings you specify in AppVerifier for a particular application will remain active anytime you run the program until it is removed from the list of applications in AppVerifier. This helps to run programs repeatedly while working out issues.

The first four tests in AppVerifier look for issues that might be found at the kernel level. Because of this, the best output from these tests can be acquired only with the use of a separate kernel debugger. The kernel tests are designed to generate access violation errors when they encounter an error in the program being tested so that the kernel debugger will break in at precisely that point in the application's execution. If you run an application through AppVerifier without a debugger attached and one of the kernel tests finds an error, the application will appear to crash.

To run the app using a debugger, just set all the options and tests desired in AppVerifier and then launch the application with a debugger according to the directions for that debugger. For example, to debug Myapp.exe with NTSD (the Windows XP system debugger), go to a command line and type **ntsd myapp.exe**.

Any debugger can be used. The assumption is that the user running the tests is familiar with using a debugger. If you are not comfortable with using a debugger, you should have problems investigated by an experienced developer, who can then run the application with a debugger.

Testing for Logo Compliance

The Designed for Windows logo program identifies products that have been proven to maintain a high level of compatibility with Microsoft Windows. Application Verifier contains several tests that directly relate to the Designed for Windows logo program to make testing easier for every independent software vendor planning to submit a product for the logo. These tests are identified in the user interface by a number at the end of the test name, as shown in Figure 18-3.

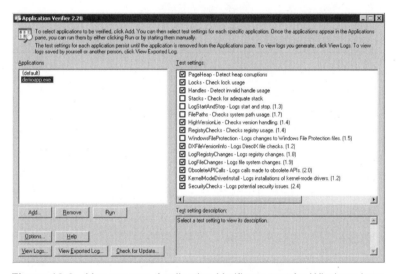

Figure 18-3   You can use Application Verifier to test for Windows logo compliance.

The numbering used in the interface indicates the specific requirement within the Designed for Windows XP Application Specification that the test setting refers to. For example, the WindowsFileProtection (1.5) test applies to section 1, requirement 5, of the Designed for Windows XP Application Specification, Support Fast User Switching and Remote Desktop, because correct use of system paths is one step toward supporting fast user switching in Windows XP and later.

Using Application Verifier during the development of applications destined for the Designed for Windows logo is strongly suggested. This tool is able to detect approximately 90 percent of the problems that Microsoft finds in products that fail the Designed for Windows logo auditing process. Using Application Verifier as a normal step in your development cycle means that you have eliminated the majority of issues that can block your product from receiving the logo. It also helps to ensure a high-quality user experience for your customers.

Application Compatibility Checklist

This section outlines a series of tests taken from the Windows XP Logo Test Framework that you can use to evaluate your application. If you are interested in applying for the Designed for Windows XP logo for your application, go to *http://www.windowslogo.com/*.

- Does the application perform its primary functions and maintain stability during functionality testing?

- Does the application remain stable when a mouse with more than three buttons is used?

- Does the application use the user's temporary folder for temporary files?

- Does the application store its temporary files only in the user's temporary folder during installation?

- Does the application store its temporary files only in the user's temporary folder during functionality testing?

- Does the application not crash or lose data when presented with long pathnames, filenames, and printer names?

- Does the application maintain stability when a file is saved by drilling down through the User1 LFNPath1 path in User1's My Documents folder?

- Does the application maintain stability when a file is saved by entering the full User1 LFNPath2 path?

- Does the application maintain stability when a file is saved using a long filename?

- Does the application maintain stability when a file is opened by drilling down through the User1 LFNPath1 path in User1's My Documents folder?

- Does the application maintain stability when a file is opened by entering the full User1 LFNPath2 path?

- Does the application maintain stability when a file is opened using a long filename?

- Does the application maintain stability when printing to a printer with a long name?

- Does the application perform primary functionality and maintain stability on a dual-processor computer?

- Does the application not crash when devices it uses are not installed?

- Does the application maintain stability when printing if no printer is installed?

- Does the application maintain stability when attempting to use devices that are not installed?

- Does the application switch the system's display mode back to the previous color mode if the application automatically changes to 256-color mode when it runs?

- Do all related kernel-mode drivers pass testing as Windows XP loads them?

- Do all related kernel-mode drivers pass functionality testing with standard kernel testing enabled?

- Do all related kernel-mode drivers pass low-resources simulation testing?

- Are proofs of Windows Hardware Quality Labs (WHQL) testing attached to the submission for all required drivers?

- Do no warnings appear about unsigned drivers during testing?

- Does the application install correctly under current and future versions of Windows?

- Does the application perform all functionality tests correctly under current and future versions of Windows?

- Does the application properly support Fast User Switching?

- Does the application properly support Remote Desktop?

- If the application installs a replacement Graphical Identification and Authentication (GINA) DLL, does the GINA properly support Remote Desktop?

- Does the application pass all functionality tests with a Windows XP theme applied?

- Does the application display normally and not lose data when focus is switched among other applications with Alt+Tab?

- Does the application display normally and not lose data when the Windows logo key and the taskbar are used to switch among applications?

- Does the Windows Security dialog box or the Task Manager display normally, and can the application be canceled or closed without losing data?

- Does the installation finish without any Windows File Protection messages appearing?

- Does the application successfully migrate from Windows 98 to Windows XP Home Edition?

- Does the application successfully migrate from Windows Me to Windows XP Home Edition?

- Does the application successfully migrate from Windows 98 to Windows XP Professional?

- Does the application successfully migrate from Windows Me to Windows XP Professional?

- Does the application successfully migrate from Windows NT 4.0 Workstation to Windows XP Professional?

- Does the application successfully migrate from Windows 2000 Professional to Windows XP Professional?

- Does the application not overwrite nonproprietary files with older versions?

- Do all application executable files have file version, product name, and company name information?

- Does the installation finish without requiring a reboot?

- Can all Test Framework testing be completed without the application requiring a reboot?

- Does the application offer a default installation folder under C:\Program Files?

- Does the application install shared files only in correct locations?

- Does installation add all necessary entries to the registry?

- Does uninstalling the application as Owner remove and leave all the correct files and registry settings?

- Does uninstalling the application as User1 either degrade gracefully or both remove and leave all the correct files and registry settings?

- Can the application be reinstalled after uninstalling it?

- Does the application default to an "all users" installation or provide an "all users" installation option when installed by Owner?

- Does the application default to an "all users" installation or provide an "all users" installation option when installed by User1?

- Does the application's installer start by way of Autorun?

- Does the application's installer correctly detect that the application is already installed and avoid restarting the installation?

- Does the application offer a correct location for opening User1's user-created data?

- Does the application offer a correct location for saving User1's user-created data?

- Does the application offer a correct location for opening User2's user-created data?

- Does the application offer a correct location for saving User2's user-created data?

- Does the application store less than 128 KB of application data in the registry for User1?

- Does the application store configuration data for User1 only in acceptable folders?

- Does the application prevent User1 from saving to the Windows system folder?

- Does the application prevent User1 from modifying documents owned by User2?

- Does the application prevent User1 from modifying systemwide settings?

- Does the application's installer either allow User1 to install the application or degrade gracefully if the installation fails?

For More Information

See the following resources for further information:

- Using the Application Compatibility Toolkit at *http://www.microsoft.com/windowsserver2003/compatible/appcompat.mspx*.

- Windows Application Compatibility Toolkit download at *http://www.microsoft.com/downloads/release.asp?releaseid=42071*.

Index

About the Author

Jerry Honeycutt empowers people to work and play better by helping them use popular technologies, including the Microsoft Windows product family, IP-based networking, and the Internet. He reaches out through his frequent writings and talks but prefers to get his hands dirty by helping companies deploy and manage their desktop computers.

As a best-selling author, Jerry has written over 25 books. His most recent include *Microsoft Windows XP Registry Guide* (Microsoft Press, 2002) and *Introducing Microsoft Windows 2000 Professional* (Microsoft Press, 1999). Most of his books are sold internationally and are available in a variety of languages.

Jerry is also a columnist for Microsoft Expert Zone, a Web site for Windows XP enthusiasts, and makes frequent contributions to a variety of content areas on Microsoft's Web site, including Office XP and TechNet. He also contributes to various trade publications, including *Smart Business* and *CNET*. Jerry is also a frequent speaker at assorted public events, including COMDEX, Developer Days, Microsoft Exchange Conference, and Microsoft Global Briefing, and occasionally hosts chats on Microsoft's TechNet Web site.

In addition to writing and speaking, Jerry has a long history of using his skills for more practical purposes: providing technical leadership to business. He specializes in desktop deployment and management, in particular using the Windows product family. Companies such as Capital One, Travelers, IBM, Nielsen North America, IRM, Howard Systems International, and NCR have all leveraged his expertise. He continues writing, training, and consulting to serve the business community.

Jerry graduated from the University of Texas at Dallas in 1992 with a Bachelor of Science in Computer Science. He also studied at Texas Tech University in Lubbock, Texas. In his spare time, Jerry plays golf, dabbles with photography, and travels. He is an avid collector of rare books and casino chips. Jerry lives in the Dallas suburb of Frisco, Texas.

See Jerry's Web site at www.honeycutt.com, or send an e-mail message to jerry@honeycutt.com.

Router

During World War I, an ingenious young patternmaker, R. L. Carter, in the little town of Phoenix, NY, looked for an easy way to do a laborious cutting job. He took a motor out of some electric barber clippers and improvised a tool that allowed him to do the job in three hours instead of the seven days it normally would have taken. He called his hand tool a hand shaper, but it was really a **router**—a high-speed motor supported vertically in a base, holding a variety of cutting bits in a collet. Carter knew he had a good thing. When the war was over, he began selling power routers, and within ten years had sold 100,000 of them.*

Carter's router is not to be confused with an **Internet router**, an electronic device that forwards data between networks via the most efficient route possible over the Internet.

At Microsoft Press, we use tools to illustrate our books for software developers and IT professionals. Tools very simply and powerfully symbolize human inventiveness. They're a metaphor for people extending their capabilities, precision, and reach. From simple calipers and pliers to digital micrometers and lasers, these stylized illustrations give each book a visual identity, and a personality to the series. With tools and knowledge, there's no limit to creativity and innovation. Our tag line says it all: *the tools you need to put technology to work.*

* From THE GREAT TOOL EMPORIUM by David X. Manners (published by E.P. Dutton/Times Mirror Magazines, Inc., 1979)

The manuscript for this book was prepared and galleyed using Microsoft Word. Pages were composed by Microsoft Press using Adobe FrameMaker+SGML for Windows, with text in Garamond and display type in Helvetica Condensed. Composed pages were delivered to the printer as electronic prepress files.

Cover Designer:	Patricia Bradbury
Interior Graphic Designer:	James D. Kramer
Principal Compositor:	Dan Latimer
Interior Artist:	Joel Panchot
Proofreader:	nSight, Inc.
Principal Copy Editor:	Shawn Peck
Indexer:	Pamona Corporation

For *Windows Server 2003* administrators

Microsoft® Windows® Server 2003 Administrator's Companion
ISBN 0-7356-1367-2

The comprehensive, daily operations guide to planning, deployment, and maintenance. Here's the ideal one-volume guide for anyone who administers Windows Server 2003. It offers up-to-date information on core system-administration topics for Windows, including Active Directory® services, security, disaster planning and recovery, interoperability with NetWare and UNIX, plus all-new sections about Microsoft Internet Security and Acceleration (ISA) Server and scripting. Featuring easy-to-use procedures and handy workarounds, it provides ready answers for on-the-job results.

Microsoft Windows Server 2003 Security Administrator's Companion
ISBN 0-7356-1574-8

The in-depth, practical guide to deployment and maintenance in a secure environment. With this authoritative ADMINISTRATOR'S COMPANION—written by an expert on the Windows Server 2003 security team—you'll learn how to use the powerful security features in the network server operating system. The guide describes best practices and technical details for enhancing security with Windows Server 2003, using a holistic approach to security enhancement.

Microsoft Windows Server 2003 Administrator's Pocket Consultant
ISBN 0-7356-1354-0

The practical, portable guide to Windows Server 2003. Here's the practical, pocket-sized reference for IT professionals who support Windows Server 2003. Designed for quick referencing, it covers all the essentials for performing everyday system-administration tasks. Topics covered include managing workstations and servers, using Active Directory services, creating and administering user and group accounts, managing files and directories, data security and auditing, data back-up and recovery, administration with TCP/IP, WINS, and DNS, and more.

Microsoft IIS 6.0 Administrator's Pocket Consultant
ISBN 0-7356-1560-8

The practical, portable guide to IIS 6.0. Here's the eminently practical, pocket-sized reference for IT and Web professionals who work with Internet Information Services (IIS) 6.0. Designed for quick referencing and compulsively readable, this portable guide covers all the basics needed for everyday tasks. Topics include Web administration fundamentals, Web server administration, essential services administration, and performance, optimization, and maintenance. It's the fast-answers guide that helps users consistently save time and energy as they administer IIS 6.0.

To learn more about the full line of Microsoft Press® products for IT professionals, please visit:

microsoft.com/mspress/IT

Inside *security information* you can trust

Microsoft® Windows® Security Resource Kit
ISBN 0-7356-1868-2   Suggested Retail Price: $59.99 U.S., $86.99 Canada

Comprehensive security information and tools, straight from the Microsoft product groups. This official RESOURCE KIT delivers comprehensive operations and deployment information that information security professionals can put to work right away. The authors—members of Microsoft's security teams—describe how to plan and implement a comprehensive security strategy, assess security threats and vulnerabilities, configure system security, and more. The kit also provides must-have security tools, checklists, templates, and other on-the-job resources on CD-ROM and on the Web.

Microsoft Encyclopedia of Security
ISBN 0-7356-1877-1   Suggested Retail Price: $49.99 U.S., $72.99 Canada

The essential, one-of-a-kind security reference for computer professionals at all levels. This encyclopedia delivers 2000+ entries detailing the latest security-related issues, technologies, standards, products, and services. It covers the Microsoft Windows platform as well as open-source technologies and the platforms and products of other major vendors. You get clear, concise explanations and case scenarios that deftly take you from concept to real-world application—ideal for everyone from computer science students up to systems engineers, developers, and managers.

Microsoft Windows Server 2003 Security Administrator's Companion
ISBN 0-7356-1574-8   Suggested Retail Price: $49.99 U.S., $72.99 Canada

The in-depth, practical guide to deploying and maintaining Windows Server 2003 in a secure environment. Learn how to use all the powerful security features in the latest network operating system with this in-depth, authoritative technical reference—written by a security expert on the Microsoft Windows Server 2003 security team. Explore physical security issues, internal security policies, and public and shared key cryptography, and then drill down into the specifics of the key security features of Windows Server 2003.

Microsoft Internet Information Services Security Technical Reference
ISBN 0-7356-1572-1   Suggested Retail Price: $49.99 U.S., $72.99 Canada

The definitive guide for developers and administrators who need to understand how to securely manage networked systems based on IIS. This book presents obvious, avoidable mistakes and known security vulnerabilities in Internet Information Services (IIS)—priceless, intimate facts about the underlying causes of past security issues—while showing the best ways to fix them. The expert author, who has used IIS since the first version, also discusses real-world best practices for developing software and managing systems and networks with IIS.

To learn more about Microsoft Press® products for IT professionals, please visit:

microsoft.com/mspress/IT

Get a **Free**
e-mail newsletter, updates,
special offers, links to related books,
and more when you
register on line!

Register your Microsoft Press® title on our Web site and you'll get a FREE subscription to our e-mail newsletter, *Microsoft Press Book Connections.* You'll find out about newly released and upcoming books and learning tools, online events, software downloads, special offers and coupons for Microsoft Press customers, and information about major Microsoft® product releases. You can also read useful additional information about all the titles we publish, such as detailed book descriptions, tables of contents and indexes, sample chapters, links to related books and book series, author biographies, and reviews by other customers.

Registration is easy. Just visit this Web page and fill in your information:

http://www.microsoft.com/mspress/register

Microsoft®

- -

Proof of Purchase

Use this page as proof of purchase if participating in a promotion or rebate offer on this title. Proof of purchase must be used in conjunction with other proof(s) of payment such as your dated sales receipt—see offer details.

Introducing Microsoft® Windows® Server 2003
0-7356-1570-5

CUSTOMER NAME

Microsoft Press, PO Box 97017, Redmond, WA 98073-9830

MICROSOFT LICENSE AGREEMENT
Book Companion CD

IMPORTANT—READ CAREFULLY: This Microsoft End-User License Agreement ("EULA") is a legal agreement between you (either an individual or an entity) and Microsoft Corporation for the Microsoft product identified above, which includes computer software and may include associated media, printed materials, and "online" or electronic documentation ("SOFTWARE PRODUCT"). Any component included within the SOFTWARE PRODUCT that is accompanied by a separate End-User License Agreement shall be governed by such agreement and not the terms set forth below. By installing, copying, or otherwise using the SOFTWARE PRODUCT, you agree to be bound by the terms of this EULA. If you do not agree to the terms of this EULA, you are not authorized to install, copy, or otherwise use the SOFTWARE PRODUCT; you may, however, return the SOFTWARE PRODUCT, along with all printed materials and other items that form a part of the Microsoft product that includes the SOFTWARE PRODUCT, to the place you obtained them for a full refund.

SOFTWARE PRODUCT LICENSE

The SOFTWARE PRODUCT is protected by United States copyright laws and international copyright treaties, as well as other intellectual property laws and treaties. The SOFTWARE PRODUCT is licensed, not sold.

1. **GRANT OF LICENSE.** This EULA grants you the following rights:

    a. **Software Product.** You may install and use one copy of the SOFTWARE PRODUCT on a single computer. The primary user of the computer on which the SOFTWARE PRODUCT is installed may make a second copy for his or her exclusive use on a portable computer.

    b. **Storage/Network Use.** You may also store or install a copy of the SOFTWARE PRODUCT on a storage device, such as a network server, used only to install or run the SOFTWARE PRODUCT on your other computers over an internal network; however, you must acquire and dedicate a license for each separate computer on which the SOFTWARE PRODUCT is installed or run from the storage device. A license for the SOFTWARE PRODUCT may not be shared or used concurrently on different computers.

    c. **License Pak.** If you have acquired this EULA in a Microsoft License Pak, you may make the number of additional copies of the computer software portion of the SOFTWARE PRODUCT authorized on the printed copy of this EULA, and you may use each copy in the manner specified above. You are also entitled to make a corresponding number of secondary copies for portable computer use as specified above.

    d. **Sample Code.** Solely with respect to portions, if any, of the SOFTWARE PRODUCT that are identified within the SOFTWARE PRODUCT as sample code (the "SAMPLE CODE"):

        i. **Use and Modification.** Microsoft grants you the right to use and modify the source code version of the SAMPLE CODE, *provided* you comply with subsection (d)(iii) below. You may not distribute the SAMPLE CODE, or any modified version of the SAMPLE CODE, in source code form.

        ii. **Redistributable Files.** Provided you comply with subsection (d)(iii) below, Microsoft grants you a nonexclusive, royalty-free right to reproduce and distribute the object code version of the SAMPLE CODE and of any modified SAMPLE CODE, other than SAMPLE CODE, or any modified version thereof, designated as not redistributable in the Readme file that forms a part of the SOFTWARE PRODUCT (the "Non-Redistributable Sample Code"). All SAMPLE CODE other than the Non-Redistributable Sample Code is collectively referred to as the "REDISTRIBUTABLES."

        iii. **Redistribution Requirements.** If you redistribute the REDISTRIBUTABLES, you agree to: (i) distribute the REDISTRIBUTABLES in object code form only in conjunction with and as a part of your software application product; (ii) not use Microsoft's name, logo, or trademarks to market your software application product; (iii) include a valid copyright notice on your software application product; (iv) indemnify, hold harmless, and defend Microsoft from and against any claims or lawsuits, including attorney's fees, that arise or result from the use or distribution of your software application product; and (v) not permit further distribution of the REDISTRIBUTABLES by your end user. Contact Microsoft for the applicable royalties due and other licensing terms for all other uses and/or distribution of the REDISTRIBUTABLES.

2. **DESCRIPTION OF OTHER RIGHTS AND LIMITATIONS.**

    • **Limitations on Reverse Engineering, Decompilation, and Disassembly.** You may not reverse engineer, decompile, or disassemble the SOFTWARE PRODUCT, except and only to the extent that such activity is expressly permitted by applicable law notwithstanding this limitation.

    • **Separation of Components.** The SOFTWARE PRODUCT is licensed as a single product. Its component parts may not be separated for use on more than one computer.

    • **Rental.** You may not rent, lease, or lend the SOFTWARE PRODUCT.

- **Support Services.** Microsoft may, but is not obligated to, provide you with support services related to the SOFTWARE PRODUCT ("Support Services"). Use of Support Services is governed by the Microsoft policies and programs described in the user manual, in "online" documentation, and/or in other Microsoft-provided materials. Any supplemental software code provided to you as part of the Support Services shall be considered part of the SOFTWARE PRODUCT and subject to the terms and conditions of this EULA. With respect to technical information you provide to Microsoft as part of the Support Services, Microsoft may use such information for its business purposes, including for product support and development. Microsoft will not utilize such technical information in a form that personally identifies you.

- **Software Transfer.** You may permanently transfer all of your rights under this EULA, provided you retain no copies, you transfer all of the SOFTWARE PRODUCT (including all component parts, the media and printed materials, any upgrades, this EULA, and, if applicable, the Certificate of Authenticity), **and** the recipient agrees to the terms of this EULA.

- **Termination.** Without prejudice to any other rights, Microsoft may terminate this EULA if you fail to comply with the terms and conditions of this EULA. In such event, you must destroy all copies of the SOFTWARE PRODUCT and all of its component parts.

3. **COPYRIGHT.** All title and copyrights in and to the SOFTWARE PRODUCT (including but not limited to any images, photographs, animations, video, audio, music, text, SAMPLE CODE, REDISTRIBUTABLES, and "applets" incorporated into the SOFTWARE PRODUCT) and any copies of the SOFTWARE PRODUCT are owned by Microsoft or its suppliers. The SOFTWARE PRODUCT is protected by copyright laws and international treaty provisions. Therefore, you must treat the SOFTWARE PRODUCT like any other copyrighted material **except** that you may install the SOFTWARE PRODUCT on a single computer provided you keep the original solely for backup or archival purposes. You may not copy the printed materials accompanying the SOFTWARE PRODUCT.

4. **U.S. GOVERNMENT RESTRICTED RIGHTS.** The SOFTWARE PRODUCT and documentation are provided with RESTRICTED RIGHTS. Use, duplication, or disclosure by the Government is subject to restrictions as set forth in subparagraph (c)(1)(ii) of the Rights in Technical Data and Computer Software clause at DFARS 252.227-7013 or subparagraphs (c)(1) and (2) of the Commercial Computer Software—Restricted Rights at 48 CFR 52.227-19, as applicable. Manufacturer is Microsoft Corporation/One Microsoft Way/Redmond, WA 98052-6399.

5. **EXPORT RESTRICTIONS.** You agree that you will not export or re-export the SOFTWARE PRODUCT, any part thereof, or any process or service that is the direct product of the SOFTWARE PRODUCT (the foregoing collectively referred to as the "Restricted Components"), to any country, person, entity, or end user subject to U.S. export restrictions. You specifically agree not to export or re-export any of the Restricted Components (i) to any country to which the U.S. has embargoed or restricted the export of goods or services, which currently include, but are not necessarily limited to, Cuba, Iran, Iraq, Libya, North Korea, Sudan, and Syria, or to any national of any such country, wherever located, who intends to transmit or transport the Restricted Components back to such country; (ii) to any end user who you know or have reason to know will utilize the Restricted Components in the design, development, or production of nuclear, chemical, or biological weapons; or (iii) to any end user who has been prohibited from participating in U.S. export transactions by any federal agency of the U.S. government. You warrant and represent that neither the BXA nor any other U.S. federal agency has suspended, revoked, or denied your export privileges.

DISCLAIMER OF WARRANTY

NO WARRANTIES OR CONDITIONS. MICROSOFT EXPRESSLY DISCLAIMS ANY WARRANTY OR CONDITION FOR THE SOFTWARE PRODUCT. THE SOFTWARE PRODUCT AND ANY RELATED DOCUMENTATION ARE PROVIDED "AS IS" WITHOUT WARRANTY OR CONDITION OF ANY KIND, EITHER EXPRESS OR IMPLIED, INCLUDING, WITHOUT LIMITATION, THE IMPLIED WARRANTIES OF MERCHANTABILITY, FITNESS FOR A PARTICULAR PURPOSE, OR NONINFRINGEMENT. THE ENTIRE RISK ARISING OUT OF USE OR PERFORMANCE OF THE SOFTWARE PRODUCT REMAINS WITH YOU.

LIMITATION OF LIABILITY. TO THE MAXIMUM EXTENT PERMITTED BY APPLICABLE LAW, IN NO EVENT SHALL MICROSOFT OR ITS SUPPLIERS BE LIABLE FOR ANY SPECIAL, INCIDENTAL, INDIRECT, OR CONSEQUENTIAL DAMAGES WHATSOEVER (INCLUDING, WITHOUT LIMITATION, DAMAGES FOR LOSS OF BUSINESS PROFITS, BUSINESS INTERRUPTION, LOSS OF BUSINESS INFORMATION, OR ANY OTHER PECUNIARY LOSS) ARISING OUT OF THE USE OF OR INABILITY TO USE THE SOFTWARE PRODUCT OR THE PROVISION OF OR FAILURE TO PROVIDE SUPPORT SERVICES, EVEN IF MICROSOFT HAS BEEN ADVISED OF THE POSSIBILITY OF SUCH DAMAGES. IN ANY CASE, MICROSOFT'S ENTIRE LIABILITY UNDER ANY PROVISION OF THIS EULA SHALL BE LIMITED TO THE GREATER OF THE AMOUNT ACTUALLY PAID BY YOU FOR THE SOFTWARE PRODUCT OR US$5.00; PROVIDED, HOWEVER, IF YOU HAVE ENTERED INTO A MICROSOFT SUPPORT SERVICES AGREEMENT, MICROSOFT'S ENTIRE LIABILITY REGARDING SUPPORT SERVICES SHALL BE GOVERNED BY THE TERMS OF THAT AGREEMENT. BECAUSE SOME STATES AND JURISDICTIONS DO NOT ALLOW THE EXCLUSION OR LIMITATION OF LIABILITY, THE ABOVE LIMITATION MAY NOT APPLY TO YOU.

MISCELLANEOUS

This EULA is governed by the laws of the State of Washington USA, except and only to the extent that applicable law mandates governing law of a different jurisdiction.

Should you have any questions concerning this EULA, or if you desire to contact Microsoft for any reason, please contact the Microsoft subsidiary serving your country, or write: Microsoft Sales Information Center/One Microsoft Way/Redmond, WA 98052-6399.

PN 097-0002296